China in the Asian Financial Crisis

AF763123

The widely held view of the Asian Financial Crisis is that it had no substantial impact on China. In fact, the country was far more vulnerable than most people realized, due to the high possibility of financial contagion entering the system from Hong Kong through Guangdong province. This book analyzes the severe policy challenge that it presented for China's leaders.

The crisis in Guangdong's financial institutions provided a forewarning of the difficulties that lay ahead as China's integration with the global financial system deepened. The experience of Guangdong in the Asian Financial Crisis provided a profound lesson for China's policy-makers as they planned the country's strategy for financial reform in the following years. China was able to avoid disaster by astute and difficult policy choices, in the face of fierce pressure from outside the country, as well as from different domestic interests at many different levels. The successful resolution of the crisis provided a breathing space for the leadership. It gave it time to undertake necessary reforms in the country's financial system in the decade that followed the crisis.

Peter Nolan is Founding Director, Centre of Development Studies, University of Cambridge and Director, China Centre, Jesus College, Cambridge.

Routledge Studies on the Chinese Economy

Series Editor
Peter Nolan
Founding Director, Centre of Development Studies, University of Cambridge and Director, China Centre, Jesus College, Cambridge

Founding Series Editors
Peter Nolan, University of Cambridge
Dong Fureng, Beijing University

The aim of this series is to publish original, high-quality, research-level work by both new and established scholars in the West and the East, on all aspects of the Chinese economy, including studies of business and economic history.

China and the West
Crossroads of Civilisation
Peter Nolan

Wind Power in China
Ambiguous Winds of Change in China's Energy Market
Julia Kirch Kirkegaard

Multinationals, Global Value Chains and Governance
The Mechanics of Power in Inter-firm Relations
Peter Hertenstein

China's Commercial Health Insurance
China Development Research Foundation

Finance and the Real Economy
China and the West since the Asian Financial Crisis
Peter Nolan

How China Escaped Shock Therapy
The Market Reform Debate
Isabella M. Weber

China in the Asian Financial Crisis
Peter Nolan

For more information about this series, please visit: https://www.routledge.com

China in the Asian Financial Crisis

Peter Nolan

Routledge
Taylor & Francis Group
LONDON AND NEW YORK

First published 2021
by Routledge
2 Park Square, Milton Park, Abingdon, Oxon OX14 4RN

and by Routledge
52 Vanderbilt Avenue, New York, NY 10017

Routledge is an imprint of the Taylor & Francis Group, an informa business

© 2021 Peter Nolan

The right of Peter Nolan to be identified as author of this work has been asserted by him in accordance with sections 77 and 78 of the Copyright, Designs and Patents Act 1988.

All rights reserved. No part of this book may be reprinted or reproduced or utilised in any form or by any electronic, mechanical, or other means, now known or hereafter invented, including photocopying and recording, or in any information storage or retrieval system, without permission in writing from the publishers.

Trademark notice: Product or corporate names may be trademarks or registered trademarks, and are used only for identification and explanation without intent to infringe.

British Library Cataloguing-in-Publication Data
A catalogue record for this book is available from the British Library

Library of Congress Cataloging-in-Publication Data
A catalog record has been requested for this book

ISBN: 978-0-415-30372-9 (hbk)
ISBN: 978-0-367-52339-8 (pbk)
ISBN: 978-0-203-50596-0 (ebk)

Typeset in Times New Roman
by codeMantra

For Wang Xiaoqiang
and
in memory of
Deng Yingtao

Contents

Tables

Preface

The relationship between China and the Asian Financial Crisis in the late 1990s has been little studied. In fact, the research topic is of great importance for understanding China's subsequent development path. The focal point of the relationship concerned Guangdong province and Hong Kong.

Guangdong International Trust and Investment Company (GITIC) was the first bankruptcy of a major Chinese financial institution since 1949. This case was important for helping to resolve international doubts about China's fairness and transparency in dealing with international financial institutions. The initial focus of the research was on the bankruptcy of GITIC and the restructuring of Guangdong Enterprises (GDE). The study broadened into an examination of the whole financial system of Guangdong province, including the deep inter-relationships between different parts of the system, and their complicated relationship with other parts of China as well as with Hong Kong. The research was connected intimately with the relationship between finance and the real economy, which remains at the core of China's reform and opening-up through to the present day. It provided insights into the pragmatic reform philosophy of 'groping for stones to cross the river'. It provided insights also into the practical, non-ideological approach of the Chinese bureaucracy towards solving problems, which has its roots deep in China's history since the Ancient World.

The main part of the fieldwork was undertaken by Dr Wang Xiaoqiang and myself. We were joined for important segments of the research by Professor Cui Zhiyuan (Tsinghua University) and Dr Zhou Xiaozhuang. The initial decision to research on this topic was taken by Professor Cui. What began as research on bankruptcy widened into a much broader field of enquiry as one issue led to another. It proved to be a remarkable and challenging research opportunity, undertaken in the midst of the process of dealing with the aftermath of the Asian Financial Crisis.

Summaries of our research findings were published in Chinese in *Canyue Wen Gao* (Beijing 2005, No. 23, 25 October, 1–57) under the title *'Kan shu jiu lin'* ('Cutting the trees to save the forest') and in English in Peter Nolan, *Integrating China: Towards the Co-ordinated Market Economy*, London, Anthem Press, 2008. Although I completed this book-length study in 2002, for a variety of reasons I decided not to publish it until now. The ideas contained in this study were developed through constant discussion between Dr Wang Xiaoqiang and myself.

This study is focused on the Asian Financial Crisis. The crisis had a profound impact upon China's policy-makers as they groped their way to reform the country's financial system. The bold measures taken in Guangdong to turn back the tide of the Asian Financial Crisis by 'cutting the trees to save the forest' provided the country's policy-makers with a breathing space. The impact of the crisis deeply affected the course of financial sector reform in China in the years that followed. Thanks to these reforms China was in the position to weather the Global Financial Crisis after 2008.

The study is based on fieldwork in Beijing, Hong Kong and different parts of Guangdong province. The research on red chips took place in Hong Kong in the summer of 1998. I am most grateful to Mr Kang Dian for his help in undertaking this research.

The main body of the fieldwork took place in 2000 and 2001. It involved interviews in Hong Kong in April 2000, Guangzhou and Beijing in October and November 2000, in Guangzhou, Enping, Shantou and Shenzhen in January 2001.

I gratefully acknowledge the help I was given by Dr Jin Zhang, Deputy Director, China Centre, Jesus College; Senior Research Fellow, Cambridge China Development Trust; and University Lecturer, University of Cambridge, in collecting materials, discussing the interpretation of those materials, and in complicated coordination activities.

I am grateful to Dr Carl Walter for his help in providing research materials, as well as for helpful discussion of the issues investigated in this study.

I am extremely grateful to Elizabeth Briggs for all she has done to edit numerous versions of this book over many years.

I am most grateful also to Peter Sowden, Editor at Routledge, who has been immensely supportive and patient.

For obvious reasons, the names of many of the people interviewed during the research for this study have been omitted.

In a work of this type, which covers such a wide and complicated field, it is inevitable there will be errors of fact and interpretation. It also contains many controversial opinions. I assume full responsibility on both counts.

Introduction

The widely held view of the Asian Financial Crisis (AFC) is that it had no substantial impact on China. This is attributed to the fact that China did not have capital account convertibility, that the capital inflows into China were mainly long-term Foreign Direct Investment (FDI), and that it had a strong trade and foreign exchange position. In fact, the country was far more vulnerable than most people realized, due to the high possibility of financial contagion entering the system from Hong Kong through Guangdong province.

The impact of the AFC was first through financial inflows from, and debts incurred in, Hong Kong, especially through Guangdong-based financial institutions operating there. The second, and apparently unrelated channel, was the massive internal flow of capital from elsewhere in China to Guangdong. The impact was all the greater because a large part of it was concentrated in a relatively limited part of the province, the Pearl River Delta. This area was one of the most dynamic in the world but also one that was fragile in terms of the sustainability of its growth path. This book examines the inter-connected nature of these aspects of the impact of the AFC upon China. It analyzes the severe policy challenge that it presented for China's leaders. The crisis in Guangdong's financial institutions provided a forewarning of the difficulties that lay ahead as China's integration with the global financial system deepened.

The experience of Guangdong in the AFC provided a profound lesson for China's policy-makers as they planned the country's strategy for financial reform in the following years. China was able to avoid disaster by astute and difficult policy choices, in the face of fierce pressure from outside the country, as well as from different domestic interests at many different levels. The successful resolution of the crisis provided a breathing space for the leadership. It gave it time to undertake necessary reforms in the country's financial system.

The Pearl River Delta and Hong Kong had become more and more closely tied together during the course of China's economic reforms. By the late 1990s, capital invested by Hong Kong firms employed several million people in the Pearl River Delta. A huge amount of capital flowed into Hong

Kong from around the world. It was attracted by the 'China play,' which increasingly stood at the forefront of the 'emerging markets' concept of global financial institutions. In the mid-1990s, a speculative 'frenzy' developed over the prospects that the region offered for capital from within and from outside the region, and both within and outside China. Behind the speculative boom lay the lure of explosive economic growth rates in Guangdong province, especially in the Pearl River Delta. Local government-backed investment vehicles in both Hong Kong and the mainland appeared to offer virtually risk-free lending.

The lenders felt that the fact that there was a Chinese state entity behind the borrowing institutions absolved them of the need to undertake careful project evaluation. This was an undemanding form of lending, requiring limited banking skills. The main banking 'skill' was selecting and building relationships with the most promising state 'parents.' Buying bonds of 'government-backed' mainland companies or providing them with commercial loans, appeared to offer a risk-free method of achieving high returns on capital. Guangdong, adjacent to Hong Kong, was an especially attractive part of this international lending structure. Within China capital poured into the region, attracted by the 'concept' of local government-backed investment vehicles in townships and cities in China's fastest-growing and most capitalistic province.

In the course of this speculative frenzy, the two Guangdong government-owned investment institutions, Guangdong International Trust and Investment Corporation (GITIC) and Guangdong Enterprises (GDE), as well as a large part of the province's local non-bank financial institutions (NBFIs) encountered serious repayment problems. These became insurmountable with the onset of the Asian Financial Crisis, and the consequent downturn in the region's prospects. As the surrounding economic environment deteriorated, a wide array of hidden problems came to the surface: 'When the tide goes out, the rocks appear.' This presented a massive challenge for both the Guangdong and the central government. This book analyzes the way in which China's policy-makers responded to the three-fold challenge in GITIC, GDE and Guangdong's local non-bank financial institutions. It constituted an important episode in China's long evolutionary process of reform and opening up.

In December 1997 it was announced that Wang Qishan would relinquish his position as the Governor of China Construction Bank and take up a leading position in the Guangdong provincial government. He was initially appointed a member of the Guangdong provincial Party committee and one month later was appointed to the post of Executive Vice-Governor of the province. He was part of a 'five-member leading team of the provincial Party committee' that faced the task of dealing with the crisis.

After fierce debate, the Guangdong government decided to close GITIC. The decision was announced on 6 October 1998. Only a few months later, in January 1999, it was decided that GITIC should apply to be made bankrupt through the courts in Guangzhou. These decisions caused an outcry in the international press. International bankers had wished to believe that GITIC was protected from bankruptcy by the Chinese government. Over the ensuing months, investigations by the liquidation committee went steadily deeper into GITIC's business structure. A series of creditors' meetings was provided with unfolding news about shortcomings in the management and the gravity of the financial situation at GITIC.

On 9 October 1998, just days after GITIC's closure, the crucial decision was taken to treat GDE differently from GITIC. The Guangdong government decided to restructure the company. The key reason for treating GDE differently from GITIC was the fact that through its five listed companies, especially Guangdong Investments (GDI) and Guangnan, GDE played an important role in the Hong Kong stock market. Moreover, the decision to close GITIC and subsequently to declare it bankrupt, radically reduced the pressure from international bankers on GDE. The threat of bankruptcy and a large 'haircut' was now wholly credible. Creditors mostly preferred restructuring to bankruptcy. On 15 December 1998, the Guangdong government appointed Goldman Sachs as financial advisor for the GDE restructuring. The declared intention of the Chinese government was to turn GDE into a modern company that conformed to international standards of business management. After a prolonged series of creditors' meetings, on 6 December 2000, the creditors finally agreed the restructuring plan for GDE. Alongside the bankruptcy of GITIC and the restructuring of GDE went a much less-publicized restructuring of the entire non-bank financial sector in the province. This was the third of the 'three steps' (*san bu zou*) taken to solve the problems in the province's financial sector. In its scope and implications, it was in many ways even more challenging and significant than the first two steps, since this sector was closely associated with the daily lives of a large fraction of the Guangdong population.

The complex episode involved numerous issues in the political economy of China's reform and development. These included how the Chinese government should deal with the activities of global financial institutions that involved Chinese entities and the way in which the government dealt with speculation by mainland Chinese individuals and business institutions. These questions in turn involved issues of the role of finance in the forthcoming phase of China's development: should finance be the central driver of the development process, or should finance be treated as a 'servant' that is useful, but needs to be firmly controlled? In particular, what contribution should global financial flows and financial institutions make to China's development in the period ahead? The episode involved the way in which the central government dealt with local governments' drive to expand their autonomy, both at the provincial and lower levels; the way in which the central government dealt with the incorporation of Hong Kong into the economic and political life of the mainland; and the way in which the government dealt with corruption within its own institutions. It shed significant light on the dilemmas facing the reform of large state-owned enterprises, including the function that bankruptcy can play, as well as the dangers of too simplistic and ideological an approach towards the function of bankruptcy.

It provided a vivid illustration of the role of 'moral hazard' in financial behaviour, showing that the nature and solutions of issues of 'moral hazard' are often extremely complex. 'Moral hazard' was involved in many aspects of the crisis. The term 'moral hazard' has come to refer to 'any situation in which one person makes the decision about how much risk to take, while someone else bears the cost if things go badly' (Krugman, 2000: 66). There was moral hazard in relation to the deposits made by Chinese investors in the non-bank financial institutions in Guangdong, which they thought were supported by the local government. There was moral hazard in relation to the loans from international financial institutions, which believed that the Chinese government would simply step in to support their 'own' institutions, no matter how poorly they made investment decisions. There was moral hazard in relation to the behaviour of the Chinese borrowing institutions, which the lenders believed were 'too big to fail' in relation to the Guangdong government (GITIC and GDE) or the local government (the local non-bank financial institutions). There was moral hazard in relation to those who borrowed from these institutions, as they believed that they would never be called upon to pay back 'dad's money' (*aye de qian*). However, fine considerations of moral hazard needed to be weighed against immediate issues of system survival. It was sometimes necessary to take decisions that had problematic consequences in terms of moral hazard in order to prevent the rapid spread of social and political instability.

The structure of this book is as follows. Part 1 examines the challenges presented to the Chinese government by the impact of the AFC on Guangdong. The AFC was a 'forest fire' that threatened to engulf Hong Kong, which had only just returned to China, and to leap to the mainland's fragile financial institutions through Hong Kong's 'back door,' Guangdong province. Part 2 analyses the 'three steps' (*san bu zou*) that the Chinese government took to deal with the crisis: bankrupting GITIC, restructuring GDE and restructuring the local non-bank financial institutions. These steps allowed the 'fire' to be controlled by creating a 'fire break' between the mainland and the international financial institutions. The key to this achievement was 'cutting the trees to save the forest' (*kan shu jiu lin*).

On 7 December 2000, it was announced that Wang Qishan would return to Beijing to take up the position of head of the State Council Office for Restructuring the Economic System. The Asian Financial Crisis had passed. The emergency situation at the two most high-profile casualties of the crisis in China had now been dealt with. The painful bankruptcy process at GITIC had run its course and creditors had begun to receive payments from the residue of GITIC's assets. GDE had completed a complicated process of corporate restructuring that ostensibly was turning it into a modern enterprise with international standards of management and corporate behaviour. The crisis in the local non-bank financial institutions had been resolved. The 'fire' of the Asian Financial Crisis had been extinguished and the storm had passed over Guangdong.

Part 1

The challenge

The threat of forest fire

I envision that in twenty years the level of development in Guangdong will be on a par with middle-ranking developed countries, and in fifty years we will rank among the world's developed regions.

(Governor Lu Ruihua, quoted in *SCMP*, 7 November 2000)

From 623 to 684, South China was prosperous and peaceful. The population increased, more land was occupied and cultivated, and commerce and industry became increasingly important to its economy. These sixty years were also some of the greatest for the Nanhai [southern seas] trade. [In 684] the governor of Kuang-chou, Lu Yuan-jui, was killed by a K'un Lun [merchant]. Yuan-jui was weak and ignorant. His officials were licentious and extortionate. When merchant vessels came, the officials appropriated the goods for themselves without stop...[The killing of Yuan-jui] was a dramatic climax for a period of great prosperity and brazen corruption.

(Wang, 1998: 73)

There are places where the government knows everybody's shoe size but doesn't know how much they have borrowed off-shore.

(Rudiger Dornbusch, quoted in his obituary, *Financial Times*, 2 August 2002)

World markets were still shaken yesterday even though Hong Kong appeared to have stepped back from the brink...Like the Indonesian forest fires that smoulder underground before bursting through the surface, regional economic problems have ignited new crises, sending financial turmoil, like smog, far abroad. The most serious fire burned this week in Hong Kong, when battle raged to defend the currency, the last in Asia to be fixed against the dollar.

(*Financial Times*, 25 October 1997)

> In the past we have said that China would not be affected by the Asian crisis. The renminbi is closed on the capital account. But now we have seen that there is one potential form of transmission of the Asian malaise, and that is through foreign lending.
>
> (Dong Tao, Crédit Suisse First Boston, quoted in *Financial Times*, 16 November 1998)

1 Introduction

In a bone-dry forest, fire can easily rage out of control. Convection from the fire stimulates a vicious circle of high winds that can blow the fire at high speed across substantial distances. Not only did the 'fire' from the Asian Financial Crisis threatened to engulf Guangdong's financial institutions, but there was also a serious risk of the contagion spreading from Guangdong's financial institutions to the broader mainland financial system. It also provided a serious threat to Hong Kong's financial stability. The financial crisis in Guangdong was hardly noticed outside China. In fact, it presented a deep threat to China's orderly development. By an extraordinary coincidence, the AFC coincided with the huge, long-lasting forest fires in Indonesia, which swept a pall of smoke across the whole region. The metaphor of forest fire was thrust into the forefront of people's minds during the crisis.

In the 1990s, Guangdong became one of the world's fastest-growing regions. At its core was the Pearl River Delta (PRD), an area which then had a population of around twenty-one million. It attracted a large amount of capital from across China, 'pulled' towards the local non-bank financial institutions (NBFIs) by the lure of illegal high interest rates, well above those offered by the formal banking system. The province also attracted a large amount of international capital, borrowed by the main non-bank financial institutions, notably the trust and investment companies (TICs), of which the Guangdong International Trust and Investment Corporation (GITIC) was the largest in the province. In addition, the province's red chip companies in Hong Kong borrowed large amounts from international financial institutions, away from the supervision of mainland regulatory authorities. China's red chip companies constituted an increasingly important part of the Hong Kong economy as the 1990s progressed, with a central role in the stock market.

The amount of capital, and rate of interest paid to attract it, from within and outside China, were based on the assumption that growth in the region would continue at high speed and yield high returns. In fact, Guangdong's growth encountered significant structural difficulties in the late 1990s, and a huge speculative property development boom collapsed. These difficulties affected Hong Kong also, since a large part of the growth of Guangdong was financed by investment from and through Hong Kong.

Analysis of the debate concerning the underlying causes of the Asian Financial Crisis is beyond the scope of this book. There is little dispute that the immediate cause of the crisis was the speculative activities of the international 'hedge funds.' The 1990s saw an unprecedented growth in international trade in currencies: 'Foreign exchange is the world's biggest market by a mile' (*FT*, 4 January 2002). The amount of foreign exchange traded each day rose from US$ 500 billion in 1989 to US$ 3 trillion in 2001. The world was increasingly resembling the 'casino capitalism' described by Susan Strange:

> The Western financial world is coming to resemble nothing so much as a vast casino. Every day games are played in this casino that involve sums of money so large that they cannot be imagined. At night the games continue on the other side of the world.
>
> (Strange, 1997: 1)

Those who commanded these vast sums of capital were able to direct their speculative activities towards any unstable economic situation. The size of the foreign currency trades that global financial institutions commanded was vast in comparison to the size of the economies of East and southeast Asia. Their speculative activities had massive effects on the stock markets and exchange rates of the East Asian economies, with very large effects on the real economy, especially through the impact on the size of international debts, typically denominated in dollars.

The international speculators, such as the Soros Quantum Fund and Julian Robertson's 'Tiger Fund,' spotted the underlying fragility of East Asian financial systems, and played a major role in precipitating the crisis that erupted in Thailand in July 1997. They speculated huge amounts against the Thai *baht*, playing a central role in the eventual abandoning of the fixed nominal rate against the dollar. The Thai devaluation set in motion the chain of events that became known as the Asian Financial Crisis, as 'contagion' spread from one country in the region to another. The immediate effect of the crisis was massive devaluation of currencies across the region. The knock-on effect of the devaluation was dramatic, causing a huge rise in the local currency value of dollar-denominated debt. For banks and other businesses that had large dollar debts, this was a disaster. The impact of the crisis was reflected in, and compounded by, a huge decline in stock market prices. Net private capital flows to the five main economies in the region were reversed. The group of countries most affected by the crisis saw a serious decline in the national product in 1997–8.

The onset of the Asian Financial Crisis in 1997 presented a huge challenge for the whole region, including both Guangdong and Hong Kong. The Hong Kong property market and stock market collapsed simultaneously. Intense speculation surrounded the exchange rate of the Hong Kong dollar. The red chip companies encountered severe repayment difficulties. Insolvency of the red chips presented a serious threat to Hong Kong's financial stability. The international creditors demanded that the Guangdong government and the Chinese central government treat the debts of mainland firms, whether ITICs or red chips, as China's sovereign debt. The huge debts of the red chips and the ITICs presented a potential giant burden for the Guangdong government and for the central government if they decided to treat the debts as sovereign debt. The local non-bank financial institutions within Guangdong were widely discovered to be insolvent.

The mainland's main banks faced great difficulties. They had a huge portfolio of non-performing loans, due mainly to their unpaid debts from the state-owned enterprises. It was widely recognized that the Chinese banking system was among the weakest in Asia. Moreover, as China's entry to the WTO approached, they faced the reality that they would have to compete sooner rather than later with the world's leading financial institutions. The severe financial problems that emerged during the Asian Financial Crisis carried a serious risk that the crisis would spread to the entire Chinese financial system through the 'window' of Guangdong. There was simultaneously a serious possibility that the Hong Kong financial system might be unable to cope with the stresses generated by the Asian Financial Crisis.

This set of financial problems presented a comprehensive challenge for Chinese policy-makers. The challenge was all the greater because a financial crisis can rapidly turn into a social and political crisis.

2 Guangdong in the 1990s

Central-local relations

The relationship between the centre and the provinces, as well as the relationship between the provinces and lower levels of government, has been a central theme in Chinese history. As one of the most powerful provinces, one that is highly commercialized, and one that is far from the national capital, the relationship between Guangdong and the centre has always been complicated.

Wang Gungwu's study of Guangdong's overseas trade between 221 BC and 960 AD reveals that in Guangdong there was a cycle of effective government, working in harmony with market development and social stability, which alternated with periods of bureaucratic decline into corruption and economic failure. Appointees to senior official positions in Guangdong often regarded their appointment as a licence to obtain corrupt income from their official position:

> The southern lands are very rich, and those who hold office there often succeed in becoming extremely wealthy men. The saying goes, 'The governor of Kuang-chou need only pass through the city gates [of Canton] just once, and he will be enriched by thirty millions [strings of cash]'.
>
> (from the biography of Wang K'un, an honest governor, of the mid-fifth century AD, recorded in the *Nan Ch'I Shu*, quoted in Wang, 1998: 44)

A sixth-century official source comments that a succession of Guangdong governors in the late fifth and early sixth centuries had been 'mostly avaricious and extortionate' (from the *Chen Shu* [Dynastic Histories], quoted in Wang, 1998: 45). In 684 the governor of Kuang-chou, Lu Yuan-jui, was killed by a K'un Lun (Burmese) merchant. Yuan-jui was 'weak and ignorant,' and his officials were 'licentious and extortionate': 'When merchant vessels came, the officials appropriated the goods for themselves without stop' (Wang, 1998: 73). David Faure's account of Guangdong's subsequent economic development also notes the frequent appearance of corrupt behaviour by local officials. A source of 1586 observed:

> The treasures deposited by barbarian boats at Aomen (Macao) are heaped into a mountain, and all taxation is administered by the county magistrate. If he would only touch it lightly with his fingers, the income so derived would not be insubstantial.
>
> (Faure, 1996: 4–5)

In fact, the degree of corruption waxed and waned in Guangdong in parallel with that across the whole country. In his study of the Nanhai trade, analysing the Guangdong economy to the end of the Tang dynasty, Wang Gungwu has shown how there were long periods of peace, stability and effective government that allowed the economy to prosper. From 505 to 544, Guangzhou experienced 'a brilliant period of intercourse with the kingdoms of South East Asia and the West.' At the end of this great trading period, at about 544, 'the exceptional incorruptibility of Wang Mai, governor of Kuang-chou drew comment' (from the *Chen Shu* [Dynastic Histories], quoted in Wang, 1998: 45). Wang Gungwu records that from 623 to 684, South China was 'prosperous and peaceful.' The population increased, more land was occupied and cultivated, and commerce and industry became increasingly important to its economy: 'These sixty years were also some of the greatest for the Nanhai [southern seas] trade' (Wang, 1998: 73). From 713 to 750 Kuang-chou was ruled by 'the four incorruptible governors,' and the Guangdong economy again prospered (Wang, 1998: 74–5).

Under the Communist Party of China Guangdong was regarded as having long been dominated by a powerful local political machine. It has been argued that the high degree of provincial autonomy in Guangdong in the 1980s and 1990s originated in a deal struck between Deng Xiaoping and Guangdong's 'godfather,' the late revolutionary general, Ye Jianying. Deng Xiaoping purportedly agreed to 'let native sons run the province' in return for Marshall Ye's support in the power struggle following Mao Zedong's death in 1976. In the years that followed, especially after Deng Xiaoping's 'Southern Journey' in 1992, Guangdong became 'a state within a state, a political fiefdom run by local leaders who paid only lip service to Beijing.' Smuggling 'flourished along the province's long border,' and 'capital flowed overseas from its shores.' Unregulated investment 'filled the landscape with impractical projects, many built with borrowed money.' Guangdong was widely acknowledged to be a massive source of smuggling and the main source of currency flight: 'Much of the estimated US$ 20 billion to US$ 50 billion which fled China [in 1998] departed from the province' (*Wall Street Journal*, 23 February 1999).

After 1978, a key aspect of the whole Chinese reform programme was the devolution of important aspects of economic control from the central to the local government. Local authorities were granted increased independence in macro development and planning, in resource allocation, system reform and the introduction of foreign capital. The only independent function that they formally lacked was in finance. In his one-week visit to China in the mid-1990s, Paul Volker, the former US Federal Reserve Chairman, observed that 'each of China's provinces wants to have its own central bank.' What made the problem more complicated was that the provincial government delegated the same economic decision-making powers to the city and regional level, and following this sequence, right through to the lowest units of social life – the towns and villages. A persistent driving force was the intense desire of each level in the administrative system to retain under its control as powerful a force as possible of local financial institutions, whether trust and investment companies, red chips, urban credit cooperatives (UCCs), or rural financial associations (RFAs).[1] These vehicles for raising capital from outside the locality provided the lifeblood for local development. Without them the needs of local credit could not be met. The development of local financial institutions could also be important for the personal financial interests of the local leaders. Moreover, not only the local financial institutions, but also the local branches of the main commercial banks could become a major force for illegal fund-raising. They found it hard to resist the local government's strong incentives to undertake financial activities for developing the local economy. Ultimately, it was the local government that decided the fate of the cadres working in these institutions. In the 1990s there were countless examples of local branches of the state-owned banks losing control in the face of pressure from the local government.

In efforts to re-assert control over the province, Beijing reverted to a time-honoured tradition of sending a team of leaders from the north (*Wall Street Journal*, 23 February 1999). In 1997 it sent Wang Qishan to become the province's Executive Vice-Governor, answering directly to Beijing, and 'effectively sidelined the current Governor, Lu Ruihua.' In addition, 'a phalanx of northern cadres later arrived to scramble the local government's old-boy network that had allowed chaos to thrive.' In 1998 it moved the provincial Party Secretary, Xie Fei, to 'a largely ceremonial post' in Beijing and replaced him with Li Changchun, who was originally from Liaoning province, in northeast China.

There was widespread concern within the Chinese leadership at the dangers posed for Guangdong's development by the growing tide of criminality and corruption in the 1990s. In his meeting with the Guangdong delegation to the National People's Congress on 10 March 1999, Premier Zhu Rongji emphasized the need to 'regulate the economic order according to law, and combat economic crime' (quoted in Cheng, 2000: 443). There were several inter-related aspects to the crime problem in Guangdong. In particular, the boundaries of 'economic' and 'non-economic' crime were often blurred. Few people failed to notice the irony that China's fastest-growing, most free market and richest province should also be the one with, apparently, the most serious problem of crime and corruption. This provoked discussion and reflection. Although many measures were taken in the 1990s to try to tackle this problem, Guangdong's internal rectification campaigns 'failed miserably in stamping out corruption' (Cheng, 2000: 47).

Reform and opening up

Guangdong province is situated in coastal south-eastern China. Historically, Guangdong was closely linked to the international economy through the trade with southeast Asia. Ships from its ports had long plied the routes across the 'Southern Seas.' Guangdong is also the province from which by far the largest number of overseas Chinese originated. Under Maoist planning, the province was substantially cut off from the international economy. The policies of 'reform and opening up' after the early 1980s allowed Guangdong to recapture its historical function in the Chinese and the international economy.

From 1979 to 1999 under the policies of reform and opening up, Guangdong's GDP grew at 13.8 per cent per annum. Its real growth rate from 1990 to 1999 was over 15 per cent per annum (SSBG, GTN, 2000: 59). The rate of industrial growth in the 1990s reached more than 20 per cent per annum (SSBG, GTN, 2000: 59). In the late 1990s the province had a population of around seventy-three million permanent residents. If it had been ranked separately as a 'country,' Guangdong would have been considered the most outstanding performer among all developing countries, including even the Asian Newly Industrializing Countries. By the late 1990s, Guangdong had achieved the level of GDP per capita of a middle-income country. Its structure of output and employment had been comprehensively transformed. The province had become one of the world's most important centres of industrial production and exports.

Of all China's provinces, by the late 1990s, Guangdong had become the most thoroughly integrated with the international economy, with an explosive growth of exports and inflow of international capital. The province's high-speed growth stimulated large-scale movements of capital from elsewhere in China to the province. Hong Kong played a vital role in the process of the reintegration of Guangdong with the international economy. It both helped to transform, and was itself hugely transformed by, this process.

Despite the province's exceptional growth performance, by the mid-1990s it faced serious difficulties in achieving the structural change needed to sustain its growth.[2] The AFC burst upon a province that was already entering a challenging phase in its development. The pattern of growth in Guangdong caused it to be especially vulnerable to the impact of the AFC.

International trade

For over 1,000 years, foreign trade was a crucial part of the Guangdong economy. Over many centuries, Guangdong's relations with other parts of the country, and with the South China Seas, were central parts of the province's economic life:

> [Before 960 AD] the South China Sea was the main trade route of what may be called the Asian east-west trade in commodities and ideas. It was the second Silk Route. Its waters and island straits were as the sands and mountain passes of Central Asia; its ports were like the caravanserais. It became to the southern Chinese what the land outside the Jade Gate was to the northern Chinese.
>
> (Wang, 1998: 3)

Although there were periods in which the central state tried to restrict trade with foreigners, such as the early Ming dynasty, for most of the last 2,000 years international trade operated free of government controls, other than the levying of import duties. Guangzhou, Guangdong's capital city, remained at the centre of the thriving trade with southeast Asia, except during the relatively brief periods of government restriction on trade with foreigners.

At the start of the reform process in the late 1970s, Guangdong's exports totalled around US$ 2.2 billion, amounting to 13.6 per cent of the province's GDP (at the official rate of exchange) (Chan *et al.*, 1999: 79). In the first half of the 1980s, export growth was still slow. From the mid-1980s onwards, alongside the acceleration of FDI, exports began to grow at high speed. By 1990 exports had increased their share of Guangdong's provincial GDP to over 34 per cent (Chan *et al.*, 1999: 79). However, even more dramatic changes were to take place in the 1990s. Guangdong's exports more than tripled from US$ 22 billion in 1990 to US$ 75 billion in 1997, growing at an average annual rate of 19 per cent. By 1994, Guangdong's exports amounted to 44 per cent of China's total national exports. This was a 'quite astonishing dominance for a single province,' with only around 5 per cent of China's total population (Chan *et al.*, 1999: 86). By 1993, exports stood at 63 per cent of the province's GNP (at the official rate of exchange). This compares with an average figure of 13 per cent for low-income countries, 16 per cent for middle-income countries and 15 per cent for high-income countries (SSBG, GTN, 2000: 28).

By the late 1990s Guangdong had become one of the world's major manufacturing bases for a wide range of consumer goods. In 1998 it exported US$ 13.2 billion-worth of textiles and garments; US$ 5.4 billion-worth of footwear, headgear, wigs and similar products; US$ 3.3 billion-worth of plastic and rubber products and US$ 2.7 billion-worth of leather and travel goods. It exported US$ 2.2 billion-worth of metal products, US$ 4.1 billion-worth of different sorts of instruments (including medical and musical), US$ 8.2 billion-worth of miscellaneous manufactures and US$ 24.2 billion-worth of machinery and different types of electrical products. Among these totals, the province exported US$ 15.5 billion-worth of household electrical products, US$ 1.7 billion-worth of clocks and watches and US$ 570 million-worth of electronic toys and games (SSBG, GTN, 2000: 488–90).

Hong Kong was by far the main immediate destination for Guangdong's exports, taking over 39 per cent in 1995 (SSBG, GTN, 2000: 487). However, a large fraction of these was either directly re-exported or 'processed' in Hong Kong and then re-exported with a 'Made in Hong Kong' label attached. A large fraction of the re-exports was to the United States. Direct exports to the United States accounted for 23 per cent of Guangdong's exports in 1995. Thus, the United States had become by far the largest single market for Guangdong's exports.

The explosive export growth of the Guangdong economy was of a classically 'dependent' type. Guangdong's export growth was based around processing and assembly of materials supplied by customers or foreign investors. By 1995, US$ 42 billion-worth of Guangdong's total exports were officially reported to consist of such products, amounting to 74 per cent of Guangdong's total exports in that year (SSBG, GTN, 2000: 485). One estimate calculates that by 1994, the exports from foreign-invested enterprises and the 'processing sub-contractors' made up 60 per cent of total export values from the province (Chan *et al.*, 1999: 91). Thus, the core of Guangdong's explosive export growth in the 1990s can be considered as a *de facto* giant export-processing zone, in which the entrepreneurial capabilities of the indigenous firms played only a small role in export success. Rather, the core of Guangdong's export-oriented economy consisted of a myriad of small-scale enterprises that constituted the 'external firm' within the supply chain of foreign firms, mainly those of overseas Chinese business people.

Capital flows

In the late 1980s and 1990s, Guangdong became one of the world's leading recipients of international capital both through loans and foreign direct investment (FDI). A veritable 'flood' of international capital was attracted to the region. Indeed, the intensity of the 'flood' was even greater in the sense that the vast bulk of it was concentrated in a relatively small area, the Pearl River Delta, with a population of around twenty-one million.

Foreign investment

Guangdong was granted special privileges in the early years of the reforms, but until the mid-1980s, the province's export growth rate still lagged behind most of the rest of China. The key turning point came in 1985–6 when the central government decided to ease radically the restrictions on foreign investment along most of coastal China.

Alongside the liberalization of restrictions on FDI went a powerful set of 'push' factors stimulating the migration of capital from Hong Kong, Taiwan and other areas in southeast Asia. In each of these cases, rising costs of labour and land were reducing competitiveness in labour-intensive manufactures. Overseas Chinese formed the core of the ensuing explosion of inward investment into Guangdong, and, especially, the Pearl River Delta. The advantages of Guangdong as the prime location for investment from overseas Chinese included its location next to Hong Kong, with its magnificent natural harbour, and the closeness of kinship and linguistic ties, since Guangdong was the main 'sending' area for overseas Chinese. Over the centuries, many millions of people from Guangdong had migrated to different parts of the 'Southern Seas' and become central parts of the economy within the respective countries that provided them with a home. Now the capital was migrating back to the mainland in a powerful fashion.

Over the whole period from 1979 to 1999, a total of US$ 87 billion in FDI was 'actually used' in Guangdong (SSBG, GTN, 2000: 505–9). This made Guangdong one of the world's leading recipients of FDI. The total of 'actually used' FDI amounted to over US$ 1,100 per person within the province in the late 1990s. Within the total of US$ 87 billion of 'actually used' FDI, Hong Kong accounted for 74.4 per cent, Macao for 0.3 per cent and Taiwan for 3.6 per cent. However, much of the capital from Taiwan was channelled through Hong Kong, so in practice it was hard to differentiate the two sources accurately. Around 78 per cent of the FDI actually used in Guangdong in the period 1979–99 was from Hong Kong, Macao and Taiwan together. By 1999, foreign-invested enterprises produced RMB 674 billion (US$ 81 billion) in gross industrial output value, amounting to 59 per cent of Guangdong's total industrial output value (SSBG, GTN, 2000: 310–11). In other words, the province's development was hugely 'dependent' on international capital and entrepreneurship. Moreover, within the total, enterprises funded by overseas Chinese investment from Hong Kong, Macao and Taiwan were hugely dominant, accounting for 40 per cent of total industrial output value.

Dongguan City, in the Pearl River Delta, is a striking example of the role of overseas Chinese in the development of Guangdong province. By 1998 it had a cumulative total of FDI amounting to around US$ 10 billion, for a population of just 1.45 million. This exceeded the stock of FDI in Turkey, which stood at US$ 8.4 billion in 1999, with a population of sixty-four million, and which was one of the fastest growing middle-income countries. Dongguan received US$ 1.2 billion in FDI in the five years 1994–8 (inclusive), almost all of which came from Hong Kong. However, the vast bulk of this was actually from Taiwan, but channelled through Hong Kong. Dongguan had no fewer than 40,000 Taiwanese living and working in the city. It had become the *de facto* capital of Taiwanese investment on the mainland. Dongguan's GDP per capita of the resident population grew from around US$ 700 in the late 1980s to US$ 3,300 in 1999. Massive overseas investment, especially from Taiwan, had pulled Dongguan into the ranks of an upper middle-income 'country.'

International loans

During the late 1980s and in the early 1990s, innumerable Guangdong-based institutions established 'window' companies in Hong Kong. These formed a major channel for the province to gain access to international capital markets. After the reform and opening up, different departments of government and different ministries, from the provincial, city and county level, poured into Hong Kong and Macao, to establish 'window' companies that would 'open-up to the outside world,' through developing foreign trade, bringing in international skills and capital, and developing trade, real estate and finance (SSBG, GTN, 2000: 29). In addition to their success in attracting FDI, Guangdong-based institutions attracted a large amount of international capital through loans and other channels. Over the whole period from 1979 to 1999, official data recorded that Guangdong-based institutions received US$ 17.9 billion in 'actually used' foreign loans, of which bank loans totalled US$ 14.4 billion (SSBG, GTN, 2000: 503). In addition, it received over the same period, a total of US$ 6.2 billion from other sources, including US$ 4.1 billion in advances on processing and assembly business (SSBG, GTN, 2000: 503). On numerous occasions GITIC and GDE issued bonds in international capital markets. More than forty international trust and investment companies (ITICs) at various levels of the Guangdong government, as well as the red chips listed in Hong Kong and up to 1,000 'window' companies in Hong Kong, all borrowed heavily from international commercial banks through various channels. The borrowings by Guangdong's 'window' companies in Hong Kong were not required to be registered with the mainland authorities and a great deal of offshore borrowing was undertaken illegally. Therefore, it is not known how large the total international borrowings were by the 'window' companies and other Guangdong entities operating in Hong Kong.

Internal capital flows

It is almost impossible to document the extent of inter-regional capital flows within China. However, we shall see from evidence presented in the main body of this book that a major and little-studied part of the process of Guangdong's high-speed growth consisted of the large-scale attraction of funds from other parts of China to the province's main growth poles, principally the Pearl River Delta. The main channel for such movement of capital was the 'off-balance-sheet accounts' (*zhang wai zhang*), which offered illegal high interest rates far above the strictly controlled official interest rates, in order to 'pull in money' (*gaoxi lanchu*). These were mainly offered by the various forms of local non-bank financial institutions, especially the rural financial associations and urban and rural credit cooperatives. They were also frequently offered illegally by local branches of the main commercial banks. They made use of the high-speed growth story of Guangdong and created a variety of myths, giving depositors from all over the country promises of abnormally high returns from investing in Guangdong, China's 'super-high growth' region, nurtured and stimulated by its economic relations with neighbouring Hong Kong. By the time of the Asian Financial Crisis, Guangdong's local non-bank financial institutions had amassed the equivalent in RMB deposits of around US$ 10 billion. A significant fraction was in the form of '*gaoxi lanchu*' deposits from elsewhere in China. The principal source of these funds is likely to have been from state-owned enterprises seeking a higher return on capital than their own business could offer.

Enping county in the Pearl River Delta is a striking example of these problems. Enping's rural credit cooperatives (RCCs), followed by the local branch of China Construction Bank, used simple stories of building cement factories in Enping, promising an annual interest rate of more than 30 per cent ('high interest to attract funds,' *gaoxi lanchu*), and attracted as much as RMB 10 billion from all over the country. Similar fund-raising miracles took place among Guangdong's NBFIs such as the urban credit cooperatives (UCCs) and rural financial associations (RFAs) especially in the fast-growing Pearl River Delta area. In the mid-1990s, the investment rate in Guangdong was over 40 per cent. In addition to investment in manufacturing, Guangdong needed a large amount of investment in environment, education, medical care, infrastructure, research and development and ordinary housing. However, an investment return of over 30 per cent could not be sustained, even if the demand for cement in Enping had continued to grow rapidly and the cement plants had been better managed. It was only a matter of time before a payment crisis emerged.

The only explanation of this behaviour is high risk speculation. The 'game' was similar to the standard 'Ponzi' scheme. In 1920, Charles Ponzi devised a scheme to arbitrage postal coupons, buying them from Spain and selling them to the US postal service at a profit. To raise capital, he promised investors a 50 per cent return in ninety days. The greedy investors swarmed in. He paid the earlier depositors with cash collected from those coming later. The scheme could only last a finite period of time, as it relied entirely on collecting ever-larger amounts from each generation of depositors. Eventually, Ponzi was imprisoned for defrauding 40,000 people of US$ 15 million. Variants of the Ponzi scheme have regularly appeared in different locations. Ponzi schemes were a key part of the Savings and Loans disaster in the United States in the 1980s. Deregulation of the Savings and Loans (thrift) sector 'allowed the thrifts access to unprecedented amounts of cash – albeit at exorbitantly high interest rates – with which to fund their investment projects and finance their shopping sprees' (Calavita *et al.*, 1997: 25). A major part of their activity was funding 'acquisition, development and construction' (ADC) of housing developments, which are 'among the riskiest investments a financial institution can make' (Calavita *et al.*, 1997: 39). These were 'essentially Ponzi schemes':

> The only way for an ADC scheme to fund interest on deposits and cover withdrawals was to grow rapidly and pay the old depositors with the funds provided by new depositors...It was for this reason that the most catastrophic thrift failures grew the fastest and consistently reported the highest profits throughout the mid-1980s.
>
> (Calavita *et al.*, 1997: 42)

For a given period, and within a particular area, the Ponzi game can be played as long as the amount of money that people are induced to deposit is sufficient to pay the high returns that are promised to the previous depositors. Many of the early participants in Enping's 'Ponzi game' made large amounts of money. The only way for the scheme to continue was to raise the rate of interest to induce further depositors. Unfortunately for the financial authorities, the greater the quantity of funds that people were induced to deposit, attracted by the super-high rates of return, the more serious the payment crisis that, sooner or later, was bound to take place. As in the typical Ponzi scheme, the process was accompanied by extensive criminality and corruption. The phrase used by the local people, *shui luo shi chu* ('as the tide retreats the rocks appear') to describe the payment crisis all over the province after 1998 is most appropriate. It appeared before the overall payment crisis in Guangdong, due to large-scale runs on Enping's financial institutions, and was dealt with during the 'three steps' to resolve Guangdong's financial crisis (see Part 2).

Real estate

Real estate bubbles have occurred regularly across all types of economy. The financial crisis in Guangdong was closely related to the bubble in real estate. The collapse of the bubble in the mid-1990s meant that even before the AFC, Guangdong's local NBFIs faced severe difficulties.

Real estate investment boomed in Guangdong in the early 1990s. Total real estate investment increased from the equivalent of US$ 1.6 billion in the Seventh Five Year Plan (FYP) (1986–90) to US$ 17.6 billion in the Eighth FYP (1991–5) (SSBG, GTN, 2000: 158). Its share of the total fixed investment in the province rose from 8.2 per cent in the Seventh FYP to 19.4 per cent in the Eighth FYP, reaching 24.2 per cent in 1995 (SSBG, GTN, 2000: 158). The geographic concentration in the value of real estate construction was striking. For example, in 1999, the PRD, with 29 per cent of the province's population, accounted for 92 per cent of the total provincial real estate investment, while the cities of Guangzhou and Shenhzen alone accounted for 72 per cent of the provincial total (SSBG, GTN, 2000: 160). The amount of floorspace under construction rose from 91 million square metres in 1990 to 213 million square metres in 1995, an annual average growth rate of 19 per cent (SSBG, GTN, 2000: 157). Although there was high-speed growth of real estate construction in order to meet real demand growth, there was an accompanying bubble in real estate prices.

Employment and standard of living

The official data on the formally registered population of Guangdong province show a large structural shift out of the farm sector into the secondary and tertiary sectors, consistent with high-speed industrialization, and substantial growth of real output and income. Over the period 1980 to 1999, Guangdong province's GDP per capita (at the official rate of exchange) rose from US$ 280 to US$ 1,400 (SSBG, GTN, 2000: 92). Guangdong had emphatically moved into the ranks of a 'middle-income country.' The economic boom in Guangdong in the 1990s was accompanied by a large growth in savings by both urban and rural residents. By 1999, total savings by residents in banks and non-bank financial institutions in Guangdong were estimated to be RMB 735 billion (US$ 89 billion), of which urban savings were estimated to be RMB 561 billion and rural savings were RMB 174 billion (SSBG, GTN, 2000: 211).

Behind these data lay a pattern of employment growth and income distribution that rendered the province vulnerable to socio-economic instability in the event of a financial crisis. The extraordinary speed of the province's development had resulted in a distinctive pattern of growth that produced severe social tensions. If the financial crisis had been allowed to spill over into the social sphere, the potential consequences would have been severe. Recent history has revealed all too vividly how quickly a financial crisis can descend into a much deeper social and political crisis. The examples of Indonesia in the late 1990s and Argentina in 2001 both demonstrate how rapidly such a 'contagion' can spread from the financial system to the social system and then to the political system. Well before either of these events, advisors within the Chinese government were acutely aware of these types of danger.

The development process in Guangdong was uneven. The PRD formed the focal point of the province's high-speed development during the era of reform and opening-up.[3] In 1999, the PRD contained twenty-one million permanent residents (29 per cent of the population of the whole province) (SSBG, GTN, 2000: 121). In other words, it had the same population as a medium-sized developing economy, such as Malaysia or Taiwan, each of which had a population of twenty-two million in 1998. In 1999 the PRD accounted for 71 per cent of the province's total investment in fixed assets and 85 per cent of the total provincial gross industrial output value (SSBG, GTN, 2000: 160, and 325–6). The PRD accounted for only 22 per cent of Guangdong's farm population, but it contained 45 per cent of its non-farm population, and 58 per cent of the total number of 'staff and workers' (i.e. those employed in the 'formal' sector) (SSBG, GTN, 2000: 136). The nine administrative districts that make up the PRD had an average (unweighted) per capita GDP of US$ 2,900, ranging from US$ 1,630 in Jiangmen to US$ 4,300 in Shenzhen (SSBG, GTN, 2000: 99). Seven of the districts had an average per capita GDP of over US$ 2,000. In other words, by the late 1990s, the PRD had achieved 'take-off.' It constituted a 'Little Tiger' to compare with the other 'Little Tigers' of East Asia. It was now an upper middle-income 'country' (see Table 1.1).

Even within China's richest and most highly developed province, Guangdong, there was a large group of poor districts. In 1998 the seven poorest districts in the province had an average (unweighted) GDP per capita of US$ 580, and contained twenty-seven million people (36 per cent of the provincial total). In other words, this poor area was the equivalent of a medium-sized developing country. Within this group there was a sub-group of three exceptionally poor districts, with an average per capita GDP (unweighted) of just US$ 400, containing twelve million people (16 per cent of the provincial total). During the period of the fastest growth that the province had ever seen, the degree to which capital was 'trickling down' to the poor regions within the province was quite limited. The highest returns from capital were to be obtained principally from the already more highly developed PRD in the centre of the province. Naturally, there was a powerful stream of migration from the poor areas around the province to the PRD.

Like some other East Asian economies, the high-speed growth in the Pearl River Delta was heavily reliant on foreign capital and entrepreneurship. However, the fact that it was part of a much larger political entity caused its development path to be quite different from East Asian late-industrializing economies. During the similar development phase in fast-growing East

Table 1.1 Comparative economic indicators: the Pearl River Delta (PRD), Guangdong and China, 2001

	GDP (RMB billion)	*Fixed assets investment (RMB billion)*	*Exports (US$ billion)*	*FDI (US$ billion)*
China	9,593.3	3,689.8	266.2	46.8
Guangdong	1,055.647	354.726	95.42	15.755
PRD cities[a]	849.528	252.724	90.862	13.843
PRD cities/China (%)	8.86	6.85	34.13	29.58
PRD cities/Guangdong (%)	80.47	71.24	95.22	87.86

Source: 'The myth of the Pearl River Delta', *Shenzhen Commercial Daily*, 22 April 2002: B2.

a These are Guangzhou, Shenzhen, Zhuhai, Foshan, Jiangmen, Dongguan, Huizhou (only including Huicheng District, Huiyang City, Huidong County and Boluo County) and Zhaoqing (only including Ruizhou District, Dinghu District, Gaoyao City and Sihui City).

Asian countries such as South Korea, Taiwan, Hong Kong and Singapore, there was tight control over in-migration. In sharp contrast, there was large-scale migration into the fast-growing Pearl River Delta region both from other parts of Guangdong itself as well as from other regions of China. The very success of Guangdong in becoming a global base for labour-intensive manufactures created a vicious circle from which it was difficult to extricate itself. The major factor that had driven other East Asian countries to move up the value chain into higher value-added areas of production, had been the exhaustion of rural surplus labour, and the ending of the 'Lewis' phase of development (Lewis, 1954). This helped to stimulate a trend increase in real wages, pushing firms into higher-value forms of production. It also stimulated governments to spend more on the upgrading of human skills to facilitate the move up the level of industrial sophistication to higher value-added forms of business activity.

By the late 1990s there were around fifteen to sixteen million migrants in Guangdong from within and outside the province. They mainly worked in the PRD and, to a lesser degree, in the Han River Delta. The Pearl River Delta contained around twenty million locally registered employees. Most of the migrants did not possess a local '*hukou*' or residence permit. This meant that they were second-class citizens without access to state education, health or other welfare services.

The impact on the labour market of around fourteen to fifteen million migrants employed in the Pearl River Delta, constituting close to one-half of the total workforce, was enormous. In some of the most highly industrialized and fast-growing areas within the PRD, the share of migrants in the local workforce was even greater. For example, in Dongguan county in 1997, the number of migrant workers was estimated to be 1.31 million, compared with a local workforce of just 0.88 million. In other words, migrant workers accounted for almost 60 per cent of the total workforce in the county (Yeung, 2001: 110). Moreover, by 1999, the number of migrants in Dongguan was reported to have risen to around three million, accounting for over 75 per cent of the total workforce in the county.

There was little change over many years in real wages in the low-wage segment that dominated the manufacturing sector in the Pearl River Delta. Nominal wages in the Pearl River Delta were unchanged throughout the whole decade from the late 1980s to the late 1990s, suggesting a substantial fall in real wages (Chan *et al.*, 1999: 89). In Dongguan average nominal wages for unskilled workers in the mid-1990s were significantly above those in the mid-1980s, but still were only around RMB 300 (US$ 36) per month or around US$ 1 per day (Yeung, 2001: 132). It is hard to imagine that there had been much growth in real wages over the previous decade. In other words, the real wages of many millions of employees in the region had certainly not risen significantly during the phase of high-speed growth, and may even have fallen. This is consistent with such information as is available about the main features of the labour market in this region.

Public order

According to the Guangdong Public Security Bureau (PSB) the number of criminal cases reported in the province in 1994 was 4.9 times greater than in 1987, and for serious crime the number reported (107,000 cases) had increased 13.7 times compared with 1987 (Che, 2000: 329). One analyst described the public order situation in the province as 'grim' (Zhang, 2000: 205). There was deep concern at the rise of organized crime. In the 1990s it was the province with the fastest level of economic development that experienced the most severe increase in crime (Che, 2000: 348).

By the mid-1990s, around one-half of those arrested in Guangdong were members of criminal gangs. Triad societies from Hong Kong, Taiwan and Macao had established themselves in the province (Che, 2000: 330). This made it easier for criminals to escape capture by fleeing to other parts of Asia through Triad networks. In 1994–5, the PSB reported that it had eliminated 849 criminal syndicates, and arrested 3,600 members of these gangs (Che, 2000: 330). There was a marked concentration of criminal activity in the Pearl River Delta. Although it contained only around 30 per cent of the province's population, by the mid-1990s it was estimated to account for around 74 per cent of the total number of criminals arrested in the province (Che, 2000: 330).

A major factor at the centre of the crime wave was the large number of migrant workers in the province, especially in the PRD. By the late 1990s there were probably around fifteen million migrant workers in Guangdong alone, a large fraction of whom were concentrated in the Pearl River Delta. In the mid-1990s, around 60 per cent of the criminals arrested came from outside Guangdong province. In some cities in the PRD, such as Shenzhen, Zhuhai, Foshan and Dongguan, 'outsiders' accounted for 80 per cent of arrested offenders (Che, 2000: 330). However, one consequence of the high proportion of migrants involved in crime is that they could relatively easily escape to other parts of the country. Most of the criminal offences in Guangdong were aimed at obtaining wealth from the victims. These included both violent crimes against the person as well as crimes involving bribery, corruption, embezzlement and deceit (Che, 2000: 348).

The highly developed nature of criminal activity in the province is indicated by the fact that in 1995, it accounted for 47 per cent of the national total of counterfeit money seized by the Public Security Bureau (Zhang, 2000: 205). The province ranked third in the country in terms of seriousness of drugs trafficking and abuse (Zhang, 2000: 205). In 1997 alone 600 drugs gangs were dealt with and 3,000 drugs cases came before the courts (Zhang, 2000: 205).

The Guangdong government was concerned about the relatively low level of human capital in the province, which was closely related to the problems of social order and criminality. A large fraction of the migrant worker population had only a low educational level. The real incomes of this large group probably fell during the 1990s. Their migration helped provide some addition to family income in the sending areas. However, the rapid expansion in their employment at a constant or falling real wage produced widening inequalities in income and wealth within the PRD. The class structure in the region was strongly polarized.

The issue of public order in the province was related also to the self-reinforcing cycle of low value-added development. The paradox has already been noted, that Guangdong was China's fastest-growing and richest province, but was also its most corrupt and most criminalized province. However, a related paradox is that among the advanced regions of China it had one of the lowest levels of educational attainment. According to 1996 data, among permanent residents of the province, only 1.9 per cent of those employed had received a college education, compared with 3.5 per cent in Jiangsu province and 13 per cent in Shanghai (Zhang, 2000: 206). During the phase of high-speed growth from the mid-1980s to the late 1990s, the province was relatively slow in upgrading its human capital. Government expenditure on culture, health, education and science was only 3.1 per cent of provincial GDP in 1978. In the late 1990s, it was even lower, standing at only 2.9 per cent in 1999 (SSBG, GTN, 2000: 58–9). In 1999, there was still only one doctor per 657 people in the province and one hospital bed per 483 people, hardly any higher than in 1990 (or even 1980). Indeed, in the poorest districts in Guangdong, namely Meizhou and Heyuan (with a combined population of 7.9 million), there were 850 and 1,000 people per doctor, respectively, compared with 156 per doctor in Shenzhen (SSBG, GTN, 2000: 578).

These were slow rates of progress in expanding human capital for a country moving from relative backwardness to middle-income level.

Smuggling

Smuggling formed a particularly important aspect of corruption in Guangdong. In 1998, the Public Security Bureau reported that smuggling cases in Guangdong made up 40 per cent of the national total (Zhang, 2000: 205). In 1999 Premier Zhu Rongji urged Guangdong's leaders to crack down on smuggling activities in the province. A number of investigations were carried out. From August 1998 to January 1999, the Guangdong authorities dealt with over 3,000 smuggling cases involving goods worth RMB 2.2 billion (Gu, 2000: 247). A significant part of the smuggling to and from Guangdong province concerned Hong Kong. Electrical products and luxury cars, which both had high tariffs, were smuggled into the mainland from Hong Kong in large quantities. Drugs from the Golden Triangle in Burma, antiques and counterfeit CDs, were all smuggled into Hong Kong in large amounts from the mainland (Che, 2000: 335). In order to tackle the huge problem of smuggling in Guangdong, the provincial government established a special police task force, the Guangdong Smuggling Investigation Bureau, with 2,700 special police officers (Gu, 2000: 247). In October 1998 it was reported that a case of smuggling automobiles into China involved the naval bases and the police together in Shantou in Guangdong, and Beihai in Guangxi (Cheng, 2000: 45).

Up until the Shantou case (see below), the most serious case in Guangdong was that at Zhanjiang. The case was one of 'collective corruption': '[It] involved over 200 government officials, with twelve cadres at the office or bureau-level, and four cadres at the division level' (Huang, 2001: 40). The smuggling ring involved 'a chain of command from the front line of customs, boundary police, commercial inspectors, and harbour affairs, all the way up to the municipal city government and Communist Party Committee' (Huang, 2001: 40). The case involved over RMB 10 billion (US$ 1.2 billion) in corruption and RMB 6 billion (US$ 720 million) in tax evasion. The operation involved smuggling steel, oil and cars worth RMB 30 billion (US$ 3.6 billion). After the trial, the head of the Zhanjiang customs administration, Cao Xiukang, was sentenced to death, and a further twenty-five people were punished, including the city's Party secretary, and several Hong Kong residents (Zhang, 2000: 204).

Another highly publicized smuggling case in Guangdong was that in Huidong county. This case illustrates the depth to which corruption had penetrated the government and Party system, making regulation and investigation work from higher levels extremely difficult. It involved the Party secretary, the head and deputy head of the county, the heads of the Public Security Bureau and the Industry and Commerce Bureau, as well as the director of the anti-smuggling office. They had allowed 16,000 cartloads of smuggled goods through after receiving payment of RMB 46 million (US$ 5.5 million) (Reported in *Liaowang*, 22 March 1999). A similar case was that of Shao Rucai in 1999. Shao concurrently held the posts of head of the Financial Bureau, the Tax Bureau and the State Asset Management Bureau of Guangzhou (Reported in *Nanfang Ribao*, 2 February 1999). In early 2001, a central government investigation was launched into suspected smuggling and corruption in Shantou City in eastern Guangdong. Around 300 investigators from the Party's Central Inspection Committee conducted a huge investigation in Shantou.

A major problem associated with smuggling was the loss of foreign exchange. Throughout the 1990s there was a gap between the increase in the country's foreign exchange reserves and the persistent large trade surpluses. In 1998 Premier Zhu Rongji declared that a major goal in the fight against the loss of foreign exchange was to bring to justice smugglers and those who had cheated the state of its foreign exchange (Cheng, 2000: 45). Guangdong was at the centre of this process, given its massive involvement in the international economy. In March 2001, seven people were sentenced to death in Guangdong for their part in a huge tax fraud. The *Financial Times* commented: [the scandal] 'reinforces a sense that corruption is withering the root and branch of China's ruling Communist hierarchy' (*FT*, 3 March 2001).

The seven included two tax officials and a former prosecutor. They were found guilty of using receipts from shell companies with no staff or premises to claim RMB 58 million in tax rebates (*FT*, 3 March 2001). The sentence was thought to be the tip of the iceberg in an investigation that spread across eleven provinces and autonomous regions. Premier Zhu Rongji reportedly described the export rebate fraud as an 'outstanding social and economic problem' and the crackdown in 2000/1 as 'an urgent economic struggle.' The export rebate scam was carried out mainly by faking export certificates to claim a rebate on the full 17 per cent in value-added tax levied on manufactures. Sometimes more elaborate methods were used, including packing container ships full of cases filled with sand to provide the impression that goods were leaving the wharf (*FT*, 3 March 2001).

Criminal behaviour among government and Party officials

The Guangdong Party and government were long aware of the rising tide of corruption in the province. It established the Guangdong People's Procurate Anti-Corruption Bureau (GPPACB) in 1989. In the following ten years the Bureau investigated no fewer than 20,000 corruption cases. In 1998 alone, it investigated 1,700 government officers allegedly involved in corruption (Gu, 2000: 249). The vast bulk of corruption cases (over three-quarters) took place in enterprises, typically involving state-owned assets. In the period 1994 to 1996, 7,085 people in the province were found guilty of various corrupt practices, mostly relating to financial matters. In 1996 alone, there were 4,255 cases of people found guilty of corruption (Zhang, 2000: 204).

The political level of those involved in corruption cases rose as the decade progressed. In 1996, Ou Yangde, Deputy Chairman of the Standing Committee of the Provincial People's Congress, was convicted of accepting bribes of RMB 530,000 (US$ 64,000) (Zhang, 2000: 204). Shortly afterwards, another Deputy Chairman, Yu Fei, was dismissed from his post and stripped of his Party membership. Yu Fei was found to have used his position to acquire land for his children at 'unreasonably low prices' and then to have re-sold the land for a large profit. Through these 'power-backed transactions,' Yu Fei was accused of gaining RMB 28 million (US$ 3.4 million). From 1985 to 1996 land sales in Guangdong amounted to over RMB 1,370 billion, but the provincial government only reported revenues of RMB 953 billion to the State Council. The central government wanted to know how the remaining RMB 417 billion (US$ 50 billion) could be accounted for (Cheng, 2000: 46–7).

In the mid-1990s, rumours circulated that important positions in Guangdong were for sale at the prefectural government level and below: 'A corrupt official had to accumulate a fortune to acquire a lucrative strategic position, but he could expect to make an even larger fortune during his tenure' (Cheng, 2000: 42). The Guangdong government's seriousness of purpose in eliminating corruption can be seen from the massive province-wide inspection of 1997/8. Within a year, 4,258 inspection and audit teams visited 9,913 enterprises. 'Readjustments' in leadership positions involved 3,048 people, among whom 1,123 lost their positions or were demoted (Cheng, 2000: 40). The provincial government organized major campaigns to strengthen ideological and educational work. In 1996 it devised a ten-year programme to raise the educational level of the province's cadres. In 1999 the provincial government announced a scheme to send 300 senior cadres abroad for specialist training. Local governments in several cities began similar schemes of their own (Cheng, 2000: 43–4).

There were difficulties in pursuing anti-corruption work. In the first place, by definition, the cases involved participation by the government and Party bureaucracy. The people concerned were able to use their positions to try to inhibit investigations. Moreover, the police force was often heavily involved in corruption. A further problem was that even if there was a successful investigation, there was no guarantee that the judiciary would fairly try those arrested. The judiciary was widely acknowledged to be corrupt. For example, in 1997, Zhang Yongku and Zhong Naiting, head and deputy head of the executive division of the Shenzhen People's Court, were convicted of taking bribes of RMB 280,000 (US$ 34,000) and RMB 440,000 (US$ 53,000), respectively (Zhang, 2000: 205, from Liu, 1998: 287–8). In 1997 also, Zeng Sheng, as a member of both the standing committees of the Party and the Political and Legal Affairs Bureau of Huazhou City, as well as head of the city's Public Security Bureau, was sentenced to death after he was found guilty of having received RMB 3 million (US$ 360,000) in bribes (Zhang, 2000: 205, from Liu Zhifeng, 1998: 282–7). In the same year, Cheng Yuwu, head of the armed police squadron in Huilai county was given a death sentence suspended for two years for directing his squadron to protect smuggling operations (Zhang, 2000: 205, from Liu, 1998: 465).

3 Linkages between Hong Kong and Guangdong

Relationship between internal and external capital flows

The process of migration of Chinese people from the mainland to southeast Asia has been going on for thousands of years. Overseas Chinese people constitute a crucial part of the economies of the region. In the 1990s in the Philippines, the overseas Chinese accounted for only one per cent of the population, but controlled over one-half of the stock market. In Indonesia the equivalent proportions were 4 per cent and 75 per cent, and in Malaysia, 32 per cent and 60 per cent. By 1996, it was estimated that the fifty-one million overseas Chinese 'controlled an economy worth US$ 700 billion – roughly the same size as that of the 1.2 billion Chinese mainlanders'

The two apparently unrelated flows of 'hot money,' one internal and one external, which were analysed above, had a complex relationship. Beginning from opium smuggling, Guangdong has always been the first to reform and open up during the historical process of China's modernization. Around two-thirds of the thirty million overseas Chinese in southeast Asia (excluding those in Taiwan) originated from Guangdong.

In 1976, when China had just begun to reform and open up, Fairbank proposed the concept of 'China on the sea': 'Today, Guangdong is again in the lead in China's international trade. China on the sea has fully developed, including the British colony of Hong Kong, Singapore, Taiwan, and tens of thousands overseas Chinese in Kuala Lumpur, Penang, Bangkok, Manila, Colombo and other areas' (Fairbank, 2002: 176). Fairbank's insight is helpful for us to understand the way in which relations between Guangdong and the overseas Chinese evolved in the 1980s and 1990s. These extensive relationships wove a network of manufacturing connections, with 'the workshop in the back and shop in the front,' not only through direct links between Guangdong and Hong Kong, but also including indirect investment through Hong Kong from overseas Chinese in Taiwan, Thailand, Singapore and elsewhere in southeast Asia. This developed within only a short period of time after 1980.

The same logic applies to the way in which, in the opening-up of China's finance, Guangdong in particular, was first and foremost developed rapidly on the basis of such a network of 'China on the sea.' The two flows of 'hot money' both from home and abroad are not simple textbook transactions. They interwove with each other, supplemented each other, and brought out the best in each other in the special channels of material flows, human flows and capital flows and on the basis of credit networks. The participation of overseas Chinese businessmen with strong business reputations enhanced the credibility of investment projects and fund-raising stories within China. For example, Enping is well-known in the country for raising funds by its stories. It is a bleak place almost without any decent factories. However, it has large-scale and luxurious leisure facilities that are up to international standards, invested in and managed by overseas Chinese and catering for foreign business people or high-rank government officials. This sharp contrast makes one suspect that the special business functions of these facilities went beyond simply consuming the services that these facilities provided. Against the background of high-speed growth of the export processing industry, countless cases of borrowing, both domestically and internationally, contributed, directly and indirectly, to Guangdong's speculative bubble.

The nature of long-distance migration the world over is that certain regions and sub-regions develop strong traditions of migration and networks that facilitate further migration ('chain' migration). For example, within Guangdong province, the Chaozhou-Shantou region in the eastern part of the province is the area with the largest single concentration of overseas migrants.[4] These had emigrated over many centuries. By the 1990s there were estimated to be around ten million Chaoshan people living in the Chaoshan region and around ten million living overseas. Even within the Chaoshan district there are large differences in the extent of migration among different counties.[5] In other words, the Chaoshan people account for around one-third of the whole overseas Chinese population (excluding Taiwan). Among their number are some of the most famous overseas Chinese business people. The most notable of these is Li Jiacheng (Li Kah-hsing). By far the largest concentration of Chaoshan people overseas is in Thailand. The Chaoshan people originally came to southeast China from all over the Chinese interior. They speak a distinctive dialect which is incomprehensible to most Chinese, not only to those from other parts of China, but also those from other parts of Guangdong. The Chaoshan people within China and overseas in southeast Asia, with their own language and kinship networks, form a 'country without borders.' This 'country' includes dense networks of capital flows across borders among the Chaoshan people. One may speculate that this dense network forms a *de facto* 'international currency region' among the Chaoshan people. There must be only a slim chance for government officials at higher levels to penetrate and control fully cross-border capital flows within such a closed network.

Capital flight had become a major issue for the Chinese government by the time of the AFC. It has been estimated that capital flight in 1997 and 1998 amounted to US$ 36.4 billion and US$ 38.6 billion, respectively (*FT*, 21 August 2002). Much of the capital flight was thought to have been channelled through Hong Kong, especially through the innumerable Chinese window companies operating there, as well as through the overseas Chinese businesses operating in both Hong Kong and the mainland. A leading US expert in the field believed that the bulk of the FDI coming into Hong Kong represented 'illegal capital flight from the mainland that has gone abroad and established itself as a foreign entity' (Raymond Baker, quoted in *Far Eastern Economic Review*, 21 June 2001). The main motive for the illegal capital outflows was in order to avoid paying taxes. Capital flight strongly stimulated corruption, since an extensive network of illegal activities was necessary to enable the complex processes of false official documentation involved. The most common method of shifting the capital was through falsification of prices of imports and exports, with the proceeds paid into foreign bank accounts.

The impact on Hong Kong was also serious, since it undermined the city's reputation. Hong Kong was an easy target for such money laundering due to the combination of low taxation, sophisticated banking facilities and the absence of currency and exchange controls. In addition, banks only defined activities as 'money laundering' when the activity included the proceeds of crime such as narcotics and gambling. Even in these areas, Hong Kong had been 'notoriously slow to prevent use of the city for money laundering.' In the 1990s it faced the possibility of sanctions from the OECD if it failed to take a tougher stand after almost 3,000 intensive investigations over four years failed to produce more than forty-nine convictions. Under Hong Kong laws at that time there was almost no chance of laying charges, let alone penalizing the lawyers, accountants and bankers handling most of these transactions. Despite the administration's best efforts, 'local lawmakers almost unanimously rejected the proposed tougher laws which they feared would put careless or gullible bankers or accountants behind bars' (*Far Eastern Economic Review*, 21 June 2001). This environment created a fertile soil for capital flight from the mainland, through the inter-meshing of mainland entities operating in Hong Kong with local Hong Kong financial institutions.

Red chips[6]

Rise and fall of the 'red chips'

The most important form of mainland business presence in Hong Kong at the time of the Asian Financial Crisis was the so-called 'red chip.' The red chips were mainland-based firms that were registered and listed in Hong Kong, but retained at least 30 per cent ownership by their mainland parent entities, usually mainland governments and departments (Table 1.2). During the 1990s, the 'red chip' concept grew at high speed. The red chips were subject to Hong Kong regulation, as that was their place of registration, as well as their main business operations. The 'H' share companies also grew rapidly, but these Hong Kong-listed companies were registered in the mainland, and, therefore, were under the regulation of the mainland authorities. From the point of view of the Hong Kong regulatory authorities and from the point of view of many analysts, the red chips were considered to be real firms, with all the associated autonomy of business behaviour. In fact, the red chips were still essentially SOEs. Although they were subject to some significant controls from their mainland parents, they also had considerable autonomy to develop their business activities. They were firms that had no clear boundaries to their expansion.

Table 1.2 Background of key Hong Kong-registered mainland Chinese companies

HK-registered mainland Chinese companies	*Ultimate Chinese shareholders (department or government)*
Beijing Holdings Ltd	Beijing City
Tsinlien Co. Ltd	Tianjin City
Shanghai Industrial Investment (Holdings) Co. Ltd	Shanghai City
Y.F. International Ltd	Chongqing City
China Liaoning Ltd	Liaoning City
H.HK Holdings Co. Ltd	Heilongjiang province
Zhong Ji Ltd	Jilin province
Inner Mongolia Hing Yuen (HK) Co. Ltd	Inner Mongolia Administrative Region
Hebei Enterprises Ltd	Hebei province
Hong Kong Heng Shan Co. Ltd	Shanxi province
Zhong Shan Co. Ltd	Jiangsu province
Zhejiang Fuchuen Co. Ltd	Shanxi province
China Shandong Group Ltd	Shandong province
Hua Gan Enterprises Ltd	Jiangxi province
Anhui Co. Ltd	Anhui province
Henan Hong Kong (Holdings) Ltd	Henan province
Yi F. Trading Co. Ltd	Hubei province
Hunan Sunshine Holdings Ltd	Hunan province
Gui Jiang Enterprises Ltd	Guangxi Zhuong Administrative Region
Guangdong Enterprise (Holdings) Ltd	Guangdong province
Hua Hai Co. Ltd	Hainan province
Jialing International Holdings Ltd	Sichuan province
Yunnan and Hong Kong Co. Ltd	Yunnan province
Gui Da Co. Ltd	Guizhou province
Lishan Co. Ltd	Shaanxi province
Gansu Co. Ltd	Gansu province
QHL Trading Co. Ltd	Qinghai province
Kachant Development Ltd	Ningxia Administrative Region
Xingjiang Development Ltd	Xingjiang Administrative Region
China Tibet Qomolangma Trade & Travel Ltd	Tibet Administrative Region
Shen Gang Ltd	Shenyang City
Dalian International (Holdings) Co. Ltd	Dalian City
Kwok Nea Development Ltd	Nanjing City
Ning Shing Development Co. Ltd	Ningbo City
Xing Xia Co. Ltd	Xiamen City
Ever Eagle Co. Ltd	Wuhan City
Yue Xiu Enterprises (Holdings) Ltd	Guangzhou City

(Continued)

HK-registered mainland Chinese companies	*Ultimate Chinese shareholders (department or government)*
Shum Yip Holdings Co. Ltd	Shenzhen City
Crown Smart Ltd	Xian City
China International Trust and Investment Corp. HK (Holdings) Ltd	State Council
China Everbright Enterprises Holdings Co. Ltd	State Council
Yuan Min Gardens Development Ltd	State Planning Commission
China United Telecom Corp. (HK) Ltd	State Economic and Trade Commission
China Venturetechno International Co. Ltd	International Science, Technology & Industrial Commission
China National Education Development Ltd	State Education Commission
APT Satellite Co. Ltd	International Science, Technology & Industrial Commission
Winner Industrial Ltd	State Sports Commission
China Resources (Holdings) Co. Ltd	Ministry of Foreign Economic Relationship Trust
China Everbest Machinery Enterprises Co. Ltd	Ministry of Machinery
CEIEC (HK) Ltd	Ministry of Power
China Metallurgic (HK) Co. Ltd	Ministry of Metallurgy
MCI (HK) Co. Ltd	Ministry of Chemicals
China Power International Holdings Ltd	Ministry of Electricity
China Merchants Holdings Co. Ltd	Ministry of Communications
COSCO (Hong Kong) Group Ltd	Ministry of Communications
China Railway Services (Hong Kong) Ltd	Ministry of Railways
CCECC (HK) Ltd	Ministry of Railways
Telpo Communications (Group) Ltd	Ministry of Telecommunications
China Overseas Holdings Ltd	Ministry of Construction
Joshek Development Ltd	Ministry of Construction
Double Resources Ltd	Ministry of Coal
Zhen Xing Medicine and Publication Enterprises Co. Ltd	Ministry of Health
Weddy Co. Ltd	Ministry of Commerce
China Legal Service (HK) Ltd	Ministry of Justice
China National Aviation Corp. (Group) Ltd	Civil Aviation Administration of China
China Zhaoyang Building Materials Co. Ltd	State Construction Bureau
China Statistics Consultants Ltd	State Statistical Bureau
China International Travel Service HK Ltd	State Tourism Bureau
Lung Tin International Ltd	International Business Cooperation Bureau
China Travel Services (Holdings) HK Ltd	State Chinese Nationals Office
Bin Hai Water Treatment (HK) Consultancy Co. Ltd	State HK Macau Affairs Office
China Overseas Space Development & Investment Co. Ltd	Aviation Industry Co.
China Aerospace International Holdings Ltd	Aviation Industry Co.
CATIC (HK) Ltd	Aviation Industry Co.
Silver City International (Holdings) Ltd	Ammunition Industry Co.
HK Resources Engineering Co. Ltd	Electricity Co.
Yuan Neng Industrial Co.	Nuclear Industry Co.
Sinopec (Hong Kong) Ltd	Oil and Petrochemical Co.

HK-registered mainland Chinese companies	*Ultimate Chinese shareholders (department or government)*
China Hua Neng Group Hong Kong Ltd	Huaneng Enterprise Co.
CNPC Hong Kong (Holdings) Ltd	Oil and Natural Gas Co.
China Ocean Oilfields Services (HK) Co. Ltd	Offshore Oil Co.
China Non-ferrous Metals Holdings (HK) Ltd	Non-ferrous Metals Co.
Tian Li International Co. Ltd	Tobacco Co.
HK Jing Yuen Development Co. Ltd	Jing An Tools Co.
HK Xing Xing Investment Development Co. Ltd	Xing Xing Enterprise Co.
Fortune Hand Industries Ltd	China Science Council
China Youth Travel (HK) Co. Ltd	State Youth Organisation
Shui Hua Development & Enterprise Ltd	Ministry of Light Industry
Eternal Sky Investment Ltd	Ministry of Textiles
Hong Kong-Macau Regional Office, Bank of China	Bank of China
China Construction Bank, HK Branch	China Construction Bank
Industrial & Commercial Bank of China, HK Branch	Industrial and Commercial Bank of China
Agricultural Bank of China, HK Branch	Agricultural Bank of China
China Insurance HK (Holdings) Co. Ltd	China People's Insurance Co.

Source: Kang, 2000.

Although red chips were Hong Kong listed companies, their place of registration was not confined to Hong Kong (Kang, 2000). The operations and business activities of red chips were mainly located in mainland China. The major shareholders (or parent companies) of red chips were mainland Chinese companies, but the ultimate owners of red chips were mainland Chinese government authorities including central government departments and provincial/local governments. Most red chip companies were established in Hong Kong with initial financial assistance from the mainland. Most of the personnel of the red chips and their parent companies were seconded from the mainland: 'Strictly speaking, red chips are extensions of governmental organizations operating within investment and cash-raising guidelines laid down by a holding company and a controlling government body' (De Trenck *et al.*, 2000: 44).

In the early years of economic reform, roughly from 1979 to 1991, more and more provincial and city governments were allowed to open representative offices in Hong Kong as 'window' companies through which to gain a better understanding of the international business environment, and to benefit from the fast-growing cross-border trade. Guangdong Enterprises (GDE) was in the forefront of this process. According to official data, by 1997 there were ninety-six Hong Kong registered mainland Chinese companies. Of these, forty-one had mainland city or provincial governments as their ultimate shareholders, thirty-six had mainland ministries or other government departments and nineteen had mainland companies (Kang, 2000: 21–2, and Table 1.2). Basically, each province and administrative region had one

Hong Kong registered company. Fifteen of the main cities, including Beijing and Shanghai, each of the main ministries, and each of the four main commercial banks had one red chip company. Among the large industrial companies, AVIC (Aviation Industries of China) had three red chip companies. Twelve other leading industrial companies, including Sinopec, CNPC (China National Petroleum Corporation), CNOOC (China National Offshore Oil Corporation) and China Non-Ferrous Metals Holding Company, each had one Hong Kong red chip company.

The Hong Kong offices of mainland entities gradually expanded their activities in the 1990s, diversifying away from trading into other sectors. Alongside this process, they began to diversify their sources of finance away from simply commercial lending and trade credit. As they began to tap the capital market for more funds, so the concept of the 'red chip' came into being. The term 'red' chip, as opposed to 'blue' chip, indicated the strong mainland backing of governments and leading firms that were regarded as guarantors of the business expansion and ultimate financial soundness of these companies.

The mainland parentage of the red chips made them attractive not only due to the apparent security that it offered, but also because it provided a powerful potential source of financial gain to investors through the assets that the parent could inject into the Hong Kong entity:

> Most of these businesses have the potential to become giants and it is easy to see why. Take Guangdong province, the government can inject whatever assets it likes into their window company [GDE], thus building a massive conglomerate in the process.
>
> (*Capital Markets*, 1996)

These assets were typically unavailable for direct investment by international investors. The asset injection was typically 'at a price that was favourable to minority investors' (*Capital Markets,* 1996). They were regarded as having more autonomy than H-share companies. They were also regarded as being better in terms of corporate governance than other mainland companies: 'Underpinning asset injections, and a key factor in red chip success, is strong operational and financial management.' Overall, red chips were perceived to be 'subject to higher standards than B-shares' and 'more responsive to investor queries than H-shares' (*Capital Markets*, 1996).

During the 1990s, one red chip after another floated on the Hong Kong stock market. By 1997 there were over seventy red chips floated on the Hong Kong stock market (Table 1.3). Over the course of the 1990s, the red chips raised large sums from stock market flotations and further asset injections from the parent companies on the mainland (Table 1.4). By 1996–7, a veritable red chip fever had gripped Hong Kong. At the end of 1996, the journal *Capital Markets* commented that global investors were 'riding the Red Chip wave with a fervour' as the 1997 handover of Hong Kong approached

(*Capital Markets*, 1996). During the peak of the 'red chip frenzy' the initial IPO was typically followed immediately by a large rise in the stock price of the floated company (Table 1.5).

Table 1.3 List of red chip companies

Red chip companies	*Time of IPO or shell-purchase*	*Holding of top shareholder (%)*
China Aerospace International (0031)	1993	50.4
Shougang Concord Century (0103)	1993	36.2
Cosmos Machinery Enterprises (0118)	1997	No data
Continental Mariner Investment (0119)	1992	58
Guangzhou Investment (0123)	1992	42.12
Guangdong Brewery (0124)	1997	72
China Merchants China Direct Inv. (0133)	1993	28.79
CNPC (Hong Kong) (0135)	1993	51.1
Jinhui Holdings (0135)	1991	55.87
CCT Telecom Holdings (0138)	1994	12.77
Great China Holdings Ltd (0141)	1992	52.87
China Merchants Holdings (Int'l) (0144)	1992	1.7
Shenzhen International Holdings (0152)	1994	44.99
Beijing Development (Hong Kong)(0154)	1993	47.85
China Everbright (0165)	1987	51.92
China Assets (Holdings) (0170)	1992	20.06
Silver Grant International Industries (0171)	1993	48.2
The Ka Wah Bank (0183)	1986	57.83
Denway Investment (0203)	1993	33.2
Shen Yin Wanguo (HK) (0218)	1993	53.59
Min Xin Holdings (0222)	1987	30.13
ONFEM Holdings (0230)	1991	53.39
China Everbright Technology (0256)	1991	42.5
China Everbright International (0257)	1993	66.6
Poly Investments Holdings (0263)	1993	41
CITIC Pacific (0267)	1990	30.15
Top Glory International Holdings (0268)	1993	50.5
Guangdong Investment (0270)	1987	43.32
China Resources Enterprise (0291)	1992	52.02
China Travel International Inv. HK (0308)	1992	60.2
Ng Fung Hong (0318)	1995	54
GITIC Enterprise (0340)	1997	75
Union Bank of Hong Kong (0349)	1986	60.5
Shanghai Industrial Holdings (0363)	1996	64
ITC Corporation (0372)	1993	30.2
Hualing Holdings (0382)	1993	39.1
Beijing Enterprises Holdings (0392)	1997	66.51
Stone Electronic Technology (0409)	1993	50.51
Founder (Hong Kong) (0418)	1996	46
Paladin Ltd (0495)	1992	48.37
China Foods Holdings (0506)	1993	51.1
China Apollo Holdings (0512)	1995	73.6

(Continued)

Red chip companies	*Time of IPO or shell-purchase*	*Holding of top shareholder (%)*
COSCO International Holdings (0517)	1994	60.2
Shougang Concord Technology (0521)	1988	46.9
Hong Kong Holdings (0535)	1989	35.8
Chu Kong Shipping Development (0560)	1997	75
Wing Shan International (0570)	1993	No data
Shum Yip Investment (0604)	1997	61.45
Yugang International (0613)	1994	50
CIG-WH International (Holdings) (0621)	1995	32.01
Tysan Holdings (0687)	1993	23.4
China Overseas Land & Investment (0688)	1992	58.73
Shougang Concord International (0697)	1991	39.6
Chun Wo Holdings (0711)	1997	24.48
FPB Bank Holdings (0717)	1993	No data
Shougang Concord Grand (Group) (0730)	1991	55
Shanghai Growth (0770)	1993	13.2
Tianjin Development (0882)	1997	66.21
Zhu Kuan Development (0908)	1998	70
China Telecom (Hong Kong) (0941)	1997	76.5
Legend Holdings (0992)	1994	68
Simsen International Corporation (0993)	1994	21.78
GZI Transport (1052)	1997	74
Guangdong Tannery (1058)	1996	71.5
ING Beijing Investment (1062)	1994	No data
China Pharmaceutical & Inv. (1093)	1993	57
China Resources Beijing Land (1109)	1996	44.2
China National Aviation (1110)	1997	70.1
CASIL Telecommunications (1185)	1997	61.01
Cosco Pacific (1199)	1994	59.02
Guangnan (Holdings) (1203)	1994	62
Oriental Metal (Holdings) (1208)	1994	35.4

Source: Kang, 2000.

Table 1.4 Capital raising history of red chip companies (HK$ million)

Method	*1993*	*1994*	*1995*	*1996*	*1997*	*1998*
IPO	1,005.6	1,705.39	1,869.75	2,007.49	39,279.68	142.38
New share placement	9,394.78	6,279.31	313.1	12,554.68	26,820.78	16,440.84
Consideration share issue	–	1,502.2	3,710.41	2,086.39	9,361.07	2,276.32
Rights issue	2,511.66	1,799.78	–	359.65	2,174.35	468.26
Convertible issue	5,285.32	749.25	489.14	–	7,182.27	–
Total	18,197.36	12,035.93	6,382.4	17,008.21	84,818.15	19,327.8

Source: BNP Peregrine Research (1999).

Table 1.5 Red chip IPOs in 1997

Company	*Listing Date*	*IPO price (HK$)*	*Fully-diluted PER (X)*	*New shares issued (m.)*	*Capital raised (HK$ m.)*	*Public offer over-subscription (X)*	*First day trading closing price (HK$)*	*% Increase/decrease*
GZIT (1052)	30 Jan	3.23	22.1	250	807.5	529	4,088	51.1
Shum Yip (0604)	7 Mar	1.85	10.6	250	462.5	438	4.53	144.9
GITIC (0340)	26 Mar	1.05	9.4	100	105	892	4.38	317.1
Chu Kong Shipping (0560)	23 May	1.2	9.8	188	225.6	480	3.6	200
Beijing Ent. (0392)	29 May	12.48	19.35	150	1,872	1,276	40.5	222.1
Guang-dong Brewery (0124)	8 Aug	1.8	25	350	630	38.5	2.8	55.6
CATIC (1185)	11 Aug	1.18	9.83	150	177	71.01	3.33	182.2
China Telecom (0941)	23 Oct	11.68	27	2,600	30,368	35.2	10.55	−9.7
Tianjin Dev. (0882)	10 Dec	6.6	11.47	182	13,322	10.01	8.2	24.2
CAAC (1110)	17 Dec	1.63	12.5	376	613	18	1.63	0

Source: Hong Kong Stock Exchange and various newspaper reports.

The crucial part of the speculative fever was the 'asset injection story': 'Investors bought into the asset injection story, regardless of whether the acquired assets were revenue-generating and earnings-enhancing or not' (Kang, 2000). On the eve of the red chip frenzy, Jurgen Ulrich, the head of the top-ranked China research team at CLSA (Crédit Lyonnais Securities Asia) evaluated the red chip companies as follows:

> Overall, investors support Red Chips because they believe capital is put to good use. Red Chips have not squandered money or abused the trust of investors. They acquired good assets at undervalued prices and a great deal of corporate finance enhanced the earnings per share picture. This is the major reason why the stocks have been pushed into the stratosphere. The average H-share and Hong Kong blue-chip do not have the ability to inject assets in such a manner. Strong organic growth and asset injections are a powerful combination.
>
> (quoted in *Capital Markets*, 1996)

The asset injection model gave a strong incentive for insider dealing and cross-investment among the red chip network. Forewarning of decisions about IPOs and asset injections provided the opportunity to make riskless 'bets,' at least until the whole market collapsed. There were strong incentives for investment banks in Hong Kong to 'spin' the 'hot red chip stocks' to favoured clients in the hope of winning other business from them. It is, self-evidently, impossible to investigate the details of the process through which shares were allocated for red chips' IPOs and asset injections during the 'red chip frenzy.'

The red chip wave 'crested with the offering of Shanghai Industrial Holdings in May of 1996.' The subsequent rise in share price of nearly 400 per cent 'had investors rubbing their hands with glee.' There was a massive incentive for preferential allocation of shares in IPOs to insiders within the given red chip firm itself, and within the network of the red chip companies as a whole. Then came the 'tidal wave of orders for the November IPO of China Resources Beijing Land.' The issue was priced at US$ 100 million, but there was US$ 7 billion in demand for the stock, which rose 70 per cent on the first day of trading. The journal *Capital Markets* commented: 'Riding high on the HKSE bull run and the popularity of stellar IPOs, Red Chips look unbeatable as 1997 enters the frame' (*Capital Markets*, 1996).

The 'Red Chip Fever' intensified in 1997. When GITIC listed a red chip subsidiary, GITIC Enterprises, in Hong Kong in March 1997, at the height of the red chip frenzy, it was more than 800 times over-subscribed. The shares rose more than 300 per cent on their debut. For the Hong Kong investors, this appeared to be a risk-free 'speculation.' The other red chips were also keen to participate in the flotation and obtain easy profits. The IPO of Beijing Enterprises was oversubscribed by a staggering 1,275 times. Shortly after it was listed the stock market price surged from the initial IPO price of HK$ 12.48 to HK$ 65. China Everbright's share price doubled within two months following its announced asset injection in June 1997, trading on a P/E ratio of 3,000. The Hong Kong China-Affiliated Corporations Index reached an all-time high of 4,200 on 9 August 1997. The red chips accounted for 10–20 per cent of the Hong Kong stock market's capitalization, but contributed to over 30 per cent of the market's daily turnover in the first half of 1997 (Kang, 2000: 14). In 1997, the peak year, the red chips raised a total of around HK$ 85 billion (Table 1.4).

In the period prior to the AFC, the leading red chips, with 'high quality parentage,' found it easy to borrow from the Hong Kong banks. One commentator observed: 'Fundamentals rarely matter in Hong Kong, where the local stock exchange is sometimes referred to as only the second place in the city that allows legalized gambling after the Hong Kong Jockey Club' (quoted in *FT*, 23 July 2002). During the 'red chip frenzy,' the element of 'gambling' appeared to be relatively small. Rather, the crucial issue was how to use connections to obtain access to a limited supply of shares that would almost certainly be a 'winner' on their flotation.

On the strength of their soaring market capitalization and their 'high quality parentage,' Hong Kong banks were highly enthusiastic about lending to the red chips. Up until the crash in 1997, the banks 'urged them to borrow more.' All the big Western banks in Hong Kong had the same policy towards the red chips: 'just lend as much as possible.' China-backed firms in Hong Kong 'set up very substantial banking facilities with, in addition to Chinese banks, Western banks, which, during most of the 1980s and the early 1990s, were falling over each other to offer attractive financing arrangements' (De Trenck *et al.*, 2000: 47). The banks 'did not require anything more than a paper report concerning the purpose for which money was being loaned.' The bankers never went to see the project concerned, except for very large projects, of more than 'several million dollars.' It was 'easy to put together a very large borrowing package by borrowing several millions each from different banks.' The banks' main consideration in making lending decisions to the red chips was 'the background of the company concerned,' namely the mainland parent. Before the crash 'red chip companies in Hong Kong could borrow huge amounts without the necessary papers,' but after the crash it was 'very hard to borrow even with the necessary papers.'

Because the borrowings were undertaken in Hong Kong by Hong Kong-registered firms, it was not necessary to register them with the mainland's State Administration of Foreign Exchange (SAFE). The red chips' total borrowings were unknown. However, the Chinese government believed that the total international borrowings were around US$ 20–25 billion, much of which was from Hong Kong-based banks. In the early and mid-1990s, the red chips expanded rapidly into speculative investments, especially the property sector, much of which was financed with bank loans. Moreover, the red chips invested in each other's listed companies, forming a 'house of cards,' in which the collapse of one red chip could have a powerful ripple effect throughout the sector.

Guangdong had a special place of importance among the red chips. Guangdong Enterprises (GDE) had become one of the most significant firms in Hong Kong. One of its red chip subsidiaries was a constituent stock of the Hang Seng Index. Guangnan, also a floated red chip subsidiary of GDE was one of the leading middle-sized firms in the territory, which had been selected by Morgan Stanley Dean Witter as one of the top fifty SMEs worldwide.

By September 1997, the red chips began their dramatic downturn (Table 1.6). By the middle of 1998, the price of most red chip companies had fallen by over 80 per cent from their peak in mid-1997, with the odd exception, notably China Telecom and Legend. The Hang Seng China-Affiliated Corporations Index plummeted from the peak of 4,200 in August 1997 to just 595 in August 1998. The price of former investor favourite, China Everbright Holdings, fell from HK$ 25.6 at its peak to just HK$ 2.3 in August 1998. The steep decline in the Hong Kong stock markets radically reduced the value of the red chips' share portfolio, and their debt-servicing ability came under intense pressure. Banks drastically scaled back their lending to the red chips, and sought repayment of outstanding loans. Many red chips were forced to make large asset disposals in order to service their borrowings. They attempted to cut costs and recall accounts receivable. The collapse of GITIC and the restructuring of GDE made it virtually impossible for the red chips as a group to gain access to new bank funding or to raise funds through new share issues: the 'red chip frenzy' was over.

Table 1.6 Red chip share performances data

Company	*Closing price as at 12 August 1998*	*Peak price after 3.97*	*% Decline*
Hang Seng Index	6,859	16,820	59.22
Hang Seng China-Affiliated Corporations Index	595	4,200	85.83
ONFEM (1208)	0.161	3	94.63
Poly Investment (0263)	0.212	3.25	93.48
Oriental Metals (0230)	0.28	4.225	93.37
Shougang International (0103)	0.112	1.65	93.21
Everbright International (0257)	0.66	9.1	92.75
CMIC (0119)	0.78	10.542	92.6
CITIC Ka Wah Bank (0183)	1.93	24.2	92.02
Shougang Concord Grande (0730)	0.3	3.65	91.78
Denway Investment (0203)	0.255	3.1	91.77
Shenyin Wanguo (0218)	0.38	4.375	91.31
Everbright Technology (0256)	0.54	6.2	91.29
Guangdong Investment (0207)	1.1	12.3	91.06
China Everbright Holdings (0165)	2.325	25.6	90.92
Shougang Technology (0521)	0.255	2.725	90.64
China Aerospace (0031)	0.69	7.1	90.28

Company	*Closing price as at 12 August 1998*	*Peak price after 3.97*	*% Decline*
Shougang International (0697)	0.285	2.9	90.17
China Overseas (0688)	0.68	6.75	89.93
China Resources (0291)	4.725	39.2	89.8
CNPC (0135)	0.63	6.1	89.67
Beijing Enterprises (0392)	6.85	65	89.46
Top Glory (0268)	0.495	4.625	89.3
China Travel (0308)	0.69	6.4	89.22
COSCO Pacific (1199)	2.075	19.2	89.19
Guangzhou Investment (0123)	0.53	4.9	89.18
Minxin Holdings (0222)	0.6	5.292	88.66
Shum Yip Enterprise (0604)	1.4	12.2	88.52
Hualing Holdings (0382)	0.23	1.95	88.21
Union Bank (0349)	3.325	27.9	88.08
Guangnan Holdings (1203)	1.71	13.6	87.43
China Merchants Holdings (0144)	3.5	26.7	86.89
Founder (HK) (0418)	1.38	9.1	84.84
China Pharmaceutical (1093)	0.495	2.95	83.22
Shanghai Industrial (0363)	10.2	60	83
Stone Electronics (0409)	0.51	2.825	81.95
CITIC Pacific (0267)	9.7	53.25	81.78
China Foods (0506)	1.85	6.9	73.19
Beijing Development (0154)	1.21	3.925	69.17
Ng Fung Hong (0318)	4.75	13.8	65.58
Legend Holdings (0992)	1.7	3.825	55.56
China Telecom (0941)	9	16.8	46.46

Source: Kang, 2000.

By the middle of 2001, there had been some recovery in the red chip prices, but they were still on average far below the peak reached during the 'fever' of 1997. The overall price index for all Hang Seng China-Affiliated Corporations stood at only around one-quarter of the peak reached in March 1997. With certain exceptions, leading individual red chip companies remained at only a fraction of the price they had reached during the 'fever.' For example, the issue price of Beijing Enterprises in 1997 had been HK$ 12.48. The stock reached a peak of HK$ 65. By mid-1998 it had fallen to just HK$ 6.85, but by mid-2001 it still stood at only HK$ 8, well below the original issue price. The total market capitalization of the red chips reached US$ 42.9 billion in May 1997 (De Trenck *et al.*, 2000: 80). In May 2001, the total red chip market capitalization stood at US$ 18 billion (MSDW, *China Strategy*, 14 May 2001), less than one-half of its peak value.

Positive function of the red chips

The red chip experiment can be viewed as part of the process of reforming China's SOEs, since in most cases the enterprises that were injected into the red chips were from the portfolio of assets owned by the local government or other mainland government entity that owned the red chip's parent.

The red chip companies gave the managers from the mainland the opportunity to operate in a capitalist environment. Hong Kong is a sophisticated high-income economy, with a highly developed system of government regulation. The red chips' managers, almost all from the mainland, learned at first hand the importance of independent accounting by globally respected firms, the function of independent directors, meeting shareholders' demands for transparent company operation, and the importance of dealing with an independent media. The leading red chips all came under intense analysts' scrutiny, with their business strategies and prospects subject to minute examination in the harsh spotlight before international fund managers.

The red chips were successful at raising funds from international capital markets up until the collapse of the bubble in 1997. From 1993 to 1997 inclusive, the red chips raised a total of over HK$ 138 billion from the stock market, including IPOs, new share placements, consideration share issues, rights issues and convertible issues (Kang, 2000: 24). The capital market fund-raising by the red chips in the mid-1990s totalled less than HK$20 billion per year up until 1997. Then, during the height of the red chip frenzy in 1997, the red chips raised HK$ 85 billion, as numerous bundles of assets were brought to the market under the red chip umbrella. The red chips formed a major channel through which international investors could invest indirectly in mainland companies, to which direct access was denied, or which were floated on the fledgling and highly speculative domestic stock market. Paradoxically, the overseas stock market in Hong Kong also generated a huge bubble. After peaking at HK$ 85 billion in 1997, the total capital raised by the red chips on the Hong Kong stock market collapsed in 1998 to under HK$ 20 billion (Kang, 2000: 24). We have seen also that the red chips may have raised as much as US$ 20–25 billion in borrowings from international banks in Hong Kong. These were huge sums that had the potential to play an important role in Chinese development. They could, for example, have played a powerful role in spearheading the catch-up process in China's high-technology industries which languished far behind those of the high-income economies in the early twenty-first century.

Through their capital-raising activities and through their business experience acquired in Hong Kong, the red chips helped to transform their state-owned parents. In this sense they made a positive contribution to the 'transition' process from the administratively planned economy towards a form of market economy.

Shortcomings of the red chips

Insofar as the red chip experiment was intended to produce a set of internationally competitive 'conglomerates' such as Li Ka Shing's Cheung Kong Holdings, then the red chip experiment failed. In fact, despite the public statements of purpose, the main reason for the existence and growth of the red chips was simply to raise revenue for their parents and for the constituent companies. The red chip concept peaked in 1996/7 during the 'frenzy,' driven by investors' speculative instincts. These instincts were responded to by more and more IPOs and asset injections from the mainland entities, responding to and, in turn, feeding the speculative frenzy. Neither side was interested in the long-term business rationale of the entities, which were thrown together at high speed with the advice of the international investment bankers, whose primary interest was short-term profits from a successful flotation or asset injection. Once the attraction of red chips as vehicles for cheap asset injection had passed, investors began to view them as 'real' firms, and saw little to attract them in the long-term business model of the red chips.

When investors started to look upon the red chips as regular firms, rather than vehicles for speculation, they found them sadly lacking in competitive capability. One expert commented that the red chips had 'all the bad features of Japanese *keiretsu,* but none of the good ones' (Li Qingyuan, Hong Kong Securities and Futures Commission, interview). The red chips are quite different from the Japanese conglomerate models, or indeed, the Korean *chaebol* model, lacking powerful core businesses that have a serious chance of becoming globally competitive large firms with long-run viability. Although they have important differences, they are closer in form to the overseas Chinese conglomerate. At the heart of the most successful Korean and Japanese business groups is typically a set of globally competitive firms that have the scale, technical and marketing capabilities to attempt to compete in global markets. By contrast, throughout much of southeast Asia, a group of highly diversified overseas Chinese conglomerates developed, often based around family networks. These typically had little capability or ambition to compete in the long-term with the leading firms based in the advanced economies. Rather, they were organized around the opportunistic acquisition of a diversified set of businesses, in none of which the headquarters had a deep industrial knowledge, and none of which had a serious hope of becoming globally competitive players. The headquarters typically did not have a long-term commitment to the businesses, but bought and sold them in a speculative fashion rather than running them with a view to long-term competition. Often, a major part of the business attraction of a particular investment was the opportunity for rent-seeking in the highly government-regulated economies of southeast Asia. Property investment typically formed a large part of their investment portfolio, with close government ties often forming an important part of success in access to, and development of, land.

The rise and fall of the red chip concept should force a more realistic approach to the viability of the East Asian conglomerate form, especially that of the overseas Chinese. In this sense, the 'red chip' experiment was valuable as a negative learning experience that helped to guide the future path of

Chinese enterprise reform. A major failing of the mainland Chinese reform process was that it unleashed a tendency to pursue short-term profits in any type of business activity, rather than attempting to build a globally competitive firm in areas of core business competence. On the mainland in the 1990s this was stimulated by the availability of rents deriving from different forms of government intervention and protection from global competition. In Hong Kong, the tendency was unleashed in the red chips, even though the economy was the least protected and the most open in the world. The free market in Hong Kong provided huge amounts of capital to the red chips as a reward for the benefits they might derive from their fortunate parentage, in other words, a reward for their lack of transparency. The same environment provided an ideal climate in which the red chips could indulge in speculative investments in a wide range of sectors, especially the property and stock markets.

The very absence of transparency constituted a major attraction of the red chips to international investors. The essence of the 'asset injection' model was the fact that the parent was the Chinese state, or its local branch, which was able to sell state assets to the advantage of the international investors. A major attraction was the possibility that through their non-transparent parentage, the assets that were injected would be underpriced: 'The red chip bubble was driven by the illusion of government protection and favouritism. Now we realize that this was, indeed, an illusion' (Li Qingyuan, Interview). The government background combined with the Hong Kong stock market flotation, and the speculative bubble, created great possibilities for insider dealing. It provided a powerful incentive for the allocation of shares in IPOs through illegal processes, giving advantage to 'insiders.' It also created a strong incentive for insider dealing through the possession of advance knowledge of forthcoming asset injections before the market obtained the relevant knowledge. Moreover, the decisions about forthcoming asset injections would be made by the parent within Chinese legal jurisdiction, not in Hong Kong, so that the incentive for insider dealing was not confined to the Hong Kong office of the red chip.

An important part of the asset injection model involves the fact that a significant, but ultimately unknown, fraction of dealings in red chips involved red chips themselves, buying each other's shares, benefiting from shared knowledge within the red chip community in Hong Kong. The speculative red chip fever resembled the race track, in which different participants in the betting process have different degrees of insider knowledge about the outcome of the next race, including the fact that the result may have been fixed in advance. Moreover, as in race track betting, much speculation was founded on rumours that quickly circulated. Hong Kong's rumour-mill connected with the stock market was notoriously active.

The red chips remained essentially SOEs. They were registered in a capitalist economy, Hong Kong, and were formally subject to supervision by the Hong Kong regulatory authorities. However, they all had ultimate control in the hands of the mainland parent, each of which was some form of state-owned entity. This was a source of strength in the sense that the parent could inject assets from the mainland. However, it was also a source of weakness with regard to the nature of management appointments, management objectives and the monitoring of the behaviour of the red chips by the parents. One experienced observer from the mainland commented bluntly:

> As long as the red chips remain essentially SOEs, then the problem of the red chips cannot be resolved. Goldman Sachs should have insisted on the privatization of GDE. It has no way out as an SOE. Unless it is privatized, any restructuring will be only temporary, and will have to be restructured again within a few years.
>
> (Li Qingyuan, Interview)

In some senses, the degree of management autonomy for red chips was significantly less than for the subsidiaries of a privately owned or publicly quoted East Asian conglomerate, such as Cheung Kong Holdings. The senior managers of the city and provincial red chips were all appointed by their respective governments. The main strategic decisions, such as which companies were going to be injected into the red chip, and the appointment of management at their main invested companies, were in the hands of the respective governments that owned the red chip's parent. One of the few red chips that significantly escaped from this type of relationship with its parent was CITIC Pacific. After CITIC Pacific's purchase of a 20 per cent stake in China Light and Power, the share of the parent company, CITIC Beijing, fell to only 26 per cent. CITIC Pacific had effectively ceased to be a 'red chip' and become a Hong Kong 'blue chip' company. Moreover, it was run by a 'real entrepreneur,' Larry Yung, the son of Rong Yiren, chairman of the parent company, CITIC Beijing.[7]

However, in another sense, the red chips had far more autonomy, in that they had the independence to raise capital from international financial institutions, and to use these funds with limited monitoring from the mainland to build a boundary-less business empire in Hong Kong. Like the profligate son of a wealthy parent, who can often also borrow against the name of his parent, they had a considerable degree of autonomy in the way in which they used these borrowings.

The red chips operated in a form of 'supervisory vacuum' in Hong Kong (Wu, 2001: 152). Within the mainland there was a whole set of regulatory structures that in some form could monitor the state-owned enterprises. These included the CPC, the judiciary and the 'ministry' or 'department' within which the enterprise was located. In Hong Kong, it was not possible for mainland supervisory bodies to exercise control over Hong Kong registered, 'mainland' firms. It was very hard to investigate suspected offences or impose the same disciplinary penalties on those who broke the rules in a separate jurisdiction. The Hong Kong authorities found it difficult to exercise control over mainland-based entities in the same way that they would do over locally owned private companies. Indeed, there was little sign that the Hong Kong authorities were interested in monitoring mainland firms operating in Hong Kong beyond the avoidance of major scandals: 'Both the method and channel of supervision have not been very effective and have contributed towards the resulting status of the majority of the PRC-owned enterprises in Hong Kong existing in a supervisory vacuum' (Wu, 2001: 152).

Liberated from the constraints of much of the normal supervision in the mainland, with inadequate monitoring from the Hong Kong authorities, doing business daily with some of the most affluent people in the international business world, and with the temptation of huge quantities of capital flowing into the increasingly independent enterprises with new-found independence, the red chips became 'out of control,' 'totally free.'

To a considerable degree the red chips were able to exploit shortcomings in the regulatory environment for all firms in Hong Kong. The system of non-executive directors was one such shortcoming. Following the normal practice in Hong Kong, many non-executive directors had a large number of non-executive directorships, and often were themselves active business people. They were frequently chosen for their connections rather than their ability to defend the interests of shareholders. It was impossible to expect such people to devote the time necessary to monitor closely and objectively the behaviour of the companies on whose boards they sat.

The supervision of the red chips caused serious headaches for the Chinese government. Premier Zhu Rongji recognized the need for the red chips to be 'more strongly supervised and led.' The Chinese government tried to get the China Securities Regulatory Commission (CSRC) to exercise supervision over the red chips. However, international practice required that the listed company be supervised by the local regulatory authority where it was listed.

The red chips were in a different position in terms of regulation than the H-share companies. In the case of the H-shares, both the company registration and the assets were in the mainland, but the company was floated on the Hong Kong stock exchange. This was not a regulatory problem for the Chinese Securities and Regulatory Commission (CSRC). However, the red chips had their 'parents' and many of their assets in the mainland. The red chip companies grew up in the mainland. But the companies were registered and floated in Hong Kong. This caused a great deal of difficulty for the CSRC. From the mainland perspective, the red chips were state-owned enterprises, but in Hong Kong they were regarded as private enterprises. The kind of problem that arose was: does the red chip company have the right to establish a subsidiary? The assets are not owned by the red chip. They are, ultimately, mainland-owned assets. On the mainland, the CSRC had the duty to preserve the rights and interests of the property owned by the Chinese people, but the CSRC needed also to ensure that the rights and interests of minority shareholders were secured.

International trust and investment companies (ITICs)

'Trust' companies have an important niche function in the financial system of most economies. During the course of China's financial sector reforms, 'trust and investment' companies (TICs) expanded to enter segments of the financial market that were not reached by the large state-owned banks. The TICs came from two main sources. The first was from the financial sector. The main financial institutions, almost all, established TICs at each level in the financial system from the centre in Beijing down through the province, prefecture and county. The big four banks almost all established literally hundreds of trust and investment companies, each one of which was an autonomous 'legal person.' A parallel system of TICs developed, originating in the government system, again cascading down from the central government in Beijing to the province, prefecture and county.

In the early days of the reforms the TICs gave local governments a mechanism for raising development funds from outside the local budget and separately from the state banking system. Local governments were unable to have their own banks, but they could have the next-best thing, the TICs, which quickly performed the function of quasi-bank institutions. The TICs were under the formal supervision of the People's Bank of China (PBOC) and needed a licence from the PBOC to operate legally.

In the late 1980s the total number of TICs reached over 1,000. A first round of 'rectification' of the TICs had taken place as early as in the mid-1980s, followed by a second round in the late 1980s and early 1990s. By 1991 the number of TICs had reportedly fallen to 375. By 1993 the number had risen again to over 700 (Xiao Gang, 2000, Interview). A further 'rectification' began in 1994. In 1996, there were reported to be 322 TICs. In 1996 the central bank conducted an investigation into 570 non-bank financial institutions, which resulted in the closure of around 130 of the TICs. However, the weakness of the central bank's regulatory powers was indicated by the fact that many of those that had powerful sponsors were soon re-approved, 'despite their distressed financial condition' (Moody's, 1998a). The PBOC 'lacked the necessary independence and authority in pursuing disciplinary actions against unruly financial institutions.'

In addition to regular domestic trust and investment companies, a subgroup of 'international' TICs quickly developed, the so-called 'ITICs.' The ten largest ITICs together reportedly accounted for over 90 per cent of the trust and investment sector's total assets in the mid-1990s. The China International Trust and Investment Corporation (CITIC) was much larger than any other ITIC, alone accounting for two-thirds of the sector's total assets. The second tier of ITICs consisted of the large regional ITICs controlled by the leading coastal provinces and cities. These included Guangdong (GITIC), Shanghai, Shandong, Fujian, Shenzhen and Tianjin. Apart from these, there were numerous smaller ITICs.

The international trust and investment company (ITIC) sector had its origin in the establishment of CITIC in 1979. The central government allowed the company to be set up under Rong Yiren.[8] After 1949, Rong Yiren had been appointed Deputy Minister of the Ministry of Textile Industries and his family-owned assets were acquired by the state. Rong Yiren was called a 'Red Capitalist.' In January 1979, when China's reforms were beginning their long journey, Deng Xiaoping held a long discussion with Rong Yiren. Deng asked Rong to use his unique background to 'do something significant to help China's opening up and promote reform.' The decision to establish CITIC, with Rong Yiren at its head, emerged from this meeting. The Rong family continued to play an important role in CITIC through the appointment of Rong Yiren's son, 'Larry' Yung (Rong) to run CITIC's 'red chip' Hong Kong company (CITIC Pacific). He became the most famous of the red chip entrepreneurs.

The name 'international trust and investment company' was chosen by Rong Yiren. It indicates that CITIC was much more than a traditional 'trust' company, set up in order to manage funds in accordance with instructions of the initiator(s) of the trust. In the late 1990s, only around 13 per cent of CITIC's total revenue derived from pure 'trust' activity. The central government set up CITIC in order to provide a mechanism for raising funds from both domestic and international sources to fund Chinese development. Whereas the other TICs contributed to the local budget, CITIC was independent of the central government budget. The company remained a wholly state-owned entity. The main original objective of CITIC was to raise and channel funds into manufacturing. This followed the business path of the pre-revolutionary Rong family, which had focused on manufacturing rather than financial services.

Unlike the family-controlled Rong empire, CITIC developed a propensity for multiplication of subordinate entities and diversification away from manufacturing. A process of 'spontaneous multiplication' of independent accounting entities emerged, blindly following different 'interests' within CITIC. Each of these entities wanted to have management autonomy. By the early 1990s, there were over 1,000 independent accounting entities within CITIC, spread widely across the country and beyond. Each of them had developed management autonomy, but without matching financial responsibilities. The vertical proliferation of independent entities meant that 'children' gave birth to 'grandchildren,' which in turn produced more children in a cascade of autonomous entities. The central headquarters of CITIC had lost a great deal of management control to subordinate entities, including its Hong Kong 'red chip' arm, CITIC Pacific. Many of these were diversifying horizontally into high-risk businesses, including property speculation, currency futures, commodities futures, securities market speculation and derivatives.[9]

In the mid-1990s, prior to the AFC, CITIC went through a radical reorganization. The key elements were a drastic re-centralization of business control and a sharp reduction in the range of businesses that CITIC engaged in. They carefully studied the examples of leading Western business restructurings. The leadership introduced far-reaching institutional reforms, guided by their close study of Western management theory and the practice of running large modern enterprises (Qin, 2004). The number of subordinate entities was cut drastically, with wholesale culling of several hundred formerly independent companies under CITIC. Numerous partially owned subsidiaries and associated companies were turned into wholly owned subsidiaries. The only subsidiaries that were left as independent business were those for which there was a proven business reason to do so. Financial control over subordinate entities was tightened dramatically, turning them into closely monitored profit centres. CITIC carefully studied examples such as Siemens, in which there is a daily clearing of accounts across the entire global company for each business unit. A fundamental re-assessment of the role of risk in the company's operations was undertaken, leading to major changes in the company's internal rules and behaviour. For example, speculation in currency futures was stopped, with only rational hedging to reduce currency risk permitted. In place of numerous city securities companies under CITIC, a single unified securities business with tight central control was established. The branches of CITIC's securities business were no longer allowed to take positions in the securities market. This became the sole prerogative of CITIC headquarters.

The tendencies evident at CITIC by the early 1990s, and the large efforts required to restructure the company in the mid-1990s, were pointers to the difficulties that lay in store for other NBFIs across China. The large-scale reforms undertaken at CITIC enabled it to survive the AFC relatively unscathed. Its unique position as an experimental entity directly under the central government allowed it formally to have a high degree of operational autonomy. This enabled it to undertake substantial internal reform prior to the AFC. The other local trust and investment companies were closely controlled by their respective local authorities, and lacked either the incentive or the autonomy to achieve such a radical restructuring.

In the 1980s and 1990s, the central government allowed the 'CITIC' model to be extended to the localities and to various state entities. A crucial function for the ITICs was raising funds on international capital markets. In order to control the nation's international debt, throughout the reform period, ministries and local governments were prohibited by law from directly borrowing from overseas, including prohibitions on issuing international bonds. Instead, they used the ITICs as their international fund-raising vehicles to support the developmental objectives of local governments and state entities, including infrastructure building, support for key industrial projects and acting as a conduit for the acquisition and absorption of foreign technology. The total assets of the trust and investment companies amounted to only around 3 per cent of the combined assets of the banks. However, the ITICs played an important role in international fund-raising.

By the time of the onset of the AFC it was estimated that the international trust and investment companies (ITICs) as a whole had legally registered international borrowings of around US$ 30 billion. A large part of this debt was with Hong Kong banks. In addition, it is thought that there were further international borrowings that totalled approximately the same amount as the legally registered borrowings. It is likely that the total of the borrowings of the ITICs was around US$ 60 billion, equivalent to almost 60 per cent of China's total foreign exchange reserves at that time. Guangdong's ITICs occupied a central role in the ITIC sector. The province had no fewer than fourteen ITICS on the eve of the AFC. Guangdong International Trust and Investment Corporation (GITIC), owned by the Guangdong provincial government, alone had borrowed almost US$ 5 billion from international lenders.

In 1997 and 1998, three in-depth studies of the ITICs were undertaken by independent external researchers, with a focus on the larger ITICs which had borrowed heavily on international markets (World Bank, 1997; Moody's, 1998a; Mitchell, 1998a, 1998b, 1998c). They concluded that the ITICs had fundamental problems.

Weak regulation

Although some ITICs had contributed to the development of their local economies, the majority of them suffered from 'gross mismanagement, lax regulatory supervision, and even outright corruption and embezzlement.' They had not only acted as their local governments' funding vehicles and investment arms, but had also 'at times acted as tools of personal enrichment.' Many of them had ventured into 'speculative activities in the property and securities markets,' and 'incurred huge losses.'

By the late 1990s, many problems had appeared in the trust and investment sector, which caused great concern to the central government. The ITICs had crossed the line from legitimate 'trust' business into commercial banking, attracting deposits through high interest rates, confident in the belief that they would be bailed out by their superior organs if they encountered financial difficulties. They experienced a spontaneous expansion of subsidiaries and associated businesses, with low levels of monitoring by the headquarters. They entered a wide range of speculative financial sector businesses, such as futures markets and derivatives. They were frequently a mechanism through which criminal business activities took place. The high interest rates offered to attract deposits ('*gaoxi lanchu*') were only sustainable provided the ITICs were able to obtain high returns. This pushed them into speculative activity, much of which was sustainable only as long as the relevant markets, such as property development and futures, were booming.

Supervision of the trust and investment sector by the central bank was 'woefully deficient,' due to 'frequent interference from the ITICs' powerful owners,' as well as due to 'inadequacies in the central bank's local branches.'

The ability of the official financial sector regulators, the PBOC and SAFE, to discipline the ITICs was made difficult by the presence of powerful local government owners. The focus of the PBOC's regulatory activities was on 'the bigger and more important banking sector, leaving the ITICs and the non-bank sector in a regulatory vacuum.' The regulatory vacuum allowed some of the ITICs to 'become mere speculative vehicles for their sponsors,' or, in some cases, they were 'even involved in illegal or fraudulent activities, including embezzlement of public funds' (Moody's, 1998a).

The problem of inadequate supervision by the PBOC was far from being the simple inadequacy of legislation, a problem that was slowly being addressed. Rather it involved the culture and the supervisory capabilities of the regulatory agency. It also depended on the extent of the resources available to it. The challenge for the PBOC was immense. The PBOC had to change from being the controller of China's money supply to being the regulator of financial services in a turbulent, high-growth, emerging market economy, in which the Communist Party was still at the centre of power. The size of the challenge would be daunting in any country but in a vast country such as China it was still greater, with powerful local interests intervening in the ability of the PBOC to undertake its regulatory activities effectively. The PBOC had around 2,000 offices throughout China. Formal regulatory procedures were steadily improved during the reform years. However, Moody's concluded that 'the quality and extensiveness of the supervisory system has not been high, due to the central bank's lack of experience and resources, which hinders the pace of progress.' They noted that although violations were often found during examinations, disciplinary actions were 'rarely taken.' Moreover, they noted soberly that the quality of supervision at some of the PBOC's provincial and municipal branches was 'questionable' because their loyalty was 'divided between the head office in Beijing and the local governments.' The PBOC's head office admitted that 'severe interference by local governments' was 'rampant at many of PBOC's local branches' (Moody's, 1998a).

Defective internal control mechanisms

The lack of adequate internal control mechanisms compounded the difficulties for the central authorities. Not only was the ITICs' behaviour influenced by weak regulatory supervision, but within the ITICs there were 'deficient internal monitoring and reporting systems, lack of risk awareness and risk management skills, and a loose organizational structure.' One of the best-known cases was that of the China Agricultural Development Trust and Investment Corporation (CADTIC), the borrowing and investment arm of the Ministry of Agriculture. CADTIC was investigated by the central authorities and closed down in 1996. However, it was re-opened after only two months, but then had to be closed again only two months later in early 1997, to the embarrassment of the central government. The central bank's investigation pointed to 'management corruption and property speculation' as the main reasons for CADTIC's failure: 'Lack of an internal control system enabled some of the company's senior managers to embezzle company funds for personal uses.' It also allowed its 'freewheeling subsidiaries,' particularly in Hainan province, to 'borrow heavily to speculate in the local property market, which later collapsed and left the company holding many worthless real estate projects in which it had invested' (Moody's, 1998a).

Following the closure of CADTIC in early 1997, the central government announced tighter regulations in an attempt to prevent the repetition of such incidents. The new practices adopted by some ITICs included establishing control over lending and investment authorities at the head office, setting forth explicit lending authority to subsidiaries, and separating loan origination and credit approval functions. However, putting new rules into place and enforcing them are not the same thing: 'Achieving adequate internal controls requires not only the set-up of a system, but also the fostering of a corporate culture that is always vigilant for potential risks'... [This is] 'likely to be a gradual process for the Chinese financial institutions' (Moody's, 1998a).

Deteriorating financial fundamentals

After explosive growth in the early 1990s the ITICs as a group achieved significantly slower growth from well before the Asian Financial Crisis. By the early 1990s they had shifted away from their traditional business policy of lending and investment, towards the more commercially oriented but riskier businesses, such as property development and stock brokerage. In the early 1990s there was huge over-building in China's main coastal cities, leading to a serious slump in property prices. This substantially strained the finances of most of the ITICs. They also suffered due to the sharp devaluation of the *renminbi* in 1994, which increased the repayment burden, since around 70–80 per cent of the ITICs' debts were in foreign currencies.

A critical difference between the lending of the ITICs compared with that of the domestic banks was that the majority of the ITICs' loans were made in foreign currencies (on average around 70 per cent). The ITICs generally adopted the practice of matching the currency of their loans with that of their fundings. This served to reduce the direct foreign exchange risk for the ITICs themselves, but at the cost of effectively transferring the risk to the borrowers, who were often incapable of managing such risk and repaying the ITICs. This made the borrowers highly susceptible to movements in exchange rates. Often, under the instruction of their local government owners, the ITICs extended large-scale guarantees to local companies and projects, guaranteeing their repayment of outstanding loans, the performance of projects or their purchase obligations for equipment. The majority of the guarantees were denominated in foreign currencies. GITIC was conspicuous for the high level of such guarantees relative to its total capital.

The overall asset quality of the ITICs was almost impossible to evaluate from outside: 'As with all financial institutions in China, the ITICs publicly disclose almost no useful information on their asset quality in the annual reports.' The true extent of problem loans was widely understated in the companies' official reports due to the 'loose classification of problem loans pursuant on Ministry of Finance guidelines, widely practiced restructuring and rollover of bad loans, as well as lack of a reliable internal reporting system.' By the time of the onset of the Asian Financial Crisis in 1997, the ITICs on average had loan loss reserves of just 0.6 per cent of their loan portfolio, which was significantly lower than the one per cent ceiling allowed by the regulations and even much below the 0.84 per cent average for the banks. Moody's concluded: 'In view of the substantial asset quality problems, China's financial system as a whole is vastly under-reserved, particularly the ITICs' (Moody's, 1998a).

Low and declining profitability

In the late 1990s the profitability of the ITICs was considerably greater than that of the banks. Moody's estimated that in 1996, the group of seven leading ITICs had an average return on total assets of 1.5 per cent, compared with just 0.3 per cent for the banks (Moody's, 1998a). The substantial difference in the rate of return was attributable mainly to the fact that the ITICs had a larger proportion of their income from dividends. In addition, the banks operated tens of thousands of branches across the country, employing hundreds of thousands of people, whereas the ITICs were much leaner organizations. Also the banks were required to pay 55 per cent of their income as tax, while the ITICs mostly enjoyed tax advantages granted to them by the local governments. However, the profitability of the ITICs was low by international standards, and was declining in the late 1990s due to the deteriorating quality of the ITICs' assets, especially the slump in property prices.

Irrational funding structure

The ITICs were in an increasingly difficult situation in relation to their sources of funds. Excluding CITIC, the funds from deposits accounted for less than 10 per cent of the ITICs funds. Moreover, a large fraction of these were institutional deposits which pre-determined the manner in which the deposits were to be allocated, and often were non-interest-bearing for the ITICs, simply earning a fee for undertaking the transaction. Such deposits could not be used by the ITICs at their discretion in the same fashion as a bank deposit with the commercial banks. The ITICs were prohibited by government regulations from taking retail deposits. Bonds accounted for a significant segment of their funds. The total outstanding at the end of 1996, was reported to be US$ 4.2 billion, about one-half from CITIC. However, conditions in the international bond market tightened considerably for the ITICs in the late 1990s as lenders became increasingly nervous of the long-term prospects for the ITICs. This nervousness was enhanced by the onset of the Asian Financial Crisis. As a result the ITICs were forced to turn to the inter-bank lending market and to borrowing from overseas banks for a large segment of their funds. Their investment and lending activities were often long-term, while their borrowing was often short-term, volatile and expensive: 'The resulting mismatch in both maturity and currency exposes the ITICs to undue liquidity and foreign exchange risk' (Moody's, 1998a).

Low liquidity

The balance sheets of the ITICs were 'rather illiquid,' with short-term assets accounting for only 20 per cent of the total assets in 1996. This contrasts with the banking sector's 34 per cent. The ITICs were under pressure from their owners, the local governments, to put their funds into long-term projects, but this came at the expense of maintaining an appropriate level of liquidity. Some of the ITICs (including GITIC) had only 4 per cent of their balance sheets in short-term assets, while others (such as CITIC) had around 20 per cent in short-term assets. In Moody's view, 'maintaining a liquid balance sheet is a necessary prudence in China's highly volatile operating environment, which is known for frequent credit squeezes and shortages' (Moody's, 1998a).

Inadequate capital levels

At first sight the leading ITICs appeared to have adequate capital levels, with an average reported capital-to-assets ratio of between 11 and 13 per cent in the mid-1990s. The ITICs' government owners from time to time injected capital as required by central government regulations. In addition, the ITICs were able to generate capital from their profits. However, an assessment of the ITICs' real capital position required an analysis of their true asset quality and provisioning levels. When these considerations were factored in, the real capital level was shown to be significantly lower: 'In Moody's opinion, in the event of an economic downturn, most of the ITICs' present capital would be insufficient to carry them through, and thus, support from the government owners would undoubtedly be necessary' (Moody's, 1998a). How able and willing were the local governments to provide such support?

Declining ability and willingness of the state to provide financial support

A key issue was the degree to which the government, at both the central and the local level, was willing and able to support the ITICs. As part of the central government's approach to overall system reform, it was increasingly trying to get local authorities to take responsibility for solving their own problems with distressed enterprises. As the crisis in the trust and investment company sector unfolded, local governments turned to the central authorities to bail them out of their difficulties. However, there was little sympathy for this approach at the centre. The central government had other, more pressing, demands on its scarce budgetary resources. Moreover, the central government was increasingly trying to force local authorities to take responsibility for solving the difficulties of their local state-owned enterprises, except where these were of national importance.

Moody's (1998a) carefully analysed the liabilities of the leading ITICs in relation to their respective government owners' fiscal revenues. They concluded that the ITICs' liabilities as a proportion of total government fiscal revenues amounted to around 20 per cent in the case of CITIC (in this case relative to the central government's revenues), 30 per cent for GITIC, rising to 40 per cent for Shandong, Shenzhen and Fujian ITICs, and around 70 per cent for Shanghai and Tianjin ITICs. In this respect, GITIC's problems were dwarfed by those of most of the other leading ITICs. The costs of supporting the 'local' ITICs for each level of government would be 'very high,' in addition to the governments' other fiscal obligations that could not easily be scaled down. Moody's warned that 'a more selective approach is more likely, and certainly, more practical, than simply providing blanket support to all government-controlled investment and development institutions.' If each local government had intervened to use its local budgetary revenues to take responsibility for the debts of its respective ITICs, it would have had very serious implications for its ability to carry out necessary government activities.

A further constraint on the ability of the local governments to intervene to support their local ITICs was the fact that the main part of the ITICs' debts were in foreign currency, while the revenue of the local governments was in *renminbi*, and 'in China's rather tight and onerous foreign exchange control regime, a timely rescue cannot always be assumed, even where the local governments may have sufficient *renminbi*-denominated resources' (Moody's, 1998a).

Moody's penetrating evaluation of the ITICs, published in 1998 (Moody's, 1998a) concluded that the environment in which the ITICs were operating had changed dramatically since the 1980s. This brought into question their long-term role. In the early years of the reform it was easy to understand their function, acting as a window to the outside world for the local governments, raising international capital and bringing in international technology. However, as China's development proceeded, international capital and technology began to enter China through other channels, notably foreign direct investment, joint ventures and international flotation of large mainland companies. The exclusive position of the ITICs was further undermined by the rapid growth of the 'red chip' companies in Hong Kong. These acted as another 'window' on the international economy for the local governments. Moreover, the red chip companies were advantaged due to the fact that they were not regulated by the central bank, since they were not financial institutions. They constituted powerful rivals to the ITICs. Moody's (1998a) warned that 'the proliferation of these new entities' would 'certainly create a greater potential strain on the local governments' resources if they have to support multiple protégés instead of just one in a future crisis.' Finally, there was a serious possibility that at some point China's local governments would be allowed to borrow directly in their own names, which would 'greatly undermine the purpose of the ITICs' (Moody's, 1998a).

The severe and realistic assessments provided in the evaluations contained in the international reports produced in 1997–8 (World Bank, 1997; Moody's, 1998a; Mitchell, 1998a, 1998b, 1998c) themselves helped to undermine international lenders' confidence in the ITICs, which directly worsened their situation through tightening the lending conditions they faced on international markets. The conclusion from these in-depth reports on the ITICs published in the late 1990s was that their long-term future was highly questionable. At the very least they would be gradually diluted in importance. The ITICs' fragile financial condition was finally exposed when the Asian Financial Crisis broke out in late 1997: 'The ITICs, which relied heavily on foreign borrowing, suddenly faced a sea change in the confidence of foreign creditors, resulting in severe funding and liquidity shortages.'

The closure of the Hainan Development Bank (HDB) in June 1998 fuelled the fears of international lenders. HDB was itself the product of the amalgamation of five smaller trust and investment corporations (Haikou Huaxia Finance Corporation, Hainan Province Funan ITIC, Haikou Zhejing TIC, Shuxing TIC and Sanya Jixia TIC). These were described by one international analyst as 'high flying financial institutions involved in trust, leasing, stock trading, property investment and other businesses that promised easy returns' (Mitchell, 1998a). By the time they were merged to form the HDB in 1995, they already had accumulated debts of RMB 4.4 billion, contributed by investors looking for 'easy returns.' The newly established entity, HDB, took over the entire debt and received an injection of fresh capital from the local government. It was reported that the PBOC injected a further RMB 1–2 billion at the last minute to try to prevent collapse.

HDB's difficulties were compounded by its relationship to the mushrooming credit cooperative sector. In the 1990s, more than thirty credit cooperatives were established in Hainan (*FT*, 23 July 1998). They illegally offered depositors rates of interest up to three times those of the state banks, which proved too much of a lure for many depositors to resist. Such returns were able to overcome investors' concerns about the dubious legality of such rates of interest, far above those set by the government. As the property market collapsed they faced severe difficulties, prompting heavy withdrawals by scared depositors. The difficulties were compounded when one of the cooperatives admitted its head had absconded with the depositors' money. Instead of closing the cooperatives, the provincial authorities ordered HDB to assume responsibility for their debts. This was a heavy burden. About one-half of Hainan's total deposits had been placed in the credit cooperatives. More than 60 per cent of these funds could not be traced. This was more than HDB's balance sheet could stand. Within a short period it was insolvent. Instead of placing HDB into bankruptcy, one of the 'big four' state banks, the Industrial and Commercial Bank of China (ICBC), was instructed to assume responsibility for HDB's debts and ensure payment of creditors. This added to the strain on the balance sheet of ICBC. It also seemed to show that the state would, indeed, step in to prevent the investors losing their deposits. This acted to encourage such illegal deposits, and perversely, stimulated local governments to allow their local non-bank financial institutions to continue their attempts to attract funds at high interest rates, even though there was little possibility of obtaining the returns necessary to justify such high rates.

Finally, in late October 1998, the closure of GITIC by the Chinese authorities dealt a fatal blow to the entire ITIC sector' (Moody's, July 2000). The closure marked 'the end of an era for China's once high-flying ITICs.' It was seen as confirmation of the long-standing suspicions of the ITICs' flaws and weaknesses.

Other 'window' companies

In addition to the red chips and ITICs, there were countless 'window' companies operating in Hong Kong, backed by government institutions from all over the country. According to one estimate there were as many as 1,700 'window' companies in Hong Kong from all parts of China in the late 1990s, with a disproportionately high share from neighbouring Guangdong province. All of these companies – red chips, ITICs and other window companies – formed an interconnected social and financial network, borrowing from, loaning to, and investing in, each other. They bought each other's shares. They acted as guarantors for each other's debts, weaving an 'open and gigantic network which formed a minefield of contingent liabilities.' Scholars estimated that the international debts of the mainland companies in Hong Kong totalled over US$ 80 billion. This estimation is quite believable, if we consider that GITIC and GDE alone had debts totalling around US$ 10 billion.

Employment and industrial structure

The growth of investment in Guangdong by overseas Chinese firms had a profound impact on the economies of southeast Asia. The greatest initial impact was on Hong Kong, which took the lead in the early phase of the growth of overseas Chinese investment in the mainland. The role of manufacturing in the city's economy fell at high speed. The number of employees in manufacturing in Hong Kong declined from almost one million in 1985 to less than half a million in 1994. However, the industrial capacity at the disposal of the city's manufacturers had 'increased more than fourfold by the addition of more than 30,000 factories in Guangdong employing five million workers as a result of investments over the border' (Chan *et al.*, 1999: 88). In addition, there was a large workforce employed in 'the many thousands of village industries acting as sub-contractors in the "processing trades", which were estimated to number more than 50,000' (Chan *et al.*, 1999: 88). Hong Kong had acquired a hinterland with 'a seemingly inexhaustible supply of low-cost labour available to be incorporated into the world economy to further expand its industrial base' (Chan *et al.*, 1999: 88). The emerging model was widely referred to as 'the shop at the front (i.e. Hong Kong) and the factory at the back (i.e. the Pearl River Delta).' Most analysts felt that this model had reached the limits of its development by the end of the 1990s.

Hong Kong's service sector grew at high speed during the late 1980s and 1990s. A major part of this growth consisted of the different services that facilitated the trade with the mainland, and, especially, Guangdong province: 'banking, insurance, shipping and container services and above all marketing facilities had mushroomed to make Hong Kong the services sector of the China trade' (Chan *et al.*, 1999: 89). The number of import-export houses grew from 14,000 in 1985 to more than 84,000 by 1993. The jobs created in this sector more than outnumbered those lost through the transfer of manufacturing to the mainland (Chan *et al.*, 1999: 89). Another major part of the change in the structure of employment was associated with the rise of Hong Kong to the status of principal provider of capital, either directly or indirectly, for the mainland. All the main international financial institutions established large offices in Hong Kong. The composition of the financial services sector shifted strongly towards Americanization, as the leading US institutions made Hong Kong the base for their China operations. The numbers involved were relatively small, in total perhaps a few hundred thousand, but they contributed to a large change in Hong Kong's socio-economic structure.

During the period of system reform on the mainland from the early 1980s to the late 1990s, Hong Kong grew at high speed, fuelled mainly by the immense advantages that it derived from its central position in the development of Guangdong province. Hong Kong, with the support of the mainland government, kept tight control on in-migration from the mainland. The proportion of unskilled, blue collar occupations fell steadily. In effect, these jobs were 'exported' to the mainland. Employment in old labour-intensive occupations, such as dockworkers, fell sharply, due to the increased application of labour-saving technologies. The only significant group of low-income migrants allowed to work in Hong Kong during this period were the thousands of maids recruited from the Philippines.

By the time of the return of Hong Kong to the mainland in 1997, the relationship of Hong Kong with the mainland, with Guangdong, and, especially, with the Pearl River Delta, had been transformed drastically. The formal political return of Hong Kong was taking place at the point at which the socio-economic interdependence of the city with the mainland had never been deeper. The socio-economic structure of the region of Guangdong and Hong Kong now looked vastly more complex than a decade previously.

As in Singapore, the privileged position of the main body of Hong Kong citizens was preserved by tight controls on rights to residence and work. Average incomes in Hong Kong had grown massively during this period. At the apex of Hong Kong's socio-economic structure, a few tens of thousands of people derived colossal financial benefit from their function in opening up the mainland. These included the senior managers of indigenous and global corporations based in the city. They included local Hong Kong people, highly qualified mainland citizens, and ex-patriots, increasingly from the United States. They formed a cosmopolitan elite with annual incomes of millions of US dollars each. The senior managers of global businesses in Hong Kong and leading local firms during these years earned enormous incomes. The MD of a leading global investment bank might have a salary and bonus budget of US$ 50–100 million for staff of only fifteen to twenty people. A senior financial firm manager from the mainland who used his connections to secure the contract for the IPO of a large mainland entity could expect to receive a bonus of at least one million US dollars. Even less senior managers in global financial institutions could expect incomes of hundreds of thousands of US dollars. The rise of the new elite in Hong Kong was reflected in the numerous trappings of conspicuous consumption, such as the new breed of super-luxury hotels, restaurants, shopping malls and clubs.

Within Hong Kong, a small, but significant, new underclass emerged, composed of a relatively small group of low-paid migrants in the lowliest of service occupations, and a group of mainly older workers unable to make the transition to the new demands of Hong Kong's predominantly service sector economy. Several studies in the 1990s showed that the distribution of income in the city was becoming significantly more unequal. Moreover, levels of absolute poverty increased significantly.

Far from Hong Kong being a society teeming with competitive small businesses, under the British colonial rule there grew up a comprehensive structure of cartels and organized monopolies which make a mockery of the notion of a 'competitive free market' environment in the territory: 'Hong Kong does not have anti-monopoly laws. It was deemed unsuitable because, in a colony, monopolies were granted in exchange for services wherever possible. Then monopolies were turned into franchises. Cartels were organized and tightly controlled' (Berthier, 2002: 17).

In the same fashion as in other colonial territories, the British 'enforced and protected the vested interests of the British merchants, originally a small group of former drug-dealers who reinvested their ill-gotten profits into lucrative monopolies' (Berthier, 2002: 20). As the British rulers were reluctant to spend any money in Hong Kong, 'the agreement was that they [the merchants] would be the ones financing the colony.' In exchange, they would be granted 'concessions,' that is, '...a monopolistic hold on specific trades and some pieces of land. Those privileges have never been abolished. They still permeate the fabric of the domestic economy' (Berthier, 2002: 20). Over the years, while the beneficiaries of the trade and the land may have changed, 'the principles of the regime have never been altered, and that is where the biggest problem lies' (Berthier, 2002: 20). Berthier colourfully describes Hong Kong's economic structure as follows:

> The Hong Kong residents started to realize that something must be wrong with the fact that the apartment they buy was built by company A, which runs the bus company that provides transport for the housing estate to an office block that belongs to the same company, which provides a telephone line through one of its subsidiaries, owns the supermarket, provides the power needed for the fridge that came imported through one of its subsidiaries, supplies the equipment and the stationery at your office, and is on the board of the bank which is around the corner.
>
> (Berthier, 2002: 17)

In its 2002 review of Hong Kong, the WTO laments the fact that there is an 'absence of a comprehensive policy to address anti-competitive practices and the entrenchment of a few dominant conglomerates in the domestic market' (quoted in Berthier, 2002: 18).

For example, in electricity generation, two companies were each granted a monopoly to supply different parts of Hong Kong. Hong Kong Electric supplied electricity to the island of Victoria and another, China Light and Power (CLP), controlled by Li Kashing, supplied the New Territories. Hong Kong, unsurprisingly, had the world's second most expensive electricity prices. James Tien, chairman of the Liberal Party, acknowledged: 'The scheme is a big mess...What we have is that the electricity companies used the hottest days of summer as the benchmark of the [electricity pricing] scheme to get approval for their investment' (Berthier, 2002: 19).

Hong Kong is widely thought of as a 'free market economy.' However, viewed from another perspective, it has had an immensely powerful government-driven 'industrial policy' to nurture powerful indigenous capitalist firms. In numerous sectors, most visibly property development, but also in transport, ports, telecommunications, beverages and the retail sector, a handful of oligopolistic firms dominate the commanding heights of the Hong Kong economy. The foundation of the leading business groups that comprehensively dominate Hong Kong's economy was their central role in the development of the colony's scarcest resource, land, which was made even more scarce by the policy of only allowing a tiny fraction of its potential building land to be developed for residential purposes. The economic rents that were available for developers were enormous. The process of development of Crown land was thoroughly opaque, involving an intimate interaction between the colonial government and a handful of Hong Kong families. These families were able collectively to monopolize access to the massive rents derived from land development. These rents in turn formed the foundation for their growth into immensely powerful business groups. In its own special way, the political economy of Hong Kong under the British during Hong Kong's 'Golden Age' closely mimics that of other East Asian economies such as South Korea, in which the state nurtured powerful indigenous firms by channelling rents towards them through granting access to monopolies and other special privileges. This process has been well hidden in Hong Kong behind a sophisticated smokescreen of ideology about the 'free market' and the 'invisible hand.'

At the end of the era of British colonial rule, the Hong Kong socio-economic structure was far removed from the idealized view of Hong Kong that is typically presented by its admirers. Instead of an economy dominated by teeming small- and medium-sized businesses, the British rulers permitted, and even encouraged, through various policies, the development of a dominant plutocracy consisting of a tiny handful of families. This pattern was common among British colonies, which heavily shaped the nature of their political development after independence.

By the late 1990s, Hong Kong had developed into one of the world's most unequal societies, with an immense concentration of business power in the hands of a tiny number of families. Firms run by the top ten families accounted for almost one-third of Hong Kong's total stock market capitalization (Table 1.7). The top fifteen families' firms accounted for no less than 84.2 per cent of the total Hong Kong GDP. The only other East Asian country that approached this extraordinarily high degree of dominance by a tiny elite group of families was Malaysia, also a former British colony.

Table 1.7 Family control in Hong Kong and other East Asian countries

Country	*Percentage of total value of listed assets that families control*				*Top 15 as % of GDP*
	Top 1	*Top 3*	*Top 10*	*Top 15*	
Hong Kong	6.5	26.2	32.1	34.4	84.2
Indonesia	16.6	40.7	57.7	61.7	21.5
Japan	0.5	1.8	2.4	2.8	2.1
Korea	11.4	29.7	36.8	38.4	12.9
Malaysia	7.4	17.3	24.8	28.3	76.2
Philippines	17.1	42.8	52.5	55.1	46.7
Singapore	6.4	19.5	26.6	29.9	48.3
Taiwan	4	14.5	18.4	20.1	17
Thailand	9.4	32.2	46.2	53.3	39.3

Source: Claessens *et al.*, 2000.

Even the official data on the distribution of income in Hong Kong show an extraordinarily unequal society (Table 1.8). By the mid-1990s, the bottom 30 per cent of the Hong Kong population received a meagre 7.3 per cent of personal income, and the bottom 10 per cent received just 1.1 per cent. At the other end of the scale, the super-rich top 10 per cent received 41.8 per cent of total personal income, and the top 30 per cent accounted for 67 per cent of the total. These official data show a hugely unequal society, even as recorded in the official statistics. However, they do not tell the whole story of income distribution in the city. It is hard to imagine that the data capture the full picture of the income of foreign residents working in Hong Kong, including people from the rich countries such as the immensely highly rewarded people working for international financial institutions. Nor do they capture accurately the income of the innumerable people from the Chinese mainland. It is not clear either if the data fully capture the income of the very poorest segments of the population, including the relatively small number of illegal immigrants, as well as the much larger number of low-paid workers such as the Philippino servants. Inclusion of data on all these groups would be likely to only exacerbate the degree of income inequality, huge as this already is shown to be.

The World Bank estimated that the Gini coefficient of the distribution of income in Hong Kong in the 1990s was 0.525, which placed Hong Kong among the most unequal countries in the world, on a par with Mexico (Berthier, 2002: 28). It is surprising to find such massive income inequalities in a relatively small city such as Hong Kong which drastically restricts immigration. However, if the data were to extend to include the whole of Hong Kong's hinterland, namely the Pearl River Delta, then the extent of income

Table 1.8 Official data on the distribution of income in Hong Kong (percentage)

Decile	*1966*	*1976*	*1986*	*1996*
Bottom 10%	1.3	1.9	1.6	1.1
Bottom 20%	5.3	5.4	5	3.7
Bottom 30%	9.1	10	9.4	7.3
Bottom 40%	13.4	15.5	14.8	11.9
Bottom 50%	19	22.3	21.2	17.6
Bottom 60%	25.8	30.4	28.8	24.6
Bottom 70%	33.3	39.2	37.9	33.1
Top 30%	66.7	60.8	62.1	66.9
Top 20%	57.7	49.5	50.7	56.3
Top 10%	45.5	33.6	35.5	41.8

Source: Yeung, 2004.

Notes: Derived from Hong Kong Census and Statistics Department Data.

inequality would look even more uneven. The Delta contained around fifteen million people working in labour-intensive, unskilled work, earning no more than US$ 1–2 per day. At the other end of the income distribution spectrum was the relatively tiny number of Hong Kong super-rich Chinese people and an even smaller number of super-rich global business people, working especially in global financial institutions in Hong Kong.

In addition, when considering the nature of inequality in Hong Kong, it must be borne in mind that imperfect as the data on personal incomes are, they are far more satisfactory than the data on the distribution of wealth, which are, to all intents and purposes, non-existent. We have seen that the concentration of business power in Hong Kong was extraordinarily uneven, with a tiny group of families controlling a large fraction of the entire Hong Kong economy. Corresponding to this, there must have been at least a comparable inequality in wealth distribution, which exceeded that of most countries, let alone that of comparable-sized cities. The massively unequal class structure produced by the policies of the British colonial rulers has resulted in a city with fantastic differences in the political interests of different segments of the society. Such official data show a remarkable gap between the average per capita income of Hong Kong people and their average per capita expenditure. In the year 2000, Hong Kong's average per capita income was reported to be US$ 24,000, compared, for example, with US$ 17,000 in Singapore. This placed Hong Kong firmly in the ranks of the world's richest countries. However, official data on the level of average per capita expenditure reported that in 2002, the level in Hong Kong was just US$ 13,000, the same level as Singapore. As far as the mass of the Hong Kong population is concerned, say the bottom 80 per cent, their average per capita income was far below US$ 24,000. In the late 1990s the average per capita income of the bottom 80 per cent of the population was estimated to be only around US$ 10,000: 'Its real per capita income is not far above that of its neighbours in Shenzhen and Guangzhou, where per capita incomes are the highest in China at above US$ 6,000' (Berthier, 2002: 29).

Across the border in the Pearl River Delta, many millions of workers were employed in predominantly labour-intensive factories producing billions of dollars-worth of goods each year, a large fraction of which were for export to consumers in high-income economies, particularly the United States. A large fraction of them earned no more than a dollar or so per day. As we have seen, the evidence suggests that there was no increase in the real average incomes of these millions of workers throughout the whole period of reform and opening up. The pressure of huge pent-up underemployed labour in the Chinese rural areas was simply too great. If we consider the whole region of Guangdong and Hong Kong, then it is inescapable that during the period of reform and opening up, alongside high-speed growth and massive absorption of rural surplus labour, a large increase in inequality in the distribution of income and wealth had taken place.[10]

4 Hong Kong in the Asian Financial Crisis

Coping with the crisis in Guangdong's financial institutions was an immensely challenging task. However, that task was rendered even more complex by the fact that the Chinese government resumed control over Hong Kong in 1997. Even without the hand-over, the Chinese government was concerned about economic and social stability in Hong Kong. The fact that it had now been formally returned to Chinese mainland rule, made the responsibility all the more direct and significant. We have seen in the preceding section that by the end of the 1990s there were close linkages between Hong Kong and the mainland, especially with Guangdong province. Both the causes and the resolution of the crises in the two administrative regions were inseparable.

On 1 July 1997, the Chinese government resumed sovereignty over Hong Kong after 100 years under British rule.[11] Under the formula 'One Country, Two Systems' the basic institutional arrangements in Hong Kong were to remain unchanged for fifty years. However, the mainland government was now responsible for both Hong Kong and the mainland. The impact of the AFC on Hong Kong produced large and challenging policy complications for the Chinese government.

The Asian Financial Crisis erupted only a few hours after the handover ceremonies were completed and the last British Governor of Hong Kong, Chris Patten, together with his family, had sailed out of the harbour. On 2 July Thailand floated the *baht*, which was to be the trigger for the crisis. The immediate effect of the crisis was massive devaluation of currencies across the region. Between 2 June 1997 and 27 March 1998 the local exchange rate against the dollar fell by 15 per cent in Taiwan, 31 per cent in Malaysia, 36 per cent in Thailand and 72 per cent in Indonesia. The devaluation caused a large increase in the local currency value of dollar-denominated debt. For banks and other businesses that had large dollar debts this was a disaster. The impact of the crisis was reflected in, and compounded by, a serious decline in stock market prices. Between June 1997 and March 1998 the stock market index fell by 22 per cent in Hong Kong, 31 per cent in Singapore, 53 per cent in Thailand, 65 per cent in Malaysia, 70 per cent in Korea and 96 per cent in Indonesia. Short-term funds were massively withdrawn across the region.

Net private capital flows to the five main economies in the region were reversed, changing from a US$ 93 billion inflow in 1996 to a US$ 105 billion outflow in 1998, equalling 8 per cent of the combined GDP of the countries concerned (Wade, 1998: 695).

The group of countries most affected by the crisis saw a serious decline in the national product in 1997/8. GNP per capita fell by 7.8 per cent in Hong Kong, 7.1 per cent in Korea, 8.4 per cent in Malaysia, 8.5 per cent in Thailand and 16.2 per cent in Indonesia (World Bank, 2000: 230–1). This was a massive systemic shock after such a long period of sustained high growth. Singapore and Taiwan experienced significant slowdowns in their growth rate of GNP to 1.5 per cent and 4.3 per cent, respectively (SSB, ZTN, 2000: 854; World Bank, 2000: 230–1), but were immune from the worst effects of the crisis. Mainland China experienced only a small decline in its growth rate, to a reported growth of GNP of 7.2 per cent.

The Chinese government not only had to deal with the impact of the crisis on Guangdong's financial institutions, but also the impact of the crisis on Hong Kong, the 'shop at the front' of Guangdong province. Naturally, the central Chinese government was concerned to see Hong Kong remain stable, economically, socially and politically. Many international and local observers doubted that the Chinese government would be capable of ensuring that Hong Kong remained prosperous after the handover of power. The impact of the Asian Financial Crisis tested the capabilities of the central government to the full.

Hong Kong's exchange rate regime was a key element in the way in which it was affected by the AFC. The Hong Kong dollar was floated from 1974 until 1983. In the latter year it was pegged to the US dollar at the rate of HK$ 7.8 per US dollar.[12] The Exchange Fund is Hong Kong's version of the currency board system.[13] Up until the late 1980s, the Exchange Fund lacked effective control over the level of liquidity in the inter-bank market and was not the lender of last resort of bank reserves (Ng and Chen, 1998: 137). The monetary authority's ability to alter the inter-bank interest rate in order to defend the peg was weak.

In the late 1980s and early 1990s, the Hong Kong government introduced a number of measures designed to 'improve its monetary management in order to defend the linked exchange rate system effectively and tackle speculation activities promptly.'[14] By the mid-1990s, the Hong Kong Monetary Authority (HKMA) had become the 'regulator of the payment system and the lender of last resort' (Ng and Chen, 1998: 146). In other words it had become Hong Kong's *de facto* central bank. The strengthened controls over Hong Kong's monetary management mechanism were put to the test in 1995 when the Hong Kong dollar came under speculative attack several times.[15]

A study of the Hong Kong monetary system written in 1997 concluded: 'Hong Kong's massive foreign reserves, its strengthened monetary management and its repurchase agreements with other banks in the region, make a formidable target for currency speculation' (Ng and Chen, 1998: 147). In fact this 'formidable target for speculation' was put to a severe test during the AFC. Hong Kong survived the early part of the AFC relatively unscathed. However, on 23 October 1997, the crisis erupted in Hong Kong. Speculators turned their attention towards the Hong Kong dollar. Underlying the speculation was the fact that the massive devaluation around the rest of the region had led to a large *de facto* appreciation of the Hong Kong dollar relative to the rest of the currencies in the region. Between January 1997 and January 1998 the local exchange rate against the dollar fell by 56.2 per cent in Thailand, 84.8 per cent in Indonesia, 43.4 per cent in the Philippines, 48.3 per cent in Malaysia and 12.3 per cent in Singapore: 'Suddenly Hong Kong was far more expensive than Bangkok or even Tokyo' (Krugman, 2000: 126). The continuous depreciation of the local exchange rate against the dollar in the neighbouring countries and regions implied the Hong Kong dollar constantly appreciating against the local currencies in the neighbouring countries. This directly affected Hong Kong's trade and export processing orders.

An important element in the response was the interaction with the mainland authorities. Although the mainland had resumed sovereignty over Hong Kong, under the formula 'one country, two systems,' Hong Kong was 'responsible for its own economic management.' Throughout the crisis, the People's Bank of China (PBOC) emphasized: 'The Hong Kong Monetary Authority has full responsibility for managing Hong Kong's financial system, its monetary policy and the Hong Kong dollar' (quoted in *FT*, 24 October 1997). Senior PBOC officials stated publicly that the PBOC would, if necessary, 'offer funds from its US$ 130 billion in foreign exchange reserves if needed to defend the Hong Kong currency' (quoted in *FT*, 24 October 1997). It emphasized that it did not think this would be necessary, as Hong Kong itself had 'enormous reserves.' Moreover, the wide devaluation of currencies across East Asia put pressure on the Chinese *renminbi*, which had been fixed at around 8.3 per dollar for the three years prior to the AFC. The rumours of possible Chinese devaluation increased the incentive to speculate against the Hong Kong dollar. A major consideration for the Chinese government in deciding its policy in relation to the *renminbi* was the possible impact on the Hong Kong dollar.

On 23 October Donald Tsang, Hong Kong's Financial Secretary, made the famous announcement: 'We have absolute determination to defend the exchange rate. Speculators arrived last night. We had a reasonably busy time and we have driven them away.' The Hong Kong Monetary Authority intervened in the market in order to raise interest rates sharply, which was to form a central plank of the battle against speculation in the next year or so. Overnight rates rose to around 250 per cent, and the three-month inter-bank rate rose to 41.25 per cent (*FT*, 24 October 1997). The defence of the Hong Kong dollar's peg against the US dollar was to stand at the centre of the crisis over the next few months. The maintenance of the peg was regarded as essential to Hong Kong's continuation as one of Asia's financial centres. The *Financial Times* reported: 'Mr Tsang and his team have the full backing of China, which staunchly supports the currency peg as a means of safeguarding the stability and prosperity of capitalist Hong Kong' (*FT*, 24 October 1997). One analyst compared the crisis to the Indonesian forest fires that raged at the same time:

> [They] smoulder underground before bursting through the surface... [R]egional economic problems have ignited new crises, sending financial turmoil, like smog, far abroad. The most serious fire burned this week in Hong Kong, where a battle raged to defend the currency, the last in Asia to be fixed against the dollar.
>
> (*FT*, 25 October 1997)

By the end of the week, Hong Kong had weathered the storm.

The defence of the exchange rate was to carry a high price. On 23 October, the Hang Seng Index experienced its largest-ever one-day decline (10.4 per cent). Over four days the market fell 23 per cent. The direct consequence of Hong Kong's 'financial crisis' was the collapse of the stock market and the property market. Between 30 September 1997 and 23 October 1997, in fewer than twenty days of trading, the Hang Seng Index dropped from 15,049 to 9,767, a decrease of 35 per cent. The red chips in Hong Kong backed by the mainland fell even more precipitously. Once the red chip bubble had been burst, it was impossible to re-inflate it. Over the ensuing months, the fall in red chip share prices was far greater than even the large falls of the rest of the Hong Kong stock market. By 14 August 1998, compared with the peak in 1997, the Hang Seng Index had fallen 59 per cent and the index for red chips had fallen 86 per cent. Of the forty major red chips listed previously in Table 1.6, the share price of thirty-five dropped over 80 per cent within which that of sixteen dropped over 90 per cent. The market capitalization of the red chips kept falling. This directly affected their borrowing capability. Moreover the effect on their asset portfolio was disastrous, as they had heavily purchased each other's shares to take advantage of the preceding red chip frenzy. Some of the red chips ended up worthless.

Alongside the collapse in the stock market, the Hong Kong property market dropped over 50 per cent. This had strong ripple effects. It placed further pressure on the value of the red chips' asset portfolios, in addition to that which came directly from the collapse in the stock market. Under these circumstances, even if a company had been well managed, it would have been hard to remain solvent. During the financial crisis Hong Kong enterprises with a mainland background faced especially great difficulties in repaying their debts. They had borrowed heavily with their shares or properties as collateral using a large proportion of their borrowings to reinvest in the stock market and property market. The collapsed value of their assets meant that debt repayment was especially hard.

The red chips' financial difficulties were intensified by hardening pressure for debt repayment. In a financial crisis, the level of asset liquidity becomes vital for an enterprise's survival: 'cash is king.' On 12 January 1998 Hong Kong's largest investment bank, Peregrine, filed for liquidation. Peregrine had 'fed off the growth of the Hong Kong economy.' It was called 'the father of red chips' due to its close relationship with that sector. Peregrine had assets of HK$ 24.6 billion and was ranked in the *Fortune 500*, with 2,500 employees in thirty-five offices in sixteen countries. It went bankrupt due to a shortfall of US$ 60 million in liquidity. The announcement sent panic through the market. The stock market fell almost 9 per cent on 12 January and the red chip index fell by more than 22 per cent (*FT*, 13 January 1998). The Zhengda Group, a so-called 'prince among princes,' had been one of Hong Kong's sixteen A-ranked security companies with 12,000 clients. It also went bankrupt during the crisis, because of a shortfall of HK$ 80 million in liquidity.

The international banks had their own liquidity difficulties. During the financial crisis, many international banks based in Hong Kong encountered serious losses elsewhere in Asia. Although Hong Kong's banks were in better condition than most of those across the rest of Asia, with high asset quality and a low ratio of non-performing loans, around 46 per cent of all bank loans were in the property sector.[16] The stock market and property market collapse placed heavy pressure on Hong Kong banks. In their efforts to recover their debts they encountered increasing difficulties due to the sharply rising bankruptcy rate among private Hong Kong firms. In contrast, the mainland-backed companies in Hong Kong not only had no record of bankruptcy, but also had the 'glorious tradition that the government would always repay their debts in full.' As we shall see, a major issue in the restructuring of GDE, the biggest of the red chips, was the persistent demand of the creditors that GDE's debts be treated by the Chinese government as if they were China's sovereign debts. Thus, the red chips became the focus for intense creditor efforts to recover debts, despite the fact that the fall in their share price had been greater than any other group of firms in Hong Kong.

By early 1998, it had become apparent that the battle to defend the peg was going to be protracted: 'When Hong Kong fought off an assault on its currency last October, it won the battle but not the war' (*FT*, 9 January 1998). Early 1998 saw a renewed round of speculation against the Hong Kong dollar. The Hong Kong Monetary Authority raised interest rates even further from the level that had been reached in October 1997. In mid-1997, the Hang Seng Index had reached almost 17,000. By early January 1998 it stood at just above 8,000. Property prices continued to fall. Rumours circulated that the Chinese government was about to devalue the *renminbi*. The Hong Kong Monetary Authority repeated its determination to defend the currency peg. The price Hong Kong was paying for defending the peg grew by the day. Speculation swirled around the possibility that it might be abandoned at some point. Analysts were equally afraid of the consequences. One commented: 'The fall of the peg would lead to a banking collapse in Hong Kong' (quoted in *FT*, 13 January 1998). The HKMA emphasized that despite the heavy impact on bank profits, Hong Kong's banks were still basically robust, with an average capital adequacy ratio of more than 17 per cent (*FT*, 12 January 1998).

The first half of 1998 saw no significant improvement. Although the banking sector was still overall making profits, these were much reduced, and almost all significant economic indicators were negative. Interest rates remained high in order to ward off speculation. Property prices languished at around 40 per cent lower than in mid-1997. GDP declined in the first quarter of 1998, and was predicted to fall substantially over the course of the whole year. Tourism declined drastically. The stock market continued to fall, after a brief spring rally. By the end of May the Hang Seng Index was still below the psychologically significant 9,000 mark, around 60 per cent lower than the previous year's peak. Unemployment began to rise to levels not seen in recent times in Hong Kong, and was predicted to rise to around 6–7 per cent by the end of the year.

The serious deterioration in the overall economic situation prompted heavy renewed speculation against the currency peg in mid-August: 'Financial markets seem determined to scent blood around the Hong Kong dollar...There is a widespread view building up that authorities will use the first period of calm in the markets...to abandon the peg' (*FT*, 12 August 1998). George Soros' Quantum Fund and Julian Robertson's Tiger Fund were widely thought to be the main speculators at this point. Speculators entered into a 'double play.' The hedge funds sold shares they did not own in the expectation that the price would fall. Their 'double play' involved speculation also against the currency, which drove interest rates still higher: 'The sales of Hong Kong dollars were ostentatious, carried out in large blocks, regularly timed, so as to make sure that everyone in the market noticed' (Krugman, 2000: 127). Hong Kong officials claimed that the hedge funds 'paid reporters and editors to run stories suggesting that the Hong Kong dollar or the Chinese *renminbi* or both were on the verge of devaluation' (Krugman, 2000: 127). In other words the hedge funds were 'deliberately trying to start a run on the currency' (Krugman, 2000: 127). Moreover, it is possible that the speculation against the Hong Kong dollar was part of a much wider 'play' against the currencies across the whole East Asia region: 'You could think of Hong Kong as only the centrepiece of a play against much of the Asia-Pacific region, indeed quite possibly the largest market conspiracy of all time' (Krugman, 2000: 127).

From the end of July through to the middle of August this strategy paid off for the speculators. Alongside the predicted rise in interest rates, the Hang Seng Index fell from around 8,600 to around 6,600 on 13 August, compared with almost 17,000 at the peak in mid-1997. This was a second serious crisis for the Hong Kong government, with sentiment in the Special Administrative Region (SAR) deeply negative, amid widespread nervousness and uncertainty. For a while it looked likely that the speculation against the Hong Kong dollar would succeed: 'After all, what could Hong Kong do? Its stock market was large compared with that of most developing countries, but not compared with the resources of the hedge funds' (Krugman, 2000: 127–8).[17] Moreover, the conspirators were secure in the knowledge that there was almost no chance that the Hong Kong government would introduce controls on capital flight: 'All in all, it looked like a brilliant plan, with very high chances of success' (Krugman, 2000: 128).

The Hong Kong government was afraid that Hong Kong citizens would lose confidence and move en masse into US dollars. At the time of the 'bloodbath' on the Hong Kong stock market in October 1997, the *Financial Times* had written: 'Should local depositors switch deposits in sufficient volume, even Hong Kong's mighty US$ 80 billion foreign exchange reserves, backed by China's holdings of US$ 120 billion, would find it hard to hold the peg' (*FT*, 24 October 1997).[18] On 14 August the Hong Kong government launched an unprecedented move to hit back at the speculators. It believed that four or five of the major hedge funds were engaged in a systematic ploy to destroy the peg against the US dollar. In mid-1998, the global hedge funds were estimated to have resources of around US$ 400 billion, more than double the combined stock market capitalization of Thailand, Indonesia and South Korea at the start of the AFC. They had a large ability to influence outcomes in such economies, which were small compared with the speculative resources at the disposal of the hedge funds. In a totally unexpected move the government used an estimated US$ 13–14 billion to intervene directly in the stock market to buy blue-chip shares. Joseph Yam, Head of the HKMA, said: 'We are going to hit the speculators where it hurts' (quoted in *FT*, 17 August 1998). The immediate effect was to ward off the speculative attack and thwart the 'double play' against the stock market and the currency. Following the intervention, it was reported that the Hong Kong government owned 10 per cent of HSBC, 11 per cent of Swire Pacific, 9 per cent of Cheung Kong and 7 per cent of both Hutchison Whampoa and HK Telecom (*FT*, 1 September 1998).

China's official newspapers warned the international hedge fund speculators against spreading 'lies and rumours about a possible devaluation of the *renminbi* with the objective of undermining the Hong Kong dollar' (quoted in *FT*, 31 August 1998). The Chinese government reiterated that it would 'answer any request from the Hong Kong government for assistance in its battles against speculators' (*FT*, 31 August 1998). Spokesmen for the Hong Kong government emphasized that the consequences of abandoning the dollar peg would be disastrous for Hong Kong. One warned that it could lead to Hong Kong becoming a 'second Indonesia' (quoted in *FT*, 31 August 1998). The hedge funds were widely thought to have been 'wounded' by the government's actions. The government's intervention was heavily criticized by extreme free market economists, such as Milton Friedman, who called the intervention 'insane' (quoted in Krugman, 2000: 128). The Heritage Foundation 'formally removed [Hong Kong's] designation as a bastion of economic freedom.' Newspaper stories linked Hong Kong with Malaysia, which had just imposed draconian capital controls (Krugman, 2000: 128).

By early September 1998, the Hong Kong government had warded off the immediate speculative threat to the currency. However, the position still remained dangerous. The Hang Seng Index stood at only around 8,000. The property market remained stuck at a low level. National output was falling and unemployment rising to new record levels. The mood was still tense. Hong Kong's Financial Secretary, Donald Tsang, recognized that this could provide the environment for further speculation from the hedge funds. He announced that the territory would continue to fight on if necessary: 'I can go right down to the US$ 12 billion needed to cover my issued currency' (quoted in *FT*, 14 September 1998).

The situation still appeared dangerous when, towards the end of September, it was revealed that Long-Term Capital Management (LTCM),[19] the US hedge fund, was close to collapse and threatened with liquidation: 'Its complex mathematical bets on discrepancies among different bonds and derivatives had come spectacularly unstuck. Its capital had been virtually wiped out as it paid out billions in collateral on loss-making positions' (*FT*, 25 September 1998). It had built up a total on-balance-sheet market exposure of around US$ 200 billion (*FT*, 26 September 1998). The amount of off-balance-sheet exposure was thought to be 'on a similarly impressive scale' (*FT*, 3 October 1998). The hedge funds were not subject to any requirement to disclose the nature of their investments: the central bankers were likened to 'indulgent parents' who 'may have allowed these offspring to grow into unruly teenagers that they can no longer understand or control' (*FT*, 25 September 1998). Investment banks 'allowed [the hedge funds] to retain a veil of secrecy... enticed by the opportunity of lucrative business' (*FT*, 25 September 1998). The major US banks which had loaned vast amounts to Long-Term Capital Management realized that if LTCM was forced to unwind its derivatives positions, they might be 'taken down' along with LTCM.

It was revealed that LTCM had suffered a 40 per cent drop in its net asset value in August alone, and 50 per cent over the year to date (*FT*, 25 September 1998). On 23 September the Federal Reserve intervened to organize a US$ 3.75 billion rescue package from the major US banks. A consortium of banks took over ownership of 90 per cent of LTCM. The rescue raised fundamental issues about 'crony capitalism' and 'moral hazard' in the West. There were close personal relationships between the senior officers of LTCM and the Federal Reserve. The board included a former vice-chairman of the Fed, a close personal friend of the (then) head of the Fed, Alan Greenspan. Some of the heads of the banks that bailed out LTCM had personal investments in the bankrupt company. Former Fed Chairman, Paul Volcker, asked: 'Why should the weight of the federal government be brought to bear to help out a private investor?' (quoted in *FT*, 3 October 1998).

LTCM's collapse forced the hedge funds to liquidate positions in riskier markets and prompted banks to withdraw credit lines or raise the interest rate on funds loaned to the hedge fund: 'The hedge funds are just not in a position to take big speculative positions in the near future. The cost has just become too high' (a banker, quoted in *FT*, 14 October 1998).

The International Monetary Fund (IMF) estimated earlier in 1998 that the hedge funds had about US$ 100 billion under management, which was leveraged between four and seven times, which meant that they had a total of 'between US$ 400 billion and US$ 700 billion worth of positions in global markets' (*FT*, 14 October 1998). This was estimated to have fallen to between US$ 200 billion and US$ 350 billion by early October (*FT*, 14 October 1998). The amount that the hedge funds needed to set aside as collateral against bank loans had also risen from about 30 per cent to around 70 per cent of the loan's value. The implications for Hong Kong were enormous: 'This means that there is unlikely to be a repetition of the big speculative attack on the Hong Kong stock market in August' (*FT*, 14 October 1998). Krugman notes that the 'the whole Hong Kong issue faded away, because a bizarre series of events around the world forced the hedge funds themselves to curtail their activities' (Krugman, 2000: 129). In other words, it is an open question whether Hong Kong would have been able to resist further speculative attacks in the absence of the collapse of LTCM.

By late 1998, the threat of disintegration of the Hong Kong financial system in the face of international speculation had receded. But Hong Kong was still in the grip of a recession of unprecedented severity. Although the Hang Seng Index climbed back from its lowpoint in August 1998, at the year-end, it still stood at under 10,000. The Hang Seng 'China-Affiliated Corporations Index' began in July 1993 at 1,000 and climbed to a peak of 4,200 on 9 August 1997. By year-end 1998 it stood at just 1,072. Hong Kong's GDP grew by 5.3 per cent per annum from 1990 to 1997. This high-speed growth was rudely interrupted by the AFC. In 1998, GDP fell by over 5 per cent at constant prices, and per capita GDP fell by over 6 per cent. The official unemployment rate reached 4.7 per cent in mid-1998. In 1999, Hong Kong began to pull out of the worst of the recession and GDP grew by 3 per cent in real terms. However, the Hang Seng Index at year end (12,869) was still far below the peak. The property market remained heavily depressed, far below the peak, and unemployment increased to 6.3 per cent.

During a time of extreme economic turbulence in Hong Kong the Chinese government was forced to develop an approach towards the crisis in GITIC and GDE. The Hong Kong economy had become hugely important for Guangdong. Also, Guangdong's firms had come to play an important role in the Hong Kong economy. The most important of these by far were the giant Guangdong companies GITIC and GDE. They both faced a disastrous deterioration in their financial situation during the Asian Financial Crisis. Although the Chinese government had no direct role in deciding economic policy in Hong Kong, it was deeply concerned to ensure that the SAR remained economically, socially and politically stable following the return of sovereignty to China. It, therefore, needed to consider closely the impact that its actions, with respect to GITIC and GDE, might have upon the economic and political situation in Hong Kong. Until the end of 1998, it was walking a knife-edge. Even in 1999, the situation was tense. Only in the year

2000 did Hong Kong resume strong growth. Real GDP rose by around 5 per cent, and in mid-year the Hang Seng Index climbed back to its peak of 1997 (though it slid back at the year-end).[20]

Hong Kong eventually managed to withstand the severe trial of the AFC after resisting the powerful attacks one after another from the international speculators. This was due not only to the Hong Kong authority's 'bayonet charge' against the international speculators; it was due also to the fact that the mainland authorities adopted the correct policy to deal with the mainland-backed enterprises in Hong Kong, particularly the ITICs and the red chips in Hong Kong, which together had huge international debts.

The mainland government could not directly intervene in Hong Kong's economic affairs, but they had responsibility for the Special Administrative Region (SAR) now that it was back under Chinese sovereignty. Concern for the crisis in Hong Kong deeply influenced China's analysis of the policy options available to them in dealing with the crisis. In explaining why the Guangdong government decided to save GDE, but not GITIC, Wang Qishan said that the Chinese government regarded the issue as 'one beyond mere economic considerations.' He pointed out: 'GDE is a group company registered in Hong Kong and involves five listed companies. We must consider the stability of Hong Kong's market.' He said that he not only 'did not want to throw Hong Kong's stock market into turmoil,' but also that 'China should make a contribution to the stability of Hong Kong.' As a result, among the twenty-eight red chips whose share price dropped more than 88 per cent (Table 1.6), only GITIC's Guangxin Enterprises was in liquidation, and that was due directly to the bankruptcy of GITIC. The reason that this was the sole bankruptcy among the red chips was the fact that the mainland government as well as the local governments and institutions all over the country, following the pattern of the GDE restructuring (see Part 2), contributed a huge amount of cash, injected a large quantity of high-quality assets and saved these giant companies that were teetering on the brink of bankruptcy. Therefore their actions, in response to the 'challenge' posed by the AFC, saved the Hong Kong economy from disaster, which would have had wider repercussions for the whole of East Asia.

The deep interaction between the debts of the mainland-based companies and Hong Kong's financial markets made the response of the Chinese government to the insolvency of its firms especially sensitive, requiring great skill to avoid damaging Hong Kong's interests. In order to consider the interests of ordinary Hong Kong citizens, it was necessary to consider the interests of the Hong Kong financial community as well.

5 Guangdong in the Asian Financial Crisis

From mid-1997 onwards, Guangdong began to feel the impact of the Asian Financial Crisis. An important part of the impact of the AFC was mediated through Hong Kong. The Guangdong government faced serious difficulties in trying to restructure the province's economy, and achieve a new growth path after fifteen-odd years of high-speed labour-intensive expansion principally led by investment from overseas Chinese business people. In addition, it was experiencing serious problems due to the end of the real estate boom, which had played such an important part in the growth process of the 1990s. This had a major impact on the balance sheets of all financial institutions, not least of those of Guangdong-based companies operating in Hong Kong.

The crisis affected the inflow of international capital. It exposed the business practices of the numerous 'window' companies established by different Guangdong entities in Hong Kong: 'The crisis revealed that these companies suffered from loose control and low levels of management, that they had serious internal corruption and had lost a great deal of the state's assets' (SSBG, GTN, 2000: 29). This affected the inward flow of capital. International commercial bank loans dropped from US$ 1.7 billion in 1998 to just US$ 704 million in 1999. The amount of agreed FDI fell steeply from US$ 24.8 billion in 1995 to US$ 9.2 billion in 1998 and US$ 6.2 billion in 1999 (SSBG, GTN, 2000: 501).

The Asian Financial Crisis had a strong impact on Guangdong's exports. The explosive growth of the early and mid-1990s was halted in its tracks. The province's exports to East Asia were especially severely hit. The core regions of the Pearl River Delta experienced substantial declines in both the volume of orders and unit prices to most countries in the region. Compared with the period from January to June in 1997, export orders fell 4.9 per cent and prices fell 5.3 per cent for seventy-three export-processing enterprises in Shenzhen and Baoan from July to December 1997. In 1998, for ninety-two enterprises in Shenzhen and Dongguan, which produced mainly for export to southeast Asia, export orders decreased by an average of 30 per cent and export orders to Japan decreased by an average of 20 per cent. In the first quarter of 1998, exports to Thailand and Indonesia from Jiangmen declined 35.4 per cent and 11.2 per cent, respectively. Exports to southeast Asia and South Korea from Guangzhou declined 25 per cent and

78 per cent, respectively. The impact of the slump in exports was felt mainly in the Pearl River Delta, which had been the focal point of the explosive growth in the 1990s.

The growth rate of the Guangdong economy was significantly affected. In the early part of the 1990s, Guangdong achieved a real average annual industrial growth rate of 28 per cent (SSBG, GTN, 2000: 82). Between 1996 and 1999 the rate more than halved to around 12 per cent per annum (SSBG, GTN, 2000: 82). The reported growth rate of provincial GDP dropped from an average annual rate of 16.6 per cent in 1990–7 to 10 per cent in 1997–9 (SSBG, GTN, 2000: 84). The growth of energy production slumped from around 28 per cent per annum from 1990 to 1997, to negative growth in 1998 and 1999 (minus 4.1 per cent and minus 10.3 per cent, respectively) (SSBG, GTN, 2000: 199). This suggests that the real extent of the slowdown in output growth was greater even than the official data indicated.

The real estate market sharply altered even before the onset of the AFC. The bubble in real estate prices had stimulated the explosive growth in real estate investment. After 1995, the growth rate of investment in real estate sharply declined, falling to an average annual growth rate of just 6 per cent in the period 1995–9 (at current prices) (SSBG, GTN, 2000: 158). The amount of floorspace under construction grew from 213 million square metres in 1995 to 224 million square metres in 1999, a real increase of only 1.2 per cent per annum (SSBG, GTN, 2000: 157).

In the early phases of rural reform in the late 1970s and early 1980s, Guangdong's rural population experienced high rates of growth of real per capita consumption, increasing at 11.4 per cent per annum in the years 1978–85 (SSBG, GTN, 2000: 93). In the early 1990s, both the urban and the rural populations achieved rapid advances in the real growth of per capita consumption. From 1990 to 1995, both groups experienced a 'golden age' of improvement in their living standards, with real increases in per capita consumption reported to be 12 per cent per annum for rural dwellers and 15.1 per cent for urban dwellers (SSBG, GTN, 2000: 93). However, the picture changed abruptly from the mid-1990s onwards. From 1995–9 Guangdong's urban population achieved a growth rate of real per capita consumption of 4.4 per cent per annum, far below that of the first half of the decade. For the rural population real per capita consumption slowed drastically, and in the years 1997–9 there was barely any increase at all, growing just 2 per cent in total in these years (SSBG, GTN, 2000: 93).

We have seen that Guangdong's export processing industry was propped up by an army of migrant workers. The recession in Guangdong's processing industry had a significant impact on the demand for migrant workers. There were social disturbances in many districts, due to such issues as overdue salary payments and unemployment. Although the effects were contained within manageable limits, the Guangdong government was acutely aware that it was sitting on a potentially explosive situation that could erupt if the impact of the AFC were allowed to spread more deeply into the region's political economy.

Prior to the AFC there were serious underlying difficulties with the management practices of Guangdong's non-bank financial institutions, including the TICs, red chips, rural financial associations and urban credit cooperatives. These often included problems of the low technical quality of management. They involved also the widespread absence of a repayment culture among borrowers; extensive off-balance-sheet transactions; low quality auditing; speculative lending and investment, especially during the property 'bubble' and the boom in the Hong Kong stock market of the early 1990s. The macro-economic environment in Hong Kong and Guangdong province deteriorated significantly during the AFC. This had a serious impact on the balance sheets of Guangdong-based financial institutions. At every level, borrowings that had been made on the assumption of a continuation of past rates of growth and returns, suddenly appeared unrealistic and unattainable. The drastic worsening of economic prospects for the region exposed the myths of super-normal returns that were the foundation of the Ponzi-type financial behaviour. The 'high tide' of continuous high-speed economic growth had receded leaving the 'rocks' exposed. Without the foundation of real annual growth rates of over 20 per cent, people no longer believed the myth of returns of 30, 40 or even 50 per cent. If people no longer believed in these returns, then the Ponzi game was over and people would no longer be willing to pour capital into the region. Both domestic and international creditors began to worry that their investment would never be recovered and asked for immediate repayment. A payments crisis hit the whole of Guangdong's non-bank financial sector.

The pressure on Guangdong's financial institutions was intense. Even without the AFC, local NBFIs faced severe difficulties trying to repay depositors. The AFC greatly intensified these difficulties. The international creditors demanded that the Guangdong government treat the international obligations of Guangdong-based financial institutions as if they were China's sovereign debt. The terms on which the international banks were willing to lend to Guangdong-based financial institutions hardened. In the immediate aftermath of the AFC, the interest rate charged by the international banks for lending to red chips is estimated to have risen on average by around 25 per cent (Research Department of GDE, 1999: 232). The AFC made it impossible for Guangdong-based financial institutions to 'borrow their way out' of the crisis.

GITIC, the province's flagship 'trust and investment company,' was the main vehicle through which the provincial government raised money on international markets to help fund the province's development efforts. By the autumn of 1998, GITIC was in great difficulty. In 1998 it was only able to meet its repayment obligations thanks to large-scale help from the Guangdong provincial government. The Guangdong government did not know the full extent of GITIC's liabilities, but it knew that GITIC was fundamentally insolvent. It was aware that the sums involved were extremely large relative to the size of the provincial budget. GITIC's international debts were eventually found to total around US$ 4.4 billion, more than one-half the size of the provincial budget (around US$ 8 billion in 1998). Assets were eventually found to be only US$ 2.6 billion. By early October 1998, the provincial government had reached a point of crisis in dealing with GITIC's escalating difficulties. Providing further help for GITIC was beyond the province's capabilities.

Apart from GITIC, Guangdong also had a further twenty-four trust and investment companies, also with substantial international debts, though far short of those of GITIC. The other TICs also experienced intensifying repayment difficulties during the AFC. Both they and the international creditors were watching intently to see the way in which the Chinese government would respond to the crisis at GITIC. Would the Guangdong government take responsibility for GITIC's international debts, and treat them as sovereign debt? Would they seek for an alternative way out of the crisis?

As well as GITIC, Guangdong province had another 'flagship' financial services company, Guangdong Enterprises (GDE). GDE was the province's 'window' company in Hong Kong. It was the model for the later development of the whole genre of 'red chip' companies which were established by local governments and central departments from across the country. It had five floated subsidiaries, one of which, Guangdong Investments (GDI), was a constituent of the Hang Seng Index. By May 1998, GDE was in deep trouble. The Guangdong government's internal report revealed that out of GDE's total assets of HK$ 35.7 billion, bad or doubtful debts amounted to HK$ 22.8 billion. The situation worsened as the year wore on. By September, GDE reported in desperation to the Guangdong provincial government that its debts exceeded its assets by HK$ 4.5 billion. GDE was basically insolvent. To be faced with the insolvency of its two main flagship financial institutions was a huge problem for the Guangdong government. The international debts of the two institutions together were eventually found to total around US$ 10 billion. It was beyond the capacity of the province to solve the problems of GITIC and GDE. For the central government also their insolvency posed a massive problem. Meeting the repayment needs of these two institutions would have posed a challenge for even the central government's budget. However, to acknowledge the international debts of GITIC and GDE as China's sovereign debt carried the extreme danger that this would set a precedent for the settlement of the international debts of all of China's other TICs and red chips. This would have been little short of disastrous.

Alongside the problems associated with GITIC and GDE, as well as with the trust and investment companies and the red chip companies as a whole, there were simultaneously severe problems with other types of local non-bank financial institutions. Powerful forces combined to drive their growth in the 1990s in Guangdong province, and, indeed, across the whole country.

Household savings rose rapidly. In Guangdong province alone, between 1990 and 1999 urban residents' bank savings grew from RMB 48 billion to

RMB 560 billion (US$ 68 billion) and rural deposits grew from RMB 26 billion to RMB 174 billion (US$ 21 billion) (SSBG, GTN, 2000: 211). The fixed rate for household demand deposits in state banks was 1.98 per cent in mid-1996 falling to 0.99 per cent in mid-1999. For one-year time deposits the respective rates were 3.33 and 1.98 per cent (SSB, ZTN, 2000: 642). It was tempting for individual depositors to seek higher returns for their savings. The domestic stock market presented many problems for individual investors, including extensive insider dealing, a high degree of volatility for individual stocks and a preponderance of partially floated enterprises that were predominantly state-owned, with low transparency. Investment funds were still in their infancy, and also faced many regulatory difficulties including illegal behaviour that undermined investors' confidence.

Enterprises also had huge deposits in the state banking system. By 1999 these had grown to RMB 735 billion (US$ 89 billion) in Guangdong alone, and RMB 3,718 billion (US$ 450 billion) across the country as a whole (SSBG, GTN, 2000: 2110; SSB, ZTN, 2000: 639). There was a strong incentive for SOEs to channel their financial resources into high-yielding investments with quick returns, rather than try to construct long-term competitive businesses in the face of intense competition with other Chinese firms in low value-added products, and increasing competition with multinationals in high value-added goods and services. This process was given added impetus by the immense amount of illegal use of funds by insiders in positions of power within the enterprises. There were powerful incentives to use poorly monitored company funds to undertake private speculative investments with other people's money.

At every level of local government, from city to county to township, officials wished to develop their own local financial institutions that could mobilize local funds, and draw in funds from elsewhere, to promote local development. For much of the 1990s, there was heavy pressure from the fast-growing areas to 'pull' funds into these areas, from individuals and from enterprises, as well as from financial institutions elsewhere. This was the mechanism commonly referred to as '*gaoxi lanchu*' (high interest rates to pull in deposits). Guangdong's Pearl River Delta was in the forefront of this process.

The cities developed their own form of local NBFI, the urban credit cooperative (UCC). In the absence of adequate provision by the official banking system for local small- and medium-sized enterprises, which boomed in the 1990s, local governments strongly encouraged the growth of the UCCs in order to meet the financing needs of local SMEs. Guangdong took the lead in this process. Initially, the establishment of a UCC required the approval of the PBOC in Beijing, but approval subsequently was permitted from the Guangdong branch of the PBOC. By the late 1990s there were almost 200 urban credit cooperatives in Guangdong province and 836 prefecture-level UCCs across the whole country (PBOC, 2000: 24). However, each of the UCCs typically had many sub-branches. Prior to the restructuring,

Guangdong had over 1,000 local branches, a great many of which were independent accounting units. The PBOC reported that at the end of 1999, the prefecture-level UCCs across the whole country had a deposit balance of RMB 96 billion (US$ 11.6 billion) and liabilities of RMB 121 billion (US$ 14.6 billion) (PBOC, 2000: 25). The UCCs also encountered serious difficulties in the 1990s. They operated within a low-repayment culture. They extensively sought loans outside the regular channels through 'off-balance-sheet' borrowing at interest rates above those of the main banks. There were many runs on local financial institutions, causing serious social disturbances among depositors, and great difficulties for the regulatory authorities. As the AFC hit Guangdong, the balance sheets of the UCCs sharply deteriorated, and many of them became insolvent. This prompted numerous runs on the UCCs, which caused widespread urban disorder.

The main traditional channel of rural credit had been the rural credit cooperatives (RCCs), which had existed since the 1950s. They were under the supervision of the Agricultural Bank of China and were supposed to operate according to strict rules, such as the ratio of deposits to lending. Despite being formally regulated by the Agricultural Bank of China up until 1996, they were deeply enmeshed in the 'low repayment' culture across the country. A report in 2001 said that the bad debts of the RCCs amounted to 'well over 50 per cent of assets.' The 40,000 RCCs accounted for 12 per cent of all deposits nation-wide. They were reported to have a total of RMB 1,050 billion (US$ 126 billion) in outstanding loans at year-end 2000 (*FT*, 18 July 2001).

In the 1990s, a new form of rural NBFI grew at high speed, the rural financial associations (*nongcun jinrong jijinhui*) (RFAs). They originated in Sichuan Province, where they grew rapidly in the 1990s (Holz, 2001). They were not 'banks' and were not required to have a licence from the PBOC. They operated without any vertical control mechanism at all. Instead they were 'under the supervision of the local government.' Technically, the RFAs were non-profit mutual aid organizations. Their members were all technically shareholders in receipt of dividends, rather than 'banks' taking deposits and paying interest. In fact, the differences were 'largely semantic' (Holz, 2001: 198). They were typically staffed by directors with little financial expertise. Although formally 'mutual aid associations,' in fact most RFAs were set up and run by the local government. The formal legitimacy of the RFAs was confirmed by the Eighth Plenum of the Thirteenth Central Committee of the Communist Party of China in November 1991 (Holz, 2001: 210). Local authorities insisted that the RFAs were 'outside the sphere of influence of the PBOC, as the RFAs were simply 'mutual aid organisations' (Holz, 2001: 208). At the provincial level, local governments and departments were urged to 'let the rural cooperative funds develop as quickly as possible' (Holz, 2001: 210). Following the encouragement from the central and provincial governments, the RFAs grew at high speed. Over one-fifth of villages across the country had established RFAs by the mid-1990s.

The RFAs attracted large amounts of funds away from the official rural credit cooperatives. Incomplete data show that their total deposits grew from around RMB 8 billion in 1990 to around RMB 200 billion (US$ 24 billion) in 1997 (Holz, 2001: 202).

A typical county in the Pearl River Delta of Guangdong province had fifteen to thirty 'townships,' each with a population of around 30–50,000 people. The province as a whole had over 900 townships, most of which had their own rural financial association by the late 1990s. Deng Xiaoping's 'Southern Journey' of 1992 was followed by high speed growth of rural non-bank financial institutions. A new category of financial service worker emerged, the 'broker' who scoured the country in search of deposits at illegal, high rates of interest. The frenzied search for funds by the local NBFIs placed great pressure on local branches of the state-owned banks to do the same in order to compete for deposits.

When Vice-Premier Zhu Rongji became head of the PBOC in 1993, he tried hard to control unregulated local financial activity. However, local governments used Deng Xiaoping's 'Southern Journey' to support the growth of local NBFIs and to resist regulatory control. Pictures of Deng Xiaoping making this journey adorned the offices of NBFIs throughout Guangdong province. Support for their growth was defended as 'doing something for reform,' as encouraged by Deng Xiaoping. Local leaders argued that opposing the growth of local NBFIs was tantamount to 'opposing reform.' Across the country, but especially in Guangdong province, the growth of the RFAs was intimately associated with the local government function in promoting local development: 'The RFAs were founded on the initiative of the rural department in the government from top to bottom' (Mei, 2000: 5). The local government appointed the managers, with most of the personnel coming from the locality concerned, typically being relatives of the local government and Party officials (Mei, 2000: 6): 'funds were often directed at the local government's will to areas of little or no commercial value.' Over 80 per cent of the deposits in the RFAs were directed towards local 'government projects,' such as roads and bridges (*Caijing*, 5 May 2001).

The extraordinarily high economic growth rate in Guangdong in the 1990s, especially in the Pearl River Delta, convinced depositors that it was reasonable for the NBFIs in the region to offer annual interest rates of over 30 per cent. In the Pearl River Delta, in the 1990s, there was widespread, high-speed privatization of town and village SME enterprises. Moreover, the foundation of industrial growth in the region became investment by overseas Chinese entrepreneurs. A significant part of local NBFI lending involved channelling funds collected through '*gaoxi lanchu*' from across the country into these small- and medium-sized enterprises.

Alongside this went an explosion of real estate development in Guangdong, strongly concentrated in the PRD, and, to a lesser extent, the Han River Delta. This provided the opportunity for huge profits. A central part of the real estate development boom was the large-scale transfer of land from agricultural to industrial and residential use. Across the whole of Guangdong, the amount of arable land fell by almost 12 per cent from 1985 to 1998 (SSBG, GTN, 2000: 275). In the highly developed counties of the PRD, such as Dongguan, farmland virtually disappeared. In China land is owned by the 'community,' either the city or the rural township. In the 1990s in densely populated areas that were undergoing high-speed development, there were huge rents to be gained from the *de facto* privatization of the rental streams from land development. Access to loans from the local NBFIs was a central part of the process of real estate 'development' in Guangdong. Innumerable routes were available to channel the gains into the hands of a relatively small group of people at the apex of the local power structure. The location of Guangdong, and the heavy involvement of overseas Chinese family relations, meant that it was possible, through money-laundering, for a large proportion of the gains to be channelled out of the country into offshore accounts.

As long as the growth process was sufficiently rapid, the local NBFIs were, broadly speaking, able to remain solvent and the regulators saw little need to interfere. However, from the middle of the decade onwards, well before the onset of the AFC, the process began to unravel. It became increasingly obvious that the underlying pattern of deposit-raising and lending was only sustainable under special conditions that no longer applied. The collapse of the property bubble after 1995 punctured confidence in the local NBFIs. As savers rushed to withdraw deposits the NBFIs were revealed to be massively insolvent: 'As the tide recedes, the rocks appear' (*shui luo shi chu*). These problems intensified with the onset of the AFC and the deteriorating macro-economic environment in Guangdong. The bubble of confidence in the region's high growth and high returns was pricked. The old Ponzi game could not continue, using new deposits to repay the old debts at an increasingly high rate of interest. Frequent runs took place. Once some institutions had encountered a payment crisis and restricted deposit withdrawal, the contagion effect began to work, leading to more urgent runs on a widespread basis across Guangdong. This in turn caused more serious payment difficulties and eventually evolved into a self-reinforcing credit crisis. Even though not officially their responsibility, the PBOC was forced to intervene and provide funds to solve the problem. This then raised deep issues of moral hazard, since it encouraged reckless lending by local RFAs, in the expectation that the PBOC would step in to solve the liquidity crisis.

In May 1997, RFAs in Zhanjiang, Jieyang and several other districts within Guangdong encountered a payment crisis. The situation was made sharply worse by the closure of the Hainan Development Bank in 1998 which caused large-scale migration of deposits from local non-bank financial institutions to the four commercial banks.[21] By 1998, RFAs in Maoming, Shantou and Shanwei had also encountered widespread payment crises. ITICs in various locations also met with payments crises which ranged from individual deposits to international debts, from the securities business to enterprise bonds: 'First came the restriction on money withdrawals. The amount of withdrawals permitted fell from thousands to hundreds per day. Later, it was even impossible to withdraw ten *renminbi*. This caused large-scale runs. To a certain degree, systemic risks exploded.' In Shantou, large-scale runs spread even to the state-owned commercial banks. In Huadu, a UCC was besieged by a mass of protesters. It was threatened that water and food supplies would be cut off if the UCC failed to provide money. Violent fighting even took place. The credit-payment crisis in the small and medium local financial institutions spread over the whole province. Over sixty large-scale runs took place. Runs frequently developed into serious riots. Angry depositors even camped outside the provincial government headquarters in Guangzhou, demonstrating in protest.

6 The threat of contagion for China's financial system

On the first day that Wang Qishan walked into his office in the Guangdong provincial government, the first issue for him to deal with was the urgent debt problems at GITIC and GDE. The debts of GITIC and GDE not only far exceeded the respective value of their assets, but also were beyond the payment capabilities of the Guangdong provincial government. Should Guangdong ask the central government for help? The central government had to consider not only a single GITIC, but the 329 ITICs all over the country that had been borrowing from all over the world. The central government had to consider not only a single GDE, but also the fact that among the twenty-nine red chips in Hong Kong whose share price had fallen by over 88 per cent, only two did not belong to the GDE Group. Could the central government save them all? Apart from the issue of the budgetary capability of different levels of government, there were also at every level and in every direction, complex issues of moral hazard to consider. The challenge posed for China's policy-makers by the insolvency of Guangdong's non-bank financial institutions during the AFC extended far beyond the province itself. There was a serious threat of contagion for the whole country's financial institutions.

The widespread interpretation of the impact of the AFC is that China escaped unscathed due to the fact that the *renminbi* was not convertible on the capital account. For example, Paul Krugman's account of the AFC asks the question:

> Why didn't the world's most populous country, very much part of the Asian miracle, get caught up in the crisis along with everyone else? Were China's policies better than those of its neighbours? Did it suffer less from the sins of crony capitalism?
>
> (Krugman, 2000: 144)

He answers emphatically in the negative:

> China's economic growth has been astonishing, but then so was the growth of everyone else in the region until the crisis. On every other

> dimension China looks worse, not better, than its neighbours: more bad banks (there may well be no truly solvent banks in China), more nepotism, more corruption.

Krugman's explanation for China's apparent ability to avoid the contagion effect of the crisis is simple:

> What spared China was the fact that, unlike its neighbours, it had not yet made its currency 'convertible': that is, in China you still needed a government licence to change *renminbi* into dollars, a licence you would not get if your purpose was merely to speculate against devaluation.
>
> (Krugman, 2000: 144)

This lack of convertibility meant that 'the kind of high-speed currency crisis experienced elsewhere, in which everyone rushed to convert their domestic currency into dollars before a devaluation, and in so doing forced a devaluation to happen, could not happen' (Krugman, 2000: 144). It meant that unlike its neighbours, China remained 'free to print money at will.' That in turn meant that 'the country was insulated from bank runs – because people believed that the government would rush cash to threatened banks – and also that it could try to offset any slump in demand by spending and lending more' (Krugman, 2000: 144).

However, the fact that the *renminbi* was not convertible on the capital account did not mean that China escaped the risk of financial contagion from the AFC. Absence of full convertibility was a necessary, but not a sufficient, condition for avoiding the possibility of contagion. The Chinese government was deeply nervous about the possibility that the crisis in Guangdong's financial institutions would spread to other parts of the Chinese financial system.

The AFC meant that international creditors faced the prospect of huge debt write-downs across Asia. They turned towards Chinese borrowers to recover at least part of what they had lost elsewhere. They hoped that a large part of the borrowing by Chinese institutions other than the central government would be covered by central government support, even though it was not sovereign debt. Prior to the AFC, the Chinese government had intervened to ensure repayment of international creditors by insolvent state-owned enterprises (SOEs). One mainland expert observed: 'This was a really stupid thing for us to have done.' Despite the fact that throughout the reform period there had been no Chinese defaults on international debts incurred by Chinese enterprises, the rate of interest charged by international institutions for their loans contained an element of 'pricing for risk.' It had typically been significantly above the rate set for genuine sovereign debt. It was now inconsistent for international bankers to demand that the Chinese government treat the debts of its SOEs as 'sovereign debt,' when they had profited over many years from loans at interest rates appropriate to non-sovereign debt. In many cases, the international debt had been accompanied by a local government 'comfort letter.' As we shall see, this was far from being a guarantee of debt repayment. The contents of the brief document amounted to nothing more than the conventional statements of support given by politicians around the world for their local or national companies.

Under the basic principles of Chinese enterprise reform pursued since the early 1980s, China's SOEs were independent companies, responsible for their own profits and losses, freely entering into market transactions, including those in capital markets.

The international creditors placed intense pressure on the Chinese government at both the provincial and the central government level to treat the debts of China's state-owned financial institutions as the country's sovereign debt. They appealed to past precedent and to the threat to international bank lending if the Chinese government allowed the debts of its enterprises to go unpaid. The essence of the reform process, strongly advocated and supported by Western scholars and policy-makers, was that Chinese SOEs should be forced to accept the 'hard budget constraint,' and not be propped up by the state. This was inconsistent with the international creditors' demands that the Chinese state should step in to repay the SOEs' debts, whether domestic or international. To do so would incur 'moral hazard.' In other words, the international financial community welcomed the 'soft budget constraint' if it ensured that their debts were repaid in full without a 'haircut.'

The fierce debate within Chinese policy-making circles about whether to continue or break with past practice of state support for insolvent Chinese firms in repaying their international debts was a watershed in China's relations with the international economy. Fear of the wide and far-reaching potential 'domino' effects from continued state support was a critical influence on the Chinese response to the AFC.

The most immediate and obvious threat of contagion was to the other international trust and investment companies (ITICs) and the red chip companies. The crisis that unfolded at GITIC immediately threatened the entire ITIC sector, about which international banks had already become more nervous in the late 1990s. At the start of the AFC it is estimated that the officially registered liabilities of the ITICs were around US$ 30 billion. However, there may have been a further US$ 30 billion in non-registered international debt from the ITICs, with the total ITIC debt equal to around one-half of China's total foreign exchange reserves at the time of the AFC. The official size of the whole trust and investment sector's assets in 1994 was US$ 47 billion (World Bank, 1997: 7), far short of their estimated liabilities. The subsequent bankruptcy of GITIC was to reveal that a large fraction of the ITICs' assets were of low quality, many were completely worthless, and a substantial fraction was highly illiquid.

The simultaneous payments crisis at GDE deeply undermined confidence in the entire red chip sector. This was highly significant for Hong Kong's economic stability. The red chips accounted for 10–20 per cent of the Hong Kong stock market's capitalization, but contributed over 30 per cent of the market's daily turnover in the first half of 1997. The impact of the AFC on the red chips was dramatic. By August 1998, the stock price of the red chips fell from their peak in 1997 by around 80 per cent or more. Even the best performers among the red chips, Legend and China Telecom, fell by 56 per cent and 46 per cent, respectively. This drastically reduced their access to bank finance, and greatly intensified the pressure from bankers for debt repayment from the red chips. They were forced as a group to sell assets, including shares and property, which further intensified the depression in the Hong Kong property and stock markets. The bulk of the red chips faced a difficult struggle. Whatever the underlying failings in their management previously, the AFC greatly increased the pressure for them to follow illegal paths in order simply to survive. On the eve of the AFC, Chinese policy-makers were afraid that the total red chip foreign currency borrowings might be as high as US$ 20–25 billion.

Throughout the early phase of the restructuring of GDE, the international creditors insisted that the Chinese government should treat GDE's international debts as if they were, indeed, China's sovereign debt. If the Chinese government had accepted that GITIC's international debts should be treated as China's sovereign debt, it would have been almost impossible to avoid the same argument being applied to GDE, and then to the main body of TICs and red chips. This was a frightening scenario. It would have had major consequences for the central government's budget, as well as greatly intensifying pressure on China's foreign exchange reserves.

The AFC coincided with, and accentuated, a trend towards large unofficial outflows of foreign currency. Because of the limitations on convertibility of the *renminbi*, there could not be a direct international speculative attack. However, the devaluations across Asia greatly fuelled expectations that the *renminbi* would be forced to devalue. The speculative attacks on the Hong Kong dollar reinforced these fears. These factors helped to drive down the black-market value of the *renminbi*. In September 1998, the official exchange rate stood at RMB 8.27 per US dollar. In Beijing, the black-market rate was reported to be RMB 8.8, and in Guangzhou, as low as RMB 10 to the dollar (*FT*, 14 September 1998). Fears about the possible devaluation of the *renminbi* helped to stimulate large-scale capital flight. The Chinese government was shocked by the revelation that in the first eight months of 1998, China's trade surplus stood at US$ 31.3 billion, but its foreign exchange reserves recorded almost no increase at all, stagnating at around US$ 141 billion. Large-scale forging of trade documents, enabling domestic entities to shift foreign currency offshore, was at the centre of the process.

As well as the TICs and the red chips, there were deep problems in the local NBFIs across China. Guangdong's problems were the most severe, but the difficulties were widespread. The central government was well aware of the potential contagion from the Guangdong crisis to the much wider problems of the NBFIs across the country. The central driver of their expansion had been that they offered the possibility for the local governments to develop their own financial instruments, independently of the formal banking system.

However, the threat was even more serious. In the mid-1990s, despite the growth of the NBFIs, the formal banking sector still accounted for around 70 per cent of the total assets in the Chinese financial system (World Bank, 1997: 7). The formal banking sector faced profound problems well before the onset of the AFC. The relationship between China's state-owned banks, its state-owned enterprises and the weakness of its public finances stands at the centre of its political economy in the early twenty-first century. China's savings soared during the economic reforms, rising from RMB 42 billion in 1978 to RMB 5,032 billion (equivalent to over US$ 600 billion) in 1996. Of this total around 77 per cent was deposited in banks and 12 per cent was held in cash. The banks then lent a large part of the money to the state-owned enterprises.

Before the onset of the AFC the Chinese government was well aware privately of the seriousness of the problem of non-performing loans (NPLs) at its major banks. Already, in 1992, it was reported officially that 22 per cent of bank loans were 'non-performing.' In early 1998, Dai Xianglong, governor of the PBOC, acknowledged that the share of NPLs in the Chinese banking system stood at 25 per cent (the equivalent of around US$ 250 billion) (Lardy, 1998: 206). However, most commentators believed that the true level of bad debts was much above this figure. Indeed, Moody's believed that the true levels of bad loans at the 'big four' banks were 'much worse than the most pessimistic of the official indications' (*FT*, 16 July 1998). In 2001, in preparation for the listing of the Bank of China's (BOC) Hong Kong assets, it was revealed that BOC's non-performing loans accounted for 28 per cent of bank assets (*FT*, 12 May 2001). The BOC was widely regarded as 'by far the strongest and best run among the top four banks' (*FT*, 12 May 2001). The announcement that the BOC had NPLs as high as 28 per cent of assets lent support to the likelihood that the level of NPLs at the other three 'big four' banks was much higher than had previously been acknowledged. After the revelations about the NPLs at BOC, the consensus of international expert opinion was that the overall NPL level of the Chinese banking system was probably as high as 40 per cent of bank assets (*FT*, 12 May 2001).

As the AFC unfolded, it was widely acknowledged that 'China had significantly more serious problems in its banking, financial services and industrial sectors than those which had led to the crisis in South Korea' (*FT*, 23 November 1998). One expert warned that 'until it reformed those institutions, China would have to weigh up carefully the risks of opening up its economy' (Fan Gang, Director, National Economic Research Institute, quoted in *FT*, 23 November 1998). The Asian crisis emphasized the danger of liberalization prior to establishing robust domestic financial institutions. However, it was widely recognized that the creation of robust financial institutions would take time, and 'China would have to pace carefully the shift to a more liberal capital regime' (*FT*, 23 November 1998). One commentator stated bluntly: 'The implication of this is that liberalization of the [Chinese] financial system is today impossible. It would lead to a financial collapse as people pull their money out of the evidently bankrupt banks and shift to more remunerative alternatives.' George Soros evaluated the situation even more dramatically: 'If the Chinese *renminbi* had been convertible, the Chinese banking system would have collapsed' (Soros, 2000: 216).

The problems in the formal banking sector were not confined to the major banks. In the 1990s, local city banks had proliferated. In the year 2000 it was reported that China had a total of eighty-eight city commercial banks (*shangye yinhang*). By international standards, at the end of the 1990s, the whole city commercial bank sector was insolvent. At the end of 1998, the sector had total assets of RMB 494 billion, but bad debts officially totalled RMB 471 billion, a staggeringly high ratio of bad debts to assets (*FT*, 6 June 2000).

In 2002, Standard & Poor estimated that if the NPLs of the local non-bank financial institutions and the city commercial banks were added up together with the NPLs of the major commercial banks, the bad debts of China's financial system were as high as US$ 518 billion, equivalent to 50 per cent of China's GDP in 2001.[22] This compares with a ratio of NPLs to total loans of just 3.2 per cent for the world's top twenty banks in the year 2000.[23] In fact, before and during the financial crisis, large national financial enterprises such as China Agriculture Trust and Investment Corporation, China Enterprise Investment Foundation and Hainan Development Bank were closed down one after another.

At the time of the AFC, Chinese household savings had reached around US$ 720 billion (equivalent in RMB). Most outside observers believed that the Chinese banking system was basically insolvent. A large fraction of its lending was to entities that would find it hard to repay their debts to the banks if required to do so. On the other hand, most of the banks' liabilities were short-term, essentially household deposits: 'This is the classic recipe for collapse' (Chang, 2001: 130). Over the long term, Chinese policy-makers had plans to improve comprehensively the operating mechanism of Chinese banks. However, at the time of the AFC the system was still in a precarious position. Periodically, there had been runs even on the country's main commercial banks. The local branches of the major state-owned banks had many large-scale runs including the Enping Branch of the China Construction Bank (see Part 2). In April 1999, in Zhengzhou (Henan province) there was a run on the Bank of Communications, China's fifth largest bank, sparked by rumours of fraud at the bank. There were panic withdrawals from the seventy branches in the area, and within a few days, the bank had lost the equivalent of US$ 108 million in deposits (Chang, 2001: 129). The superior levels of the bank pumped in funds to stem the haemorrhage, keeping the branches open day and night.

The massive deposits of China's households in the country's main banks were termed the 'tiger in the cage.' Throughout the AFC, the central government was acutely aware of the possibility of contagion spreading from the international financial system to the fragile domestic banking sector. In November 1997, the central government called a high-level National Financial Work Conference in Beijing to discuss the challenges China's financial and banking system were facing against the backdrop of the AFC (Lardy, 1998: 202–9). The meeting was addressed by President Jiang Zemin, Premier Li Peng and Vice-Premier Zhu Rongji. The meeting focused on the similarities between China's weak financial system and those elsewhere in Asia, and sought to identify a set of policies that could reduce the risk of a financial crisis in China. In the wake of the meeting a number of important financial system reform measures were announced. These included reorganizing the PBOC along regional lines to reduce local political interference in bank lending decisions; a large capital injection into the big four banks; the establishment of four asset-management companies to remove a large body of NPLs from the books of the big four banks; introducing risk into the pricing of loans (though there were still strict limits on the rate of interest that could be charged); closure of unauthorized financial institutions and stricter enforcement of exchange control regulations by the State Administration of Foreign Exchange Control (Lardy, 1998: 207–8). Most remarkably, at the conclusion of the Financial Work Conference, an editorial appeared in *People's Daily* which acknowledged that 'criminal activities in banking are rampant' (quoted in Lardy, 1998: 206).

7 Conclusion

The Asian Financial Crisis presented a major challenge to Chinese policy-makers. This was almost invisible outside the country. Most Western analyses of Chinese policy during the AFC focused on the possibility that China might be forced to devalue the *renminbi*. Much attention also was devoted to the implications of the insolvency of GITIC and GDE for the possibilities of debt recovery for the international creditors. Another set of analyses concentrated on the impact of the AFC on Hong Kong, focusing on the attack on the currency peg. Within China, central policy-makers were deeply worried about the insolvency of the huge number of local non-bank financial institutions, with those in Guangdong in the front line. There was also great concern about the fragile condition of the other TICs and red chip companies across China. China's policy-makers were deeply apprehensive that the contagion might spread from the NBFIs to the main banks, arguably the most fragile in East Asia.

In fact, the insolvency of GITIC, GDE and Guangdong's small-scale financial institutions were intimately inter-related. Moreover, the solution to the wider insolvency of the TICs and red chips was directly dependent on the Chinese government's policy towards GITIC and GDE. The way in which these problems were resolved also had a profound bearing upon Hong Kong's ability to survive the AFC. The Chinese government did not directly decide policy in Hong Kong, but it had a heavy responsibility for the SAR, which had just returned to Chinese sovereignty. Indeed, the AFC broke out only a few hours after the hand-over ceremony. The challenge to Chinese policy-making was all the greater because of the speed with which the AFC unfolded, and the pace at which the different stages of its development took place. This illustrated powerfully for the Chinese government the incredible dangers of high-speed 'close' integration with the international financial system. Guangdong was the 'workshop at the back,' but Hong Kong the 'shop at the front,' through which the 'fire' of international financial contagion threatened to sweep through China.

We saw above that the total debts of the mainland firms in Hong Kong may have been as high as US$ 80 billion. This presented a considerable challenge to China's policy-makers when the AFC erupted. It meant that the fortunes of Hong Kong and the mainland were inextricably intertwined:

> In the past we have said that China would not be affected by the Asian crisis. The *renminbi* is closed on the capital account. But now we have seen that there is one potential form of transmission of the Asian malaise, and that is through foreign lending.
>
> (Dong Tao, Crédit Suisse First Boston, quoted in *FT*, 16 November 1998)

The main location for that foreign lending was Hong Kong. The Chinese government had only limited means either to control the amount of borrowing undertaken by its own firms once they had 'escaped' to Hong Kong, or to control the purposes to which the huge borrowings were put.

The most important question for Chinese policy-makers to decide was: to what extent the central government, provincial government and the sub-provincial governments should take responsibility for the domestic and international debts of the insolvent red chips and ITICs? This caused intense debate in the media and among scholars. 'Moral hazard' was everywhere.[24] From the point of view of the borrowing parties in Guangdong, GITIC and GDE were wholly owned by the provincial government and the provincial government had direct responsibility for their borrowing activities. GITIC and GDE had continuously received both direct and indirect support from the provincial government. From the perspective of the international creditors, China's large state-owned enterprises had no record of bankruptcy.[25] The mainland's government at different levels and its firms had always paid back their international debts. It is because they knew of the close relationship between the enterprises and the Guangdong government that the international creditors competed with each other to lend to these 'ideal clients.' Lending to borrowers such as GITIC and GDE appeared to have the advantage of sovereign debt in terms of repayment risk, but to carry an interest rate corresponding to commercial loans. The international banks had made a great deal of money over many years from this relationship, especially from the biggest players, such as GITIC and GDE.

China's policy-makers faced the twin challenges of whether they had the money to fully repay the international debts and whether, if they had the money, they should do so. For the former question, at one level the answer was simple. The Guangdong government did not have its own foreign exchange. The only possibility was to seek help from the central government that managed China's foreign exchange payments. The first action taken by the Guangdong government was to apply to the central government for emergency help. In previous cases, the central government had stepped in and paid in full the international debts of the enterprises that were closed down. Such cases included the China Enterprise Investment Foundation,

China Agricultural Trust and Investment Corporation, and the Hainan Development Bank. But at the critical moment of the AFC, in order to support the Hong Kong dollar in resisting the attacks from international speculators, the Chinese government promised gravely that China would not devalue the *renminbi.*

During the AFC, a promise not to devalue the *renminbi* against the US dollar was tantamount to a promise to sustain the large appreciation of the *renminbi* relative to the hugely depreciating currencies in neighbouring countries. This inevitably had a large negative impact upon China's exports, foreign exchange earnings and the foreign exchange reserves which supported the credibility of the *renminbi.* It was impossible to control this impact, or, at that time, to know what the size and duration of the impact would be. That depended on the duration and depth of impact of the AFC, which was unknowable. Against this background, the central government's foreign exchange reserves were a precious resource. If the central government had paid in full the international debts of GITIC and GDE as it had done for insolvent SOEs in the past, it would have strongly encouraged the international creditors, who were desperate for cash in order to survive, to press even harder against the red chips in Hong Kong and the ITICs all over China (including China International Trust and Investment Corporation) for debt repayment. During the AFC, paying international debts equivalent to around one-half of China's foreign exchange reserves within a short period of time would have meant disaster for the promise not to devalue the *renminbi.*[26] That in turn would have had incalculable consequences for the course of the AFC. Thus, the challenge facing Chinese policy-makers was not only intimately connected with the future of both Hong Kong SAR's and the Chinese mainland's political economy, but also that of the whole of the rest of East Asia, and, in turn, that of the whole world.

The challenges for China's policy-makers were made even more complex because the full extent of the risks was unknown. At that time, the exact extent of the international debts of the ITICs and red chips was unknown. Moreover, another huge danger was that it was impossible to determine the *renminbi* payment risks. The ITICs all over China and the red chips also had a large amount of *renminbi* debt. Even the local branches of each of the major commercial banks all over China competed for deposits through '*zhang wai zhang*' (off-balance-sheet accounts), promising interest far above the official rate. The RCCs, UCCs and RFAs all over the country and also various kinds of non-bank financial institutions had accumulated debts that were impossible to repay, through all kinds of means including 'Ponzi-type' schemes. No one knew the extent of these debts. The expectation of super-normal growth speed was shattered by the AFC. This had unfortunate implications for the financial enterprises not only in Guangdong but also in the whole country. These huge debts had been accumulated with the promise of high returns though these had been impossible to estimate. Now there was suddenly a dramatic call for cash by both domestic and international creditors. This constituted a massive payments crisis.

The financial crisis entered Guangdong through Hong Kong and a widespread payment crisis immediately erupted in Guangdong. If the payment crisis in Guangdong had not been dealt with properly, it is likely that the crisis would have rapidly spread into the heartland of China through red chips in Hong Kong, various kinds of non-bank financial institutions in Guangdong, the ITICs all over China, the local branches of the state-owned commercial banks, and the dying local non-bank financial institutions all over the country as well as the hugely complex chain of borrowing, lending and payment among these financial institutions. There would have been a big financial 'fire.' It would have been difficult to extinguish this 'fire.'

In theory, as long as the *renminbi* was not convertible on the capital account, then the financial crisis that took place in the other Asian countries ought not to have been a danger for China. Under normal circumstances, even if there is a serious local *renminbi* payment crisis within a limited area, it can be resolved by simply printing more money. But in the dangerous environment of the AFC, the payments crisis in Guangdong shook people's confidence. The government had innumerable urgent issues to deal with in solving the deep problems in the financial sector, including *gaoxi lanchu* ('pulling in money'), *zhang wai zhang* ('off-balance-sheet accounts'), widespread illegal fund-raising, the bad debts of the mushrooming UCCs and RFAs as well as the commercial banks – all these meant that the Chinese financial authorities were extremely busy as a 'fire brigade' (Hu, 1999). In this kind of special crisis, it is easy to understand that the central government's answer to the appeal for help from the Guangdong provincial government was: 'Whoever gives birth to the child must take responsibility for the child.'

The common thread of the challenges facing China's policy-makers during this crisis was the extreme complexity and huge dangers of integrating China with the global economy at a time of unprecedented size and volatility of international flows of capital. Even with China's tight controls over foreign exchange and without convertibility on the capital account, it proved impossible to 'sterilize' international capital flows, and prevent them interacting with the domestic financial system. Ultimately, the unstable global structure deeply threatened China's social and political stability. Advanced capitalism in the age of globalization has produced a 'Frankenstein monster' in the shape of the global financial revolution that comprehensively shapes global economic development. However, no-one understands it fully. There is no consensus on the degree to which it should be regulated. No-one knows how to regulate it even if they wished to do so.[27] The free market in financial flows since the 1980s has produced a succession of crises in both rich and poor countries, but their consequences in the latter are far more severe than in the former.[28]

The experience of Guangdong in the AFC provided a profound lesson about the difficulties that the Chinese government faced in integrating China into the high seas of massive and largely unregulated international capital flows. Handling this situation was one of the biggest challenges that they had faced during the long road of system reform since the 1970s. The solution could not be found in any textbook.

Notes

1 In recent years the local government financing platforms *(zhengfu rongzi pingtai)* have assumed this function.
2 There were intense discussions among Guangdong government officials about ways in which to enhance the international competitive capability of Guangdong's largest firms in the face of the challenge on the 'global level playing field' after China's entry to the WTO. The province closely investigated ways to shift the production structure towards higher value-added products. There was serious concern about the relatively backward state of the province's higher education system in relation to the achievement of this stated goal. The pollution problem in the Pearl River Delta was widely recognized also to be so serious as to cause a major obstacle to attracting high technology firms to the region. Analysis of these structural issues in the long-term development strategy of Guangdong would take us beyond the main focus of the book.
3 In the late 1970s Guangdong province had a total of ninety-eight counties (*xian*). Just six counties (Panyu, Nanhai, Shunde, Taishan, Xinhui and Zhongshan) in Foshan Administrative District, which is at the heart of the Pearl River Delta accounted for over one-third of the total provincial output of commune and brigade-level enterprises (Nolan, 1983: 29). The average per capita income in the six counties in the Foshan District was twice the provincial average and four times greater than in poor counties in the north of the province (Nolan, 1983: Table 16). In the late 1970s as the impact of market forces began to get under way, output growth was much faster in the central Pearl River Delta counties than in outlying parts of the province (Nolan, 1983: Table 29).
4 The Chaoshan region extends from Shantou (literally the 'head') to Shanwei (the 'tail'), around 150 kms to the west of Shantou. It includes four main parts, Shantou, Chaozhou, Jieyang and Shanwei.
5 For example, Chaoyang county has around two million locally resident people, but is thought to have as many as four million overseas Chinese.
6 I am greatly indebted to Mr Kang Dian, former Director of Guangdong Enterprises and Chairman of Guangnan, for his research in this area (Kang, 2000) and for extensive discussions with him, which has enormously assisted me to understand the 'red chip' question.
7 Larry Yung became a true 'entrepreneur,' adopting an ostentatious and high spending lifestyle: 'The trappings of being a red king were very attractive indeed. Larry Yung was seen fox-hunting with British aristocrats around his landed property in England. He owned racehorses and family mansions around the world. His high-stake bets at the Hong Kong Jockey Club made headlines in the territory.' More significantly from a business perspective, during the red chip bubble, he bought 10 per cent of CITIC Pacific shares for himself at a 25 per cent discount on the market price. This angered the institutional investors, who dropped CITIC Pacific from their portfolios, helping to drive the company's shares downwards. He had used the market capitalization of CITIC Pacific as collateral for his bank borrowing. The collapse in the Hong Kong stock market added to his difficulties, and the banks sharply contracted their credit lines. Yung was personally bankrupted by these events. This even further sullied the reputation of the red chips as a class of investment.
8 Between them, the Rong brothers controlled one of China's largest pre-revolutionary business empires. The mainstay of their empire was a dozen or so cotton mills (Shenxin Cotton Mills) and the various flour mills in the Fuxin and Maoxin Flour Mill companies (Bergère, 1986). The Maoxin-Fuxin-Shenxin Group was organized as a joint stock company, but it 'operated as a family-run

business' (Bergère, 1986: 158). The Rong family directly occupied three-fifths of the senior management positions in the company, including the subsidiaries, and most of the remaining top management positions were filled by close relatives (Bergère, 1986: 158).

9 A much-discussed example arose at CITIC in 1994. In that year a trading dispute exposed the lack of controls exercised by the head office in Beijing over its Shanghai subsidiary. CITIC Shanghai became involved in a settlement dispute regarding its metal futures trading with some international brokers. The brokers claimed that CITIC had not met the margin calls of its trading position and was therefore in default. An internal investigation by CITIC revealed that senior officers at CITIC Shanghai were engaging in proprietary trading without authorization, and were also falsifying monthly reports sent to CITIC headquarters. The unauthorized trading had been going on for about a year before it was discovered. CITIC subsequently took remedial action to establish internal procedures that were intended to prevent this behaviour recurring. However, Moody's report of the incident (Moody's, 1998a) noted that it 'illustrated the weakness of CITIC's internal auditing system as well as its loose controls over the activities of its subsidiaries.' In Moody's view this was 'by no means an isolated incident.' Rather, it was 'indicative of a system-wide phenomenon.' Moreover, it emphasized that CITIC was 'considered to be the most established and sophisticated ITIC' (Moody's, 1998a).

10 I have not seen a study which attempts to make such an estimate for the whole region in question, but the logic behind this statement seems hard to disagree with.

11 Hong Kong had first come under British colonial rule in 1841.

12 To a substantial degree this was done in order to provide a stable environment given the uncertainties over the hand-over of Hong Kong to the Chinese mainland.

13 The Exchange Fund was established in 1935, but became a central component of the linked exchange rate system after 1983. Unlike a typical currency board, the Fund does not issue domestic currency to be circulated in the economy. Instead, it issues Certificates of Indebtedness (CIs) to be held by designated local note-issuing banks (currently, these are HSBC, Standard Charter and the Bank of China) to cover their note issuing. The fixed exchange rate applies to the rate at which the designated banks acquire CIs in order to issue notes or the rate at which they redeem them. Through this procedure, the Exchange Fund maintains 100 per cent matching international reserves against the local currency issued. However, after the 1983 reforms, the exchange rate in the foreign exchange market continued to be determined by market forces. For most of the 1990s, the rate in the market was persistently somewhat above the fixed rate.

14 The key step in this process was the establishment in 1993 of the Hong Kong Monetary Authority (HKMA), which merged the Exchange Fund and the Commissioner of Banking, to become a 'quasi central bank' (Chen and Ng, 1999: 213). Under a succession of measures taken at this time, the HKMA increasingly assumed the function of 'lender of last resort' to the banking system (Ng and Chen, 1998: 143). It also greatly increased its control over liquidity and short-term interest rates (Ng and Chen, 1998: 143).

15 Speculative attacks 'usually take the form of either forward contracts to sell Hong Kong dollars or sales in the foreign exchange market of Hong Kong dollars borrowed from the banking sector' (Ng and Chen, 1998: 146). The main considerations in speculation are the interest cost and rate of depreciation of the Hong Kong dollar. The response of the HKMA to the speculation takes the form of market sales of its US dollar reserves, which drains the inter-bank liquidity and pushes up the inter-bank interest rate (Ng and Chen, 1998: 147).

16 In 1996, 20.3 per cent of loans and advances were to the building and construction sector and 25.7 per cent were to the residential sector. The latter figure is exceptionally high, having risen from just 6.3 per cent in 1981 (Chen and Ng, 1999: 217).

17 It was reported that the combined short position of the alleged conspirators was about US$ 30 billion, which would be the equivalent of short-selling roughly US$ 1.5 trillion in the US stock market (Krugman, 2000: 128).

18 In their careful analysis of the Hong Kong monetary system, written prior to the AFC, two Hong Kong economists had outlined the circumstances under which Hong Kong might be forced to abandon the currency peg. They considered what might happen if there were to be a large volume of rapid outflows of capital, which could be triggered by 'a sudden loss of confidence in the exchange rate regime or in the economy as a whole or by some kind of political situation' (Ng and Chen, 1998: 148). This would be likely to involve portfolio capital outflows and the collapse of the stock and real property markets. The market rate of the Hong Kong dollar would depreciate rapidly, and the Exchange Fund would intervene by selling US dollars for Hong Kong dollars in the foreign exchange market: 'The inter-bank interest rate would rise drastically and whether this would help to check capital outflows depends on whether the market perceived the resulting interest rate differentials to be adequate to compensate for the risk of holding Hong Kong dollar assets.' When Hong Kong's foreign exchange reserves had been exhausted, 'the authority would have no other option but to devalue the exchange rate or abandon the linked exchange rate regime' (Ng and Chen, 1998: 148).

19 The *FT* commented: 'The hedge funds have developed a uniquely paradoxical private language... "Long-term" capital means a slender wedge of short-term capital leveraged to an unlimited degree. And, of course, there is the brilliantly propagandist misnomer: "hedge" fund' (*FT*, 3 October 1998).

20 However, in 2001 GDP growth was just 0.6 per cent, and in 2002 was only around 3 per cent (*FT*, 9 January 2003). By the end of 2002, the unemployment rate had climbed to almost 8 per cent, and the property market remained at only around 40 per cent of the level reached prior to the AFC. It is estimated that the fall in the value of property had 'wiped out US$ 360 billion in household wealth,' or more than 200 per cent of GDP, between 1997 and the end of 2002 (*FT*, 9 January 2003). In early January 2003, Hong Kong Chief Executive, Tung Chee-Hwa, said: 'Our economy is facing difficulties unprecedented since World War II' (quoted in *FT*, 9 January 2003).

21 Only three years after it was established, Hainan Development Bank was closed due to several massive runs.

22 The average recovery rate was estimated to be 15 per cent ('NPLs of China's banking sector will continue for ten years', *Xin Bao*, 11 June 2002: 20). There were unofficial estimates that 70 per cent of the county-level financial institutions had total arrears of RMB 3,000 billion. If we add the arrears in the town and village-level financial institutions as well as the arrears in social security funds, China's total hidden bad debts amounted to RMB 10,000 billion. This estimate was so widely referred to that the Minister of the Ministry of Finance, Xiang Huaicheng, came forward to deny it (Liao Meixiang, 'Local debts and banks' NPLs are overlapping', *Xin Bao*, 3 June 2002: 2).

23 By September 2002, the capital adequacy ratio was 8.5 per cent for BOC, 4.57 per cent for ICBC, 3.79 per cent for CCB, 1.44 per cent for ABC. The average capital adequacy ratio for the world's top twenty banks was 11.5 per cent.

24 During our fieldwork, the term 'moral hazard' appeared constantly in analyses of the crises, from the highest to the lowest level of policy-maker and practitioner.

25 In fact, it is hard to find examples of state-owned enterprises anywhere in the world that go bankrupt. Almost always, the government rescues the insolvent SOE.

26 In the first half of 1998, China's foreign exchange reserves were US$ 145 billion and the total official international debts were US$ 138 billion.

27 This was vividly revealed by the fact that the capitalist system was almost brought to its knees by Long-Term Capital Management. This firm based its trading activities on the models of two of its partners, Robert Merton and Myron Scholes, who had won the Nobel Prize for Economics in 1997, for their work on option pricing. In order to 'save' the system, the US Federal Reserve undertook actions that were deeply problematic in terms of its own declared principles of operation. They were widely criticized for being 'crony capitalist' and deeply problematic in terms of moral hazard.

28 For a scathing critique of the consequences of capital market liberalization promoted by the Washington Consensus, see Stiglitz, 2002, especially pp. 59–69.

Part 2

The response

Three steps (*san bu zou*) to control the fire

> [The Fire] began this morning in the King's bakers house in Pudding Lane ... Having stayed, and in an hour's time seen the fire rage every way...; and the wind mighty high and driving it into the city, and everything, after so long a drougth, proving combustible, even the very stones of the churches; ... so I was called for and did tell the King and Duke of York what I saw, and that unless his Majesty did command houses to be pulled down, nothing could stop the fire. They seemed much troubled, and the King commanded me to go to my Lord Mayor from him and command him spare no houses but to pull down before the fire every way.
>
> (Samuel Pepys on the Great Fire of London, 1666, in Pepys, 1995: 269)

> One cannot deny the impact of the closure of GITIC and of the Asian Financial Crisis on GDE, but the internal causes were determinative of GDE's downfall. GDE's problems already existed before the Asian Financial Crisis reared its ugly head. GDE was only protected by man-made 'bubbles'. When the storms of the Asian Financial Crisis swept through southeast Asia, they also swept away the bubbles covering GDE's problems, leaving them unavoidably exposed.
>
> (Wu, 2001: 9)

> GITIC's bankruptcy revealed the 'suspected rot throughout hundreds of China's non-bank financial institutions – the highly-leveraged and under-performing investment companies that have become increasingly integrated into the international financial community and are now helping to suck China into the Asian economic crisis'.
>
> (*FT*, 8 October 1998)

> I have never seen such deep corruption in any country or company as I found in GDE. There must be companies like GDE and GITIC in every province of our country. Not only the ITICs, but all sizes and types of company have equally serious problems. If the international media knew the true situation at GITIC, they would know we took the correct decision to close it.
>
> (Anonymous, Chinese official)

1 Introduction

In order to prevent the spread of forest fires, foresters cut large swathes of trees to act as fire breaks. In urban fires in medieval and early modern times, the main way to prevent a fire spreading was by pulling down houses in the path of the advancing conflagration. In the face of the Asian Financial Crisis (AFC), the Chinese government took a sequence of three inter-related policy measures ('the three steps') to attempt to solve the crisis in Guangdong's financial institutions, and prevent the spread of contagion to the rest of the country. These were: first, the bankruptcy of GITIC; second, the restructuring of GDE; and third, the restructuring of the local non-bank financial institutions (NBFIs). Each of these steps facilitated the succeeding step.

During the Asian Financial Crisis huge problems emerged in Guangdong's leading NBFIs. Guangdong International Trust and Investment Corporation (GITIC) and Guangdong Enterprises (GDE) were at the forefront of these problems. They were both owned by the Guangdong provincial government. The insolvency of GITIC and GDE attracted great attention in international financial circles, not least because they had total debts of around US$ 11 billion. In addition, a 'hidden' crisis emerged in the small-scale local NBFIs of Guangdong province. A large number of the rural financial associations, the urban credit cooperatives and many of the rural credit cooperatives were revealed to be insolvent. This stimulated 'bank runs' across the whole province and widespread social disorder as angry depositors were unable to withdraw their deposits. These events posed a severe challenge for the leadership both in Guangdong and in Beijing.

The Chinese central government was increasingly concerned about the difficulties within Guangdong's financial institutions. In December 1997, shortly after the onset of the Asian Financial Crisis, the central government sent Wang Qishan, then President of the China Construction Bank, to become a member of the Guangdong provincial Party committee. One month later he was appointed Executive Vice-Governor of the province. On Wang Qishan's very first day in the post, the first issue that he had to deal with was a request from GITIC and GDE for the provincial government to provide them with funds to pay their immediate debts. In March 1998 Li Changchun was appointed as the new provincial Party secretary.[1]

The two appointments were part of the central government's drive to 'crack down on corruption and clean up Guangdong's overstretched financial institutions' (*FT*, 21 October 1998). These problems were associated with the lack of discipline that the Guangdong government had permitted to develop during the boom years of the 1990s after Deng Xiaoping's 'Southern Journey' (*nan xun*).

Dealing with the impact of the AFC upon Guangdong's financial institutions was the core task of the provincial government over the next two years. The main task was to prevent the province experiencing a financial collapse such as was taking place in the countries surrounding China. A by-product of the 'three steps' to resolve the financial crisis in Guangdong was the exposure of massive financial corruption and financial crimes. Simply cleaning up the NBFIs' accounts directly affected the vested interests of criminal groups and individual criminals. Each of the 'three steps' involved 'a life and death struggle between good and evil,' with the reality that at the end of the struggle for many of the people involved there waited criminal conviction, prison and, even, the death sentence. The Governor of Guangdong province, Lu Ruihua, required in public that the government leaders at each level 'duly investigate and deal with cases that violate the law and regulations, and fight against financial crimes.'

Throughout the crisis Wang Qishan appeared frequently before the public and the mass media in Guangdong and Hong Kong. Standing behind him was the 'five-member leading team of the provincial CPC committee.'[2] These included the team-leader Lu Ruihua, Governor and Vice-Secretary of the provincial CPC committee; Chen Shaoji, Vice-Secretary of the provincial CPC committee and Secretary of the political and legislative committee; Liu Fengyi, Vice-Secretary of the provincial CPC committee and Director of the of organization department; Wang Qishan himself, member of the standing committee of the provincial CPC committee and Executive Vice-Governor; and Wang Huayuan, member of the standing committee of the provincial CPC committee and Secretary of the provincial disciplinary and supervisory committee.[3] Implementation of the 'three steps' was under the direct leadership of the political and legislative committee, the organization department of the CPC, and the disciplinary and supervisory committee. Alongside the bankruptcy of GITIC, restructuring of GDE and restructuring of over 800 local financial institutions, the 'three steps' included a massive clean-up of corruption and criminality. This was only possible due to the leadership of such a politically powerful team.

Outside China, the main attention was focused on GITIC and GDE. Within the province, dealing with the problems in the local financial institutions was the main focus of government attention. In responding to the crisis, the central government, the Guangdong provincial government and the People's Bank of China (PBOC), both in Beijing and through its local branch, were intimately involved in the various measures to rectify the situation. The central government coordinated closely with the Guangdong government in formulating the responses to the crisis. In early 1998, the Guangdong government held a work conference to analyse the threat presented to the province by the AFC. Afterwards, it established a working group under the chairmanship of Wang Qishan, to lead the province's response to the unfolding crisis. The Guangdong government promulgated an overall package (*yi lan zi*) to deal with the whole NBFI sector as an integrated problem of financial system risk. The plan was entitled 'Guangdong province's programme for managing risk in the local small and medium financial institutions and the rural financial associations.'

Surviving the crisis involved an intense policy effort by both the Guangdong and the central governments. It was a day and night battle in the midst of immense pressure on all sides, both from within and from outside China. Underlying the difficulties in the financial sector in Guangdong was a set of problems that had developed through the policy of experimental reform in China's financial institutions. The AFC demonstrated vividly the huge dangers of a simplistic belief in the pursuit of a free market model of financial reform, in a world of turbulent, volatile international capital markets. The impact of the AFC upon Guangdong also demonstrated the complexities and difficulties involved in the path of gradual, experimental reform. There was no easy 'first choice' for China's reform path.

The conception of the 'three steps' to solve the crisis was an *ex post* concept used to describe what the Guangdong government did in order to solve the crisis. The working team of Guangdong province adopted the term 'three steps' in accordance with the actual sequence of measures adopted to deal with the crisis: GITIC bankruptcy, GDE restructuring and the closure of over 800 small and medium financial institutions within the province. It was not a detailed *ex ante* plan that was worked out in advance. Wang Qishan described the Guangdong government's response to the crisis as a 'choice of no choice' (*mei you xuanze de xuanze*). The Guangdong provincial government, supported by the central government, took two years to resolve the payment crisis across Guangdong and prevent the AFC spreading into the heartland of mainland China. In the midst of the raging fire the steps taken were the only way in which to ensure system survival and stop the contagion from the AFC spreading deep into the Chinese financial, social and political systems.

The bankruptcy of GITIC and the restructuring of GDE provided a unique opportunity to look closely at the nature of China's large state-owned enterprises. The bankruptcy and restructuring processes were conducted substantially in the public domain, which provided a unique opportunity for an in-depth analysis of the large Chinese firm at the end of the 1990s. None of these was more important than the giant state-owned banks, which are at the heart of the whole economic system. However, their internal structure and operating mechanisms were a closed book to researchers. By looking in detail at the case of GITIC and GDE one can gain a deeper insight into the challenges that faced China's policy-makers in their reform of the giant state-owned banks as well as of other state-owned firms.

2 The first step

The bankruptcy of Guangdong International Trust and Investment Corporation

Most Western experts considered that the Chinese government mishandled the problems at GITIC. They viewed the closure of GITIC as part of a general pattern of debt repudiation at China's financial institutions, which augured badly for their reform:

> There are many reasons for the historic failure of GITIC, but the one that stands out, especially in the minds of the creditors, is that Beijing forced that institution to repudiate its debts when they could have been paid with the help of its parent, Guangdong province ... The way the People's Bank of China (PBOC) closed GITIC reinforced the notion that debt repudiation is acceptable in the People's Republic.
>
> (Chang, 2001: 142)

In fact, as this Part of this book will show, if the Chinese government had treated the debts of GITIC as China's sovereign debts, it would have started a cumulative process that might well have been not only disastrous for Guangdong province but might also have spread to the rest of the non-bank financial sector on the mainland. It might even have spread to the formal banking sector. It would have posed a serious threat to China's foreign exchange reserves, and, hence, to China's ability to sustain the international exchange rate of the *renminbi*. It was likely also that it would have had a serious negative impact on Hong Kong, during the worst economic crisis it had ever experienced. The Chinese government's response was deeply considered, albeit that many of the key decisions needed to be taken at high speed. It was based on a pragmatic and thorough evaluation of the entire complex of factors that related to the policy responses. It was a further example of the process of 'system reform' in China, viewing the process of reform as an inter-related set of complex variables, not a set of textbook models.

What was GITIC?

The evolution of China's trust and investment sector followed the lead taken by China International Trust and Investment Corporation (CITIC), which set the pattern for the development of the whole sector. The sector made many important contributions to Chinese development, but large-scale problems developed in the 1990s. GITIC became the symbol for these problems.

GITIC was established in 1980 by the Guangdong government, with permission from a special order from the State Council. In 1983 it obtained a licence from the PBOC to engage in financial services business and from the State Administration of Exchange Control (SAEC), predecessor to the State Administration of Foreign Exchange (SAFE), to engage in business involving foreign currencies. Guangdong province does not possess its own large commercial banks. The major banks were a part of the national banking system, supervised by the head offices in Beijing. GITIC became the *de facto* 'development bank' of Guangdong province, broadly analogous to state-owned development banks elsewhere in Asia. In its role as 'the primary borrowing instrumentality of the Guangdong government' GITIC was intended to play a central part in Guangdong province's own state-led industrial policy of import substitution and export promotion. Its financial services activities were supposed to 'assist Guangdong in building its basic industry and infrastructure' and to support the growth of 'those enterprises which manufacture export products, earn foreign currencies directly or indirectly, or manufacture products for import substitution.' To be eligible for a loan or guarantee from GITIC, a project had to be included in the Guangdong plan. In the case of 'projects that are of particular importance to the Guangdong government,' GITIC could be required to make a particular loan or extend a particular commitment, 'whether or not it satisfies GITIC's normal lending and guarantee criteria' (Merrill Lynch *et al*., 1996: 17).

Up until the Asian Financial Crisis, international investors had a strong appetite for lending to GITIC. They were confident in the region's growth prospects and in the support they believed would be forthcoming from the Guangdong government. They considered these to be almost risk-free investments but with the great advantage of a rate of interest and perceived security of return associated with much more risky investments. When GITIC launched its 1996 Yankee bond, it sold out within fifteen minutes. Through the mechanism of external borrowings and debt issuance, GITIC was responsible for raising the majority of the foreign currency funds obtained by Guangdong government–controlled entities. By late 1998, GITIC had borrowed over US$ 1 billion from international banks and secured around US$ 800 million in bonds and floating rate notes, as well as acting as guarantor on borrowings of almost US$ 2 billion. It had grown into a vast sprawling business empire, spanning financial services, real estate, equities, leasing and trading.

In May 1994 *Business Week* carried a cover story on Huang Yantian, GITIC's President. The article was entitled 'Inside the world of a red capitalist: Huang Yantian's financial powerhouse is helping to remake China.' The article said:

> [Huang] bears little resemblance to the old-style bureaucrats used to mouthing political bromides or giving hostile speeches, savvy in the

> ways of Western finance, Huang and other new managers like him are members of China's new class of 'red capitalists'. They are politicians, tycoons and dealmakers all in one: [Huang's] office is a revolving door of American, Japanese, and other foreign bankers, eager for a piece of lucrative financing or corporate deals in China's wealthiest province.

Business Week contrasted GITIC's ability to raise international finance with that of China's main commercial banks:

> Old-fashioned state banks ... are strapped for cash, mainly because they still have to bail out unprofitable state enterprises ... Enter GITIC, with its arsenal of the latest financial techniques, in everything from risk management to currency-linked borrowing ... 'When we talk about sophisticated things, they understand us', says Guangzhou-based Timmy Chan, Vice-President and South China operations head of Citibank.

Huang's ambition was to 'turn GITIC into a state-of-the-art investment house.' He told a visiting senior official from Lehmann Brothers: 'We want more foreign capital. As you invent new financial products, come and introduce them to us.'

The *Business Week* article emphasized Huang Yantian's personal contribution to GITIC's rise. When Deng Xiaoping opened Guangdong to foreigners in 1979, Huang worked as a secretary to the Vice-Governor of the province. He worked his way up through the company, becoming President in 1990: 'From that position he has been the ultimate salesman for Guangdong.' During the road show for GITIC's US$ 150 million Yankee bond in 1993, Huang impressed fund managers. David P. Walker, Managing Director of CSFB (Hong Kong), said: 'Huang can sit down with a guy and let him know that [Huang has] got his finger on the pulse of what's happening.' *Business Week* pointed out that a key reason for a positive view of GITIC was its intimate relations with the Guangdong government:

> The way that Huang runs GITIC is one of the reasons that McDonalds selected it out of fifteen contenders to be its joint-venture partner. Since GITIC itself is part of the government, the company has unequalled *guanxi*, or connections, among local officials. As a result, Huang's company has buildings located throughout the city in prime spots for hamburgers and restaurants. Moreover, GITIC knows exactly how to work the system to get restaurant, construction, and business licences quickly.

Business Week emphasized Huang's 'global' lifestyle:

> Over dinner at the restaurant in his headquarters, Huang boasts about how service has improved. He tells a guest that he has made waiters wear gloves when handling expensive bottles of wine so their body heat won't disturb the contents.

Mounting pressure of insolvency during the Asian Financial Crisis

Well before the AFC, there was increasing concern in the international press about the financial condition of the ITICs as a whole. In 1995 the Chinese government had closed Zhongyin Trust and Investment Corporation, but due to its small scale, it was little noticed. In January 1997, the China Agricultural Development Trust and Investment Corporation (CADTIC) collapsed. CADTIC had been established by the Ministry of Agriculture and, at one point, had been the country's second largest ITIC. At its closure it was found guilty of tax evasion, illicit trading, property speculation and high-interest lending banned by the PBOC. Foreign analysts asked the question: 'If such a large ITIC, with powerful backers, could fail, how stable are the others?' (Mitchell, 1998a). However, creditors were reassured by the fact that debts of the CADTIC were assumed by the China Construction Bank. It was reported that the PBOC had set aside US$ 200 million to meet the foreign debt obligations of the failed company. It appeared as if the failed ITICs' international debts were being treated as if they were China's sovereign debts. International lenders' fears were exacerbated by the collapse and closure in June 1998 of Hainan Development Bank (HDB), but once more the debts to the international creditors were met by Chinese state-owned entities.

GITIC faced serious problems prior to the AFC. The collapse of the property bubble harmed GITIC's investments as well as damaging the balance sheets of many of the companies to which it had made loans. The Asian Financial Crisis had a considerable effect on GITIC, which had a large fraction of its investments and loans in real estate, hotels, tourism and construction. In 1998, GITIC faced a bunching of debt repayments and a deteriorating business environment. It encountered escalating difficulties in making scheduled repayments to financial institutions. Alarm bells were sounded in the international press in July 1998, when GITIC reportedly missed a payment of US$ 14 million to sixteen of its creditor banks (*FT*, 23 July 1998). GITIC eventually paid up 'but not before causing sleepless nights for creditors' (Mitchell, 1998a).

Close attention was turned upon the general condition of the trust and investment companies. A World Bank report helped to unsettle investors:

> Off-balance-sheet accounts are not usually reported. Consolidation is generally inconsistent and reported bad debt reserves are not adequate … The true financial condition of the TICs and ITICs cannot be determined by analysis of their published financial statements. Many are rumoured to be actually insolvent, although their financial ratios may appear strong.
>
> (World Bank, 1997)

Another in-depth report produced a bleak evaluation of the prospects for the ITICs as a group (Mitchell, 1998a). It noted that the nationwide growth slowdown in the late 1990s had seriously damaged their earnings prospects. It pointed out that at the top seven ITICs, their liquidity was low, with cash, marketable securities and other short-term assets accounting for only 20 per cent of total assets, compared with 34 per cent for the state banks. It noted that they were heavily exposed to the property market through loans and direct investment during the property boom of the early 1990s: 'Now empty buildings stand everywhere in China, constructed with money which will not be recovered for years, if ever' (Mitchell, 1998a). This analysis focused on GITIC as one of the most vulnerable of the leading ITICs.

GITIC's crisis intensified during 1998. Right up until the final decision to close GITIC, the senior management did not believe that closure was a serious option. They believed that the company was 'too big to fail': 'They were in the middle of a crisis, but didn't realize it was a crisis.' GITIC's leadership believed that the provincial government would ultimately step in to rescue the company. They thought that the survival of GITIC was a matter of 'reputation' (*xinyu*) for both the provincial and the national governments. The GITIC leadership fought tenaciously through different channels to save the company right up until the end. The leadership fought 'day and night' to get back their loans from their debtors. GITIC had almost 300 different locations in which it had made loans or investments. The company used its relationships with the different local governments under which the enterprises operated, to press them to ensure repayment from the debtor firms. GITIC was able to use a wide variety of extra-legal means to ensure debt repayment. However, these efforts at debt recovery were far from sufficient to meet its escalating repayment commitments.

The Asian Financial Crisis meant that the international banks, especially those based in Hong Kong and the Hong Kong branches of global banks, faced serious problems in obtaining repayments of their loans in East Asia outside China. They turned their focus towards their loans to the Chinese mainland-based companies in order to obtain repayments from the only government in the region that appeared to have given unqualified support to domestic institutions in the repayment of their international debts. Although the Guangdong government asked the foreign banks to 'give a breathing space to GITIC due to the Asian Financial Crisis,' the terms available from international financial institutions hardened during the crisis. GITIC's mounting payments difficulties in 1998 'owed much to the decision by Japanese bankers to reduce their overseas lending to remedy overstretched balance sheets at home' (*FT*, 16 November 1998).

Increasingly GITIC turned to high-interest, short-term loans in order to pay its debts, hoping that this would enable them to survive a temporary period of difficulty. In its attempt to raise funds, GITIC exceeded its short-term foreign exchange quota set by SAFE. GITIC thereby moved increasingly into illegal financial operations in order to try to survive. However, these operations were insufficient to solve GITIC's repayment obligations. Eventually, GITIC found itself unable to pay the interest on around US$ 500 million in short-term debts. By the late summer of 1998, it was clear that GITIC was insolvent.

Mitchell's (1998a) analysis of the ITICs concluded: 'GITIC's accounts, like too many Chinese financial institutions, exhibit questionable asset quality, weak capitalization and suspect earnings quality … GITIC provides no information about non-performing loans, which it most likely grossly underestimates.' He noted that the quality of GITIC's equity investment portfolio was 'indeterminable.' Moreover, GITIC's Bank of International Settlement (BIS) adequacy ratio was 'even less determinable':

> In line with market standards, GITIC does not disclose its BIS ratio. Although equity as a percentage of funding amounted to 13.4 per cent at the end of 1997, this is almost certainly inadequate in light of GITIC's lenient classification of non-performing loans.

GITIC's liquidity levels were 'equally poor': at the end of 1997, liquid assets accounted for 'just 3.4 per cent of total assets.' In 1997, GITIC reported the lowest profitability of the top five ITICs. Two-thirds of its profits were derived from financial services and real estate. As a result GITIC was 'exceptionally vulnerable to a real estate slump.'

Mitchell asked the question, 'Should investors therefore be worried that the People's Bank of China will liquidate GITIC, in the course of its ongoing clean-up of the country's ITICs?' He answered:

> Probably not. As the investment vehicle of one of China's premier industrial powerhouses, GITIC will continue to play a major role in channelling overseas investment into southern China. As a result of this near-monopoly, strong political and financial support in case of need is virtually assured.

In other words, Mitchell felt able to assure international financiers that their investments were secure due to central and/or Guangdong government support. They could continue to lend without fear of default, and, therefore, did not need to directly concern themselves whether their loans were being used well or badly.

By September 1998, it had become clear that the problems of the ITICs as a whole were worsening. The US rating agency Moody's Investors Service downgraded CITIC and six other trust companies, including GITIC. It warned that both the central and local governments faced increasing difficulties in dealing with the problems of restructuring loss-making state-owned enterprises and of rising urban unemployment. They concluded that this would weaken the governments' ability to support the ITICs (*SCMP*,

7 October 1998). GITIC 'tried to reassure investors' by making a public announcement that they had repaid almost US$ 180 million in syndicated loans to foreign banks.

The fast-unfolding payments crisis presented severe policy challenges for both the Guangdong government and the central government. It was hoped initially that GITIC's problems could be solved through support from the provincial budget. GITIC was able to make its repayments in 1998 mainly due to the fact that it received large-scale financial support from the Guangdong government. On 2 September 1998, the provincial government provided GITIC with RMB 110 million to stave off the crisis, and on 18 September, it provided a further RMB 105 million to ensure that it met its repayment obligations. However, it was eventually realized that the scale of GITIC's problems was beyond the capabilities of the provincial budget.

The central government and the Guangdong government were both aware that GITIC and GDE together had massive liabilities, of several billion dollars. They were unaware of the full extent of those liabilities or the weakness of GITIC's assets. However, they knew that GITIC's liabilities were extremely large in relation to the province's financial resources. Moreover, the Guangdong government had also to deal with the insolvency of the other TICs, as well as the insolvency of the huge number of rural financial associations, and urban credit cooperatives within Guangdong. As with GITIC, the provincial government had no idea of the full extent of either the foreign exchange or the *renminbi* debts of the maze of Guangdong's financial institutions, whose complex inter-relationships only increased the uncertainty and fears of the provincial government, and intensified the concerns of the central government.

The debts of GDE, GITIC and the other NBFIs in the province were eventually revealed to total the equivalent of around US$ 20 billion, compared with a provincial output of around US$ 100 billion in 1998 (SSBG, GTN, 2000: 59). This sum was more than twice the level of the provincial government's revenue of around US$ 8 billion in 1998 (SSBG, GTN, 2000: 59). Moreover, numerous other Guangdong-based red chips and 'window' companies had borrowed from international markets through Hong Kong. The total international liabilities of Guangdong-based financial institutions and red chips were unknown but substantially exceeded the officially registered figures, and these were very large compared to the financial resources of the Guangdong government. In other words, the crisis in Guangdong's main NBFIs was a critical matter for the provincial government. The way in which the GITIC case was resolved would have enormous implications for the way in which the crises in other NBFIs in the province would be resolved. The potential domino effect went far beyond Guangdong's NBFIs and red chips. As we saw in Part 1, it included the possible implications for the whole NBFI sector and for red chips from across the country and, ultimately, for the whole country's financial system.

The GITIC case was a watershed in China's relations with the international capital markets. The potential 'domino' effects from GITIC were enormous in terms of the potential liabilities for the central government. The central government knew very well that the problems at GITIC were 'replicated across the country in all provinces and in all sizes of companies.' It is estimated that the total registered international borrowings of the ITICs was at least US$ 30 billion. Moreover, a large part of these was due for repayment within one or two years. However, we have seen that there was also estimated to be a further amount of at least US$ 30 billion borrowed by the ITICs from international financial institutions which had not been registered with SAFE. The red chips and other mainland entities in Hong Kong may have had further international liabilities of US$ 20–24 billion. The total liabilities of the ITICs and red chips may have been as much as US$ 80 billion, compared with total foreign exchange reserves of US$ 147 billion in 1997. In other words, taken together, these liabilities amounted to around one-half of China's total foreign exchange reserves at that time. To have accepted that GITIC's international debts should be treated as Chinese sovereign debts would have had serious implications for the country's foreign exchange reserves, including China's ability to defend the exchange rate during the AFC. Yet, the logic of the creditors' demands was precisely that the debts of all mainland-backed entities, including both ITICs and red chips, should be treated as if they were China's sovereign debt.

If the central government had stepped in unconditionally to support GITIC in order that it could meet its international repayment obligations, then it would have given a powerful signal to international financial institutions that they should forcefully pursue the other ITICs and red chips, to repay their international liabilities, in order to reduce their losses from the Asian Financial Crisis. As long as the Chinese government was willing unconditionally to underwrite GITIC and the other ITICs, as well as the red chips, then the international bankers had no incentive to soften their stance and seek debt-restructuring solutions. The consequences would have been that the Chinese government would have been forced to shoulder the responsibility for the ITICs and red chips across the country, including provinces far poorer than Guangdong.

Ultimately, the way in which the crisis at GITIC was resolved also had potential implications for the formal banking sector. It affected the confidence that the mass of the population, the country's hundreds of millions of savers, had in the country's financial institutions. It provided important lessons also to the main banks about the way in which the central government would treat their own liabilities.

The GITIC crisis had serious implications for Hong Kong. GITIC had borrowed around US$ 4.8 billion from the Hong Kong banks. However, in addition, it is estimated that the total liabilities of mainland-based firms in Hong Kong, including the other ITICs, local governments' 'window' companies and the Hong Kong red chip companies of different ministries and commissions, were around US$ 18–24 billion. We have seen in Part 1 that Hong Kong had been greatly affected by the AFC in 1998. The territory was in great difficulties due to the collapse of the property bubble, and the severe impact of the AFC on the stock market. In the words of a contemporary analyst: 'The addition of the liabilities of the mainland-based firms on top of the existing difficulties, places Hong Kong in a highly vulnerable situation. If these firms are made bankrupt, Hong Kong is finished.' The way in which the GITIC crisis was handled greatly affected Hong Kong's prospects for economic stability. Having only taken Hong Kong back into Chinese sovereignty in 1997, the Chinese government had a solemn obligation to ensure that the SAR functioned successfully under Chinese rule, even if the territory's economic policies were not under its direct control.

It was 'impossible' for the central government to repay both GITIC's and GDE's debts. The budgetary implications were enormous. There also were complicated political issues involved. Other, less affluent, provinces would have been highly aggrieved that apparent profligacy and criminality at the flagship company of China's richest province should have been supported by revenues from less affluent parts of the country. If the central government took over the liabilities of a province that had failed to monitor its own institutions, and which had allowed criminal activity within that company, what signal did this provide to other provinces, to the future behaviour of Guangdong province or, indeed, to governments at other levels in China? Should they all be allowed to use the 'name' and reputation of the central Chinese government to acquire international debts, and then turn to the central government to accept responsibility for these debts when they could not be repaid?

In other words, taking all of these issues into consideration, 'from the perspective of the whole country's situation, there was no way it could afford to pay the total international debts of GITIC': 'Obviously, any state leaders with a sense of responsibility could not consider a policy choice that would have such disastrous consequences. This was what the "choice of no choice" really meant.' Following intense debate within the Guangdong government itself, and discussions between Wang Qishan and Premier Zhu Rongji, the decision was taken to close GITIC. On 6 October 1998 the PBOC announced that it was closing down GITIC and withdrawing its licence to operate, because of its 'inability to pay maturing debts,' mostly denominated in foreign currency (*FT*, 7 October 1998). The PBOC said that it would 'take responsibility for all the rights and obligations for GITIC's debt' (*FT*, 7 October 1998). The securities operation of GITIC was to be taken over by Guangfa Securities, a local Guangzhou brokerage firm. Non-financial subsidiaries were to continue operating as normal. Payment of GITIC's debts was to be suspended until 6 January 1999. Creditors had until that date to register their claims against GITIC. It was initially thought that GITIC had international debts of around US$ 1 billion, 'much of it short-term' (*Economist Intelligence Unit*, 13 October 1998).

From closure to bankruptcy

This was by far the biggest closure that had ever taken place in China's financial sector. As we have seen, the Chinese government had closed other financial institutions, but none was as large as GITIC. In each case the central government had stepped in to rescue the lenders by assuming the liabilities through different means: 'In each case, money owed to small depositors and foreign creditors was paid back in full. Banks took over the business and the scandals were soon forgotten.' The liabilities involved in these bankruptcies were small relative to those involved at GITIC, probably less than US$ 200 million in total. The GITIC 'Notice of Closure' contained no indication that the central government would bail out GITIC. Lenders viewed this omission as 'a breaking of China's guarantee': 'Predictably, the GITIC Notice set off a firestorm in Hong Kong's financial community, which forecast dire results if all GITIC's debts were not honoured in full' (Chang, 1998).

The decision to close GITIC coincided with the annual meeting of the World Bank and IMF in Washington. It was speculated that the timing of the announcement was intended to convey the impression, not least to the IMF and World Bank, that the Chinese government was 'serious about economic reform' (*Economist Intelligence Unit*, 12 October 1998).

However, the decision provoked a flood of speculation in the international press about its implications for the rest of the Chinese financial sector. The *Economist Intelligence Unit* (EIU) warned:

> [R]elief that the matter has been taken in hand is surely misplaced. Foreign bankers have long convinced themselves that China is Asia's last safe haven. Now it is clear that it has financial problems that, by some measure, dwarf those of neighbouring countries. If China's financial system unravels, foreign bankers will not be spared the consequences … If a financial institution in China's least state-directed province is unable to repay its debts, it bodes ill for trust and investment companies in the more state-bound provinces now suffering from slowing economic growth.
>
> (*Economist Intelligence Unit*, 13 October 1998)

GITIC's closure revealed the 'suspected rot throughout hundreds of China's non-bank financial institutions – the highly-leveraged and under-performing investment companies that have become increasingly integrated into the international financial community and are now helping to suck China into the Asian economic crisis' (*FT*, 8 October 1998).

Following the closure, the initial picture was confused. At first, international creditors assumed that the PBOC would 'assume liability for most or all of GITIC's debts': 'Beijing has said foreign debt registered with it will be repaid' (*FT*, 23 October 1998). Although China's central bank 'went out of its way not to guarantee that it would honour GITIC's obligations to foreign creditors,' the appointment of the Bank of China (BOC), one of the big four state-owned commercial banks, as administrator for the closure meant that 'many international investors were initially confident they would recover their funds' (*FT*, 30 October 1998). The main immediate fear was about 'those people who bought into deals that in some way did not conform with foreign exchange rules: will they be paid in full or will they have to take a haircut?' (*FT*, 8 October 1998). International lenders were unsettled by the statement from the Vice-Minister of State Development Planning, Li Rongrong that 'in future lenders will be left to manage their own risks and losses' (quoted in *Asian Wall Street Journal*, 20 October 1998).

GITIC's closure caused intense focus on the risks involved in lending to China. China's hard currency reserves stood at US$ 140 billion in late 1998, but the country's official foreign debt now stood at US$ 130 billion. Moreover, there was great nervousness due to the fact that 'nobody knows the size of the liabilities the ITICs and their Hong Kong subsidiaries really face' (*Asian Wall Street Journal*, 26 October 1998). It was well known that international bankers had made extensive loans to the ITICs that were not registered with SAFE. Furthermore, borrowing by the overseas subsidiaries of mainland entities did not require registration with SAFE. Foreign commentators awoke to the fact that unregistered borrowings by the TICs were at least as great as those officially registered with SAFE. Merrill Lynch believed that China's actual foreign borrowings were 'at least US$ 30 billion larger than the official figure' (*Asian Wall Street Journal*, 26 October 1998). Concern was expressed also that GITIC was heavily involved with 'off-balance-sheet transactions': loan guarantees from GITIC were reported to be five times its capital figure (*Asian Wall Street Journal*, 26 October 1998). It was reported that GITIC had extensively participated in 'complicated derivatives transactions' (*Asian Wall Street Journal*, 26 October 1998).

Less than two weeks after the official announcement of the closure of GITIC, China's Minister of Finance, Xiang Huaicheng, gave an official interview which marked a dramatic clarification of central government policy towards the debts of the ITICs. The newspaper headlines announced, 'Beijing warns that it will not bail out foreign banks' (*FT*, 26 October 1998). Most international lenders to the ITICs had hoped that the central government would honour GITIC's international debts in full, as had been the case with previous closures of ITICs. However, Minister Xiang warned that 'Beijing would not act as guarantor of last resort on foreign loans' and that many other ITICs apart from GITIC would be closed. The central bank would 'settle accounts with these ITICs one by one.' Xiang said:

> Local government does not have the qualification or the resources to guarantee these loans. I say to governors of the provinces, even I do not dare to provide these guarantees, so how dare you? And the governors say: 'I did not do it. It was the mayors who did it'. Then I just say, the foreign bankers should look carefully at these loans.
>
> (quoted in *FT*, 26 October 1998)

Another senior official made it clear that the PBOC 'would not provide funds to honour obligations to international creditors, who would have to seek redress from the Guangdong provincial government.' In other words, the Guangdong government must take care of its own 'child.'

Minister Xiang Huaicheng made crystal clear that the closure of GITIC should be taken as a big signal by Chinese local governments, by the ITICS themselves as well as by the international financial institutions:

> We announced to the whole world that we are doing something real now to reform our financial system. We are also giving a big warning to all the international trust and investment corporations across the provinces to say that before you start raising loans from abroad you should be very cautious ... And that is also a lesson to investors and foreign bankers, that before you provide these loans you should study Chinese laws carefully.
>
> (quoted in *FT*, 26 October 1998)

By the end of October 1998 it had become apparent that the central government was not going to bail out GITIC, that the repayment process would be long and complicated, that the PBOC's responsibility would be confined to that of administrator of the closure of GITIC and that the legal responsibility for GITIC lay with it owners, the Guangdong government.

Executive Vice-Governor Wang Qishan hammered home the message given by Minister Xiang Huaicheng. He emphasized that a careful examination of the true situation at GITIC in terms of assets and liabilities was necessary before the Guangdong government could make a final decision about how to deal with the collapsed entity: 'When we have identified all the issues, we will be able to see a clear picture. Then the Guangdong provincial government will determine how to deal with the liabilities of GITIC' (quoted in *FT*, 30 October 1998). Wang Qishan said: '[A]ll investors' interests will be carefully considered ... The closure of GITIC shows the Chinese government's determination to enhance regulation and ensure stability in the financial system. For the long term this is a positive move.' He emphasized that the closure of GITIC should be taken as a lesson by local governments that managed the ITICs. Also, he said it should serve as a lesson for the foreign banks that loaned large sums to the ITICs: 'Foreign financial institutions should also bear responsibility in this area. Foreigners should take some responsibility and they should learn some lessons' (quoted in *FT*, 30 October 1998).

The decision to close GITIC immediately impressed some commentators with the evidence this provided of the Chinese leadership's determination to clean up the operation of its financial services sector. The *Financial Times* commented: 'You can see that Zhu Rongji means business ... China is doing everything it can to prevent a financial crisis' (*FT*, 8 October 1998). The Chinese government's decisive approach was contrasted positively with that of other governments in the region: 'By taking decisive action against high-profile institutions, China has sought to stand apart from Asian neighbours where a mixture of political paralysis and self-interested neglect has let cronyism and incompetence fester in the financial sector with disastrous consequences' (*FT*, 16 November 1998). The closure of GITIC was also viewed as a vivid demonstration of the authority of the central government over Guangdong province. The closure of GITIC was interpreted as part of the same 'cleaning up' process that required the People's Liberation Army (PLA) to give up its control over commercial activities:

> The prosperous but free-wheeling province of Guangdong, where the PLA has run extensive smuggling operations and owns businesses ranging from massage parlours to real estate, has been one of the chief targets of Beijing's drive to shut down the military's commercial operations.
> (*FT*, 21 October 1998)

In a long interview in November 1998, Guangdong's Governor, Lu Ruihua, made clear that the terms under which Guangdong-based firms dealt with international banks would be changed radically after the GITIC event. He emphasized that even in the early 1990s, the Guangdong government's policy had been that the government 'would not back bad loans made by various local governments': 'But, in fact, there was no serious implementation at the grassroots level and many foreign investors still gave money to them. Through the settlement of the GITIC problem, we want to deal with this problem once and for all' (quoted in *Agence France-Presse*, 15 November 1998). Governor Lu emphasized that Guangdong wanted to develop a stronger set of business rules, 'what we call economy by law,' making clear that all lending agreements would be between bankers and borrowers, with nobody thinking the province would bail out bad deals. Lu commented on the international bankers' claims that they had been led to believe that their loans were guaranteed by the government. He called this 'magic that is absolutely impossible.' 'That's not really the market economy,' he said.

The immediate impact of the closure of GITIC was to raise the cost of international lending to China, and reduce the volume of lending, which resulted in the cancellation of agreements to roll over loans: 'International rating agencies have been falling over each other to downgrade the credit rating for the trust and investment companies' (*FT*, 16 November 1998). The GITIC closure 'served as a wake-up call to foreign banks and prompted a reassessment of credit risk.' The lesson was appreciated by international bankers. The Chief Executive of Banque Nationale de Paris in Hong Kong said:

> GITIC was a big surprise, but I believe it's a good thing. [The Chinese authorities] had to do it to show that things are changing in China. The message [from the GITIC closure] is well received and understood by

> foreign bankers. From now on we have to be more cautious and will react in China as we do in any other country. We have to look to the financial strength of the borrower.
>
> (*Agence France-Presse*, 18 November 1998)

Moody's rating agency believed that the closure of GITIC signified that the Chinese government had undertaken a fundamental reassessment of the role of foreign capital: 'While direct foreign investment in selected industries will continue to be encouraged, overseas borrowing by Chinese companies, particularly those deemed financially weak and inefficient, will be discouraged' (Moody's, 1998b).

However, by the end of 1998, GITIC's international creditors were nervous about the extent to which they would be repaid and the extent of the 'haircut' they might be forced to accept. In November 1998, the Hong Kong Association of Banks (HKAB) made two trips to Beijing to lobby the central authorities. The Bank of China had issued a statement saying that priority would be given to those loans properly registered with SAFE (*China Economic Review*, 23 November 1998). However, by the end of November it was still not clear to what extent foreign creditors would receive re-payment of such loans. The Secretary of the HKAB said: 'Foreign banks have begun to lose patience' (quoted in *SCMP*, 25 November 1998). In December 1998, overseas creditors were still 'largely in the dark' as to how GITIC's massive debts would be covered (*Agence France-Presse*, 14 December 1998). They still nourished the hope that GITIC's owner, the Guangdong government, would assume full responsibility for all GITIC's international liabilities.

In order better to evaluate the options available to the government after the closure of GITIC, Wang Qishan took the unprecedented step of commissioning one of the global 'big five' accountancy companies, KPMG, to undertake a rough and ready high-speed audit. KPMG became the first international accountancy firm to penetrate so deeply inside a Chinese state-owned enterprise. Moreover, it had the technical capability to probe much more deeply into many aspects of the firm's behaviour than would have been possible even for domestic supervisory bodies. The 'fast and dirty' audit, undertaken within ten days by KPMG shortly after GITIC was administratively closed, immediately showed that GITIC's accounts contained a great number of 'bubbles.' It provided a much more accurate picture of the full extent of GITIC's insolvency than was hitherto available.

KPMG was shocked at the level of accountancy procedures at GITIC. It was quickly obvious that the value of GITIC's 'assets' was far less than had been officially declared. KPMG made the government aware that the final extent of GITIC's liabilities was far greater than had initially been feared due to the effect of extensive contingent liabilities arising from the complex web of cross-guarantees for debt undertaken by GITIC's subsidiaries. By mid-November it was reported that the final figure for GITIC's indebtedness was likely to be around US$ 3 billion, more than twice the initial estimates

(*SCMP*, 13 November 1998). These investigations greatly increased the Chinese leadership's nervousness about the full extent of the indebtedness of the ITICs and red chips, and, therefore, the full extent of their commitments if they wished to treat GITIC's (and GDE's) debts as if they were China's sovereign debt.

KPMG's investigation showed that the difficulties at GITIC were attributable to more than simple incompetent management. They revealed that GITIC had serious criminal activity, supporting the suggestions in previous reports of central government investigation teams. What message would be conveyed to Guangdong's government, to the management of GITIC and to the management of all the other ITICs, if the central government stepped in to use its own resources to resolve the financial crisis at GITIC? It would suggest that the central government was prepared to use the resources of the whole Chinese people to underwrite not only commercial incompetence but, even more significantly, to underwrite criminality and theft.

GITIC's leaders did not believe that there was sufficient reason to bankrupt the company. While many of them eventually accepted that it might be necessary to close GITIC temporarily, they believed that it should have been restructured and then re-opened, 'just like a shop.' This was, indeed, a widespread pattern in the wake of the Asian Financial Crisis, as the original owners and operators fought tenaciously to keep control of their companies. In one company after another across the region, prolonged restructuring over many years, in negotiation with the main creditors, led to company survival rather than bankruptcy, typically with various channels of state support, including extensive intervention in the legal process. The Guangdong government supported GITIC's leaders for a long time in this struggle against bankruptcy.

After intense and anguished debate in the period after the closure, the Chinese government decided that GITIC should declare itself bankrupt in the Guangdong courts. GITIC's leaders had been surprised when the company was closed. They were shocked when it was declared bankrupt.

Bankruptcy

Following the enquiry undertaken by the PBOC, GITIC filed for bankruptcy in the Higher People's Court of Guangdong province on 10 January 1999. The fact that GITIC itself filed for bankruptcy was highly significant. For the leaders of GITIC it was a humiliating loss of face to petition the court to be declared bankrupt. For the international creditors, it took control out of their hands. It gave them no possibility of pursuing the option of debt restructuring. One international investment banker closely involved in lending to GITIC reported that he had set considerable store by the statement by Chinese authorities that GITIC could 'not be made bankrupt' by its creditors. He had never considered the possibility that GITIC might itself apply for bankruptcy.

On 16 January the court ruled that GITIC and its three wholly owned subsidiaries were bankrupt, and GITIC entered the liquidation process. It was reported that GITIC had assets of US$ 2.6 billion, against liabilities totalling US$ 4.4 billion, far larger than had originally been estimated (*Dow Jones*, 14 January 1999). This was by far the biggest bankruptcy in the history of the People's Republic of China. GITIC was China's second largest trust and investment company. Only CITIC was larger. The bankruptcy of GITIC marked the first occasion on which the Chinese government had refused to bail out a large state-owned enterprise. The worst fears of the international creditors were now confirmed. Their last hope after the closure, that the Guangdong government would step in to assume responsibility for GITIC's liabilities, had gone. They now realized that they would have to pursue their claims through the mechanism of formal court-based bankruptcy. The 'rules of the game' for lending to China had clearly and unambiguously changed.

The Chinese leadership in Beijing was publicly clear about its goals in relation to the signals it wished to give from the closure and bankruptcy of GITIC: 'Closing insolvent financial institutions demonstrates the strong determination of the Chinese government to, on its own initiative, settle and ward off financial risks' (Foreign Ministry spokesman, Sun Yuxi, quoted in *Dow Jones*, 14 January 1999).

Shortly after GITIC applied for bankruptcy, Premier Zhu Rongji held a press conference at which he said:

> This incident is of great significance because it has sent a message to the world that the Chinese government will not repay the debts for the financial institutions or a firm if the debts are not guaranteed by governments at various levels in China.

Zhu Rongji said that foreign banks and institutions needed to make risk analyses and act prudently and cautiously in extending loans to financial firms in China: 'I think the approach adopted by China in approving the bankruptcy of GITIC is consistent with the principle of financial reform and consistent with international practice.' He emphasized: 'China is fully capable of repaying its debts, but the question is whether the debts should be repaid by the government, the answer is, of course, they should not.'

Wang Qishan met with global fund managers in early February 1999 to explain the reasons for the bankruptcy of GITIC. He said that China was determined to 'burst the bubble of perverse incentives that affected both the behaviour of foreign lenders and domestic enterprises "free riding on government credit"' (quoted in *Wall Street Journal*, 9 February 1999). He said that while Guangdong province would 'do what it could to sort out the GITIC mess,' the investors were 'in a two-way street.' He said further:

> Whoever gives birth to a child has to assume responsibility for the child. China is trying to enforce the principle of borrowing entities taking

> responsibility for their debt. One clear message from GITIC is that investors would have to make decisions based on the merits of a company and market disciplines would be brought to bear.
>
> (quoted in *Wall Street Journal*, 9 February 1999)

Policy-makers on the Chinese side believed that the decision to bankrupt GITIC had a firm basis of juridical support. This view argued that 'the governments in European capitalist countries are not prepared to unconditionally pay all the debts for their own state-owned enterprises if they are insolvent.'[4] It considered that 'since China's SOEs are legal persons, they have the right to finish their own lives by choosing to go bankrupt.'[5] Seen in this light, it was argued that GITIC's bankruptcy conformed to international practice. Moreover, it accorded with the direction of reform in China's SOEs, under which enterprises were responsible for their own profit and loss, and the government was no longer directly responsible for the enterprises' business. Under this approach if the Chinese state took responsibility for SOEs' international debts, it should also take responsibility for those of the domestic creditors. If the principle was indeed extended to domestic creditors as well, then the idea of enterprise responsibility for its own profit and loss would be rendered meaningless. If GITIC's debts had been taken as the responsibility of the Chinese government, then it would have given a signal to all Chinese SOEs, that their debts were not their responsibility, a disaster from the moral hazard perspective.

GITIC's bankruptcy sent a powerful signal for the further reform of China's SOEs:

> No matter how big they are, how well-known in the world, no matter how glorious their history might be, no matter how badly they performed or why, they could no longer rely on being rescued by the government, which would step in to pay their debts.

The decision not to support GITIC represented a milestone in the evolution of the Chinese state:

> A Chinese state-owned enterprise, which is what GITIC was, is owned by the whole people of China, not by the province of Guangdong. The Chinese state represents the whole people of China, of which Guangdong is just a part. Its debts can be viewed as the debts of the whole Chinese people.
>
> (international banker, interview)

The central government's refusal to take responsibility for the whole of GITIC's debts, which were effectively those of the whole Chinese people, marked a 'critical and landmark case in the development of the post-Soviet-style Chinese state, overturning the whole notion of the state and its structure up to that point.' At the time, and long afterwards, many leaders of large

Chinese state-owned enterprises had reservations about GITIC's bankruptcy and the government's refusal to pay its international debts. This was not simply out of concern that they might share the same fate as GITIC. The government continued to intervene in the decisions of both financial and non-financial SOEs. The leaders of SOEs were unwilling to take full responsibility for their enterprise's performance, even though it might have been insolvent or bankrupt.

The response of the international financial community to the decision for GITIC to declare itself bankrupt was confused and self-contradictory. On the one hand the anger of international bankers mounted as it became clear that they would be unlikely to recover more than a fraction of the money they had lent to GITIC. However, it was hard to deny the benefits that the decision would bring to Chinese financial system reform.

The international bondholders and their advisors felt that the Chinese government had betrayed promises contained in the bond prospectuses. GITIC raised funds from international markets through two major US bonds, one for US$ 150 million in 1993 and one for US$ 200 million in 1996. The 1996 bond prospectus was issued as GITIC's problems were entering their final phase. Already there was serious concern within the central government about the nature of GITIC's management. However, potential bondholders were reassured by the apparent repayment guarantees contained in the bond prospectuses.

In the 1990s, the Chinese central government had repeatedly issued directives, and even passed formal legislation, forbidding provincial and municipal governments from providing guarantees for the repayment of international loans to enterprises. The Guangdong government had been explicit that GITIC's borrowings from the international bond market would 'not be guaranteed by China or the Guangdong government' (CSFB, 1993: 3; Merrill Lynch *et al.*, 1996: 5). However, the Guangdong government had issued so-called 'comfort letters,' which emphasized the closeness of its relationship to GITIC and the responsibility that it took towards GITIC's international financial obligations. In October 1993 and September 1996 it issued identical letters to GITIC to re-assure the potential purchasers of two different bonds. The letters said:

> Should GITIC experience difficulty in paying the principal amount or interest on the bonds after the completion of the offering, the Guangdong government would provide support and would instruct relevant debtors to fulfil their obligations to ensure that GITIC's external obligations would be repaid or would designate relevant entities to bear the obligations.
>
> (CSFB, 1993: 5; Merrill Lynch, 1996: 5)

The carefully worded documents did not say that the Guangdong government would assume responsibility for GITIC's debts. However, they gave the strong impression that they would ensure through different channels that the debt obligations were honoured fully. The period around the closure and bankruptcy of GITIC was marked by intense internal debate among China's leading policy-makers. One strongly held view was that the Chinese government should abide by the spirit of the commitments to international lenders, not just have regard to the letter of the agreements. The spirit of the comfort letter was, self-evidently, that at some level the Chinese state would ensure that creditors were repaid.

One international investment banker closely involved in the negotiations prior to the issue of international bonds has detailed recollections of the conversations surrounding this issue. Such discussions were crucial to the way the bond was presented to global purchasers. His recollection is that he was given explicit commitments from the PBOC in Guangdong that the PBOC itself would 'assist in repayment of GITIC's foreign currency debt,' through allowing GITIC's use of swap centres to obtain the necessary foreign currency, through the funds of the PBOC itself or through the Guangdong provincial government funds. Finally, if all else failed, the bankers were assured that the State Council would step in to 'fix the problem.' The bankers were assured that provision of a formal letter of guarantee of debt repayment was unnecessary:

> China is not a federal state. Provinces have no formal autonomy, so a promise from a local branch of a central government entity such as the PBOC is as meaningful as a promise from the same entity's head office in Beijing.

The bankers involved in the international bond issues were assured that China's foreign debts had always been met in the past, and would continue to be met in the future. It did not require a formal letter of guarantee to ensure that this would be the case in the future.

During the boom years for the Guangdong economy in the 1990s, the international bankers were avid to lend to GITIC. In the mid-1990s, the international credit rating of both CITIC and GITIC was triple-A. Much of the international commercial bank lending to GITIC and other ITICs was based on 'relationships.' International bankers talked proudly of their success in 'relationship' lending to Chinese institutions.

One senior banker in a Hong Kong-based bank estimated that only about one-fifth of his bank's loans to GITIC (and GDE) before the AFC had been made on 'the strength of the company' At least three-fifths of his bank's lending had been justified only on the basis of *de facto* government guarantees. For over eighteen years, the local governments had effectively guaranteed repayment of loans without any defaults. Prior to GITIC's bankruptcy, the principal bankruptcies in the Chinese financial services sector had each been followed by the respective governments bailing the company out and ensuring repayment of its debts to international bankers.

Repayment of debt had been in full, including both principal and interest. The international banks always looked for support for their lending from the local government. This did not need to take the form of a written comfort letter. It could take many forms, including speeches and even the ubiquitous *ganbei* at the end of the celebration dinner. The banker complained that he had believed that these *de facto* guarantees were 'promises not representations.'

At the same time as anger mounted among the international creditors at the prospect of a 'haircut,' it was impossible for international commentators to deny that the decision for GITIC to enter bankruptcy was positive for the reform of China's financial system.

The *Wall Street Journal* commented: 'Mr Wang [Qishan] was most certainly correct to point out that once moral hazard has been removed from the equation, China's sovereign credit and indeed the entire atmosphere for investment there will be much healthier' (*Wall Street Journal*, 9 February 1999). Frederick Hsu, an economist at Goldman Sachs, said: 'The only way you educate people is to have them burned. That's the free market way to solve the issue' (quoted in *Washington Post*, 12 January 1999). For Moody's, the lessons to be drawn by international financial institutions from the collapse, closure and bankruptcy of GITIC were 'rather straightforward': 'The era of "name lending" in China is over: [Foreign creditors] now need to analyse a Chinese borrower with the same vigour and thoroughness as they would analyse borrowers elsewhere' (Moody's, 1999). This view was echoed by other commentators. Shortly after GITIC was declared bankrupt *The Wall Street Journal* carried an article under the title 'Tough credit could be a boon for China - sounder foreign debt would grow more' (*Wall Street Journal*, 15 January 1999). It commented: 'Raising capital from abroad will be tougher for Chinese companies following a string of high-profile loan defaults, but that's good news for China.'

The bankers themselves recognized that the GITIC bankruptcy would 'change the way international lenders do business in China' (*Washington Post*, 12 January 1999). One international banker whose bank had loaned money to GITIC commented:

> If this is the chemotherapy for the ills of the financial system, it's incredibly important. But, the downside is we do exactly what they are suggesting we should do, that we treat all loans on a commercial basis assuming no government support.
>
> (quoted in *Washington Post*, 12 January 1999)

Goldman Sachs' economist, Frederick Hsu, said: 'Hopefully, after this there will be a cleaner boundary between the government and Chinese companies or financial institutions, and foreigners will base their decisions on intrinsic creditworthiness instead of political connections' (quoted in *Wall Street Journal*, 15 January 1999).

Jurgen Lemmer of Germany's Commerzbank responded to the closure of GITIC by announcing that his bank would curtail its China lending in response to the decision. He said that since the Chinese government was 'not willing to back up loans,' the bank planned to 'make sure that in future it does business only with partners it knows can repay their debts "without [a government] stamp".' The *Wall Street Journal* commented dryly:

> We don't know exactly what was going through Mr Lemmer's mind at the time. What it sounds like is that the moral hazard route having failed, an annoyed Commerzbank is now vowing to go back to responsible lending practices. Next time they will insist on collateral or proof of the lender's ability to repay. Imagine that.
>
> (*Wall Street Journal*, 9 February 1999)

Having been willing to lend freely as long as the government acted as *de facto* guarantor, the banks responded sharply to the changed atmosphere following the administrative closure of GITIC. The announcement that there would be a distinction made in terms of repayment between officially registered and unregistered debt shocked the foreign banks. It signalled that there was a fundamentally new situation. They responded by squeezing credit lines to Chinese companies, further exacerbating an already tense situation, and leading to a string of difficulties in the already deeply indebted ITIC sector. The decision to bankrupt GITIC and for the government not to honour the *de facto* commitment that foreign bankers believed to have been given 'changed the rules of the game.' Foreign bankers now had to 'look carefully at the cash flow and general state of the company.' This meant that the foreign bankers were 'definitely reluctant to lend to Chinese entities.' They believed that if GITIC reverted to being a true 'trust' company, it 'would not have much business.'

Some international commentators emphasized that bankruptcy is a normal part of the capitalist economy. There was no reason why a certain species of capitalist, namely international bankers lending to East Asia, should have been exempt from this reality. For example, Stiglitz' analysis emphasized the positive function of workouts and bankruptcy:

> In standard market economics, if a lender makes a bad loan, he bears the consequences. The borrower may well go into bankruptcy, and countries have laws on how such bankruptcies should be worked out. This is the way market economies are supposed to work … Bankruptcy is an unwritten part of every credit contract … Bankruptcy does not violate the 'sanctity' of the credit contract.
>
> (Stiglitz, 2002: 201 and 209)

During the AFC, the IMF undertook massive lending to East Asian governments, which was often directly or indirectly geared towards ensuring that international creditors were repaid. This constituted a massive form of moral hazard: '[R]epeatedly the IMF programs provided funds for governments to bail out Western creditors. The creditors, anticipating an IMF bailout, have weakened incentives to ensure that the borrowers will be able to repay' (Stiglitz, 2002: 2001).

Across much of the rest of East Asia, Western bankers wished the IMF to stand by and ensure that their loans were repaid. In the case of GITIC they wished the Chinese government to perform a similar rescue function to ensure that they were repaid. Nowhere did they wish to take responsibility for their bad lending. Having criticized the 'crony capitalism' of East Asia, international bankers contradictorily wished their own financial interests to be protected by international financial institutions and, even, by the Chinese government: 'moral hazard' should be avoided by others but not oneself.

The Guangdong high court

Following GITIC's submission of bankruptcy papers to the Guangdong provincial high court, the liquidation process was in the hands of the court. From 1987 to 2000, Guangdong had over 1,000 bankruptcies annually. However, these were all relatively small cases, dealt with by the local, middle-level courts. Since this was China's first major bankruptcy since 1949, handling the case was a big responsibility for the Guangdong high court. The case involved huge international debts and attracted intense scrutiny from the international media.

A panel of three people – the judge, Huang Xiong and his two assistants – oversaw the case. On 16 January 1999, Huang Xiong declared GITIC bankrupt in an open, public, written judgement read to the court. Huang believed that the decision to declare GITIC bankrupt was correct. He was pleased that the international response to the decision was generally positive. Through this case, he believed China took 'a big step towards a situation in which the independence of the law is upheld.' The court took great care to follow the requirements of Chinese law.

The court carried out the bankruptcy of GITIC in accordance with Chinese law.[6] This meant, fundamentally, the 1986 bankruptcy law. However, although GITIC was a mainland-registered company, its bankruptcy was of considerable international significance, since 82 per cent of its debt was owing to international creditors. The relatively small amount of around RMB 6 billion (around US$ 700 million) was owed to domestic creditors. The Chinese government was concerned that the liquidation of GITIC should be in accordance with international practice and should be perceived as transparent and fair by its international creditors. This was a major reason for appointing KPMG as the accountants to work for the liquidation committee in auditing the GITIC accounts. This decision was controversial within China. KPMG was paid high rates compared to domestic standards, and it opened up the possibility for the first ever in-depth probe by a non-Chinese entity into the workings of a large Chinese state-owned company, the results of which would be exposed to full public gaze, including the international media.

The principal part of the bankruptcy referred to that of the GITIC headquarters, GITIC proper, which itself had twenty-six wholly owned subsidiaries. In addition to the main bankruptcy of GITIC, three of GITIC's mainland subsidiaries were declared bankrupt separately, namely GITIC Shenzhen, Guangdong Leasing Company and GITIC Enterprise Development Company. GITIC's two Hong Kong red chip subsidiaries were closed and declared bankrupt under Hong Kong law, namely Guangxin Enterprises and Guangxin (Hong Kong). These were thought to have accounted for as much as one-third of GITIC's total foreign debts (*SCMP*, 13 November 1998).

A major difficulty for the court in dealing with the GITIC case was the fact that in the 1990s China had no law on trusts. Not until 23 January 2001 was a set of 'regulations' published by the PBOC to clarify the way in which China's trusts should conduct their business. The regulations required that trust companies should obtain central bank approval and have a valid business licence in order to operate. Trust companies were allowed to obtain commissions for 'conducting capital business,' for real estate and other asset transactions as trust business, and for 'operating investment funds.' The new rules specifically forbade trust companies from accepting deposits, from issuing bonds or borrowing overseas (*Legal Media Group*, 23 January 2001).

Prior to that, the absence of a set of trust regulations or a trust law allowed the trust and investment companies to enter a wide range of fields. GITIC did undertake traditional 'trust' business. However, its main businesses were outside the 'trust' field as normally defined. At the time of its closure, GITIC was involved in securities underwriting, securities trading, commercial banking and investment banking. GITIC was a form of 'one-stop shop' universal financial services company, which had been denied to regular commercial banks by strict government legislation to separate the main types of financial services from each other, along the lines of the US Glass-Steagall Act (repealed in the late 1990s). This wide range of banking services undertaken by an NBFI caused great difficulties for the court from a legal point of view. It also meant that dealing with the GITIC case in terms of accepted international legal practice was difficult, since GITIC was not a 'trust' company in the usual terms understood in international legal practice.

A further matter of special difficulty for the court was the fact that China's 1986 bankruptcy law did not envisage the possibility of 'restructuring' the bankrupt enterprise so that it might recover and survive. This was in sharp contrast with the US bankruptcy law. Under the US bankruptcy law's 'Chapter 11,' bankrupt US firms are allowed to have a stand-off with the creditors while the company's business is reorganized with a view to restoring it to commercial viability. Many US commentators believe this provides for an unfair advantage for companies in Chapter 11. It is also highly problematic from the standpoint of 'moral hazard,' since it greatly reduces the threat of bankruptcy as a consequence of poor performance. It is estimated that among US companies that appeal for 'restructuring' under the protection of Chapter 11, 20 per cent 'survive,' compared with only around 10–15 per cent under the judicial-based bankruptcy systems of the EU and Japan. Moreover, among large US companies the proportion is far higher, standing at around 80–90 per cent (*FT*, 31 January 2001). Clearly, one of the fundamental drivers of the capitalist system, the so-called 'hard budget constraint,' hardly exists for the largest US firms. In some case, US companies have been bankrupted and placed under Chapter 11 bankruptcy law on more than one occasion.

A major pressure on the court was the need to consider issues of 'social stability.' GITIC had over 30,000 'natural person' individual account holders. These depositors were apprehensive about the safety of their deposits. The period leading up to the closure of GITIC had been marked by runs on other NBFIs in Guangdong. In addition, there were 80,000 stock owners who were buying and selling shares through GITIC. Furthermore, there were 500 GITIC employees who became unemployed when the company was declared bankrupt. The fact that the Guangdong people's high court 'must pay attention to issues of social stability' put an added burden upon the court in dealing with the GITIC bankruptcy.

The court decided that issues that concerned social stability should be the ultimate responsibility of the state. The Guangdong government provided 780 million *renminbi* (equivalent of around US$ 94 million) to the Bank of China as administrator of GITIC after the closure, in order to meet the immediate demands of individual creditors, and ensure that social order was maintained. The Bank of China thereby became one of GITIC's creditors. An official spokesman said: 'There is no question of harming GITIC's other creditors. The government is simply adopting the policy to ensure social stability and to simplify the settlement process by replacing many creditors with a single one' (quoted in *AFX*, 9 April 1999). The Guangdong provincial government provided around five million *renminbi* to form a settlement payment to each of GITIC's redundant employees. In accordance with the state's redundancy regulations, this amounted to around three times their annual income, amounting to around 40–45,000 *renminbi* per employee.

An important function for the court was to establish the liquidation committee (*qingsuanzu*), which was composed entirely of representatives from mainland entities. A main function of the liquidation committee was to hold creditors' meetings. Since GITIC had over 300 creditors, most of whom were international institutions, this was a complex logistical and management task. It was the first time such an undertaking had been carried out in relation to a large Chinese company. The court had responsibility for ensuring that the chairmanship of the creditors' meetings rotated among the creditors in a way that was perceived to be fair by the different types of creditors. The liquidation committee had responsibility for confirming the extent of repayments available to the creditors in the light of their validation of the assets of GITIC and their progress in reclaiming debts from GITIC's debtors. Where there were disagreements between the creditors' meeting and the liquidation committee, the court had the responsibility of adjudicating. Numerous such adjudications took place during the course of the bankruptcy. A large number of the disagreements arose over areas that were not adequately covered by the 1986 bankruptcy law. Interpreting the law and making decisions in areas not adequately covered by the law formed an important function for the court. The court bore a heavy responsibility in keeping the bankruptcy process moving forwards smoothly, to the mutual satisfaction of all sides, in the face of the ambiguity of GITIC's business activities, the absence of a trust law and the shortcomings of the original bankruptcy law.

The GITIC case broke new ground in leading China towards better bankruptcy practices. The lessons were not only for domestic institutions but also demonstrated to international businesses and foreign governments that China was serious about following international best practice. In addition to its full members, the court appointed professional advisors to assist the liquidation committee in its complicated tasks. These were the international accountants, KPMG (one of the global 'big five' accountants) and the Hong Kong-based law firm Johnson, Stokes and Master. The court then had the function of supervising the liquidation committee's subsequent work.

The decision to allow an international firm of accountants deeply inside a Chinese company was extremely sensitive, especially as the Chinese company was insolvent and was known to the government at different levels, through their own investigations, to be highly corrupted. Although international accountants had been involved in all the foreign listings by Chinese companies, they did not, through that process, penetrate deeply inside the parent company. There were strong feelings expressed by different interest groups within China that the bankruptcy process should be kept tightly controlled within the Chinese mainland's own institutional framework. It was felt that it was inappropriate to allow a foreign entity to investigate deeply inside a Chinese company, exposing behaviour that could be embarrassing for the Chinese government, as well as potentially leading to the criminal prosecution of people involved in the case. Not only was the decision widely criticized on these grounds, but also because the fees charged by a leading international accountancy firm seemed outrageously high to the ears of mainland people. Gradually people in China began to understand the benefit of high-quality international involvement. The international expert advice received throughout the liquidation process by the liquidation committee was of great importance in ensuring that the bankruptcy accorded with international norms.

The Guangdong government under Wang Qishan stressed that the high price paid to international firms working on the GITIC bankruptcy was worth paying, for the high quality of the advice that was received, benchmarking China's procedures vividly against global standards. It was a bold decision, since it meant that one of China and Guangdong province's showcase businesses was placed under the microscope and subjected to intense scrutiny according to global standards. The provincial government was well aware that the picture that would be painted would not be a pretty one. However, such an exposure was regarded as necessary if China were to advance towards a more civilized and morally acceptable business environment. In the early stages of GITIC's bankruptcy there was an outcry from the international bankers. Increasingly, as the case developed, there were strong statements of support for the broad path chosen by the Chinese and Guangdong governments in dealing with the GITIC insolvency.

Liquidation committee

Under the 1986 Bankruptcy Law the liquidation function was undertaken by a committee appointed by the court: 'The liquidation committee is responsible for preservation, valuation, administration and distribution of the debtor's assets' (Standing Committee, China National People's Congress, 1986: Article 24). The bankruptcy law provided that the liquidation committee should be selected 'from among the personnel of the department in charge of the debtor, the personnel of government finance departments and other professionals' (Bankruptcy Law, 1986: Article 24). In the case of the bankruptcy and liquidation of GITIC, the committee consisted of ten people, mainly from senior positions in different departments within the Guangdong provincial government, including Dong Hong, Deputy Secretary General of the Guangdong government. A representative from Guangfa Securities Company was also included, 'due to the importance of the securities business in the GITIC liquidation.' The committee was chaired by Wu Jiesi, assistant to the Governor of Guangdong province.

In practice, many tasks of the liquidation committee were undertaken by the advisors to the committee, namely the accountants, KPMG, and the legal advisors, Kingson, from mainland China, and Johnson, Stokes and Master, from Hong Kong. The three advisory entities worked closely together in advising the liquidation committee. Under Chinese law, the court had the right to overrule the recommendations of the liquidation committee. However, the constant input of advice from the three entities was crucial to ensuring that this important test case for Chinese bankruptcy was carried out in a professional way that accorded full legal protection to the rights of the creditors. The liquidation committee was concerned to carry out the liquidation in accordance with internationally accepted practice. This was especially important as around four-fifths of GITIC's total debt was held outside China.

Since this was the first major bankruptcy in the history of the People's Republic of China, none of the domestic Chinese parties at first fully appreciated what a bankruptcy involved. A major difficulty for the liquidation committee was to obtain repayment of loans to other mainland entities. The initial response of most of the mainland debtors to GITIC on hearing of the bankruptcy was pleasure. Most of the debtors in which GITIC had invested or to whom GITIC had made loans believed that GITIC's bankruptcy absolved them from the need to repay their debts.

A key decision that the liquidation committee was required to take was the extent to which they placed the different parts of GITIC in bankruptcy. Their initial belief was that it would be appropriate for the real estate segment of the business to survive and the rest of GITIC's mainland operations to be bankrupted. It was decided to attempt also to keep the securities segment, which included nine separate companies, as a going concern. The liquidation committee entrusted the operation of GITIC's nine securities companies to Guangfa Securities Company, with the objective of selling the entities to the highest bidder.

Accountants

The controversial decision to employ an accountancy firm with a global reputation to advise the liquidation committee was crucial to the bankruptcy process. Not only did the Guangdong government decide to employ an international firm, but they chose to employ one of the 'big five,' that dominated global accountancy at that time. This decision was crucial to gaining the trust of the international creditors. KPMG had enormous international experience in bankruptcies. The decision was highly significant for China. The Guangdong government's goal in appointing KPMG was to ensure that the bankruptcy followed 'normal' international procedures and accorded with Chinese law. By appointing KPMG, the Guangdong government wished to make it clear that it intended 'to protect creditors' interests and to try to repay the heavy debts GITIC owes its victims' (quoted in *FT*, 29 May 2000). KPMG's objective was to ensure that the repayment of debts was 'handled according to Chinese law and international bankruptcy practice' (Louis Choi, KPMG, quoted in *China Daily*, 29 March 1999).

KPMG's investigations revealed a shocking picture of combined technical incompetence and criminal behaviour. It is widely acknowledged by accountants that fraud is much easier to perpetrate in financial services than in physical production companies. The latter have physical ratios that can be used to cross-check financial data. In sharp contrast, a financial services company provides a much greater opportunity for deception in the company's accounts. Not only was there large-scale deception in relation to GITIC's true financial situation. There was also a serious problem of technical incompetence. GITIC had become involved in almost every aspect of financial services, in most of which it had little in-house expertise. Financial services business depends crucially on expert judgement. However, it is often difficult to disentangle fraud and incompetence. 'Poor judgement' in making loans may sometimes be intentional, if the loans are made to related parties. 'Incompetence' in collecting debts can in fact be a cover for insider theft by a related party.

KPMG felt that there was evidence that the development of GITIC could be divided into four stages. In the first stage, GITIC concentrated mainly on building long-term projects, consistent with its objective of 'developing Guangdong province.' In the second stage, it borrowed increasing amounts from international capital markets. In stage three, it began to experience increasing financial difficulties and relied more and more on short-term loans to finance the repayment of its long-term investments, hoping that the crisis would pass. Once it entered the fourth stage it had lost the confidence of its creditors and was only able to survive through borrowing short-term at high interest rates. This was only sustainable for a short while and, ultimately, required state intervention if it was to survive. The pressure for criminal actions intensified as the property market collapsed and the pressure of the AFC intensified.

In most bankruptcies, the incumbent managers know far more about the business than do the incoming accountants. In this case, KPMG found that the managers often had poor knowledge of the business they were supposed to be running. One manager told KPMG: 'I have only been a manager in this business for eight years, so I don't know too much about it.' In part, this may have been an intentional display of apparent naivety. However, in part it reflected a genuine problem, namely, that KPMG found a business structure at GITIC that was extraordinarily complex. One of the reasons for the slow progress in restructuring was that it took a long time to understand the real nature of GITIC.

KPMG found that GITIC's accounts were in 'a terrible state.' KPMG's staff involved in the GITIC liquidation had 'never seen such a mess in company accounts.' At the time of its liquidation the GITIC balance sheet showed that it was still making a profit. In fact, KPMG wrote off one billion RMB (the equivalent of US$ 120 million) in assets immediately, due to 'errors' in the balance sheet. GITIC was regularly recording as assets in 'accounts receivable,' loans that were long overdue and on which no interest or repayment of principal had occurred for many years. This was not simply a matter of Chinese accountancy rules differing from international rules but, rather, was 'bending the existing Chinese accountancy regulations to give a false picture of GITIC's profits.' Chinese accountancy rules require debts to be written off after three years of non-payment, but GITIC kept rolling over old loans or providing new loans to keep the 'accounts receivable' picture looking much healthier than it really was: 'Everyone knew the accounts were being incorrectly drawn up, but nothing was done to change things.' The inflated balance sheet picture enabled staff bonuses within GITIC to be inflated and increased the company's ability to borrow and make loans. Instead of using accountancy procedures as a mechanism to exercise financial control over the business, GITIC used its accounts as a 'mechanism to pay higher bonuses to its staff.'

From the early 1990s, GITIC's annual reports were audited by the firm called 'Guangzhou Certified Public Accountants.' The annual reports noted that these audits were carried out:

> in accordance with the Accounting Standards of Enterprises, the Finance Standard of Enterprises, other regulations of accounting and financial systems and the Proposed Auditing Routines of Certified Public Accountants which are used by the central government of the People's Republic of China, as well as generally accepted auditing standards and procedures.

The GITIC bankruptcy cast serious doubt on the honesty and quality of China's auditing standards. However, Guangzhou Certified Public Accountants was wholly owned by the Guangdong provincial government and under the supervision of Guangdong provincial finance bureau. The firm it was auditing, GITIC, was also owned by the Guangdong provincial government.

KPMG found that there was 'negligible due diligence' in making loans or investing in other companies. The attitude of the invested companies was that funds from GITIC were the equivalent of state aid. Ironically, the international creditors wished the Chinese government to provide 'state aid' to GITIC to ensure that they were paid their outstanding debts. It appeared to be 'hard to get any of the subsidiaries or associated companies to remit any profits to the GITIC headquarters.' The subsidiaries and associated companies viewed their generation of profits to be the result of their hard work, whereas they considered that GITIC simply pulled in funds from global capital markets using the name of Guangdong province without any business effort. Therefore, it was 'unreasonable' to ask the borrower or the invested company to hand over its hard-earned profits to GITIC.

KPMG encountered large problems with 'ambiguity' in asset ownership. Some key assets were the subject of ferocious legal disputes over their ownership. Large assets, such as the prime site, 63-storey hotel in Guangzhou, were owned by several different entities as a joint venture between more than one GITIC subsidiary and external partners. Untangling the legal minefields involved in such cases took a great deal of time and expense. The legal tangles over the property rights of several large investments precluded their easy sale. Had the property rights not been so entangled, it is even possible that their sale might have enabled GITIC to postpone or even avoid bankruptcy.

At the start of the bankruptcy process, many Chinese experts thought that the whole process would be completed within only a few months. There was much sensitivity about the length of time needed to conclude the process, since the fees that KPMG were paid were far above those of domestic accountancy firms. Obtaining an agreement with the creditors about the restructuring and repayment process was a long drawn-out affair, lasting almost two years. In fact, large-scale bankruptcies almost always take a long time to complete. By the end of 2000, most Chinese people closely involved with the case had come to the realization that in almost any circumstances, bankruptcy of a large entity is likely to be a long, complicated procedure. This was, in itself, an educational process.

KPMG found that the relationship between GITIC and its subordinate entities was 'a mess.' At the time of the closure, the Guangdong government, the owner of GITIC, didn't even know the number or identity of GITIC's subsidiaries. GITIC's public documents stated that it had 136 subsidiaries. In fact, KPMG's investigations revealed that there was a total of 240 subsidiary companies, of which 105 were domestic and 135 were abroad, including over one hundred subsidiaries in Hong Kong alone. A major complication was the fact that many of GITIC's shareholding companies and subsidiaries were 'independent legal persons,' which had 'their own legal standing' and continued to operate after the closure and declaration of bankruptcy (*FT*, 29 May 2000).

The liquidation committee found that GITIC had made loans to businesses owned by people employed by GITIC, formerly employed by GITIC or closely related to GITIC employees. A major area for such 'related party' loans was in real estate. A further complication for the real estate loans was that many of them were associated with property development on land originally owned by the Guangdong provincial government. Often, the developments were made highly profitable due to an advantageous sale price and/or a change of use subsequent to purchase by the company concerned. The sale price and the permission for change of use were determined by departments within the provincial government. This made the task of the liquidation committee, which was mainly composed of senior officials from the Guangdong provincial government, especially sensitive.

GITIC's bankruptcy emphasized the complicated, inter-related nature of large bankruptcies. A bankrupt company is a debtor. However, it is also a creditor from the point of view of entities to which it has lent money or in which it has invested. GITIC had a total of 242 confirmed debtors at the end of the year 2000. KPMG estimated that the debtor companies employed a total of 'several hundred thousand people.' Of these, only thirty-one were operating normally. Eighty-seven had ceased business or were in liquidation and 124 were in difficulties but were still trading. The Chinese government was concerned that numerous large-scale bankruptcies such as GITIC would have much larger repercussions across related businesses, including debtor firms. This was especially so during a time of economic recession such as the one that affected the most advanced and prosperous parts of Guangdong during the AFC, mediated especially through the effect of export orders from Hong Kong.

Any large bankruptcy always has knock-on effects on firms associated with the bankrupt company. However, in the GITIC case, many of the companies to which GITIC had loaned money or in which it had invested, felt that they had no obligation to repay GITIC. They regarded the loans as having been made by the state, in the guise of GITIC, which was a state-owned firm. They regarded these as 'free assets' that had no need of repayment. Moreover, many of the firms in which GITIC had invested were themselves SOEs that were deeply in debt. Almost two-thirds of GITIC's outstanding debt was from SOEs. Many of these regarded the bankruptcy of GITIC as a godsend, since there would now be no need to repay their debts. They were surprised to be pursued for their own debts to GITIC. This also was an educational process for large Chinese firms about the real meaning of bankruptcy. The bankruptcy process can lead to financial difficulties and even to the serial bankruptcy of the numerous firms that have been invested in or received loans from the principal firm undergoing bankruptcy. Just as the international creditors were avidly pursuing GITIC for debt recovery, so GITIC's liquidators pursued GITIC's debtors, aggravating their difficulties. The greater the degree of international debt repayment, the greater the effect on those to whom GITIC had loaned money or in whom they had invested. The more speculative their ventures, and the harder they were hit by the downturn in the local economy, the more damaging was the impact on the business environment in Guangdong of the liquidation committee's pursuit of GITIC's debts.

The GITIC case demonstrated just how widespread the extent of such inter-related business difficulties was likely to be. This was already well known in the analysis of large bankruptcies in advanced capitalist countries, but it was a new phenomenon for China to consider. The implications of large bankruptcies, the so-called 'hard budget constraint,' were much greater than many Chinese economists had realized. In this respect also, the GITIC bankruptcy provided an important educational tool for Chinese policy-makers.

A normal difficulty in bankruptcies, which applies as much to GITIC as to any bankruptcy, is the timing of asset disposals. Whatever mismanagement there was in the GITIC case, the firm was strongly affected by the downturn in the surrounding market, notably real estate and share prices. A liquidation that proceeds as rapidly as possible may not serve the interests of creditors, as assets may be sold at 'fire sale' prices that 'mark-to-market' but do not reflect their true long-term value. There may also be businesses that can be salvaged from within the overall structure. In normal times these may be profitable. They may yield a better return for creditors by being salvaged, turned around and then sold, than through high-speed disposal or break-up.

Mainland lawyers

Kingson was founded in 1994, emerging from a former state-owned law firm. Although it was one of China's leading law firms, its size was not remotely comparable with that of the global giants in this fast-consolidating industry. In the year 2000, Kingson had just three partners, sixty staff and twenty lawyers. Kingson played an important role in advising the Guangdong government about the legality of different possible steps to deal with the GITIC problem. Advice from high-quality law firms was crucial for the liquidation committee, since few of the committee were legal experts.

Numerous complex legal issues arose during the bankruptcy. Immediately, there arose the issue of the validity of the government's decision to close (*guanbi*) GITIC prior to the liquidation through the courts. The reason given by the PBOC for the decision to close GITIC was its inability to pay its international creditors. Kingson concluded that this was a dubious decision in terms of Chinese law. The PBOC issued the licence for financial institutions. If GITIC had broken the rules of the PBOC, then it could have legally been closed for infringement of the government's regulations, although the PBOC's 'administrative regulations' (*xingzheng guiding*) were not in fact 'law.' GITIC could not have its licence withdrawn simply for failure to pay its debts. Non-payment of debts required that the company be taken to court and that it cease functioning due to bankruptcy and liquidation. In fact, there were several ways in which GITIC failed to observe the regulations of the PBOC, including 'chaotic financial management' and 'failure to observe foreign exchange regulations.' However, these were not the reasons given for the closure. So, from a legal point of view, in the heat of the moment, the government did not choose the legally correct path to close GITIC.

In its work for the liquidation committee, Kingson regarded its key duty as protecting the creditors' interests. One of the lawyers involved in the case had received advanced training in Western liquidation law, having studied for the LLM at a leading UK university and specialized in liquidation law. This training geared the lawyer towards serving the interests of the creditors first. An important part of the legal process of dealing with GITIC's debts was to ensure social stability while simultaneously observing the law and maintaining the confidence of the international creditors in the fairness of the liquidation proceedings. Kingson advised the Guangdong government to use its financial resources to purchase the debts of 'natural persons' and then to take its place in the liquidation process as one of the creditors (see above). In this way, the interests of social stability were met, with the interests of the individual depositors met first, but without the individuals being given a superior claim on GITIC's recoverable assets over other creditors. This enabled the twin goals of social stability and meeting the requirements of the bankruptcy law both to be achieved.

China's 1986 bankruptcy law was framed at a time when China was in the early stages of emerging from the planned economy. The law was brief, consisting of only forty-three provisions, with many aspects of bankruptcy left ambiguous or uncovered. For example, the provision dealing with the function of the creditors' meeting required the meeting to confirm the validity of the company's debts: 'The creditors' committee is authorized to examine evidence concerning claims, to determine whether the claims are secured or unsecured and their respective amounts' (Bankruptcy Law, 1986: Article 15). However, it gives no indication of which entity has the right to collect and provide this information. The creditors' meeting cannot itself undertake this function since it means that it would verify the claims of its own members. In most countries, the liquidator, appointed by the court, has the duty to undertake such validation. Moreover, the argument is circular, since creditors can become members of the creditors' meeting only if they have already established a valid claim: 'logic is useless in trying to explain this regulation.'

A major area of legal difficulty arising from the GITIC case, upon which Kingson advised the liquidation committee, was the absence of a trust law in China, despite the explosion of 'trust and investment companies' in the 1980s and 1990s. The absence of trust law produced a problem in relation to the funds deposited with GITIC. The depositors felt that they were entitled to the immediate return of their deposits. However, Kingson advised the liquidation committee that funds 'entrusted' to GITIC should not be treated as entrusted property. Rather, they were no different in principle from a bank deposit. According to this interpretation, the 'trust deposits' should be included as part of the bankrupt company's assets for the purposes of the liquidation.

The social context of the GITIC bankruptcy threw up some unusual legal and behavioural quirks. For example, GITIC's employees had no clear understanding of the meaning of bankruptcy. This meant that they were still eating free of charge in the GITIC canteen several months after GITIC had been declared bankrupt. The employees had no concept of bankruptcy as a legal procedure and were baffled by Kingson's instruction that they must now eat outside GITIC at their own expense.

A much more serious legal issue for Kingson was the status of assets purchased with loans from GITIC or its related companies. Some major pieces of real estate in Guangdong, as well as other investments, had been built with loans from GITIC, often not repaid, or with investments from a GITIC subsidiary. The 'developers' who had borrowed funds from GITIC, or benefitted from a GITC or related company's investment, fought tenaciously to keep the properties out of the assets to be included in the bankruptcy proceedings: 'GITIC only loaned us the funds; we did the hard job of developing the company.' One of Kingson's functions was to advise the committee that it should insist on the rights of the creditors and bring such assets into the bankruptcy proceedings. Many of these were 'related party' transactions undertaken by GITIC employees involving loans to and investments in companies that were operated by GITIC employees and their relatives. These transactions were typically, and, intentionally, extremely complex. They frequently left property rights highly confused. For Kingson, interpretation of the property rights and the proper relationship of the assets to the bankruptcy was a hugely complex problem. Kingson attempted to protect the legal interests of the creditors, but it was faced with an immensely complex property rights arrangement, as well as heavy pressure from interested parties. For example, two years after GITIC had been declared bankrupt the property rights surrounding the huge 63-storey building in downtown Guangzhou was still the subject of ferocious legal wrangling and intense personal feelings. The financial interests were hugely important to the individuals involved.

A further important practical issue for Kingson was to assess whether or not outstanding debts were valid, due to the lapse of time. In mainland China a claim against a bankrupt company needed to be made within just ninety days: 'A claim filed beyond these time limits is deemed to have been abandoned' (Bankruptcy Law, 1986, Article 9). Moreover, if no claim was made against the debtor for two years, the debt ceased to be valid. Kingson spent a great deal of energy checking the validity of the claims against GITIC and those of GITIC against its own debtors. It concluded that many claims had intentionally not been made due to collusion between employees of GITIC and the debtor, a standard procedure in theft from one's own company.

International lawyers

The third set of professional advisors to the liquidation committee was the international law firm Johnson, Stokes and Master (JSM), headquartered in Hong Kong. The main reason for having an international law firm of high standing advise the liquidation committee was that in key aspects of international loans it enabled the decisions taken by the committee to be consistent with best practice internationally. This was crucial to the bankruptcy proceedings gaining trust from the international creditors. Another important reason was that, unlike even leading domestic law firms, international law firms have the resources to insure against large claims arising from negligence in giving advice. In a large case such as GITIC, the potential size of the damages might be sufficient to bankrupt a small law firm if it advised GITIC on international issues. The main function of the international legal advisors was to advise about the numerous points of conflict between domestic and international practice. The loan agreements between GITIC and the international financial institutions were governed by the law of the lending country. A large fraction of the foreign creditors made loans to GITIC through agreements drawn up in Hong Kong and so were subject to Hong Kong law.

One of the key issues in the case was the legal validity of loans made to GITIC. During the reform process, China passed a succession of laws to control the acquisition of foreign debt by Chinese entities. In 1987, with the cooperation of the IMF, China established foreign exchange control regulations requiring all long-term foreign currency loans to be approved by the state. This registration body was subsequently called the State Administration of Foreign Exchange, and all short-term loans needed to be registered with SAFE. Each long-term foreign exchange loan required individual approval on a case-by-case basis. Above a certain size, long-term loans needed to be approved by SAFE in Beijing, but below that, only local approval was required. Each province had an overall quota for long-term foreign exchange borrowings. Since it was China's fastest-growing province, accounting for around two-fifths of China's exports and one-quarter of its FDI by the mid-1990s, Guangdong received a large share of SAFE's quotas. Two of GITIC's bonds were of sufficient size to require registration in Beijing. The rest of its long-term loans were locally registered. Within Guangdong, GITIC accounted for a large share of the province's total long-term foreign exchange quota.

The fact that the loans were registered with SAFE did not mean that SAFE was required to monitor the quality of the investments undertaken by GITIC and other entities that borrowed long-term. Nor was SAFE required to consider the potential risk of fluctuations in international exchange rates that might cause repayment difficulties independently of the results of the investment in local currency terms.

Short-term loans did not require a case-by-case approval but needed to be registered with SAFE in order that the central government could monitor the country's overall level of indebtedness. Short-term loans were registered in a running account with the local branch of SAFE. SAFE approved an annual quota for the maximum permitted short-term loans in the running account at any point in time. As long as the quota was not exceeded, there was no problem. Since the loans were short-term, the account was constantly being renewed with fresh loans. Each entity that had a running account with SAFE for short-term loans needed to make a monthly report to check that they were within the quota.

JSM's advice was crucial to assessing the validity of various claims against GITIC from an international standpoint. Innumerable complex legal issues surrounded the process of validation of international loans to GITIC. The basic position of Chinese law, in fact, was clear. Essentially, all domestic Chinese enterprises needed to obtain approval from SAFE before entering into long-term 'international commercial loans' (Chang, 1998). International loans that had not been approved were void. This in turn meant that the contract could not be used to determine the rights and obligations of the respective parties. In order to circumvent the Chinese government's restrictions on foreign borrowing, a substantial fraction of GITIC's international borrowing was unregistered, perhaps as much as one-third (*SCMP*, 12 January 1999). One aspect of this was borrowing by GITIC's Hong Kong branches. Lenders had been advised that this did not require approval from SAFE.

However, following GITIC's bankruptcy, the legal advisors to the liquidation committee came to the conclusion that this debt also required to be approved under Chinese law. Moreover, international legal opinion strongly supported this view. One commented that the argument that Chinese procedures did not apply to branch lending outside China, 'defied the common sense interpretation of those rules and, in addition, legal theory relating to the nature of branches' (Chang, 1998). This indebtedness would be viewed as the debt of the headquarters in China, and this required approval by SAFE. Further complications were introduced by the fact that some of GITIC's debt-like obligations were cast in a different form, using modern lending techniques that were not contemplated when the relevant Chinese laws were originally drafted (Chang, 1998).

Under Hong Kong Law, if a contract was 'null and void,' then no repayment could be sought. However, in the mainland, even though a contract might be 'null and void,' repayment could be sought under the civil code on the basis that the debtor had been 'unjustly enriched' by the transaction. Under Chinese registration rules, responsibility for obtaining the requisite registration of the debt with SAFE unambiguously resided with the borrower, not the lender: 'GITIC, not its foreign lenders, had the obligation to register its debt. By failing to do so, GITIC harmed its lenders' (Chang, 1998). Under Chinese law, the debtor ought to repay to the creditor that which was 'unjustly obtained.' This meant, essentially, repaying the principal. Interest accruing on the loan was to be repaid only at the official rate. Any interest beyond this was regarded as 'unjust enrichment' and need not be repaid.

A major issue on which JSM was called upon to advise the liquidation committee was that of the legal status of different forms of loan guarantee. GITIC had 'sprinkled loan guarantees around like confetti' (*Economist Intelligence Unit*, 13 October 1998). Its guarantees were equivalent to five times its capital at the end of 1997. JSM advised the committee on over 300 different files on a case-by-case basis to determine the validity of different alleged guarantees. International bank loans invariably required a 'letter of comfort' from some mainland entity. According to the lenders these constituted a legal guarantee. However, none of the 'comfort letters' to foreign banks involved in the GITIC bankruptcy gave an unambiguous government guarantee to repay the lender in the event of default in repayment. They constituted different levels of 'moral support' from the mainland government entities, not binding obligations to step in and make repayments. In both mainland and Hong Kong law, the only valid guarantee is one that is unambiguous in relation to repayment in the event of default. Thus, instead of being repaid in full by the Chinese government entities, the foreign banks were forced to wait in line as a regular creditor in a 'normal' bankruptcy to the extent that their claims were judged to be legally valid.

We have seen that the international bankers were disappointed and, initially, angry that the 'letters of comfort' were deemed invalid. However, there was a widespread recognition that the bankruptcy process scrupulously observed Chinese law, despite its many areas of ambiguity and deficiency.

In this important sense, Chinese law made significant progress through the means of the GITIC bankruptcy. The decision to appoint high-quality international legal advice was crucial in guiding the liquidation committee through the tortuous legal issues involved.

Creditors' meetings

In addition to the claims against the parent, GITIC's bankrupt subsidiaries (Guangxin Enterprises, GITIC Shenzhen and Guangdong International Leasing Company) had claims against them totalling RMB 10.86 billion. Each of them held their first creditors' meetings in April 1999. The liquidation committee of Guangxin Enterprises reported that the firm had total debts of RMB 1.2 billion, but recoverable assets amounted to only RMB 125 million out of total assets of RMB 722 million. The liquidation committee of GITIC Shenzhen reported that it was likely to recover only RMB 58 million from RMB 224 million in outstanding loans. The liquidators of Guangdong International Leasing Company reported that its assets totalled RMB 1.6 billion, but only RMB 229 million was likely to be recoverable.

The first creditors' meeting of GITIC's bankruptcy was held on 22 April 1999. Some of the creditors had still hoped that the liquidation committee would announce a plan to restructure GITIC, so that it would continue in operation. However, at the meeting, the liquidation committee made it clear that GITIC would be taken through the full bankruptcy procedure in accordance with the draft bankruptcy law of the People's Republic of China. The meeting confirmed that China's bankruptcy code allows restructuring plans only when creditors force bankruptcy on the company, whereas GITIC itself had entered bankruptcy voluntarily. The liquidation committee made it clear that the creditors could hope only to obtain a small fraction of the amounts they were owed. In January 1999, when GITIC was declared bankrupt, the Guangdong government announced that GITIC's liabilities totalled RMB 36.17 billion against assets of RMB 21.47 billion, giving a rough repayment rate of sixty cents in the dollar. At the first creditors' meeting it was shown that GITIC in fact only had recoverable assets to the value of RMB 6.5 billion.

It was clear that the creditors were going to have to accept a far smaller repayment rate than they had hoped for at the start of the bankruptcy proceedings. They were deeply unhappy. At the meeting, Louis Choi, one of the auditors from KPMG, said: 'From our observation, management at the company was nearly out of control. They lent money to their subsidiaries, but no-one cared if the subsidiary acknowledged the debt and no-one knew if it really received the money' (quoted in *Financial Post*, Canada, 23 April 1999). Creditors were 'stunned' and 'shocked' by the revelations made at the meeting. One commented, 'We will be lucky to get back even ten cents on every dollar we are owed.'

The liquidation committee described the accounting books and records of GITIC as being 'in a state of disarray.' Although the broad outlines of GITIC's situation were revealed at the first meeting, important additional details were provided at subsequent meetings. Consequently, the work of the liquidation committee was relatively slow as is normal in a large, complex bankruptcy anywhere in the world. The bankruptcy process for GITIC took almost two years to complete. After the first creditors' meeting on 22 April 1999, a further two creditors' meetings were held, on 22 October 1999 and 31 October 2000 respectively. The third creditors' meeting agreed to the debt restructuring proposal made by the liquidation committee. It was announced that the first repayment of GITIC's debts to its creditors would be made. They would receive an initial payment of about US$ 170 million, equivalent to 3.39 per cent of GITIC's recognized debts, with the aim of eventually recovering 'as much as one-third' of those claims deemed valid by the liquidation committee.

Liabilities

The liquidation committee gave a preliminary statement of GITIC's balance sheet at the point of bankruptcy on 16 January 1999. Registered claims against GITIC that had not yet been verified totalled RMB 38.8 billion (US$ 4.7 billion), consisting of RMB 19.6 billion for unsecured creditors, RMB 15.8 billion in guarantees and RMB 3 billion for 'letters of comfort' (Table 2.1). The book value of liabilities to unsecured creditors totalled RMB 16.6 billion (US$ 2 billion). There was a total of 569 claims submitted by creditors, of which 287 were domestic and 282 overseas. However, the overseas claims were of much larger value, amounting to 82 per cent of the total value of claims against GITIC. By the time of the third creditors' meeting in October 2000, the estimated amount admitted for proof had changed substantially. However, the changes applied mostly to certain categories of claims.

There was little change in the amounts claimed by unsecured creditors and amounts admitted for proof, in respect to loans from financial institutions, long-term trust deposits, long-term loans, floating rate loans or bonds payable. The original registered number of claims against GITIC for these items in April 1999 at the first creditors' meeting stood at RMB 16.6 billion, and by the time of the third creditors' meeting it stood at RMB 16.3 billion, only slightly lower. The proofs for these items were mostly relatively straightforward. A large fraction of these claims (82 per cent) were from international financial institutions. As we have seen, the treatment of GITIC's registered and unregistered international debts involved immense legal complexities. Initially, the creditors had hoped that all debts registered with SAFE would be treated as China's sovereign debt, and, indeed, initial comments from Chinese officials also gave this impression. After prolonged legal disputes

Table 2.1 GITIC's liabilities as at 16 January 1999 (RMB million)

	First creditors' meeting, 22 April 1999		*Second creditors' meeting, 22 October 1999*		*Third creditors' meeting, 31 October 2000*	
	Book value	*Registered amount*[a]	*Book value*	*Estimated amount admitted for proof*	*Book value*	*Estimated amount admitted for proof*
Unsecured creditors						
Loans from financial institutions	3,043	3,496	3,044	3,483	3,043	3,515
Designated deposits	321	118	321	118	321	–
Payables	1,389	2,042	953	579	953	654
Intra-group accounts payable	981	559	122	119	122	114
Long-term trust deposits	1,805	1,779	1,805	1,725	1,805	1,716
Long-term loans	3,307	4,940	3,307	4,360	3,307	4,236
Floating rate notes	2,475	3,560	3,469	3,514	3,468	3,514
Bonds payable	2,898	3,062	2,898	3,065	2,898	3,065
Securities department						
Clients deposits	320	320	323	320	323	320
Payables	21	81	22	81	22	81
Sub-total	16,560	19,957	16,262	17,364	16,262	17,215
Guarantees	–	15,779	–	6,969	–	3,885
Letters of comfort	–	3,041	–	–	–	–
Total liabilities	16,560	38,777	16,262	24,333	16,262	21,100

a Amounts registered were based on claims submitted by creditors, which had not yet been verified.

and investigation, the liquidation committee decided that there was no legal basis for this procedure.

There were large changes in the amounts admitted for proof in relation to guarantees given by GITIC. These involved a total of forty-four international creditors with total guarantees of RMB 13.7 billion, and 105 domestic creditors, with guarantees of RMB 2 billion. Frequently, changes in claims relating to these items did not involve complex issues of proof. Some of these (RMB 5.9 billion) consisted of creditors who withdrew their proofs, because the debtor concerned, who had been guaranteed by GITIC, had repaid their principal and interest in full. Another important claim against GITIC as a guarantor was in respect to the Shenzhen-Guangzhou superhighway (RMB 4.8 billion). The Superhighway Company found a new guarantor to assume the guarantees given by GITIC. The amounts admitted as proofs in respect to guarantees fell from a registered amount of RMB 15.8 billion at the time of the first creditors' meeting to RMB 3.9 billion by the time of the third creditors' meeting.

However, major problems were encountered in processing the proofs for other categories of claims. Owing to the fact that GITIC 'failed to maintain a complete set of accounting records in relation to its loans and deposits' and the fact that 'the accounting ledgers do not serve as an effective hint on the tracing of further information,' the liquidation committee needed to spend far more time than it had hoped in verifying the validity of the proofs.

Moreover, the liquidation committee found that GITIC had 'committed acts of unlawful borrowing and unlawful taking of deposits,' such as 'borrowing at an interest rate in excess of that permitted by law,' 'borrowing or taking deposits from entities which did not possess the necessary legal capacity' and 'unlawfully extending the time for repayment of loans.' Such activities 'rendered the original contracts and agreements invalid.' As a result, a lot of complicated legal problems arose, increasing the difficulties of processing the proofs.

Two of the most complex issues that the liquidation committee had to deal with were the claims of individual depositors and claims against the securities department. Around 30,000 'natural persons' had deposited around RMB 800–900 million with GITIC. The individual depositors had made their deposits in GITIC on the assumption that the deposits were guaranteed by the government. Dealing properly with so many people across the province was extremely important for maintaining social order. In addition, there were around 50,000 clients who had deposits and accounts payable to the value of around RMB 400 million with GITIC's securities department. The 'laxity of management of the securities department' and 'the lack of formal and complete procedure for registration and verification of the information of these customers' greatly complicated the task of the liquidation committee in dealing with claims against the securities department, which continued as a going concern under Guangfa Securities. In the wake of the bankruptcy the small depositors were frightened that they would lose their deposits. There were numerous demonstrations across the province by small depositors concerned that they would not be repaid. As we have seen, in order to simplify the bankruptcy procedure and maintain social order, the Guangdong government provided around 780 million *renminbi* to BOC so that it could purchase debts from individual depositors, thereby becoming GITIC's largest single creditor.

Assets

In the months prior to the first creditors' meeting, KPMG undertook a preliminary analysis of the amounts recoverable by GITIC. The main sources of recoverable assets were loans and long-term investments in subsidiaries. These constituted over 93 per cent of the total amount of estimated recoverable assets (Table 2.2).

Table 2.2 GITIC's assets as at 16 January 1999 (RMB million)

	First creditors' meeting, 22 April 1999		*Third creditors' meeting, 31 October 2000*		*Amount recovered as at 31 Oct. 2000*
	Book value	*Estimated amount recoverable*	*Book value*	*Estimated amount recoverable*	*Amount recovered as at 31 Oct. 2000*
Unencumbered assets					
Cash and bank deposits of GITIC	150	35	35	35	35
Deposits from securities dept. with banks, stock exchanges and settlement centres	–	–	188	–	–
Loans	11,307	3,976	12,029	3,868	443
Long-term investments in subsidiaries	6,875	2,134	7,314	2,981	230
Other long-term Investments	622	246	622	324	122
Other receivables	2,261	100	668	43	17
Fixed assets	27	3	27	3	1
Other assets	56	20	59	8	–
Sub-total	21,298	6,514	20,942	7,262	848
Less					
Preferential creditors:					
Staff salaries	2.4	2.4	2.4	–	–
Tax payable	3	3	3	3	–
Total	21,293	6,509	20,937	7,259	848

Loans

The book value of loans made by GITIC amounted to RMB 11.3 billion (US$ 1.36 billion). GITIC's records showed that it had outstanding loans to a total of 268 debtors. KPMG made a preliminary investigation of the recovery possibilities in order to provide information for the first creditors' meeting. It analysed the background of the debtors and the status of guarantees and securities provided for the debts. It examined the previous repayment record of the debtors, the status of the debtors' businesses and operations, the status of their assets and liabilities, and the availability of sufficient materials to prove their claims. It concluded that only RMB 4 billion of the loans was recoverable. This amounted to just 35 per cent of the total amount of loans made by GITIC (Table 2.3). By the time of the third creditors' meeting in October 2000, the book value had increased slightly to

RMB 12.13 billion. However, the estimate of the amount recoverable from its loans had fallen slightly to RMB 3.87 billion, amounting to just 32 per cent of GITIC's total loans.

The liquidation committee concluded that GITIC 'lacked an overall control of the granting of loans.' Records relating to payments and receipts were 'very disorganized.' GITIC had 'failed to conduct diligent investigation and evaluation of the background of debtors during the process of approving the loans.' GITIC had 'no system to monitor the repayment of loans and to pursue recovery of the amount outstanding.' Some debtors had 'not made any repayment of loans for a long period of time,' and GITIC 'failed to keep a comprehensive record of such loans.' The liquidation committee needed to 'search for the related source documents from accounting records for the past ten years or more.' The liquidation committee found that due to GITIC's failure either to commence recovery actions or to preserve the records of demands made against the debtors, at least thirty-five loans, with an aggregate book value of RMB 758 million (around US$ 91 million), had prior to the bankruptcy become time-barred. The creditors were informed that 'when a debtor failed to repay the amount outstanding, GITIC's usual practice was either to extend the term of the loan or capitalize the long overdue interest.'

The liquidation committee concluded that a mere 13 per cent of GITIC's total loan portfolio was 'normal.' Almost one-quarter of its loans had been made to firms that had ceased operation. One-half of the loan portfolio was made to firms that were 'in difficulty.'

As of 16 January 1999, almost nine-tenths of GITIC's total loans were overdue. Among GITIC's total portfolio of loans, only 12 per cent were not overdue. Eight per cent were overdue by one year or less, and could therefore possibly be attributed to the Asian Financial Crisis. Twenty per cent were overdue by one to three years, and 12 per cent by three to five years. No less than 47 per cent were overdue by more than five years, of which less than

Table 2.3 GITIC loans analysed according to the debtors' operations as at 16 January 1999 (RMB million)

	Normal	*In difficulty*	*Ceased operation*	*In liquidation*	*In litigation*	*Disputed*	*Total*	*%*
Manufacturing	687	3,410	1,966	49	684	86	6,882	61
Hotels/tourism	–	668	393	–	265	–	1,326	11
Trust investments	–	724	–	–	–	–	724	7
Utilities	354	254	–	–	–	–	608	5
Trading	–	175	57	53	4	159	448	4
Real estate	270	59	–	–	47	–	376	3
Finance	74	5	7	–	–	–	86	1
Others	32	393	296	–	33	101	855	8
Total	1,417	5,688	2,719	102	1,033	346	11,305	100

one-fifth were thought to be recoverable. In other words, the vast majority of the overdue loans could not be attributed to the AFC.

Over three-fifths of GITIC's loans were to the manufacturing sector. Of these, less than 10 per cent were 'normal.' One-half were 'in difficulties,' and almost two-fifths had ceased operation, were in liquidation, in litigation or disputed. In the hotels and tourism sector, there were no 'normal' business operations at all. Fifty-five per cent of loans to the hotels and tourism sector were to businesses that had either ceased operation or were in litigation, and the remainder were all 'in difficulties.' A mere 16 per cent of GITIC's loans had valid security. Three-fifths were unsecured, and the remainder had either invalid or doubtful security.

This was a remarkable record of bad lending. Although the growth rate had slowed somewhat compared with the boom years of the early 1990s, Guangdong's real GDP was still growing at over 10 per cent per annum in the years 1996–8 inclusive, and secondary industry was growing at over 12 per cent per annum in these years (SSBG, GTN, 2000: 82). Guangdong escaped the drastic downturn in economic activity of much of East Asia in 1997–9. To have undertaken so much bad lending in such a high-growth economy was remarkable. What is at least as remarkable is that international financial institutions rushed headlong to lend to GITIC and to buy its bonds.

Long-term investment in subsidiaries

GITIC's business structure prior to the bankruptcy was opaque. GITIC was known to have long-term investments in over one hundred wholly owned and joint ventures. However, apart from the ten main wholly owned subsidiaries and a handful of partially owned companies (Merrill Lynch *et al.*, 1996: 31) little was known about the full dimensions of GITIC's equity investments. The liquidation committee revealed that GITIC had thirty wholly owned, directly held subsidiaries. These in their turn had thirty-three subsidiaries, of which twenty-six were wholly owned, and seven had holdings of between 50 and 80 per cent. In addition, GITIC had fourteen other major long-term equity investments. The liquidation committee revealed that GITIC's subsidiaries in turn had ten wholly owned overseas subsidiaries, and a further ten companies in which they held substantial equity shares.

The liquidation committee concluded that the management of GITIC and its group companies and the inter-relationship between the group companies were 'confusing.' The business operation 'seriously contravened the laws and regulations.' The allocation, re-allocation or transfer of investment projects between the group companies 'almost invariably failed to comply with the legal formalities,' so that 'there was a lack of legal documentation in support of these transactions.' Consequently, there 'often existed inconsistencies among the legal documentation, the information on record, the true intent of the management, the actual operation of the business and the sharing of risks and returns.' Unsurprisingly under these conditions, there was a protracted legal argument about the ownership of entities in which GITIC had invested. Sometimes, these were complicated by the fact that GITIC subsidiaries had in turn established joint ventures with loans from GITIC itself.

The book value of GITIC's long-term equity investments at the point of bankruptcy totalled RMB 6,875 million (equivalent to US$ 828 million). Of this amount the liquidation committee estimated that RMB 2,134 million was recoverable, amounting to just 31 per cent of the total amounted invested.

Forty-four per cent of GITIC's long-term equity investments were in businesses that had gone into liquidation and 40 per cent were in businesses that were 'in difficulties.' It was estimated that less than one-third of the investments in firms 'in difficulties' was recoverable. Among these businesses, the recovery rates from the real estate sector were especially low, estimated at less than one-fifth. For those businesses 'in liquidation' the estimated recovery rate was a mere 10 per cent. Just 13 per cent of GITIC's investments were in 'normal' businesses. This was a remarkable record of poor investment, given that the bulk of the investment was in businesses located in one of the world's fastest-growing economies.

A large fraction of the invested businesses that were in liquidation were in the real estate sector. The real estate sector in Guangdong encountered serious problems in the late 1990s. GITIC had thirty invested companies in this sector, most of which had gone into liquidation. The liquidation committee concluded that the accounting records of the real estate companies were 'disorganized' and could 'not be taken to have fully and accurately reflected the financial position of these companies.' The liquidation committee found that in many cases, GITIC's real estate companies had not obtained certificates of land use rights or property ownership for real estate under construction. It found that in many cases, properties had been completed and delivered to the purchasers, but the procedure of obtaining ownership certificates had not been completed. This presented a legal obstacle to recovering investments made by GITIC and involved a great deal of litigation to obtain even partial recovery of the investments. By the time of the second creditors' meeting, the liquidation committee had concluded that for GITIC's non-bankrupt real estate subsidiaries, the capital investment and receivables totalled RMB 1.6 billion, of which only RMB 597 million was recoverable, only 36 per cent of the total amount. By far the most important was Guangdong Trust and Real Estate Development Corporation, with capital investment and receivables from GITIC totalling RMB 1.22 billion. At the time of the second creditors' meeting, the liquidation committee estimated that only RMB 475 million (39 per cent) was recoverable.

The recovery rate was highest in the hotels and rented property sector. By the time of the second creditors' meeting, it was estimated that 100 per cent of the RMB 1.6 billion in capital investment and receivables was recoverable from this sector, with the possibility of several of the investments being sold as going concerns. However, even here the liquidation committee found major problems. There were difficulties of low occupancy rates due to the downturn in tourism as well as 'intense competition' due to over-investment in hotels in Guangdong during the boom years. GITIC's main hotels had occupancy rates of around 55–60 per cent at the time of the bankruptcy. However, much more serious was the uncertainty over titles to the buildings. GITIC invested heavily in massive hotels which were held jointly in the names of three of GITIC's direct subsidiaries. This complex arrangement resulted in complicated uncertainties over title to the properties. It was anticipated that protracted legal disputes would be necessary to resolve these.

GITIC's capital investment and receivables for other long-term investments totalled RMB 637 million, of which the liquidation committee estimated only RMB 138 million (21 per cent) was recoverable by the time of the second creditors' meeting. The most important of these investments was the Yun Fu Cement Plant, in which GITIC invested RMB 554 million (US$ 67 million). Almost RMB 530 million of this amount consisted of 'accounts receivable' from Yun Fu. It ceased operation, with 'little residual assets' and 'huge liabilities.' A mere RMB 130 million (24 per cent) was estimated to be recoverable. The liquidation committee found that Yun Fu's accounting records were 'disorganized' and that there existed a 'huge discrepancy between the balance of accounts receivable as recorded by Yun Fu Cement and GITIC's records.'

As we have seen, three of GITIC's subsidiaries were declared bankrupt separately from GITIC on 16 January 1999. These were GITIC Shenzhen, Guangdong International Leasing Company and Guangxin Enterprises. The liquidation committee found these companies to be 'seriously insolvent' and envisaged that the chances of recovering the invested capital were 'extremely slim.' In addition, they found that funds invested by GITIC and recorded in the current accounts of these subsidiaries were unsecured. GITIC's capital investment and recoverables from GITIC Shenzhen, totalled RMB 928 million, of which the liquidation committee estimated (for the second creditors' meeting) just RMB 158 million (17 per cent) to be recoverable. GITIC's capital investment and recoverables from Guangdong International Leasing Company totalled RMB 745 million, of which just RMB 96 million (13 per cent) was estimated to be recoverable. GITIC's capital investment and recoverables for Guangxin Enterprises totalled RMB 730 million, of which just RMB 128 million (18 per cent) was estimated to be recoverable.

Of the almost US$ 90 million invested in its overseas subsidiaries, a mere 7 per cent was estimated to be recoverable. Almost nine-tenths of GITIC's total investments in its overseas subsidiaries had been allocated to businesses that went into liquidation. In other words, around US$ 80 million of overseas investment from GITIC's headquarters had simply disappeared.

Long-term investment other than in subsidiaries

The recovery rate for GITIC's long-term investment in businesses other than its subsidiaries was estimated to be 39 per cent, a marginally higher estimated recovery rate than that for its subsidiaries. Seventy per cent of the value of these investments was in businesses that were 'in difficulties,' for which the estimated recovery rate was only 28 per cent. Estimated recovery rates were less than 30 per cent for all the main categories of investment in unlisted companies. The liquidation committee hoped to be able to obtain funds by making use of the property of debtors to GITIC. The prospects were uncertain. In several cases, involving investments of hundreds of millions of RMB in each case, GITIC's legal title to the property was unclear. This included assets such as a 1,000-acre plot of land, in which GITIC had invested RMB 350 million (US$ 42 million), for which the legal title appeared not to have been transferred to GITIC. A mere one per cent of the long-term investments in property other than in subsidiaries (totalling over RMB 1.2 billion) was thought to be recoverable.

Summary

By the time of the third creditors' meeting, on 31 October 2000, the book value of GITIC's unencumbered assets was calculated to be RMB 20.9 billion (around US$ 2.5 billion). The estimated recoverable amount was calculated to be RMB 7.3 billion, 35 per cent of the book value of unencumbered assets (Table 2.2). Wang Qishan had urged government departments to do what they could to get debtors under their control to pay back their debts to GITIC: 'Those who refuse to pay will be seriously punished by law' (quoted in *AFX*, Asia, 27 May 2000). However, by the time of the third creditors' meeting, only RMB 848 million had in fact been recovered.

At the third creditors' meeting, the liquidation committee recommended making a first distribution to creditors. The total amount to be distributed was RMB 713 million, with each creditor receiving 3.38 per cent of the amount of its proof. When announcing that the creditors were likely to receive a 3 per cent distribution in November 2000, Louis Choi, of KPMG, commented that 'it could be years' before GITIC's creditors received the next tranche of repayments (quoted in *FT*, 9 August 2000).

The international creditors were 'exasperated.' The liquidation committee estimated that GITIC's recoverable assets would amount to RMB 7.3 billion, representing just 37 per cent of GITIC's recognized debts and 20 per cent of the amount originally claimed by GITIC's creditors. By the time of the third creditors' meeting most of GITIC's foreign creditors had written off their exposure to GITIC. This is hardly surprising, considering they had 'waited more than two years for less than 2 per cent of what they were originally owed' (*SCMP*, 1 November 2000).

In February 2002, the liquidators raised RMB 350 million (around US$ 40 million) from the sale of GITIC's 75 per cent stake in the 63-storey Jiang

Wan New City complex in central Guangzhou. The liquidation committee had placed a value of RMB 870 million on the complex, but there were attached bank debts estimated at around RMB 400 million. The sale of this asset left only one other substantial asset left to sell, namely the Guangdong International Building. By early 2002, three years after GITIC had been declared bankrupt, and with almost all its assets now disposed of, the creditors had received back only around RMB 900 million, or around US$ 100 million (*SCMP*, 1 February 2002), equivalent to just 4.3 per cent of the amount eventually 'admitted for proof' and 2.1 per cent of the amount originally claimed by creditors. This was, indeed, a severe 'haircut' for the creditors.

The Chinese government and the international creditors

The way in which the Chinese government dealt with the GITIC case had wide repercussions on the attitude and bargaining strength of the international banks. The immediate effect of forcing the international banks to be responsible for their own lending decisions was a loud outcry: 'The banks squealed betrayal. They argued that they had a gentleman's agreement with the government. In return for suspending their better judgement and lending to non-transparent trusts, their loans would be backed by the government' (*SCMP*, 15 August 2000). Credit lines to mainland firms 'dried up almost overnight.' In 1999, foreign lending into Guangdong province fell 51 per cent to US$ 1 billion, most of which was lent to the Chinese operations of multinationals. This in turn exacerbated the cash flow problems of the ITICs.

However, the effect was more complicated. By forcing GITIC into bankruptcy, where its dismemberment was governed by the 1986 Bankruptcy Law, the government 'absolved itself of responsibility for the company's 39 billion *renminbi* debt' (*SCMP*, 15 August 2000). Foreign creditors had little say in GITIC's liquidation process. The decision-making power rested with the liquidation committee: 'The move set an intimidating precedent, considering the limited recourse available to foreign creditors under this law' and 'the last thing foreign banks wanted to see was other troubled trusts in court' (*SCMP*, 15 August 2000). International banks were reluctant to push a succession of ITICs into bankruptcy, since the GITIC case showed how prolonged, complicated and unrewarding such a process would be for them. Consequently, they were forced to moderate their claims against the ITICs as a group and accept substantial 'haircuts' from one ITIC after another. They did not dare to force them into bankruptcy. This, in turn, greatly reduced the magnitude of the insolvency problem that the Chinese government had to deal with.

At least as important, it forced the international creditors to adopt a more conciliatory approach towards the GDE restructuring. After the GITIC bankruptcy, the threat was always in the back of the creditors' minds: 'Do we want to go through another long, complicated bankruptcy and suffer an even bigger "haircut" than we might gain through agreeing to debt restructuring?'

One financial journalist asked: 'Who played their hand better in the wake of GITIC's bankruptcy, the government or foreign banks? The answer has to be the government' (*SCMP*, 15 August 2000). In fact, the journalist suggested that the Chinese government had even more to fear from a wave of ITIC bankruptcies, due to the effects this might have had on the commercial banking sector: 'But foreign banks did not call Beijing's bluff, and as each day passed the government's position grew stronger' (*SCMP*, 15 August 2000). At the time of GITIC's bankruptcy, China was still under the influence of the Asian Financial Crisis, but the picture had sharply changed by the middle of 2000. By then the government was in a much better position to bargain with creditors.

What kind of firm was GITIC?

China's 'trust and investment companies' were a creative response to the challenges facing China's policy-makers as they wrestled with the complex issues involved in reforming the planned economy. GITIC was at the forefront of this process, located in the front line of China's deepening integration with the global economy, which was itself undergoing tremendous change.

A 'window' company for Guangdong province?

In the earlier stages of reform, China was emerging from long years of isolation from the international economy. At this stage GITIC performed some important functions in linking the local economy with the outside world, including activities such as leasing equipment and acting as an international trading company.

GITIC's domestic leasing business was conducted through its wholly owned subsidiary, Guangdong International Leasing Corporation (GILC), incorporated in 1983, which invested US$ 250 million in acquiring imported equipment for lease. The equipment was supplied to over 200 enterprises in a wide variety of industrial sectors in Guangdong. In 1988, the Guangdong government approved the establishment of GITIC's wholly owned subsidiary, Guangxin International Trading Corporation (GITC). Rights to engage in foreign trade were only gradually reformed in the 1980s and early 1990s, so GITIC had considerable advantages due to its allocation of foreign trade rights. Import and export trading accounted for 36 per cent of GITIC's operating income in 1988. As the economy liberalized in the 1990s, the relative importance of these 'window' functions began to atrophy. By 1995, 'trade,' including both domestic and foreign, accounted for only 8 per cent of GITIC's total operating income. However, GITIC continued to enjoy some special advantages in conducting foreign trade. For example, as a licensed non-bank financial institution, it was able to open its own letters of credit, which was able 'to simplify the import process for many of its customers' (Merrill Lynch *et al.*, 1996: 27).

A development bank for Guangdong province?

At first sight GITIC appeared to be a *de facto* local development bank working closely with the Guangdong government to serve the province's development interests. GITIC's investment policy was guided by the provincial government's development objectives. In many countries, both developed and developing, financial institutions supported by the local government have played an important role in supporting local economic development. Unlike a commercial bank, GITIC had limited rights to take deposits, other than those held on trust. Certain of GITIC's deposits were funds deposited by business enterprises and the public at interest rates fixed by the PBOC. However, revenues derived from these deposits were an insignificant source of income. GITIC obtained relatively small amounts of capital from the Guangdong government and also generated income from its own operations, which the Guangdong government permitted it to retain. GITIC's operating income in the mid-1990s was only around US$ 300 million, with pre-tax profits of around US$ 25 million. In 1995, 49 per cent of GITIC's operating income was from interest on loans.

Borrowing was the main source of GITIC's funds. It borrowed heavily from both domestic and international commercial banks, as well as from export credit agencies. GITIC was authorized to issue bonds and notes in both the domestic and the international market. From 1986 to 1996, GITIC issued seven international bonds. It issued a total of US$ 390 million (equivalent) in Japanese *yen*-denominated bonds, and US$ 550 million in US dollar-denominated bonds. At the end of 1995, the official figure for GITIC's borrowings totalled US$ 1,168 million, of which US$ 844 million was from foreign financial institutions.

Loans and guarantees

GITIC was the channel for mobilizing a large volume of capital from international markets to support the development of Guangdong province. GITIC's total loans and guarantees grew from less than RMB 6 billion in 1988 to RMB 36 billion (US$ 4.3 billion) in 1995. The bulk of these were in foreign currency. Between 1985 and 1995 GITIC provided loans and guarantees for over 300 major projects in Guangdong province. GITIC's principal loans at the end of 1995 included US$ 353 million to the Shantou New Era Photo Material Company for the purchase of a colour film production line from Fuji (Japan). This accounted for around one-quarter of GITIC's total loans outstanding in 1995. Other important loans included US$ 112.5 million for the construction of GITIC Plaza, GITIC's own headquarters, including a five-star hotel and residential facilities, US$ 63.7 million for the construction of Riverside New City, a building with a four-star hotel, residential and office facilities and US$ 43.9 million to the Yun Fu Cement Company for the purchase of a 680,000-ton cement plant.[7] At the end of 1995, the ten largest guarantees accounted for 87 per cent of the total value of GITIC's total guarantees. They included US$ 1,166 million for the Shajiao (Plant C) Power Development Corporation, for the construction of a 3 x 660 MW power plant and acquisition of power generation equipment and US$ 800 million for Hopewell China Development (Super Highway) Limited, for the construction of the Guangzhou-Shenzhen-Zhuhai super highway.[8]

As can be seen from the above, GITIC's main orientation in the allocation of its loans and guarantees was towards sectors with potentially large positive externalities, which often were 'lumpy,' with long gestation lags. In other words, the principal function of GITIC's loans and guarantees was to facilitate the economic development of Guangdong province. In this sense GITIC was acting as a traditional state or regional development bank. Over US$ 1.2 billion of GITIC's loans and guarantees were for the urgently needed development of Guangdong's electric power sector, to meet the pressing electricity needs of the province's booming economy. GITIC was able to provide substantial support for key manufacturing projects, such as the Shantou New Era Photo Materials Company, the Yun Fu Cement Company and the Maoming Acrylic Fibre Company. GITIC's loans and guarantees to the real estate sector were quite large absolutely (US$ 518 million in 1995), but they constituted only around 12 per cent of its total portfolio in the mid-1990s. By this time GITIC's total loans and guarantees had reached US$ 4.3 billion, which represented a large contribution to the province's economic development.

Equities

It is a common practice across the world for local state-owned development banks to take equity shares in local businesses. Naturally, the investor hopes that these businesses eventually will be profitable and yield dividends. However, the whole point of a development bank is that the investment would be unlikely to have been made by the private sector. Hence, the time horizon over which to expect a return from the investment may often be longer than would be the case if the investment was financed purely from the private sector, or the positive externalities may be thought to justify the investment.

In 1981, GITIC began investing in equity shares in domestic enterprises. The investments were handled by three subsidiaries: Guangxin Industrial Development Corporation, Guangxin (Huiyang) Enterprises Corporation and GITIC Shenzhen Corporation. By the mid-1990s, GITIC had made equity investments in more than 200 projects, including over one hundred infrastructure projects, some of which were key state and provincial projects (Merrill Lynch *et al.*, 1996: 24). It invested in over thirty hotel developments, including some of its own projects, such as Guangdong International Hotel and the Furama Hotel in Dalian. The portfolio included minority shares in a wide array of industrial activities.[9] GITIC was the 100 per cent owner of

Yun Fu Cement Plant and Shenzhen Biological Engineering Company. At the end of 1995, the book value of GITIC's equity portfolio stood at US$ 180 million. But in 1995, the income of GITIC's equity investments was reported to be just US$ 6.3 million.

GITIC formed a number of business relationships with foreign companies, including equity investments and joint ventures, both inside and outside China. These included the establishment of an equity joint venture with McDonald's Corporation in 1992. Under this agreement GITIC operated, on a non-exclusive basis, fast-food outlets for McDonald's in Guangdong, with twenty-one outlets operational by the end of 1995.

Universal financial services company?

Although GITIC did carry out traditional trust business, in keeping with its name (i.e. the Guangdong International Trust and Investment Corporation), taking deposits from both domestic and foreign entities and individuals, and loaning the deposits to third-party borrowers, its trust business never provided more than 3 per cent of its revenue. In the 1990s, like almost all other SOEs, GITIC was allowed increasing autonomy to retain profits and develop an independent business strategy. By the mid-1990s, GITIC had developed into a multi-sectoral financial services company. It made loans and undertook large-scale financial guarantees. It was an underwriter and a securities broker. It was a commodities trader, including futures markets. It had ambitions to enter the insurance industry.

Its investment banking services were conducted through two units: the Securities and Finance Department and GITIC Shenzhen (SZ). GITIC was one of the first institutions to act as a securities broker in Guangdong province. GITIC became a non-local member of the Shenzhen and Shanghai stock exchanges in 1992 and 1993 respectively, entitling it to broker A and B shares in each of them. GITIC (SZ) was one of the founders of the Shenzhen stock exchange. By 1995 GITIC was the third and fifth largest brokerage in Guangzhou and Shenzhen respectively. GITIC sponsored listings of A and B shares on both the Shenzhen and Shanghai stock exchanges. After 1993 GITIC assisted several Guangdong-based SOEs to convert into joint stock companies, of which eight listed on the Chinese stock markets. For each of these listings, GITIC was the underwriter. GITIC was the first entity in Guangdong to issue domestic bonds. GITIC fund management activities began in 1986 with a joint venture in Hong Kong. In 1992 it became a partner in a Shenzhen-based fund management company. In 1993 its own subsidiary, Guangxin Fund, was listed on the Guangzhou stock exchange. By 1995 investment banking accounted for 14.5 per cent of GITIC's pre-tax profits. GITIC was a full member of the commodity exchanges in Guangdong, Beijing, Shanghai, Zhengzhou and Suzhou. It set up trading units in Wuhan, Zhengzhou and Taizhou, trading over one hundred commodities. In 1994 GITIC entered the commodities futures trading business.

Prior to its bankruptcy, GITIC was in discussion with international insurance companies to establish joint venture companies to offer life insurance services in Guangdong. In addition, it signed a memorandum of understanding with 'each of a European and American insurance company' to form a Sino-foreign joint venture to offer life insurance services in Guangdong, subject to approval of the PBOC. Naturally, the hope was that as a state-owned entity owned by the Guangdong government, GITIC would receive such approval.

By 1995, none of GITIC's diversifications into financial services other than loans and guarantees had developed into a large-scale business. However, GITIC assumed the character of a universal financial services company. By developing its financial services skills in securities broking, underwriting, bond issuance, fund management, futures trading and life insurance, GITIC was trying to construct a professional, integrated business with strong 'economics of scope' between different activities in the sector. Although the initial development was supported by GITIC's privileged relationship with the Guangdong government, the objective was to construct a financial services business that could be a competitive firm in the sector earning secure long-term profits.

Real estate development company?

One of GITIC's 'development' functions was building 'infrastructure.' This could, in principle, include land development for various purposes to meet the province's wider 'development' needs. From early in its life, GITIC was involved in real estate development. However, as the property boom got under way, GITIC used its increased autonomy to rapidly expand its activities in the property sector.

Up until the early 1990s, GITIC's real estate business was conducted through a single wholly owned subsidiary, Guangdong Trust and Real Estate Development Corporation (GTRED). Subsequently, it established a further six real estate development companies. GTRED remained the largest of these. GITIC provided a full range of real estate services, including design, construction, material supply and decoration, as well as sales, lease, property registration and management. By the mid-1990s, GTRED had grown into the largest real estate developer in southern China. It had offices in Guangzhou, Shenzhen, Zhuhai, Shantou and Huizhou, and joint ventures in Guangzhou, Zhuhai, Hong Kong, Thailand and Macao. Almost 100 per cent of GITIC's real estate developments were in Guangdong, and 79 per cent were in Guangzhou, which was the centre of the Guangdong property boom in the early 1990s.

By 1995, GITIC had completed more than 200 real estate projects, with a total floor area of over ten million square metres. The projects included hotels, commercial buildings, residential districts and residential buildings. GITIC's real estate projects were mainly funded through bank loans or pre-sale agreements. It constructed over five million square metres of commercial development and ten urban residential districts. It invested in and financed the construction of over thirty hotels. Several of GITIC's hundreds of real estate developments involved an investment the equivalent of tens of millions of US dollars. Guangxin Riverside City Hotel and GITIC Plaza, both in Guangzhou, and the Furama Hotel in Dalian, each involved an investment the equivalent of almost US$ 100 million. Many developments involved individual investments of several tens of millions of US dollars.

By 1995, GITIC had a 'land bank' of over ten million square metres, including over eight million in Guangzhou itself. A large proportion of this was acquired in the 1980s 'at relatively low cost.' In addition, in 1993, the Guangdong government designated certain areas of land for sale at 'discounted prices' to developers of affordable housing in Guangdong. GITIC was in a strong position to acquire additions to its land bank through this channel. Such developments were subject to controls on profit margins exercised by the Guangdong Provincial Construction Committee. After the luxury property market collapsed in Guangdong in the mid-1990s, GITIC turned increasingly to the construction of affordable mid-rise residential real estate developments for sale to home owners. GITIC's main objective in real estate was to develop buildings for immediate sale. However, it kept certain key projects as income properties. GITIC's real estate management income in 1995 totalled US$ 109 million.

The attractions of involvement in the real estate sector enormously increased in the 1990s. In the economic boom in Guangdong in the mid-1990s, real estate demand soared, with high rates of property price inflation. The sector offered high returns during the upswing in the property price 'bubble' until the mid-1990s.

In addition, the 1990s saw a widespread process of *de facto* (and, often, *de jure*) privatization of land in Guangdong's fast-growing areas, especially the Pearl River Delta. Former farmland was turned over to commercial and residential property on a massive scale. The land had formerly been owned by local communities or by the local government. Local authorities had the right also to decide on re-zoning of land from one purpose to another. In suburban areas, this was mainly farmland, and in built-up areas it included large swathes of formerly low-rise residential public housing, low-rise factories, shops and administrative buildings. There were huge opportunities for profiting from the combined process of high-speed development and privatization.

GITIC was a state-owned large enterprise with an intimate relationship with the provincial government. Its senior management team was drawn almost exclusively from this group of people. Due to this background, it had privileged access to land allocation for property development enabling it to make exceptionally large profits in this sector during this period. It was at the centre of the process of land privatization and re-allocation to new purposes to meet the needs of the booming economy. This structure provided a huge temptation to speculate in the land and property market with other people's money. It also provided a large opportunity to use 'insider theft' to benefit from GITIC's intimate relationship with the provincial government. This could be done through obtaining land relatively cheaply, and benefitting from insider knowledge and influence to achieve re-designation of land for different, more profitable, purposes. Many complex issues relating to GITIC's property investments arose during the bankruptcy proceedings. Typically, property rights were ambiguous. Property acquisitions and development took place through a complex network of GITIC's subsidiary and related companies.

Business behaviour

Absence of focus

GITIC developed in a haphazard fashion with little conception of its 'core business,' seizing opportunities as they arose. Through its privileged relationship with the Guangdong government it was able to raise capital easily on international markets, as long as international lenders were confident that the provincial government would treat GITIC's international debts as if they were China's sovereign debt. The same privileged relationship enabled GITIC opportunistically to enter numerous business fields that had little obvious relationship with each other, but which offered the possibility for high returns. By the time of the bankruptcy it had become a sprawling structure involving a wide array of business activities.

Mismanagement

Investigations conducted at GITIC shortly before the company was closed in October 1998 revealed a textbook picture of corporate mismanagement. There was a proliferation of subsidiary companies, each of which had a high degree of operational autonomy. The strong incentive for proliferation of subsidiaries is indicated by the duplication of subsidiaries, each engaged in the same line of business. Each of them could use the name of GITIC as a means to raise capital and to obtain access to potentially profitable investments, and they formed a network of mutual investments and guarantees. The company failed to establish a centrally controlled system of financial control which is the key to effective management of a modern large corporation. Projects were undertaken and investments made without any form of professional appraisal from higher levels. Profits were retained routinely by subsidiaries. GITIC failed to establish a corporate culture or provide a clear vision of the company's strategy. There was no conception of where GITIC's core business capabilities lay, or how the company could enhance those capabilities.

The Liquidation Committee report cited negligent business practices as 'a primary cause of the firm's failure.' The investigation showed that the senior management of GITIC was 'ignorant of its own situation.' Key data on debts and assets 'didn't make sense.' Data presented to the investigation were 'continually changing.' During the bankruptcy process, it became clear that over 90 per cent of GITIC's investments were bad debts. The investigation 'couldn't find the companies to whom loans had been made and in which investments had been undertaken,' but GITIC still kept the items in the accounts as 'assets.' It is easy to attribute GITIC's failure to management incompetence. However, there were other factors at work, including, as we shall see, criminal behaviour.

Distorted accounts

The category 'non-performing assets' is a perennial problem in the accounts of firms in developing countries. It had even become a central issue in the evaluation of the crisis that faced the Japanese financial system after 1990. One Asian banking expert commented, 'The non-performing assets classifications can be stretched to accommodate the most appalling situations' (Delhaise, 1998: 115). The report by KPMG revealed a huge discrepancy between the company's assets and its debts. A large portion of the company's loans and investments were non-recoverable. GITIC's accounts routinely inflated the firm's earnings and profits by, for example, including long-overdue debt repayments in 'accounts receivable' rather than as bad debts that should be deducted from reported profits.

Government monitoring

The central government and GITIC

The central and local governments in Guangdong constantly interacted during the crisis. The appointment by the central government of Wang Qishan to the position of Guangdong's Executive Vice-Governor reflected the gravity of the situation in the eyes of the central government. Guangdong's policies towards the crisis at GITIC and GDE were shaped through constant central and local government interaction over an issue that had enormous implications for China's internal reform process and for its relations with the outside world. GITIC became an issue of great importance for China's most senior political leaders. It was a crucial issue for Premier Zhu Rongji in his campaign to clean up China's financial system, which was necessary in order that China could survive its increasing integration with the global financial system. The GITIC case was important also in terms of the wider course of political developments. The ability to obtain support from powerful provinces such as Guangdong has always been a key ingredient in the battle for power in the centre of Chinese politics. The way in which the central authorities dealt with Guangdong's flagship company directly affected the relationship of Guangdong with the centre. The course of events was watched closely by other provinces, which were also trying to increase their autonomy during the evolving reform process.

Like other ITICs, GITIC was under the supervision of the PBOC. The PBOC in Beijing detected violations of its rules from quite early in GITIC's existence. It sent work teams repeatedly to Guangdong to try to put things right. A large part of the management team was replaced in 1993, following a PBOC investigation. In 1997, the central government warned GITIC that it would remove its foreign exchange quota entirely if it didn't change its leadership. It said that GITIC had become a 'borrowing machine,' not a real company. In June 1997 a new General Manager, Mai Zong, and a new Deputy General Manager, Zhu Yong, were finally appointed. The question that must be asked is: why, despite in-depth knowledge of the failings in GITIC's business behaviour, was the PBOC unable, as regulator of the industry, to intervene effectively until GITIC finally became insolvent?

The Guangdong government and GITIC

The closeness of GITIC's relationship with the Guangdong government was explicit: 'GITIC is a non-bank financial institution, wholly owned and directly controlled by the Guangdong government' (Merrill Lynch *et al.*, 1996: 13). Its articles of association stated that it was 'owned by the Guangdong government on behalf of the people.' It was established 'to promote the development of the Guangdong economy.' Its annual and long-term plans were made 'in accordance with the state economic development plans adopted by the National People's Congress and the provincial development plans of the Guangdong government.' GITIC's plans were subject to approval by the Guangdong Provincial Planning Commission. Major investments and loans made by GITIC were included in the Guangdong provincial economic development plan. The primary functions of GITIC, as set forth in its articles of association, were:

> To raise and utilize domestic and foreign funds, to engage in international and domestic financial activities, to provide loans and make investments in and outside China for the purpose of assisting the modernization of Guangdong province and to import advanced technology, equipment and management expertise.
>
> (Merrill Lynch *et al.*, 1996: 13)

GITIC was given special rights and status within Guangdong. GITIC sat at the centre of economic decision-making in Guangdong. The President and Executive Vice-President of GITIC participated in major meetings concerning the province's economic development and investment plans. GITIC assisted the Guangdong government in undertaking feasibility studies, market surveys and financial projections. Due to its ownership by the Guangdong government and its close involvement in the planning process, GITIC often had 'first priority in selecting and undertaking many projects as a lender or an investor' (Merrill Lynch *et al.*, 1996: 13). GITIC was also 'consulted with respect to the debt financing plans of the Guangdong Provincial Planning Commission' (Merrill Lynch *et al.*, 1996: 13).

Almost all of GITIC's loans, guarantees, equity investments, lease financing or other services were supposed to be made through an 'interactive process with the Guangdong government' (Merrill Lynch *et al.*, 1996: 17). Initially, 'substantially all projects' undertaken by GITIC were included in the Guangdong provincial development plan, which was eventually included in the national plan. GITIC was required to carry out many projects that were selected 'for their social utility.' GITIC then conducted a 'detailed feasibility study' to determine if the projects were 'economically feasible' (Merrill Lynch *et al.*, 1996: 17). GITIC 'worked closely' with the Guangdong government to 'determine the package of loans, guarantees, equity or lease investment appropriate for each project.'

GITIC's selection of real estate development projects was supposed to be made in accordance with the Guangdong provincial economic development plan established by the Guangdong Provincial Planning Commission. GITIC's equity investment policy was 'based on the economic needs of Guangdong, as expressed through the Guangdong economic development plan and the State plan,' as well as on 'GITIC's assessment of market demands and the ability of the enterprises to operate economically' (Merrill Lynch *et al.*, 1996: 24). GITIC's import of advanced technology and raw materials was in line with provincial development plans, which were in turn strongly geared towards stimulating the province's export growth.

External pressure on GITIC's leaders came from several different directions. Major projects in which GITIC invested were part of the formal Guangdong provincial planning process. An important part of GITIC's investments were in other SOEs. Great pressure was exerted through the Guangdong government from different interests within the province to invest in projects that might benefit those interests. Many of these projects turned out to have negligible returns or even to be complete write-offs. There could be numerous reasons for this, not simply bad project selection by GITIC.

By the time of its closure, GITIC had invested RMB 80.8 billion (around US$ 9.7 billion) in around 400 enterprises across Guangdong province. GITIC's leaders estimated that 73 per cent of the total value of GITIC investments was decided by the Guangdong government, rather than by GITIC. In other words, GITIC's investment autonomy was heavily constrained by government intervention. GITIC was, clearly, regarded by the Guangdong government as substantially their own investment vehicle to support 'provincial development,' as defined by the government itself. GITIC's involvement in large 'dragon' projects (*longzi xiangmo*), such as the Guangzhou-Shenzhen highway, for which GITIC was the guarantor, and the Gongyuan Photographic Material Company, in which GITIC invested US$ 450 million, was decided by the provincial government as part of its planning process.

GITIC was one of ten original state-designated 'windows' that enjoyed special privileges in securing foreign currency borrowings. All GITIC's external borrowings required the approval of SAFE and the Guangdong Provincial Planning Commission on behalf of the Guangdong government. They were required to be made in accordance with the external borrowing provisions of the State economic development plan, to be incorporated into the State's statistical monitoring system and registered with SAFE. GITIC was regarded as bearing responsibility for upholding the reputation (*xinyu*) of the Chinese state. GITIC was subject to state regulations and supervision concerning deposits and loans, and trust and brokerage services. It submitted its financial statements to the PBOC and SAFE. GITIC was required to submit an annual financial report to the Guangdong branch of the PBOC. It was required to obtain SAFE approval for its foreign currency medium-term and long-term bank borrowings and bond issues.

Formally, GITIC's financial service activities were closely regulated by independent outside bodies. Its financial service activities were under the supervision of the Guangdong branch of the PBOC. GITIC was required to conduct its financial services business in accordance with the Provisional Regulations for the Control of Financial Trust and Investment Institutions issued by the PBOC in 1986, and in accordance with the Non-Bank Financial Institutions Administration of Foreign Exchange Business Provisions promulgated by the State Administration of Exchange Control (SAEC) (later SAFE) in July 1993. The interest rates on *renminbi* loans made by GITIC were in accordance with the guidelines set by the PBOC. GITIC was also authorized to make loans in foreign currencies. For these it was required to set the interest rate 'with reference to prevailing rates in the international capital markets' (Merrill Lynch *et al.*, 1996: 17).

GITIC's domestic securities business was monitored by the PBOC, the State Commission of Economic System Reform and the China Securities Regulatory Commission. Trust business in China was not subject to any specific body of law right up until the year 2000. However, in order to be involved in this business GITIC required the authorization of SAEC (later SAFE), subject to a transaction-by-transaction report to SAEC, in the case of foreign-currency-denominated deposits and loans, and the PBOC, in the case of *renminbi*-denominated deposits and loans. In addition, GITIC's trust operations were 'subject to the supervision of the Guangdong branch of the PBOC' (Merrill Lynch *et al.*, 1996: 21).

GITIC's real estate operations were monitored by the Guangdong Provincial Construction Commission. GITIC's real estate sales made to purchasers residing outside China were subject to the approval of the Guangdong

Provincial Commission for Foreign Economic Relations and Trade. GITIC's leasing business was one of the few leasing companies authorized by the State to import and export technology and equipment. GITIC's import of equipment for lease was subject to regulation by the Guangdong Provincial Commission of Foreign Economic Relations and Trade. GITIC's overseas operations also were monitored by the Guangdong Provincial Commission of Foreign Economic Relations and Trade.

GITIC's foreign borrowings, including those from domestic branches of foreign banks, required approval from the Guangdong government, and were required to stay within approval quotas for short-term or long-term foreign currency borrowing approved by SAEC. They were required to be in accordance with the State economic development plan and the Guangdong provincial economic development plan's provisions for utilizing foreign capital. GITIC's issuance of domestic bonds required approval from the PBOC.

The leading officers of GITIC were selected by the Guangdong government. These included GITIC's Chairman, Vice-Chairman and Executive Directors. The Board of Directors was required to meet once per year and, at other times, 'to deal with important issues as they arise' (CSFB, 1993: 24). The Chairman of GITIC was appointed directly by the Provincial Governor and was closely connected with the Guangdong provincial government (CSFB, 1993: 24). Di Changyun was appointed as Chairman in 1992 and served in that position for most of the 1990s. He was formerly Secretary General of the Guangdong government and the Chief Director of the Guangdong Provincial Financial Bureau. One of the main tasks of the Board of Directors was to select GITIC's principal operating officers, including the President and several Vice-Presidents. Their appointment was subject to approval by the Guangdong government. The President of GITIC for most of the 1990s until his replacement in May 1997 was Huang Yantian. He served simultaneously as Vice-Chairman of the Board of Directors. The Vice-Presidents throughout most of the 1990s – Zhang Yonglin, Li Jiansheng, Ling Weizeng and Zhu Yiwen – also served simultaneously as members of the Board of Directors. Most of the senior managers were formerly employed by the business and finance units of the Guangdong government, such as the Guangdong Finance Bureau and the Guangdong Provincial Planning Commission, or the PBOC (CSFB, 1993: 24, and Merrill Lynch *et al.*, 1996: 32).

Moody's in-depth analysis of the TIC sector prior to their restructuring concluded:

> The lack of an appropriate and effective governance mechanism, which led to government interference and the absence of accountability, is the real culprit of GITIC's failure, and remains, to a large extent, a problem for the remainder of the ITIC sector.
>
> (Moody's, 1998b)

The lack of checks and balances on local governments meant that they were not accountable for their mismanagement of the TICs, certainly not to the public, and often (in reality) not to the central government:

> Even today, the role of the Guangdong government in the GITIC collapse has not been publicly acknowledged in the official media. This inevitably raises some concerns over whether the true causes, both financial and political, of GITIC's failure are accepted, and whether the measures taken are to the point.
>
> (Moody's, 1998b)

Moody's account of the GITIC collapse warned, 'If [the Chinese government] fails to completely separate government from business, and make the government - both central and local - accountable for its behaviour, they run the risk of repeating GITIC's collapse' (Moody's, 1998b).

The Guangdong government was deeply and formally involved in the 'failure' of GITIC. The Guangdong government failed in its duty to effectively monitor the behaviour of GITIC. It watched over the construction of a company with deep inadequacies in its behaviour. Moreover, as we shall see below, the government was responsible not only for allowing poor business behaviour in GITIC but also for the development of serious criminal behaviour within the company. How many of these failures by the Guangdong provincial government would have come to light without the AFC? GITIC was closed, but, as we have seen, the TIC sector still existed as an institutional form. Other TICs were not opened up to public scrutiny as GITIC was. GITIC's management and monitoring failures provided a unique glimpse of the possible deficiencies of other TICs and, indeed, of the whole state-owned sector.

Criminality

GITIC headquarters

During its development, the senior management of GITIC became seriously criminalized. We have seen that the senior officers in the company were appointed by the provincial government. At the top of the company stood Huang Yantian, who was President and Vice-Chairman for most of the 1990s and had been feted on the front cover of *Business Week* in May 1994. Reportedly, investigations into Huang Yantian and the other officials had begun in December 1997, months before GITIC's closure (*BBC Monitoring Service*, 11 July 2000). Following the closure and bankruptcy of GITIC, Huang Yantian and several other GITIC leaders were arrested. Among these were former deputy general managers Chen Buzhong and Xie Lisheng. Huang, Chen and Xie were charged with corruption by the Guangdong Provincial Procurator (*BBC Monitoring Service*, 11 July 2000).

Chen 'died of an illness' while being investigated. Another of GITIC's senior managers committed suicide after the closure of GITIC. Another seven leaders 'ran away,' mainly from the foreign branch offices.

It was difficult for honest managers within GITIC to function in the criminalized environment that developed in the company: 'Every day, you have offers made to "cooperate" and make money … If you start to fight it, you will never end. When society is in a mess, the efforts of a few people are useless.' A major source of pressure for criminalization in GITIC, as in all Chinese SOEs, was the tight controls on official levels of remuneration. In the 1990s the senior managers in GITIC, most of whom were Communist Party members, were still only paid RMB 2,000–3,000 (around US$ 240–260) per month. Even managers of GITIC's subsidiaries and associated companies were able to earn several times this amount, because they escaped from the strict control system of state-owned enterprises: 'The moral demand placed on Party members is simply too great, so they are forced to become corrupt.'

GITIC was penetrated by external criminals from within Guangdong province. The methods of entrapment of company officials by criminals are well known. Company officials were lured through dinners, *karaoke* and prostitutes, 'sharing illegal things together.' This could be followed by a gift of a first-class ticket to some foreign destination, such as Bangkok, with a new credit card, and a large deposit in the account corresponding to the credit card. It could be followed by a gift to pay for an operation for a relative or for foreign school or university fees for children. The entrapment method was adjusted to the particular needs of the individual being entrapped. The pay-off consisted of pressure upon the GITIC manager to use GITIC's investment funds to invest in a project owned by the criminal or in joint ventures with the criminals. Often these investments turned out to have ambiguous property rights that proved difficult to verify during the bankruptcy process. Sometimes the investments were in illegal activities. GITIC operated a chain of 'real estate developments' that were superficially 'hotels' and 'entertainment complexes,' but many of these were in fact brothels and gambling casinos.

The social origins of the criminal elements that penetrated GITIC are a source of controversy. People often speak of 'individual peasants' (*getihu*) as the source of the problem. The perception is that the *getihu* had become successful through operating in a tough, amoral market environment. They were outside the boundaries of Party discipline, were hostile to the morality the Party was supposed to represent and had no compunctions about the methods used to entrap and maintain control over company employees. Highly publicized cases such as that of Lai Changxing in Xiamen lent support to such a view. Lai was a *getihu* who allegedly corrupted a significant part of the leading body of officials in Xiamen and fled to Canada to escape arrest.

The terrible performance record of GITIC's investments was in part a consequence of incompetence, reflecting an absence of investment skills in the emerging market economy. It was also an indication of an excessively speculative approach to investments. However, to some degree it reflected the influence of non-economic factors upon investment decision-making, including both external interest pressure through the political system and straightforward criminal pressure.

GITIC's problems were obvious to people at the top of the company at a relatively early date. A meeting of senior officials of the company in 1995 was told by one of the members: 'If you don't reform yourself, someone else will do it for you.' China's central Party leadership was made aware of the problems in GITIC's senior management at least two years before the closure and was aware of the need to change the leadership. The appointment of the senior management of GITIC was the prerogative of the Guangdong provincial government. Despite the fact that the management problems were well known among the relevant senior officials, it proved impossible to change GITIC's leadership until after the Asian Financial Crisis fully exposed the depth of GITIC's problems.

It is questionable how much information about the criminalization of GITIC would have been made public knowledge without the company's closure and bankruptcy. The immediate cause of that was the Asian Financial Crisis. It was due to the severity of the impact of the Asian crisis that Wang Qishan was appointed to the position of Executive Vice-Governor of Guangdong with a mandate to sort out the mess in Guangdong's NBFIs. GITIC was a mainland company, owned by the state. It had only a small degree of influence from foreign operations, unlike GDE, which operated to a considerable degree outside the mainland. If the Asian crisis and liquidation of GITIC revealed such widespread criminalization at senior levels of the company, it raised questions about the degree of criminalization existing more widely in Chinese state-owned enterprises.

GITIC was visited by six different government investigation groups. They unearthed extensive corruption. Why, despite extensive knowledge of the level of corrupt and criminal behaviour at GITIC, was the central government unable to bring about fundamental change at GITIC until the company became insolvent during the Asian Financial Crisis?

Against this background, the decision to close and then bankrupt GITIC was, indeed, hugely significant and bold, analogous to felling a giant, greatly valued, tree. It was as 'rude' as Gulliver putting out the fire in the queen's palace in Lilliput by urinating on it. It was a highly significant decision in Chinese politics in terms of one of the key issues throughout Chinese history, namely the relationship between the centre and the regions.

Writing at the end of 2000, almost two years after the closure of GITIC, one analyst commented that it was 'still not clear how so many trust companies managed to get themselves so deeply into hock in the first place and to what degree corruption contributed to their downfall' (Tom Mitchell, *SCMP*, 12 October 2000). He noted that the debts accumulated by the mainland trusts were 'massive,' with GITIC leading the way with liabilities estimated at RMB 38.8 billion:

> It is hard to believe that so much money was lost through incompetence and bad luck alone, especially at a time when an unprecedented number of high-ranking cadres are being paraded through the mainland's courts on corruption-related charges. Yet with the exception of a brief report carried by the Shanghai-based *Security Times* in July that three former GITIC officials (including former General Manager, Huang Yantian, Shenzhen Branch Manager, Li Ji, and Shenzhen Branch Vice-Manager, Du Shizuo) have been arrested, there has been almost no mention of investigations into criminal activities at mainland trusts.
>
> (Tom Mitchell, *SCMP*, 12 October 2000)

GITIC's overseas operations

The word 'international' in the name of GITIC was not idly included. One of the main goals of GITIC was to 'become an integrated international business enterprise supporting the growth of Guangdong' (Merrill Lynch *et al.*, 1996: 27). It was intended that GITIC would be a vehicle through which Guangdong's economic development could be supported by developing its international business, opening up overseas markets for Guangdong products and attracting overseas investment to Guangdong. GITIC had a threefold international investment strategy (Merrill Lynch *et al.*, 1996: 28). First, it intended to open finance companies in international financial centres 'to improve access to foreign capital.' Second, it intended to establish branch offices in countries or areas with developed economies, 'in order better to be able to access the equipment and management capabilities required to support the development of business in Guangdong.' Third, it intended to establish branch offices in areas rich in natural resources 'which [would] be used to further the economic development of Guangdong.' All of GITIC's overseas subsidiaries were required to 'report to GITIC on their business strategies, development, management and financial position' (Merrill Lynch *et al.*, 1996: 27). They were 'supervised by the Overseas Administrative Office of GITIC.' GITIC's Hong Kong branch was supposed to 'manage and supervise the subsidiaries of GITIC in Hong Kong and Macao' (Merrill Lynch *et al.*, 1996: 28).

The bulk of GITIC's overseas operations were in Hong Kong. Its largest overseas operations were its two Hong Kong incorporated subsidiaries, Guangxin Enterprises, set up in 1985, and Guangdong International Trust and Investment Corporation Hong Kong (Holdings). In the late 1980s it established subsidiaries in Macao, the United States and Australia. It also established an office in Thailand, and joint ventures in Hong Kong, Macao, Malaysia and Thailand.

Investigations conducted after GITIC went bankrupt revealed gross mismanagement in its overseas branches. GITIC established a branch office in New York. This in turn invested US$ 30 million in a joint venture with the Guangdong Construction Bank and the Guangdong Agricultural Bank, owned 50 per cent by GITIC. After GITIC's bankruptcy, KPMG visited the company and found that it was in fact 'run by overseas Chinese people.' The Deputy Manager, appointed by GITIC headquarters, was supposed to have run the company for eight years, but 'knew nothing about the business.' The company even established a subsidiary in Houston, without the knowledge of GITIC headquarters. The company 'invested' a large amount in the purchase of properties 'owned by an overseas Chinese family.' When KPMG went to investigate in order to recover debts for the Liquidation Committee, it found that the properties had been bought originally at hugely inflated prices and then sold again 'at a loss.' The matter was taken up in the US courts: 'This gives you an idea of the overseas operations of GITIC. The officers we send there cooperate with overseas Chinese: how can we protect GITIC's interests in foreign countries?'

GITIC also established a company in Thailand, intended to be GITIC's 'window in southeast Asia.' In the 1990s Thailand required that the foreign investor could not exceed a 50 per cent ownership share in a joint venture. However, an overseas Chinese person with a Thai passport counted as a 'Thai' owner. GITIC involved an overseas Chinese person as the joint venture partner, but the relationship was fraught with difficulties. The joint venture borrowed several million dollars (US) and invested the money in an equity share in a golf course, but the golf course was never constructed. GITIC was unable to recover the investment. GITIC Thailand invested a total of US$ 30 million in real estate deals, all of which was lost and non-recoverable for the creditors.

GITIC established another company in Australia. This also invested heavily in real estate. After GITIC's bankruptcy, the company was wound up within two months, and some revenue obtained from the sale of real estate. However, the amounts recovered were far below GITIC's initial investment. GITIC's Macao branch made several real estate investments, including a relatively large one in Macao airport, which was a 'disaster.' GITIC's Hong Kong branch was involved in two fraudulent land deals involving the same piece of real estate. One of the operations alone is estimated to have lost GITIC Hong Kong around HK$ 420 million. The two officials from GITIC involved in the fraudulent transactions both disappeared.

Overall, the GITIC bankruptcy revealed a picture of widespread failure in the company's overseas operations. Different people in GITIC headquarters were in charge of different overseas operations. For example, GITIC's president, Huang Yantian, was in charge of GITIC's US operations. He was arrested and jailed after GITIC's closure and bankruptcy. Although the total sums involved were relatively small, compared to the operations of the headquarters, they revealed a picture of comprehensive mismanagement, frequent *de facto* control of business operations by overseas Chinese people from outside GITIC, and widespread fraud, often involving collaboration with senior officials of the company in Guangzhou. It requires little imagination to understand the nature of the relationship between officers in GITIC's overseas branch offices and the business 'partners' in the 'failed ventures,' such as the multi-million-dollar golf course in Thailand that was never built.

GITIC (Shenzhen)

Major problems emerged during the closure (6 October 1998) and bankruptcy (16 January 1999) of GITIC's subsidiary, GITIC Shenzhen (SZ). A separate liquidation committee was appointed to supervise the liquidation process, including four people from the provincial government,[10] and two from the Shenzhen government.[11] As in the case of the parent, GITIC, the Committee was advised by KPMG. GITIC (SZ) was established in 1980.[12] The high-speed growth of Shenzhen greatly stimulated the company's growth possibilities and ambitions. Up until the closure and bankruptcy of GITIC, it had five different general managers, each of whom tried to outdo his predecessor in achieving growth of the business.

GITIC (SZ) had a total capital of only RMB 50 million, but at the time of its closure it had a total value of business (net assets plus liabilities) of RMB 3 billion. Given the size of its business, it ought to have had RMB 200 million in capital in order to comply with the required 8 per cent capital adequacy ratio. As a trust and investment company, GITIC (SZ) was not legally allowed to obtain non-trust deposits. However, like many of the smaller NBFIs in the Pearl River Delta, GITIC (SZ) was found to have attracted large-scale illegal deposits through 'off-balance-sheet accounts' (*zhang wai zhang*). Alongside the legally recorded 'trust' deposits were much larger, formally recorded illegal deposits. The main source of deposits was 'enterprises from all over the country,' including central government SOEs and research institutes, attracted by annual interest rates of up to 22 per cent at their peak. This was more than double the official deposit rate at that time. One close observer commented:

> The institutional depositors paid a high price as they failed to get back their interest, let alone their principal. However, in the end it is the state that suffers the most, because it is responsible for both sides of the contract, while the money goes into the pockets of the individuals.

General Manager Li Ji was accused of making unsecured, non-guaranteed loans to a single related party in Shenzhen, to the value of RMB 1.3 billion. Li had previously been awarded the title of 'excellent Communist Party member.' GITIC (SZ) was found to have extended numerous loans to enterprises, totalling RMB 1 billion, that had in fact been directed into personal accounts.

Large amounts of loans were made without collateral. In May 1998, the Guangdong provincial government sent a 'Special Case Group' with a staff of thirty, to try to sort out the growing insolvency of GITIC (SZ). It found that many of the people to whom large loans had been made had simply run away 'anywhere,' taking the funds with them. The Group found it very hard to obtain debt repayment due to GITIC (SZ) up until the closure in October 1998, and 'impossible' to obtain any repayment thereafter. The Securities Department of GITIC (SZ) was found to have had RMB 300 million in trades that didn't even appear in the account books. Senior staff of GITIC (SZ) were found to have used the firm's funds to 'buy villas' as personal property speculation.

The general manager of GITIC (SZ), Li Ji, was sentenced to fifteen years in prison. In addition, three other senior officials at GITIC (SZ) were prosecuted for criminal actions at the company. All the senior managers at GITIC (SZ) had been appointed directly by GITIC headquarters in Guangzhou.

GITIC (Hong Kong)

Two managers from GITIC's Hong Kong listed company, GITIC Hong Kong Ltd, fled after the bankruptcy. They were being sought by the Hong Kong police in connection with fraudulent letter of credit, reportedly to the value of one billion Hong Kong dollars, 'the biggest case of fraud in the history of Hong Kong.'

3 The second step

Restructuring Guangdong Enterprises

Establishment and growth of GDE

In 1979 the Central Committee of the Communist Party of China and the State Council approved Guangdong and Fujian provinces being allowed to pursue special policies, including opening up to the outside world. The special policies granted to Guangdong included the right to establish business organizations in neighbouring Hong Kong. Guangdong Enterprises (Holdings) Ltd (GDEHL or 'GDE') was set up by the Guangdong provincial government in 1980.[13] It was established by the Guangdong government as a 'window' company, incorporated in Hong Kong, but wholly owned by the provincial government. GDE was 'established to assist in implementing the Guangdong government's economic development policies.' The company conducted its day-to-day business 'independent of direct control by the Guangdong government but subject to the government's periodic supervision' (GDEHL, 1998). GDE was the first such business established in Hong Kong by a mainland provincial government.

The directors and senior executives of the company were appointed by the Guangdong government, and many of them were former members of the Guangdong government. GDE's strategic planning was undertaken in consultation with, and with the approval of, the Guangdong government. The Guangdong government contributed all of the original capital (HK$ 5 million). It allowed GDE to retain all of its profits. This followed the pattern of reform of Chinese SOEs across China. The closeness of GDE's ties with the Guangdong government was emphasized by the government's injection of a further HK$ 747 million in share capital into GDE in 1998. This was further enhanced by the appointment of Zhong Guanchao, former Mayor of Foshan City, Guangdong, and a deputy to the Eighth and Ninth National People's Congress, to the positions of Chairman and General Manager of the company in 1997 (GDEHL, 1998). The company's annual report commented:

> These events are both demonstrative of the Guangdong government's commitment and support to the company to enhance the company's financial strength, assist the company in the implementation of its long

> term strategic development and to allow the company to take full advantage of its role as a Hong Kong-based 'window' company for Guangdong province to support the province's economic development.
> (GDEHL, 1998)

GDE went through three stages of development. In the first stage, from 1980 to 1985, China was in the initial phase of 'opening up' to the outside world after decades of isolation. GDE conducted international trade as an agent, operating mainly on a commission basis. Relations between Guangdong and Hong Kong developed rapidly in the 1980s and GDE functioned as a valuable 'window' through which to acquire information about the international economy and help the province to expand its international trade. In 1982, the Guangdong government launched the 'five import' scheme. Under this scheme, GDE assumed responsibility for importing capital and technology, and for the installation of major pieces of imported equipment, for attracting talented people and management experience to the province. In other words, GDE was acting as a government development agency, alongside its own profit-seeking commercial development. By 1985, GDE's turnover had reached HK$ 1.5 billion, with a profit of HK$ 4.5 million, and net assets totalling HK$ 330 million.

From 1986 to 1990, GDE moved from being a purely trading company to attracting international capital and establishing industrial enterprises. It began the large-scale import of international capital and started to develop its processing and assembly businesses. GDE was a leader in Guangdong province in the process known as *sanlai, yibu* (Yeung, 2001: 6). This business of processing, assembly and compensation trade included the following three categories. Under *laijian zhuangpei* ('assembling supplied components') Chinese partners received a net fee to assemble supplied components according to a design provided by the foreign investors. Under *lailiao jiagong* ('contract processing') Chinese partners received a net fee to process supplied raw materials into finished products, according to the foreign investors' requirements, and to deliver them to foreign partners for export. Under *laiyang jiagong* ('import processing') Chinese partners produced and exported the finished products according to the sample provided by foreign investors. GDE was centrally involved in developing these three main forms of international business ventures in Guangdong province, indeed, itself took the lead in terms of the whole of China in this field. These included Sino-foreign joint ventures, cooperative business activities and exclusively foreign-funded businesses. GDE also invested extensively in production bases for the export of a variety of products. As the leader in the process of opening up Guangdong to the international economy, and with its close relationship with the Guangdong provincial government, GDE was able to attract a large amount of capital from Hong Kong for investment in Guangdong province. By 1990, at the end of the second phase in its development, GDE had a turnover of HK$ 6.8 billion, net profits of HK$ 69 million, total gross assets of HK$ 5.7 billion and net assets of HK$ 630 million.

In the 1990s, GDE entered a new phase in its growth, by turning increasingly to the Hong Kong stock market for finance. GDE was the pioneer in the process of internationalization of mainland companies. Through the establishment of Guangdong Investments Ltd (GDI) as a listed company in 1987, GDE became the first mainland-based company to be listed on the Hong Kong stock market. This paved the way for the development of the whole genre of so-called 'red chip' companies, defined as Hong Kong–registered firms owned by mainland parents, the majority of whose business takes place in the mainland. This, in turn, paved the way for the 'H-share' strategy, under which the Chinese government selected mainland-registered companies to be floated on the Hong Kong stock market. GDE's position as the pioneer of the internationalization of mainland companies was symbolized by the fact that in 1994 its subsidiary, GDI, became the first mainland-based firm to form part of the Hang Seng Index. GDE's access to capital from the Hong Kong stock market further increased with the acquisition of four additional stock market listed companies during the 1990s. In 1997, on the eve of the Asian Financial Crisis, the market capitalization of GDE's five listed companies totalled HK$ 19.6 billion (US$ 2.6 billion). Investors in the Hong Kong stock market were strongly persuaded of the logic of buying into companies with the backing of mainland state institutions.

As the 1990s progressed, GDE widened still further its connection with international capital markets. Its access to long-term capital markets took a major step forward with the issuance in 1993 of US$ 250 million in senior notes with a ten-year term. In 1994 it issued US$ 150 million in floating rate notes with a five-year term. In 1997, it issued US$ 500 million in senior notes with a ten-year term. By 1995, GDE had a total of HK$ 15.1 billion (US$ 1.96 billion) in long-term debt, of which HK$ 6.8 billion was in the form of long-term loans from banks and HK$ 8.4 billion (US$ 1.1 billion) was in senior notes, floating rate notes, commercial paper and convertible bonds (GDEHL, 1998: 75). GDE acted as 'a leading force among domestic Chinese enterprises and Chinese enterprises abroad in its raising enormous amounts of capital, including the emission of unsecured non-national debt bonds on international markets' (senior official of GDE).

GDE's ability to raise large amounts of capital from international markets was closely related to the strong links between GDE and the Guangdong provincial government. International investors believed that they could benefit from this 'non-transparent' business structure. There were few, if any, criticisms of this relationship prior to the Asian Financial Crisis.

Structure of GDE

GDE described itself as 'one of the major Hong Kong-based diversified Chinese business enterprises' (GDEHL, 1998). Underneath the parent company there were five listed companies and numerous subsidiaries. GDE directly owned 61 per cent of the floated Hong Kong company Guangnan Holdings Ltd (Guangnan) and a 40 per cent controlling interest in GDI, another Hong

Kong listed company. By 1997 GDE had an officially recorded investment interest in over seventy subsidiaries, of which twenty-three were established in the PRC, thirty-six were incorporated in Hong Kong and the remainder were incorporated in places ranging from the British Virgin Islands and Cayman Islands to France and Jersey (GDEHL, 1998). There were also thirteen officially recorded major associated companies in which GDE held an interest (GDEHL, 1998). GDE's business activities were in trading (68 per cent of turnover in 1997), manufacturing (15 per cent of turnover), property and development (5.6 per cent of turnover), finance (6 per cent of turnover), infrastructure (3 per cent of turnover) and hotels (1 per cent of turnover) (GDEHL, 1998: 8). Its diversified business structure looked similar to that of many East Asian and Latin American conglomerates.

GDE had numerous trading units. Many of these had been established in the period when there were limited connections between domestic producers and the global market. As these contacts developed during the reform years, so the function of these units atrophied. By far the most important part of GDE's trading activities was carried out through Guangnan (see below).

GDE entered manufacturing in the mid-1980s. It described its investment strategy as 'identifying growth markets, attaining efficiencies through economies of scale, acquiring and creating brand names by emphasizing quality of product and after-sales services, and building manufacturing groups around related products' (GDEHL, 1998: 11). By 1997, GDE had invested in five timber companies, three metal products companies, four food products companies (through Guangnan), three textile companies, four beer companies, a cement company and a company producing automobile air conditioners. By 1997, GDE's reported income from manufacturing reached HK$ 2.2 billion (around US$ 290 million). The investments were all in the mainland, and were mainly in the form of controlling shares.

GDE developed residential and commercial property mainly for the purpose of sale. In the 1990s it developed and completed a number of projects both in Hong Kong and the mainland. Its main target in the mainland was to become a leading developer of housing for middle-income households: 'With the implementation of the new housing policy, the Group believes that there will continue to be significant and increasing demand in Guangdong, particularly in prime areas of prime cities, for middle-income housing' (GDEHL, 1998: 19). GDE's objective was increasingly to pursue vertical integration of its property operations:

> Through GDRE (Guangdong Real Estate) and its subsidiaries, the Group intends to perform a variety of functions required in respect of a real estate project development including design, planning and construction, sourcing and supply of building materials, and the marketing, leasing and management of completed projects.
>
> (GDEHL, 1998: 19)

By 1997, GDE's income from property development and investment had reached HK$ 819 million (around US$ 107 million).

GDE's financial business included lending, insurance, merchant banking, securities and fund management. Like GITIC it developed rapidly into diversified financial services in a way that was prohibited for the mainland's commercial banks due to China's restrictive banking legislation. Its lending activities included residential mortgages, mortgages for small-scale real estate development and commercial loans in both Hong Kong and the mainland. Through its subsidiary, Guangdong Asia Insurance, GDE engaged in general insurance, including insurance for marine cargo, fire insurance, motor vehicle insurance, household insurance, construction, cash and machinery, and employee compensation. Through its subsidiary, Guangdong Capital Holdings, GDE conducted a range of merchant banking services, including advice on mergers and acquisitions, corporate restructuring and trust management. Its securities business included stock brokerage, investment advisory services and underwriting. Its fund management business was conducted through Guangdong Investment Management Ltd, which managed Guangdong Development Fund Ltd, a floated company on the London and Hong Kong stock markets. The Fund invested mainly in industrial projects in Guangdong province, including a wide range of industrial sectors. In 1997, GDE's finance activities reportedly generated HK$ 867 million (US$ 113 million).

GDE was heavily involved in investment infrastructure projects in Guangdong province. The company believed it stood to gain large amounts of business due to its close relationship with both the Guangdong provincial government and with local governments: 'The Group believes that its ties with the Guangdong government and relationships with local enterprises and authorities have been and will continue to be the important factors in its ability to identify, evaluate and implement infrastructure projects' (GDEHL, 1998: 23). By 1997, it had participated in eight large infrastructure projects, including a bridge, an airport expressway, a toll road, a power plant and a petrochemical storage facility. In 1997, GDE's infrastructure activities reportedly generated HK$ 28 million (US$ 4 million) in revenue.

GDE's hotel business was relatively small, generating just HK$ 115 million (US$ 15 million) in 1997. It decided not to include it as part of its core business and sold off most of its hotel assets in the mid-1990s.

Guangdong Investments Ltd

In 1987 GDE purchased Union Globe Development, a Hong Kong listed company, and renamed it Guangdong Investments Ltd (GDI). GDI was the pioneer of the 'red chip' companies in Hong Kong. After 1987, GDI expanded through acquiring assets from the parent company, GDE, and investing in several projects in Guangdong province. This later became a regular pattern for red chip companies. GDI's revenue grew rapidly. Its annual turnover rose from HK$ 30 million in 1990, to HK$ 7.1 billion (US$ 924 million) in 1997 (GDEHL, 1998: 27). In November 1994, GDI became one of the constituent stocks of Hong Kong's Hang Seng index. GDI expanded into five main business areas, including manufacturing, infrastructure, travel services, real estate and trading.

By 1997, over one-third of GDI's revenue came from its manufacturing investments. It held a 72 per cent interest in Guangdong Brewery Holdings Ltd, which was listed on the Hong Kong stock market in 1997. It had ownership also of breweries in Shenzhen and Shandong provinces. It had majority ownership interests in three mainland malting companies. It held a 71 per cent interest in Guangdong Tannery Ltd, which was listed on the Hong Kong stock market in 1996. The company had expanded its business operations from simply tanning, 'into one which includes the production, distribution and retailing of brand name products' (GDEHL, 1998: 31). It owned a 57 per cent interest in Guangdong Building Industries Ltd, the holding company for Full Arts Metal Works Ltd, which engaged in the design, supply and installation of curtain wall systems, aluminium windows, doors and shop fronts, skylights and other building-related materials in Hong Kong. The company was listed on the Hong Kong stock market in 1997. GDI also had investments in companies producing cement and furniture in Guangdong province.

By the late 1990s, GDI had investments in three power stations, a toll road, two expressways and two bridges, all in Guangdong province. Their combined revenue in 1997 was HK$ 625 million (US$ 81 million).

Through one of its subsidiaries, GDI was one of four companies allowed to organize Hong Kong tours for Chinese residents. In the late 1990s, it owned and managed nine hotels and guesthouses in Hong Kong and mainland China, as well as one in Bangkok. The revenue from its travel services and hotels in 1997 totalled only HK$ 737 million (US$ 96 million).

In the 1990s, GDI acquired numerous properties in Guangdong and Hong Kong. The most significant of these included the Riverside Garden Hotel in Panyu, a satellite city of Guangzhou (with 1.43 million square metres of residential space and 190,000 square metres of commercial space) and the Teem Centre, a large commercial development in Guangzhou. In addition, it purchased from the parent company, GDEHL, a 29-storey office building in Hong Kong, and fourteen floors of another Hong Kong office building owned by GDEHL. GDI's property investments brought in a total revenue of HK$ 836 million (US$ 109 million) in 1997.

GDI invested in two joint ventures in the wholesale and retail sectors. One of these was a relatively large business, involving a 56 per cent share in Nanfang Dasha, the second largest retail chain in Guangdong province, with eight stores across China. GDI's sales revenue from wholesale and retail in 1997 totalled HK$ 2.1 billion (US$ 270 million).

Guangnan

By far the most important part of GDE's trading activities was carried out through Guangnan Holdings Ltd. Guangnan became a Hong Kong-listed company in December 1994, with 58 per cent of the equity owned by GDE. In the mid-1990s, Guangnan moved rapidly towards its goal of becoming 'a vertically integrated food business with a broad earnings base and a degree of market dominance.' Guangnan's Board of Executive Directors consisted of experienced business people who had developed their business skills in the transition from central planning in the dynamic market economy of southern China. They were mainly in their forties and fifties. The Chairman, Sun Guan, had 'over twenty years' experience in foodstuffs trading and business management.' Several of the other executive directors had twenty or more years of experience in food processing and trading (Guangnan, 1998: 37). Its three non-executive directors were senior Hong Kong business people, two of whom were bankers and one a solicitor.

In accordance with Hong Kong law, Guangnan was required to have its accounts approved by certified public accountants. Its accounts for 1997, immediately prior to the Asian crisis, were audited by Deloitte Touche Tohmatsu. Deloitte reported: '[We have] obtained all the information and explanations which we consider necessary in order to provide us with sufficient evidence to give a reasonable assurance as to whether the financial statements are free from material misstatement.' They concluded: 'In our opinion the financial statements give a true and fair view of the state of the company and the group as at 31 December 1997' (Guangnan, 1998: 40). The public accounts for Guangnan showed that in 1997 it had a turnover of HK$ 8.16 billion, profits after taxation of HK$ 302 million, assets of HK$ 6.96 billion and liabilities of HK$ 4.5 billion. Guangnan had forty-one subsidiaries listed in its annual report for 1997. These were mainly incorporated in the PRC and in Hong Kong, but included nine incorporated in the Cayman Islands, the British Virgin Islands and Bermuda. It was not uncommon for Hong Kong-based conglomerates to have such a large number of subsidiaries, including several in well-known tax havens.

Guangnan developed into a powerful vertically integrated firm in the foodstuffs and related sectors. The business was built around the fact that it was the sole authorized distributor for the export of several important foodstuffs from the mainland to Hong Kong. In 1995 it accounted for 98 per cent of the supply of fresh pond fish to Hong Kong, 90 per cent of the vegetables and 68 per cent of the poultry. It developed its own supply base for several farm products, including a majority share of China's largest prawn and pearl farming/processing enterprise. Guangnan imported fertilizers, feedstock, cereals, sugar and palm oil for the Chinese food industry. It diversified both upstream and downstream in food-related businesses. Upstream, it diversified into the production of processed food, frozen food and nutrient food. Through Chaozhou Industries, Guangnan held a controlling interest in Sino-foreign joint ventures in the farming, roasting and packaging of eel and other aquatic products. Through vertical integration within the food business, including transportation, distribution and wholesaling, Guangnan intended to expand into the more profitable parts of the value chain. Downstream, it expanded into supermarket operations. By 1997 it had over one hundred supermarkets in Hong Kong, Guangdong and Shanghai.

Between 1995 and mid-1998 it acquired, or established joint ventures with, over thirty businesses. Guangnan's annual turnover rose from HK$ 2.9 billion in 1994, to HK$ 8.2 billion in 1997, and was predicted by Morgan Stanley Dean Witter (MSDW) to reach HK$ 10.5 billion (around US$ 1.4 billion) in 2001 (MSDW, 8 June 1998). In 1997 alone, reported net income rose by 39 per cent. Operating profits (before tax) were reported as HK$ 394 million in 1997 and forecast to rise to HK$ 574 in 2001 (MSDW, 8 June 1998).

In 1997, Guangnan was one of six Hong Kong companies included by Salomon Securities in its list of 119 global 'best shares.' In the midst of the crash in the Hong Kong stock market after the Asian Financial Crisis, Guangnan was strongly recommended by MSDW as a 'defensive' share, which would 'outperform in a down market and perform in line with an up market':

> We are raising our rating on Guangnan Holdings to Outperform from Neutral. We believe the diversified food company is a defensive investment with an earnings base that is less cyclical and less sensitive to the weak yen and regional economic turmoil than the average listed company.
>
> (MSDW, 8 June 1998)

In 1998 also, MSDW selected Guangnan as one of its 'global top fifty small and medium-sized firms.' In the two years 1996 and 1997 together, Guangnan was able to raise around HK$ 1.2 billion (around US$ 160 million) from international capital markets through the issuance of new shares, and issue and exercise of warrants and convertible bonds.

GDE on the eve of the Asian Financial Crisis

GDE was a pioneer in China's economic reform and opening up to the outside world. It attracted much attention in Hong Kong, including business people, media, intellectuals and ordinary citizens. Its subsequent development path was symbolic of the whole process of China's system reform up until the late 1990s.

Between 1990 and 1996 GDE grew at high speed. Turnover rose from HK$ 6.8 billion in 1990, to HK$ 14.9 billion (US$ 1.9 billion) in 1996, and the company's assets rose from HK$ 10.7 billion to HK$ 30.6 billion (US$ 4 billion) over the same period. The company's income before taxation rose from HK$ 376 million in 1990 to HK$ 1.13 billion (US$ 145 million) in 1996

(Merrill Lynch, 1997: 25). GDE had become a large, successful Hong Kong conglomerate. Its success was reflected in the fact that its flagship subsidiaries, Guangnan and GDI, had become constituents of the Hang Seng Index.

By the end of 1997, GDE had an aggregate book value of assets amounting to HK$ 36.5 billion and a net value of HK$ 7.48 billion. In terms of the aggregate book value of its assets it had moved into the ranks of the top five companies in Hong Kong. In the words of a leading official of GDE at the time:

> In a word, GDE has made an active and important contribution to the economic development, prosperity and stabilization of Hong Kong. Its development process, taking trade as the leading force and industry as the foundation on which to develop capital management, can be used as a point of reference for the entire China-funded enterprise sector in Hong Kong.

The Guangdong government was proud of GDE's achievement as the flagship in leading the province's transition from the closed, planned economy towards the market, which was itself at the forefront of China's whole reform process. In 1998 one of GDE's leaders commented: 'With the mighty support of the Guangdong provincial government, GDE has developed vigorously and has obtained remarkable achievements with the two million dollars that were used to start the Company.' The company had some obvious weaknesses, such as a relatively large exposure to the property market and a relatively large amount of long-term debt (Merrill Lynch, 1997: 16–21). However, in this it did not appear to be fundamentally different from other ambitious Hong Kong-based conglomerates. Moreover, unlike its indigenous Hong Kong-based competitors, it had the advantage of a close relationship with both the Guangdong government and local governments within Guangdong, which gave it privileged access to the choicest opportunities for profitable growth. At its head were a group of leaders who had successfully made the transition from traditional Party cadres to international businessmen, honing their business skills in the competitive environment of Hong Kong. They now had deep knowledge of international business practice.

In an evaluation of the Hong Kong red chip companies as a whole, the *Asian Wall Street Journal* commented: 'Guangdong Enterprises is one of the oldest of China's overseas investment arms and is widely viewed as one of the best run' (*Asian Wall Street Journal*, 21 April 1998). In 1998 also, the Hong Kong government itself selected GDE as the 'best managed firm in Hong Kong.'

The arrival of the crisis for GDE

In 1996, Lu Ruihua replaced Zhu Senlin as Governor of Guangdong province. Soon after this the senior leadership of GDE was changed. Zhong

Guanchao, former Mayor and Party Secretary of Foshan City, in Guangdong's Pearl River Delta, replaced He Keqin as Chairman of GDE. On 14 November 1997 He Keqin resigned as Chairman and Director of GDI, and was replaced in both these positions by Zhong Guanchao.

After Zhong Guanchao took over as Chairman of GDE, the company became much more active in the Hong Kong stock market. In May–June 1997 Guangnan received a substantial injection of assets from the parent company. In late 1997, as the red chip fever got under way, it spun off Guangdong Brewery, Guangdong Building Enterprises and Guangdong Tannery. In November, Guangnan invested in the shares of Golden Resources, Firestone International and many other companies (*East Week*, 4 February 1999). In August 1997, GDE increased its holdings in Nam Fong International (*Nanfang Guoji*). In September 1997, GDE, in partnership with GDI, announced the acquisition of an additional interest to bring its shareholding in Nam Fong International to 28.5 per cent. The total acquisition was valued at HK$ 1.164 billion, with GDE and GDI contributing HK$ 811 million and HK$ 353 million respectively. These major investments provided a large boost to Nam Fong's share price. During the restructuring of GDE it was revealed that GDE had made book losses of over HK$ 1 billion on its investments in Nam Fong International.

In late 1997, the Asian Financial Crisis erupted. Over the ensuing months, the situation at GDE became progressively bleaker. In May 1998, GDE's financial department prepared an urgent report for submission to the Guangdong provincial government. It made clear that GDE, the province's flagship international company, faced a grave financial situation. It was finding it increasingly difficult to meet its repayment obligations.

The report said that out of GDE's total assets of HK$ 35.7 billion, bad and doubtful debts and the depreciation of on-credit accounts amounted to HK$ 11.8 billion. It estimated that these assets had already lost 70–80 per cent of their value. The situation was deteriorating fast:

> Each year, the company has to finance the payment of capital and interest as well as spend large amounts of manpower and material resources to clear the accounts, all of which greatly affect the efficiency and turnover of funds of the company.

Accounts receivable 'increase year after year' and the proportion of overdue accounts was 'rather large.' The accounts receivable rose from HK$ 8.5 billion in 1995 to HK$ 12.9 billion (US$ 1.7 billion) in 1998, an increase of over 50 per cent in just three years. Most alarmingly, overdue accounts receivable totalled HK$ 7.5 billion (almost US$ 1 billion) by 1998, accounting for 51 per cent of all accounts receivable: 'These accounts have almost become bad debts, dead loans or inactive capital, which greatly affect the company's financial turnover.'

The report stated that the 'debt-bearing capability of GDE' had reached its limit. Both GDE's total debt and the debt ratio had risen to an unsustainable level. It reported that by May 1998, GDE's gross liabilities had reached HK$ 28.2 billion. Its loans from the bank (including bonds and commercial bills) had reached HK$ 23.8 billion, accounting for 86 per cent of GDE's total liabilities, and amounting to 3.21 times the value of its net assets. In the past GDE had relied on debt to finance its current business activities, 'namely, by renewing or borrowing new loans to pay back the old debts.' However, the Asian Financial Crisis had led to a fall in the credit rating of the whole region and a general tightening of bank lending to the region. The report to the Guangdong government concluded that GDE had reached a 'critical situation,' in which it would soon be unable to meet its contractual requirements to its creditors:

> When it comes to the time that bondholders ask for redemption of their bonds, or banks require that GDE clear its due debts, or even appeals to the courts for the take-over of the company, the result would be disastrous.

In order to 'solve the current problems and avoid the risks that were approaching,' the report requested that the Guangdong provincial government should take the following steps to restructure GDE's debts. First, it should 'invest RMB 5 billion (US$ 600 million) unrequitedly in GDE for repayment of its long-term loans from the bank.' Second, it should 'give RMB 7 billion-worth (US$ 846 million) of high-grade assets unrequitedly to GDE for offsetting the corresponding accounts receivable.' Third, it should 'lend GDE HK$ 1.6 billion to counter-purchase its debts from the market.' Fourth, it should 'reduce the management fees by HK$ 0.7 billion every year during the period of restructuring the company.'

On 29 August 1998, GDE again reported to an emergency meeting of the Guangdong provincial government, requesting emergency assistance to enable GDE to repay US$ 72 million in commercial paper due by 4 September. On 9 September, GDE submitted yet another emergency report to the provincial government. This showed that there was still a shortfall of US$ 117 million in GDE's debt repayments even after meeting the repayment of 4 September. On 10 September, GDE presented another report to the provincial government, saying that the extent of poor quality and bad loans had reached HK$ 12.8 billion, amounting to 35 per cent of total assets of HK$ 36.2 billion. GDE's net assets were officially recorded as being HK$ 7.5 billion (US$ 0.96 billion). In fact, GDE reported to the provincial government that its debts exceeded its assets by HK$ 4.5 billion.

At this point the financial crisis at GDE exploded. On 6 October, the Central Bank decided to close GITIC. The closure of GITIC led the international banks to 'quickly tighten up credit and chase repayment once loans were due, as they perceived GDE to be in a precarious situation' (quoted in *Next*, 22 January 1999). This further contributed to a worsening situation at GDE.

On 8 October, the Guangdong provincial government took the decision to save GDE. The key reason for treating GDE differently from GITIC was the fact that through its five listed companies, especially GDI and Guangnan, GDE played an important role in the Hong Kong stock market. GDI was especially significant as one of the thirty-three constituent stocks of the Hang Seng Index.

The decision to restructure GDE

Confronted with the reality of the grave situation in its flagship company, the Guangdong provincial government decided to take an unprecedented step. On 10 October 1998, the provincial government engaged KPMG, one of the global 'big five' accountancy firms, to conduct an audit of GDE in order to ascertain its true financial condition as of 30 September 1998. KPMG was now centrally involved in the reorganization of both of the two main SOEs owned by the Guangdong provincial government. The audit was 'fast and dirty,' conducted at high speed in less than three weeks, in order to rapidly provide the Guangdong government with a snapshot of the company's true condition.

KPMG provided the Guangdong government with a blunt assessment of the real situation at GDE. They concluded that the company's true financial situation was 'grim.' As of 30 September 1998, the official book records of GDE showed that it had total assets of HK$ 37.1 billion, gross liabilities of HK$ 30.7 billion and net assets of HK$ 6.4 billion. KPMG reported that, using the standards of the Hong Kong Accountants' Association, GDE's total assets in fact were HK$ 15.52 billion less than they were reported in the company's official accounts. They concluded that GDE's liabilities exceeded its assets by HK$ 9.12 billion, or more than US$ 1 billion.

KPMG informed the Guangdong government that there were a number of explanations for the situation at GDE.

First, GDE had 'invested badly and in an improper way.' Part of the reason for the reduction in the true assets position of GDE was due to the fact that HK$ 5.42 billion of GDE investments were 'bad,' and HK$ 3.4 billion were 'improper loans,' totalling HK$ 8.82 billion. They informed the Guangdong government that 'most of the investment decisions were made without adequate investigation and without detailed research by the responsible company officials.' The person in charge of each particular project had taken the decisions on his or her own. They concluded that the company 'lacked an explicit investment policy.' It 'failed to give adequate supervision or management of investment projects,' and did not adopt even the most basic of measures to reduce risk.

Second, GDE had 'only a vague concept of what is of primary and secondary importance.' The 1997 annual report listed only the principal and affiliated companies, totalling over eighty (GDEHL, 1998). KPMG reported that GDE in fact had no fewer than around 500 subsidiary and affiliated companies, with a 'complicated and overlapping structure.' KPMG reported that GDE had 'neither a central management system nor a business strategy.' Each of the subsidiaries 'does things in its own way to a certain extent, and sometimes undertakes overlapping investments.' For example, both the parent company, GDE, and the subsidiary, GDI, invested in real estate, brewing, cement and construction, so that 'the company's resources cannot be rationally allocated and utilized.' GDE's main purpose was to assist the development of Guangdong province, but in fact it had invested extensively abroad, including investments in the United States, Canada, France and Thailand: 'All these investments ended in failure.' As of 30 September 1998, there were still 257 subsidiary companies in operation, including such diverse businesses as financial services, food distribution and processing, hotels, tourism, construction, many different types of manufacturing (including beer, tanning and building materials), real estate, supermarkets, retail and transportation. GDE had no conception of 'core business' and made multiple overlapping investments.

Third, GDE 'lacked systems of control and supervision.' It did not possess an internal monitoring system or a clear system of risk assessment. When GDE examined and approved loans, 'the decision was not based on the borrower's financial status or ability to repay the loan, but on the relationship between the borrower and the company, or the borrower and the individual in charge of allocating the loan.' Many of those in charge of loan allocation 'lacked common sense in financial matters.' Some branches of GDE used the company's financial resources to 'speculate in the stock market.'

Fourth, KPMG reported to the Guangdong government that GDE 'practised fraud' and that there were 'discrepancies between the accounts and actual resources.' There were numerous false accounting records. Some of GDE's officials 'do not handle matters according to economic rules and thus cause large-scale losses.' In order to cover up for their failures, they 'resort to constructing false accounts.' Such conduct would be 'regarded as criminal fraud under Hong Kong law.' However, some of GDE's officials 'consider these practices are acceptable as long as they are done for the public's sake.'

Fifth, GDE undertook 'speculative investment that caused great losses.' Some of GDE's enterprises tried to achieve high returns in a short period of time through speculative investments, including risky investments in the stock market, in futures and in real estate. Losses on these accounts were estimated at around HK$ 3.02 billion.

Sixth, 'ease of access to funding led to a high level of company indebtedness.' For much of the 1990s, mainland China was regarded as a highly desirable market for international financial institutions, making it easy for GDE officials to raise funds from abroad. This enabled them to 'loosen the investment requirements of projects,' and to 'not take due heed of the risks involved in running a business with a high level of indebtedness.' GDE's officials became 'accustomed to borrowing new money to repay the old debts in order to solve the problem of lack of funds.' This was the classic approach adopted by 'Ponzi-style' schemes across the world. GDE's approach to raising new funds was 'first to decide on the amount of financing required, then construct an assumed profit to justify the borrowing.' However, the assumed profit turned out to be unrealistic. KPMG commented: 'If the predicted profit turns out to be unrealistic, then GDE must undertake some remedial measures. Even if these measures are successful, GDE is still cheating the investors.'

On 10 December 1998 Guangnan's Assistant General Manager, Li Ruihua, was arrested in Hong Kong for 'offering advantages and conspiracy to defraud in relation to the application of letter of credit from banks.' This was a strong public signal that there were serious problems within GDE.

The Guangdong government drew its own conclusions from KPMG's report. First, it acknowledged that there was a serious shortfall in GDE's assets compared with its liabilities. Second, it recognized that GDE's problems had developed long before the onset of the Asian Financial Crisis. The shortfall in GDE's assets relative to its debts had begun to manifest itself several years prior to 1998. As was the case with GITIC, the Asian Financial Crisis had laid bare problems that had long existed within the company: 'as the tide recedes the rocks appear' (*shui luo shi chu*).

Third, the Guangdong government realized that GDE could not continue to operate in this fashion. Even GDE itself acknowledged this reality. KPMG's report showed that GDE's total cash inflow in calendar year 1997 amounted to HK$ 6.025 billion, of which HK$ 352 million was interest income, and new loans totalled HK$ 5.673 billion, or 94.2 per cent of the total. The total cash outflow during this period was HK$ 5.641 billion, of which cash outflow to pay interest and principal on debts totalled HK$ 1.561 billion, or 27.7 per cent of the total; that for management of the business totalled HK$ 1.126 billion, or 20 per cent of the total; and that for other purposes totalled HK$ 2.951 billion, or 52.2 per cent of the total. The data showed that 'basically GDE does not achieve any cash inflow through managing its business, but relies instead on new bank loans to repay the due capital and interest, and to keep the company functioning.' However, despite its precarious financial position, GDE kept borrowing money to undertake new investments. The Guangdong government was forced to conclude:

> If this continues to happen, more efforts to borrow money will only mean greater losses for the creditors until the company finally becomes bankrupt. Therefore, measures must be taken to protect the interests of creditors and to safeguard the government's credibility.

The Guangdong government faced the harsh reality that the only possible choices for GDE were bankruptcy or restructuring. KPMG projected the financial situation of GDE forward for the period from November 1998 to 31 September 1999, assuming that there was no restructuring. It projected that GDE would have a cash outflow of HK$ 9.36 billion, including HK$ 0.76 billion in cash outflow for business operations, HK$ 6.6 billion of debt repayment and HK$ 2 billion in interest repayment. The projected cash inflow was only HK$ 0.70 billion. In other words, the projected net cash outflow was HK$ 8.66 billion. However, it concluded that even if the Guangdong government made up this shortfall, it was not certain that GDE could survive until September 1999. Moreover, it calculated that the Guangdong government would need to provide around HK$ 15–16 billion (over US$ 2 billion) in order to substantially improve GDE's financial situation. This was 'obviously impossible.'

Faced with the brutal reality revealed in the KPMG report, the Guangdong government held a press conference in Hong Kong on 16 December 1998. At the press conference it announced the restructuring plan for GDE. It declared that it would form a restructuring advisory group consisting of Goldman Sachs, the US investment bank; Shearman and Sterlings, one of the leading US-based law firms; and Richards Butler, a leading Hong Kong law firm. This was the first time the Chinese state had employed an international investment bank to help restructure a Chinese firm. Executive Vice-Governor Wang Qishan said, 'The move is intended to provide an example for other state-owned firms going through structural reform.' In other words, the restructuring was intended to be more than merely debt restructuring but also a comprehensive business restructuring. At the same meeting, the co-chairman of Goldman Sachs, Henry Paulson, said that the objective of the restructuring was to create 'a commercially viable, financially independent company committed to the development of Guangdong province.' He announced that Goldman Sachs would make an equity investment in GDE of 'up to US$ 20 million.' He said that it was very seldom that Goldman Sachs made an equity investment in an advisory case like this: 'We are doing so this time because it is a very important case and we are confident it will be a successful company.'

This meeting set in motion the largest corporate restructuring in Hong Kong's history, and, arguably, in East Asia. It also made a huge impact in Hong Kong business circles and received extensive coverage in the global media. It was an event of great significance in the evolution of China's political economy. The combined effect of the bankruptcy of GITIC and the restructuring of GDE caused an immense impact upon the attitude of international financial institutions towards China.

On 24 December 1998, Guangdong's Governor, Lu Ruihua, formally confirmed that GDE would be restructured, not closed.

The restructuring process

Goldman Sachs described its role in the GDE restructuring as 'like a professional fireman, whose job was simply to put out the fire: the question of what the new house will look like is only considered after you have put the fire out.'

On 4 January 1999 GDE and Guangnan announced that they were seeking deferral of all loan principal repayments until 15 April 1999 or beyond.

The announcement followed one week after the decision to place GITIC in liquidation. The combined effect of these two events 'sent shock waves from Guangdong, shattering the banking community's confidence in PRC companies and threatening to trigger yet another wave of write-offs among local banks following last year's property slump' (*Next*, 22 January 1999). GDE and Guangnan both announced that they intended to continue to make payments of interest on all borrowing facilities.

Following these announcements, China's Minister of Finance, Xiang Huaicheng, said that Beijing 'would not bail out distressed corporations, showing that the rules of the game had changed with the PRC government saying that it would no longer be committed to honouring debts the way it previously did' (*Next*, 22 January 1999). David Carse, Deputy Chief Executive of the Hong Kong Monetary Authority, said:

> Previously banks lent to PRC companies on the assumption that loans were guaranteed by their parent companies. This assumption, now appearing illusory, led to imprudent lending. However, the rules of the game have changed and banks are now having to bear the painful consequences of this change.

The implications for Hong Kong were serious, since Hong Kong banks were estimated to have over US$ 42 billion in outstanding loans to PRC companies. Among the hardest hit was the Bank of East Asia, a 'pioneer in mainland China's banking market.' Chan Kei-cheung, the bank's Deputy Chief Executive for China, said:

> Because of lack of transparency and accounting information for verification among PRC companies, we based our lending decisions on the merit of their parent companies. Now the parent companies have declared insolvency as a result of negative equity, we feel rather helpless.
>
> (quoted in *Next*, 22 January 1999)

In early February it was announced that the Bank of East Asia had seen its profits plunge 55 per cent in 1998, after taking a HK$ 1.5 billion charge for bad and doubtful debts. The bank had made a 100 per cent write-off against all its exposure to GITIC, and made a 20 per cent provision for its exposure to all other ITICs.

To solve their escalating debt problems, Hong Kong units of mainland companies were heavily selling off assets, contributing to further depression in the already depressed stock and property markets. A large fraction of the property of red chip companies was bought at the peak of the Hong Kong property cycle. For example, in January 1999, GDI was forced to sell a residential property in the exclusive Repulse Bay Area. It sold the property for HK$ 140 million, 57 per cent less than when it was originally purchased in 1997 (*Hong Kong Economic Times*, 26 January 1999). In 1998, the banks had to make heavy provisions due to plummeting Hong Kong property prices.

The impact of the announcements on the behaviour of international banks was immediate: 'Many banks have joined a nation-wide chase for repayment covering ITICs and all PRC and red-chip companies based in Hong Kong' (*Next*, 22 January 1999). Indeed, the decision in 1998 to close GITIC had itself led to increased pressure on GDE. Liu Jinbao, Chairman of the Hong Kong Association of Banks, Deputy Chairman of the Bank of China Group and Head of its Hong Kong operations, appealed to international banks to 'run the water to keep the fish alive,' instead of tightening credit. However, most banks were not prepared to do so. A Japanese banker observed, 'Unless all creditors promise not to chase repayment, those who don't will suffer' (quoted in *Next*, 22 January 1999). Another commented:

> If there is only one bank pursuing repayment, a company may be able to honour its debts. But if two or more banks chase repayment at the same time, chances are that the company may go default. Therefore, the sooner you chase repayment, the better it will be.
>
> (quoted in *Next*, 22 January 1999)

First creditors' meeting

The first creditors' meeting was held on 12 January 1999, just two days after GITIC had filed for bankruptcy. During the restructuring, all the subsidiaries continued normal operation. The total debt of GDE was announced as being US$ 2.94 billion as of 31 December 1998, of which US$ 2.55 billion was for GDE excluding Guangnan and US$ 391 million was for Guangnan. Within the GDE Group's total debt of US$ 2.94 billion, consolidated bank debt amounted to US$ 1.91 billion and debt securities amounted to US$ 1.03 billion. The near-term financial obligations of the GDE Group as a whole for the period January to April 1999 amounted to a total of US$ 63 million for interest payments and US$ 1.17 billion for scheduled repayment of principal, of which US$ 700 million in interest and principal was due immediately, in January 1999. In addition, GDE had US$ 265 million in outstanding guarantees. GDE stated that its cash flows from its operations were 'substantially short of that required to meet those obligations.' It was admitted that the GDE group was 'only able to continue trading and make interest payments based on significant assistance from the Guangdong provincial government.' This was to be a common pattern for the red chips during the AFC. During the boom years, different interests within the red chips had profited hugely from the asset price bubble. In the crisis, the parent governments were forced to provide large-scale support to keep the red chips alive. It was the different local governments, government departments and other parent entities within China that were 'running the water to keep the fish alive.' These were, in their turn, helping to keep Hong Kong alive.

The Guangdong government proposed to undertake a 'comprehensive restructuring' in order to 'create a commercially viable, financially independent group.' The restructuring would have three components. First, there was to be financial restructuring. This would involve 'determining an optimal capital structure consistent with the group's business strategy.' This would include achieving a 'proper mix of debt and equity,' and an 'appropriate balance of short-term and long-term debt'; 'restructuring the balance sheet to achieve the optimal capital structure'; 'establishing and implementing a risk management strategy to manage conservatively the group's currency and interest rate exposure'; and 'implementing significantly improved management information systems and internal control mechanisms.' The Guangdong government said that it was 'prepared to invest new capital and cash generating assets as part of a comprehensive restructuring exercise.'

Second, there was to be a corporate restructuring. This would 'reconfirm the mission and redefine a focused corporate strategy for the group, its subsidiaries and associates.' It would identify the core businesses for the group to retain. Non-core or poorly performing assets should be disposed of or liquidated. The group should 'establish operating and financial targets based on comparable company benchmarks.' The group's 'transparency and efficiency should be increased.' The corporate structure should be 'simplified.'

Third, there was management restructuring. This was to include 'determining and implementing the optimal management organization for the group and individual companies.' The restructuring would involve 'determining and implementing the appropriate Board sizes and composition.' It would involve 'appointing the appropriate management personnel, developing new compensation arrangements, implementing management training programmes and improving internal controls and corporate governance mechanisms.'

It was reported that actions on all these restructuring fronts had already begun by the time of the first creditors' meeting.

At the meeting it was confirmed that GDE would halt all payment of principal but would continue to pay interest. Following the meeting spokespeople for the Guangdong government emphasized that the provincial government had no intention of allowing GDE to follow the same path as GITIC into bankruptcy. On the same day as the first creditors' meeting, Guangnan Holdings explained to the Hong Kong stock exchange that its gross debt amounted to US$ 391 million, and that US$ 115 million was due immediately in debt repayment.

These announcements revealed that GDE and Guangnan were effectively insolvent. The combination of this revelation with the fact that GITIC had filed for bankruptcy on 10 January caused dismay in the Hong Kong stock market:

> Red chips were hammered today and the shockwaves were felt throughout the market. It is now a question of credibility for the red chips. Investors now no longer trust the so-called guaranteed earnings of China

> and just want to be free of them. The red chips will either restructure or go bankrupt.

One analyst commented: 'There's a lot of questions about where the money went, and if it did go somewhere it should not have gone. It raises the question that there are other companies in the same situation' (quoted in *China Business Information*, 14 January 1999). Following the creditors' meeting, shares in Guangnan plummeted 53 per cent, and GDI fell 24 per cent.

Up until the 12 January creditors' meeting, investors retained confidence in the red chips, believing them to be fundamentally different from the ITICs. The GDE and Guangnan announcements destroyed their complacency: 'Red chips are no longer seen as untouchables which will always be rescued.' Analysts feared that a number of smaller ones could be eliminated, and others thought the number of red chip insolvencies could be much greater (*FT*, 26 January 1999). Analysts were even afraid that the red chips might disappear altogether. The red chips were specifically designed to raise funds from international markets. Shortly after listing they would typically return to the market for cash to pay for asset injections from the parents, usually at prices favourable to the red chip. However, this process more or less stopped around 1997. Moreover, in the late 1990s, the tax privileges enjoyed by red chips were being withdrawn, and the red chips were being separated from their parent companies. The revelation of the huge problems at GDE provided apparent confirmation of the bleak future to be faced by the red chips.

On 13 January 1999, Wu Jiesi, assistant to the Governor of Guangdong, said that the foreign banks facing losses on the mainland were themselves to blame for their predicament. He said the problems arose from their own imprudent lending policies. He said that the creditors could not expect to recover more than 50 per cent of their debts unless they agreed to 'special arrangements' for debt repayment, including extending the repayment deadline by at least two years and possibly including debt-for-equity swaps (*Agence France-Presse*, 14 January 1999). The same message was conveyed in a speech by Shanghai's Mayor, Xu Kuangdi. The closure of GITIC and the restructuring of GDE are 'signals for international lenders that there is no government guarantee on corporate borrowing. In the future banks must lend on market principles' (quoted in *Reuters*, 25 January 1999). On 28 January, the Governor of the PBOC made a formal statement that government approval of foreign borrowing did not amount to a guarantee: 'Foreign banks should now obey market forces. As for the lenders, I think they should make a strict analysis of the balance sheets and the credit-worthiness of the borrowers, not only political factors' (quoted in *Sydney Morning Herald*, 28 January 1999).

At the end of January 1999, in a rare event, foreign media were allowed to attend a meeting of the Guangdong People's Congress (GPC). The leader of the GPC, Zhu Senlin, delivered a shocking statement by bringing into the public spotlight the problems of the province's flagship corporations. He announced that the cash flow problems of GDE were attributable to 'massive losses' caused by stock market speculation financed by funds from two of its listed subsidiaries:

> GDE was doing fine operationally and even successfully expanding its operations by listing a group of well-packaged companies. However, due to bad investments, it got its fingers burned by putting its money into shares which subsequently fell badly. The Guangdong provincial government was unaware of the chaotic situation with GITIC and GDE, but it now knows well what has been going on down there.
>
> (quoted in *East Week*, 2 February 1999)

At this time also, Wang Qishan raised in public the possibility that Guangdong province might contribute its Dongjiang water project to help save GDE. This would involve injecting one of the province's crown jewels into the insolvent company in order to help save it. Local leaders in the GPC 'voiced their opposition against bailing out GDE as doing so would undermine the province's long-term growth by taking away funds needed for local development.' They were 'unhappy about the possible disruption of fund allocations for local development as a result of the provincial government's support for GDE' (*East Week*, 2 February 1999). To many members of the Guangdong government it must have appeared as deeply distasteful to channel the province's funds that could have been used for developmental purposes into saving a company that had wasted huge amounts of funds in speculation, incompetent investment procedures, fraud and theft.

Zhu Senlin's 'outburst' in such a public fashion in the GPC was thought to be closely related to tensions within the Guangdong government about the amount of provincial support that was necessary to save GDE. The provincial government had reportedly set aside around RMB 30 billion to rescue GDE, with a pre-allocation of RMB 15 billion 'to meet the corporation's pressing needs.' The responsibility for providing these rescue funds was reported to lie squarely on the shoulders of the Guangdong government rather than with the central government in Beijing: 'By clearly stating its intention against rescuing GDE, the central government is shifting its responsibility to the local authorities.' However, support from the provincial government was provided against a background of a sharply worsening macro-economic performance in Guangdong province and severe pressures on its ability to raise funds for the provincial budget. The projected provincial government expenditure to save GDE amounted to the equivalent of close to one-half of the government's entire revenue for 1998 (RMB 64 billion). It compared with the province's 1998 outlays on capital construction of RMB 12 billion, and education, of RMB 11 billion (SSBG, GTN, 2000: 207).

Speculation immediately started in the Hong Kong press about the objective of Zhu Senlin's 'stunning revelation,' with detailed discussion about its connection with internal struggles in Guangdong's leadership. Zhu's accusation that GITIC and GDE were 'out of control' was 'incomprehensible' since Zhu was considered a 'bulwark of the province's corporations, having been a former Guangdong Governor and working in the province since 1952.' As Guangdong's 'window' company, GDE was 'part of the supervisory responsibility of the provincial government and Party committee.'

In the middle of January 1999, three of the senior managers of Guangnan resigned. On 28 January it was revealed by Hong Kong's Independent Commission Against Corruption (ICAC) that Guangnan's Assistant General Manager, Li Ruihua, had jumped bail. In early February 1999, KPMG announced that its audit of Guangnan had revealed 'improper and irregular' transactions, including loans by subsidiaries to related companies without adequate disclosure of the transactions. Guangnan's Chairman, Sun Guan, said that Guangnan's directors had 'instructed internal auditors to investigate those areas of the company's business supervised by Li [Ruihua]' (*Dow Jones*, 31 January 1999).

In early February an in-depth analysis of GDE in the Hong Kong press placed much of the blame for the 'fiasco' at GDE upon the uncontrolled subsidiary structure: 'With multi-layered structure of subsidiaries beset by triangular debt, the group has encountered chaotic loan problems and even a serious drain on its assets as a result of embezzlement' (*Hong Kong Economic Times*, 6 February 1999). It estimated the total number of subsidiaries to be around 500. A substantial number of these were under municipal and county governments: 'As a result, GDE does not have the authority to manage these subsidiaries, but it has the obligation to provide loan guarantees, including guaranteeing letters of credit.' It said that many of the local subsidiaries had 'taken advantage of this to secure private gains.' The report gave the example of a key executive in GDE who issued guarantees for bills valued at US$ 60 million in the name of the subsidiary, without informing the parent listed company. As a result GDE found itself 'laden with debts incurred by its subsidiaries.' As of December 1998, GDE's contingent liabilities arising from GDE's guarantees for its subsidiaries totalled US$ 265 million, a fourfold increase compared with the amount reported just six months earlier. The article asked the question:

> Following the announcement of the appointment of Goldman Sachs for the restructuring programme, investors have expected this corporate doctor to nurture the ailing group back to health. But as a foreign advisor, can it really rectify the inherent structural and management problems of this debt-laden company?

On 8 February 1999, Sun Guan resigned as Chairman of Guangnan and was replaced by Kang Dian, who had formerly been Director-General of

CITIC. On the same day it was announced that Guangnan's General Manager, Huang Xiaojiang (James Huang), had also resigned. The company said that the reason for the changes was in order to 'ensure proper oversight of the operations and management of Guangnan.' It said that the main findings of the KPMG auditors indicated 'inappropriate accounting for various transactions and improper and irregular practices.' Trading transactions involving letters of credit opened through the company's facilities 'involve a number of Guangnan's subsidiaries appearing to buy goods from suppliers and to on-sell the goods to buyers.' However, it acknowledged that 'KPMG has been unable to satisfy itself in certain cases that goods actually existed.' Guangnan's subsidiaries appeared to have lent funds to certain PRC companies, but KPMG was 'unable to satisfy itself that these third parties are not related parties or as to the purposes of such loans.' The company also admitted that there were 'significant discrepancies in the ageing analysis of Guangnan's receivables' (*AFX*, 9 February 1999).

Guangnan announced in early February that in 1998 it had suffered a loss of HK$ 3.47 billion, following a profit of HK$ 301.8 million in 1997. KPMG concluded that in the light of its audit of Guangnan, the 1997 financial statements 'possibly required revision.' The Guangdong government asked the creditors to accept a 50 per cent debt write-off alongside a plan to inject assets worth RMB 20.45 billion into GDE and sell RMB 14 billion in under-performing assets (*AFX*, 9 February 1999). The creditors responded by saying that they would 'not accept any debt haircut' (*Agence France-Presse*, 11 February 1999). Throughout the following protracted dispute and negotiations, the creditors argued that they 'had assumed their lending to GDE was fully backed by the Guangdong provincial government,' despite the fact that the Guangdong government had never given any formal guarantee that it would repay GDE's debts in the event that the group was unable to do so from its own resources.

Second creditors' meeting

The second creditors' meeting was held on 1 March 1999. It reported on GDE's overall financial situation, the procedure for restructuring the company, the objectives of the restructuring and the principle of injecting some high-grade assets from Guangdong province. The possible assets for injection involved a variety of infrastructure projects, including the Dongjiang-Shenzhen (Dongshen) water supply project as well as the government's interests in the Shaoguan power plant, and in a variety of toll bridges and toll roads in different parts of the province.

The main objective of the meeting was to clarify GDE's financial results for the nine months to the end of September 1998 as a result of the audit undertaken by KPMG. It reported that GDE's total assets amounted to HK$ 19.39 billion (US$ 2.52 billion), and its liabilities amounted to HK$ 31.87 billion

(US$ 4.14 billion). In other words, liabilities exceeded assets by HK$ 12.5 billion (US$ 1.62 billion). The whole group registered a consolidated loss of HK$ 18.8 billion (US$ 2.4 billion) for the first nine months of 1998. Within this total, GDI incurred a loss of HK$ 2.2 billion (US$ 280 million) and Guangnan incurred a loss of HK$ 3.3 billion (US$ 430 million). Guangnan made adjustments for exceptional items totalling HK$ 3.41 billion, of which provisions for bad or doubtful loans totalled HK$ 2.28 billion (US$ 297 million).

The announcements led to loan calls from banks' lending to GDI, which triggered technical defaults on certain borrowings. This was followed by a freeze on GDI's repayment of loan principals but a commitment to continue paying interest.

GDE's consolidated bank debt as of 21 January 1999 was HK$ 14.45 billion, and debt in bond and notes was HK$ 8.03 billion, making a total of HK$ 22.48 billion (US$ 2.93 billion), of which secured debt amounted to only 13 per cent of the total. Within GDE's total debt, that of GDE Holdings was HK$ 14.58 billion; Guangnan, HK$ 2.87 billion; and other GDE subsidiaries, HK$ 5.03 billion. In addition to bank debt, bonds and loans, GDE had consolidated contingent liabilities totalling HK$ 3.21 billion (US$ 418 million).

The Guangdong government revealed that between mid-December and early February it had provided HK$ 246 million (US$ 32 million) to support GDE. Wang Qishan emphasized the difference between its treatment of GITIC and GDE:

> GITIC and GDE have similar problems but the companies have different natures and the problem of chaotic management was much worse at GITIC. GDI is listed and is a constituent of the Hang Seng Index, therefore we also have to consider the stability of the Hong Kong financial markets.
>
> (quoted in *Agence France-Presse*, 1 March 1999)

Wang Qishan said that initially, one of the reasons for deciding to support GDE, while allowing GITIC to die, was the fact that GDE's balance sheet initially seemed stronger than that of GITIC: 'But now, we see the financial situation at GDE is in the same ballpark as GITIC' (quoted in *FT*, 2 March 1999). Zhong Guanchao, Chairman of GDE, said: 'These financial results are truly sobering. However, this is an important step to get our house in order.'

The meeting confirmed that the Guangdong government was 'committed to the restructuring of GDE, subject to the understanding and cooperation of the financial creditors.' It made clear that a major objective of the restructuring was not merely to 'fix a hole in the balance sheet.' The goal was to fundamentally restructure the entire GDE group's business. This involved fundamental changes in the management system and in the entire business structure. The core of this was to shift the focus of GDI to infrastructure and property, and that of Guangnan to food and beverages. It was proposed also to combine GDE and Nam Yue, a substantially smaller company, both of which were 100 per cent owned by the Guangdong provincial government. Nam Yue was substantially smaller than GDE but also faced a dire financial situation. The meeting confirmed also that the central government had given permission for the Guangdong government to provide funds to GDE in *renminbi* which could be converted to foreign currency to service outstanding loans.

In April 1999, Deloitte Touche Tohmatsu resigned as Guangnan's auditors. On 7 May 1999 Deloitte withdrew their audit report on Guangnan's 1997 financial statement. Such a move was unprecedented in the history of Hong Kong. On 10 May 1999, the Hong Kong Stock Exchange set up a group to check the auditing work of Deloitte at Guangnan.

Relations between the creditors' steering committee and GDE and Goldman Sachs became heated, with constant rumours and counter-rumours in the newspapers. On 2 May it was reported that the Guangdong government had declared that the creditors would be required to accept a 'haircut' of 'up to 30 per cent' of their exposure (*AFX*, 3 May 1999). The creditor banks announced that they refused to accept a 'haircut.' It was reported that the steering committee had written to both Premier Zhu Rongji and the Guangdong Executive Vice-Governor, Wang Qishan, reiterating their position that they would not accept a 'haircut' (*AFX*, 4 May 1999). One banker said that the banks had 'taken a huge blow from the failure of Guangdong International Trust and Investment Corporation, and were determined not to take another one from GDE' (quoted in *SCMP*, 5 May 1999). The creditors complained that they had been excluded from a full role in the restructuring process which they said was being dominated by Goldman Sachs, the advisors to the Guangdong government (*SCMP*, 12 May 1999).

On 15 May 1999, Goldman Sachs published the results of a study by KPMG which showed that if GDE were liquidated, creditors would receive just 26 per cent of what they were owed, perhaps as little as 20 per cent for Guangnan. This was a substantially bleaker scenario for the creditors than the earlier estimates which had suggested a recovery rate of around 60 per cent. The threat of following the same path as GITIC, which had been bankrupted, hung over the whole GDE proceedings, much to the consternation of the creditors.

On 19 May, a delegation from the Hong Kong Monetary Authority, led by Joseph Yam, the Chief Executive, travelled to Beijing to meet Premier Zhu Rongji. The international media reported that the Premier had promised them that there would be 'no haircut' for the GDE creditors and that GDE would 'not be allowed to go bankrupt.' He reportedly assured the delegation that the creditors would ultimately be able to secure 'full repayment of principal and interest' on loans extended to GDE. Apparently referring to the possibility of a debt-for-equity swap, he reportedly said that the company's debt restructuring plan would 'provide an opportunity to minimize losses if creditors are willing to take a long-term interest in the group' (quoted by *AFX*, 24 May 1999). These reported statements by the Chinese Premier gave considerable comfort to the creditors. They interpreted the statements as constituting a promise that the Chinese state would take full responsibility for the debts incurred by GDE. It encouraged the creditors to pursue solutions that would lead to full recovery of their debts, i.e. 'no haircut.'

Third creditors' meeting

The third creditors' meeting was held in Hong Kong on 25 May 1999. Immediately prior to the meeting, emboldened by their meeting with Premier Zhu Rongji, the creditors reiterated that they would 'not accept a haircut.' The bankers were afraid that by accepting a 'haircut' in the case of GDE they might set a precedent for the restructuring of other mainland-owned companies. However, many were said to be 'braced for the possibility' (*FT*, 25 May 1999).

Goldman Sachs intended that the proposals brought to the meeting would 'upset the creditors.' In order to establish a starting point for negotiation, they advised the Guangdong government to make it clear that there would 'not be a bail out.' Wang Qishan made it clear that there was going to be 'pain,' and it would be shared by both sides. The advice from Goldman Sachs, who had long experience of how to play the debt restructuring 'game,' was important for the Guangdong government in their battle with the creditors, since the government was inexperienced in such procedures. Goldman Sachs' advice to be tough with the international creditors achieved the intended result. The creditors were deeply irritated. They knew very well that the Chinese side had hired a high-quality advisor. The situation was analogous to a Western film, in which the town hires the best gunslinger available to protect it from its enemies.

The key to the immensely complex proposal presented to the third creditors' meeting was the injection of the Dongshen water supply project into GDI, which was the strongest part of the GDE Group. The project supplied 75 per cent of Hong Kong's fresh water and had an estimated annual cash flow of around US$ 275 million. The water company was valued at around US$ 2.25 billion. The restructured enterprise would use newly issued shares and notes to exchange for the creditors' claims. The term of some debts would be extended. Certain other debts would be converted into equity in the restructured enterprise so as to lower the interest burden on the enterprise's debts. Wu Jiesi (2001) provides a detailed account of the restructuring proposals.

The Guangdong provincial government estimated that this proposal would mean that the creditors would receive various financial assets with an actual economic value of US$ 2.422 billion, compared with total claims of US$ 4.39 billion. They estimated that this would result in a recovery rate of 55.2 per cent, an economic loss of US$ 1.969 billion and an overall 'hair-cut' of 44.8 per cent. They estimated that the recovery rate for creditors of GDE and Nam Yue would be 56.3 per cent, compared with 45.9 per cent for Guangnan creditors.

Wang Qishan emphasized the contribution made by the Guangdong government under the proposal: 'The people of Guangdong province have offered their highest quality asset [Dongshen Water Company] in order to save the group' (quoted in *China Business Information Network*, 26 May 1999). He emphasized that there was no question of the Guangdong government injecting further assets into GDE: '[The Dongshen Water Company] represents the limit of the Guangdong's government's input, and such a limit has already gone higher than is normal in international restructuring cases' (quoted in *AFX*, 25 May 1999). He told the creditors that the Guangdong government would 'share equally in the economic pain of restructuring in order to ensure that the GDE Group is successfully restructured.' He believed that the losses of the Guangdong government were as great as those of the creditors, 'maybe more depending on the outcome of our negotiations with the banks' (quoted in *AFX*, 25 May 1999). He pointed out that 'all international restructuring cases involve some loss to the creditors.'

Wang Qishan emphasized that the Guangdong government had taken the unusual step of contributing cash over the preceding few months to enable the GDE group to continue to pay interest to its creditors while the restructuring had been under way. He said that the GDE restructuring had caused the Guangdong government to 'tighten its belt.' In the United States when bankrupt companies enter Chapter 11, creditors must accept a stop on all repayment including both principal and interest until the company emerges from Chapter 11 protection. He said that the proposed plan was the 'best deal the creditors would get.' He warned that GDE would only pay interest until the end of June 1999 unless the creditors 'showed good faith in the negotiations.'

Wang Qishan noted, 'This was another meeting with no applause. But creditors must accept the plan, otherwise the outcome would be unimaginable' (quoted in *Reuters*, 26 May 1999). He warned that he could not guarantee that there would not be further Chinese corporate bankruptcies or restructurings, 'otherwise we would not be talking about a market economy, whose most important principle is that the fittest survive and the weakest perish.' However, he stressed that as far as GDE was concerned, the proposal meant that the 'nightmare of bankruptcy can cease from tonight' (*FT*, 26 May 1999).

The counter-example of GITIC was constantly in everyone's mind, both the creditors and the Chinese government. In explaining why the Guangdong government had decided to save GDE, but not GITIC, Wang Qishan said that the government regarded the issue as 'one beyond mere economic considerations.' He pointed out that if the Guangdong government had chosen to liquidate GDE, as it had done with GITIC, then the creditors would have been likely to receive less than one-fifth of their loans. He said that he had taken special care with GDE because he 'did not want to throw Hong Kong's red chip market into turmoil ... We feel we should make a contribution to the stability of Hong Kong' (Wang Qishan, quoted in *New York Times*, 26 May 1999). He emphasized that through the restructuring, 'GDE can escape death and Hong Kong's markets can escape an earthquake.' He said that the ultimate goal of the restructuring went beyond mere debt restructuring. He wanted to 'turn the new GDE into a company like Hutchison Whampoa' (quoted in *AFX*, 25 May 1999).

GDE's Chairman, Zhong Guanchao, said at the meeting that the Guangdong government's objective was to comprehensively restructure the entire business and management of GDE, not just the debt:

> We intend to refocus our core business and dispose of other businesses, and hire the best people and adopt the best practices for our group. With the equal partnership between the government and the creditors, we are confident about creating a company that has a transparent management, prudent financial practices and that maximizes shareholder value.
>
> (quoted in *Reuters*, 25 May 1999)

The Chinese government considered that under the 'one country-two systems' agreement it had a solemn responsibility to ensure the survival of Hong Kong as a prosperous city. After two decades of high-speed growth, the Asian Financial Crisis hugely shocked the city. The AFC precipitated a collapse of Hong Kong's stock market and property market. Hong Kong's GNP fell by almost 8 per cent in 1998. The city was 'shell-shocked.' The wealth of a large fraction of its citizens had been decimated almost at a stroke. Throughout the crisis, as national currencies were devalued across East Asia, there was frenzied speculation about both the mainland's and Hong Kong's exchange rate. In early 2002, Argentina withdrew from the currency board system. Hong Kong was then the only economy with this form of strict control over the exchange rate, pegged to the US dollar. Stability in the exchange rate was crucial for the continued flow of capital into the city. By the late 1990s, the debts of red chip and other mainland firms in Hong Kong totalled around US$ 20–25 billion and on top of this were the much larger debts of the ITICs, much of which was owed to Hong Kong financial firms. If the Chinese government had not stepped in to provide support for GDE and found a way to share the burden with the international creditors, then, as Wang Qishan pointed out, the consequences would have been 'unimaginable.' The bankruptcy of GDE could have had a 'domino' effect on the huge liabilities of mainland-based firms in Hong Kong, with grave consequences for Hong Kong's financial institutions. The Chinese government was deeply concerned to prevent such an outcome.

The Guangdong government had no legal obligation to inject assets into GDE, and there was considerable resistance to doing so in some segments of the political leadership in Guangdong itself. Moreover, injecting a valuable asset into GDE risked giving problematic signals in terms of moral hazard. It softened the tough message that had been conveyed by the GITIC bankruptcy. It might encourage imprudent behaviour by other mainland-based SOEs. It might encourage imprudent lending by international financial institutions, which might now believe that there was at least a partial Chinese government guarantee of the international liabilities for mainland-based firms. However, the Chinese government considered that there was a more important immediate issue, namely, the survival of Hong Kong. Fine issues of moral hazard calculation had to be set against issues of system survival. These issues are not absent from the considerations of Western governments. In 1998, the US government organized a colossal bail-out of Long-Term Capital Management (LTCM) by the main Wall Street banks. This was deeply problematic in terms of moral hazard. It effectively condoned a massive loss of funds through a gigantic speculative operation with 'other people's money.' However, the US government judged that system survival was a higher objective. This issue was to arise in still more dramatic form with the eruption of the Global Financial Crisis in 2008.

The global media interpreted the offer at the creditors' meeting as indicating a 'softening of tone towards foreign lenders,' with 'the banks and the government sharing the losses' (*New York Times*, 26 May 1999). One reason suggested for the softening of tone was the possible embarrassment that could follow from GDE's listed vehicles being made bankrupt:

> Several of GDE's units are listed on the Hong Kong stock exchange and it is likely that if the banks choose to take GDE to court in Hong Kong - as they may if the repayment schedule is too low - they could open a Pandora's box.
>
> (*FT*, 25 May 1999)

The arrest of some of Guangnan's leaders and charges of conspiracy to defraud levelled against them was already highly embarrassing for the mainland, especially for the Guangdong provincial government. This was thought by some commentators to be a 'stick' that could be used to leverage the Guangdong government into going further towards meeting the creditors' demands than they wished to do. This was part of a complicated game of bluff and counter-bluff in testing each other's will to bargain to the end.

Both sides realized that presentation of the proposals to the third creditors' meeting would be the start of a long negotiation process over the fine details. However, an added complication was that in Hong Kong law, as in UK law, any individual creditor could force the company into bankruptcy if they were unhappy with the proposed restructuring plan as it related to them. This was especially difficult in the case of a large restructuring such as

GDE, in which there were hundreds of creditors. By contrast, in the United States, 75 per cent of the creditors can bind the remaining minority. This made the final stages of the negotiation, once the basic principles had been agreed, extremely delicate, with the possibility of the agreement unravelling right up to the final minute.

The initial response from the creditors was that the plan was unsatisfactory. The creditors stated that they believed the plan would result in their being forced to accept losses of between 20 and 40 per cent on their loans, with an average of 27 per cent losses (*Reuters*, 26 May 1999). The steering committee stated: 'The Guangdong government should stand firmly behind the group and support the group in honouring its obligations to financial creditors, as this was the basis of the group's previous borrowings' (quoted in *AFX*, 25 May 1999). The creditors were unhappy that the bulk of their financial risk stayed with the company in the shape of the proposal to issue new debt and equity. Under the plan the creditors would swap their debt for ten-year notes paying an interest coupon of 7 per cent or for preference shares which gave no voting rights and paid a dividend of one per cent per annum: 'The plan is not very fair. It seems the bankers are giving more than the government,' said one Hong Kong banker. The creditors complained that the proposals would essentially extend the repayment period for ten years at 'extremely low interest rates,' during which time they would have very little say in how the company was run.

The creditors were sceptical about the chance of reviving GDE, 'given that many of its assets are in sad shape and some former executives are suspected of corruption.' They did not believe that GDE could restructure its management and business structure successfully, as opposed to merely restructuring its debt obligations. They were nervous of the implications of the proposal for their other loans to Chinese entities: 'If we say we accept a 20 per cent haircut on GDE, we're in effect saying we accept a 20 per cent write-down on our entire Chinese portfolio.' Just as the decision to bankrupt GITIC had large implications for the way in which the GDE issue was resolved, so, in its turn, the way in which the GDE issue was resolved had large implications for the way in which the whole of the red chip and ITIC sector debts were resolved. However, as one commentator noted, 'The grim reality is that bankers have little leverage against GDE short of winding up the company.' The GITIC bankruptcy had demonstrated how unattractive a prospect that would be.

However, 'the creditors' relief seemed palpable' (*New York Times*, 26 May 1999). One advisor to the creditors commented, 'It's definitely an OK place to start negotiating. The Guangdong government didn't have to give anything. These companies are bankrupt.' The solution offered by the Guangdong government even provided the technical possibility that some of the creditors might receive the whole of their debts back in the long run, if the new stock performed well. One commentator noted, 'The Guangdong government has put down its marker. Now at least the banks know where they stand.' The steering committee representing bank lenders to GDE commented: 'The proposed preliminary framework is an important milestone but it is not satisfactory on initial inspection. It provides a starting point for further negotiation to take place between the financial creditors and the Guangdong provincial government' (quoted in *Reuters*, 26 May 1999).

In the end, the general feeling was that the creditors had little option but to accept the haircut. One banker commented:

> Notwithstanding all these guys tramping up to Beijing and all these statements that we won't accept haircuts, there's obviously going to be some sort of haircut. The government can't bail out [GDE] 100 per cent, because if they do, then they'll have to bail out everybody 100 per cent.
> (quoted in *China Securities Bulletin*, 25 May 1999)

Another commented, 'I think for the 30–40 per cent haircut, the banks will swallow it, there is no doubt about it.' Within a few days, the feeling had emerged among the creditors that there were unlikely to be major changes to the restructuring proposal. The efforts of the creditors were thought likely to focus on some increase in assets injected or in some increase in the dividend paid on the preference shares.

Some of the creditors acknowledged that the restructuring proposal was 'good from the central government's perspective,' because it was 'not sending the message that the [central] government would stand as a guarantor for any provincial debt' (Anthony Lok, Head of North Asia banking, Nomura International (HK), quoted in *Agence France-Presse*, 25 May 1999). In other words, it appeared to demonstrate that the 'parent' (in this case the Guangdong provincial government) would, indeed, have to take responsibility for its 'child.'

The stock market responded to the third creditors' meeting with a sharp fall in the shares of both GDI and Guangnan. However, the fall in GDI's shares was far smaller than in those of Guangnan. While GDI fell by 14 per cent on the news of the restructuring proposals, Guangnan plummeted by 42 per cent. Without the benefit of any asset injections, investors' initial response was highly sceptical about Guangnan's prospects. GDI was perceived by the markets as being the major beneficiary of the restructuring proposals, due to the injection of the Dongshen project, which would give it a stable source of income. However, analysts were concerned at the fact that GDI would emerge from the restructuring with a high gearing ratio and large exposure to the US dollar debt. One commented that the main objective of the package appeared to be 'to help save its parent group' (*AFX*, 26 May 1999).

The whole process of restructuring GDE was watched closely by the international financial community, in order to gauge how safe it was to resume large-scale lending to entities not directly covered by explicit central government guarantees.

After fully digesting the restructuring proposals, the creditors quickly returned to the offensive through a sequence of statements and leaked reports to the press. It was reported that on 27 May, the steering committee had agreed that it could accept 'neither the proposal nor any reduction in loan principal repayments' (*AFX*, 28 May 1999). The creditors were said to be deeply concerned at having to accept nearly half their debt in a swap for preference shares, 'whose value will depend on the situation in the stock market.' The bankers said that they were 'not used to taking equity as collateral.' The creditors were said to be preparing their own package, 'completely different to the Goldmans Sachs restructuring plan' (*AFX*, 28 May 1999). It was reported that the creditors did not rule out the possibility of liquidating GDE 'if the Guangdong government remains adamant about its debt restructuring proposal' (*AFX*, 2 June 1999). David Li (Li Guobao), Head of the Bank of East Asia, said that 'some banks will be taking an "everybody dies together" attitude if the Guangdong government refused to make concessions' (quoted in *AFX*, 2 June 1999). Another commented that he agreed with Wang Qishan's estimate that the GDE restructuring effectively amounted to a debt write-off of 50 per cent in which the Guangdong government takes around 25 per cent and the banks take another 25 per cent: 'Yes, we are sharing the responsibility, but we wonder why we [the banks] should take the responsibility?'

On 27 May it was reported that the creditor banks were 'prepared to urge the Guangdong government to punish members of Guangnan (Holdings) Ltd and GDE management who are responsible for the financial crisis the group faces' (*AFX*, 27 May 1999).

On 3 June, David Carse, Deputy Head of the Hong Kong Monetary Authority, urged the creditors to be calm. He hoped that 'both sides would get down to a negotiated compromise.' He was 'unable to see how the creditor banks would be better off if GDE were liquidated: The return to banks would be lower and there would be bigger provisions to make [in the event of liquidation]' (quoted in *AFX*, 3 June 1999). He cautioned that liquidation of GDE would have 'a significant negative impact on other mainland enterprises and would hurt their liquidity ... We should try to avoid a string of liquidations [of mainland entities]' (quoted in *AFX*, 3 June 1999). He did not need to add what was obvious, namely, that a 'string of liquidations' of mainland-based entities would be disastrous for Hong Kong.

On 7 June, David Li (Li Guobao), Head of the Bank of East Asia, confirmed that the creditors were working on a counter-proposal to put to Goldman Sachs (*AFX*, 7 June 1999). However, it had become clear that the counter-proposal would not be forthcoming until after the 15 June deadline set at the original restructuring meeting.

On 9 June 1999, ICAC announced that it had arrested eight people from Guangnan Holdings for their part in an 'enormous' alleged embezzlement. They were accused of embezzling HK$ 200 million (US$ 26 million) from

Guangnan Holdings between March 1997 and June 1999. On 9 June it initiated a court case against two of those arrested, accusing them of embezzling from subsidiary companies by issuing company cheques to other companies controlled by them, by making applications for letters of credit based on bogus transactions and using false accounting methods to cover up their crimes (*FT*, 9 June 1999). The international press reported that the arrests placed the problems at Guangnan in a new light: 'Debt problems at Guangnan – as at its parent group, GDE – had previously been attributed entirely to poor investments and broader economic problems in the wake of the Asian Financial Crisis' (*FT*, 9 June 1999). The creditors hoped that this would give them fresh ammunition with which to bargain for a greater contribution from the Chinese government. It increased the pressure they could apply using the implied threat of forcing 'a string of bankruptcies' of mainland entities in Hong Kong. How many further such revelations would there be if a 'string of mainland firms' went through bankruptcy proceedings?

On 13 June 1999, the Guangdong government announced that it would continue to pay interest to creditors of GDE for a further two months beyond 30 June, 'if creditors continue to negotiate in good faith' (*AFX*, 13 June 1999).

On 25 June 1999, two weeks after the arrest of eight of Guangnan's senior managers for alleged economic crimes, David Li (Li Guobao) Chief Executive of the Bank of East Asia, resigned as one of Guangnan's three independent non-executive directors. A few weeks later he said that the GDE and Guangnan affairs had been 'a great learning experience' for him. They had 'shattered his dream of retiring soon' and had made him 'very angry':

> I was too trusting. At the time when the Guangdong government invited me to be on the board of Guangnan, every time at the board meeting I was given a lot of information. The company's prospects looked good. I only knew later that there were so many subsidiary companies. Actually, I feel that I have been cheated. I used to think that the mainland officials worked for the country, and were not corrupt. But this time I was wrong with my judgement. This has seriously affected my reputation, and has caused me to lose face.
>
> (quoted in *Oriental Daily News*, 10 August 1999)

On 30 June, the creditors finally gave their formal response to the Guangdong provincial government's (GPG) plan to restructure GDE. The creditors refused to acknowledge that they and GPG were 'in the same boat' in respect to the problems at GDE and its associated companies. They explicitly rejected the idea that there should be 'shared responsibility for losses' between the creditors and GPG. The steering committee observed that 'the directors and principal officers of GDE and Nam Yue were appointed by, and many were officials of, GPG.' They observed that 'the strategic planning of the group was carried out in consultation with, and subject to the approval of, GPG.' They observed that 'the investments and projects of the group were developed with a view to promoting Guangdong's economic needs and development, and in the context of the province's 20-year plan.' They added:

> Entities outside the group which appear to be controlled by GPG received a large proportion of the funds lent by the financial creditors to the group, and the majority of these investments and loans made by GDE and Nam Yue now appear to be wholly unrecoverable from these entities.

The creditors demanded that the Chinese central government and/or GPG should treat GDE's international debts as if they were China's sovereign debt:

> It is the strongly held view of the financial creditors that lending to the group was extended on the clearly and mutually understood premise that GPG would support the group and ensure that it was able fully to meet its contractual obligations to the lenders.

They pointed out that since the financial difficulties of GDE had come to light, the financial creditors had been made aware of:

> ... evidence which is strongly suggestive of gross mismanagement within GDE, Nam Yue and Guangnan; wholly inadequate accounting and other records and controls; preparation of accounts for 1997 which were materially inaccurate and misleading; use of funds for purposes which are extraneous to the objects of GDE and Nam Yue and/or which were otherwise inappropriate; and a suspicion of fraud carried out within the group.

For all these reasons, the financial creditors considered that 'GPG bears responsibility for the losses which have occurred and has a responsibility to make good those losses.'

The creditors said that the restructuring proposals 'must provide for a real prospect of eventual full repayment of all outstanding indebtedness owed to the financial creditors.' The restructuring proposals:

> ... do not provide for sufficient assets to be injected into the group to provide for a real prospect of eventual repayment of all outstanding indebtedness owed to the financial creditors. As such, the proposals are not acceptable to the financial creditors.

They calculated that the shortfall in asset injection necessary to ensure full repayment of the debt was 'in the order of HK$ 1.8 billion.' They requested that:

> ... further assets and/or cash flows be identified by GPG for injection into the group, to the extent necessary so that the restructuring provides for a real prospect of eventual full repayment of all the outstanding indebtedness owed to the financial creditors.

On 4 July, Li Guobao (David Li), Chief Executive of the Bank of East Asia, reiterated that he 'refused to accept a haircut.'

After receiving the hostile response from the creditors, the Guangdong government, closely advised by Goldman Sachs, toughened its response in order to bring the creditors into line. Between the end of 1998 and May 1999 the Guangdong government had paid interest on GDE's debts totalling HK$ 3 billion (around US$ 390 million). On 9 July the government announced that it was ceasing to pay the interest on GDE's debts (*SCMP*, 9 July 1999). It said that it was doing so because the creditors had departed from the fundamental principle of the restructuring, namely the need for the banks and the Guangdong government to share the economic pain of the collapse of GDE. This meant, in turn, that Guangnan would be unable to repay interest to its creditors.

The announcement of the cessation of interest payments 'sent a chill down the back of the international creditors.' On the one hand the banks were 'furious at the government for not honouring an earlier pledge to keep interest current.' On the other hand, 'there was little the banks could do about it, short of threatening liquidation,' a step which the government 'knew the creditors did not really want to take,' since debt recovery was estimated at only 26 per cent if GDE was wound up (*Reuters*, 9 July 1999). One banker commented, 'The Guangdong government is basically calling our bluff. It's suggesting that if we ask for too much, then they will just let GDE go' (*Reuters*, 9 July 1999). GITIC had shown vividly how dangerous such a course was for the creditors. By ending interest payments 'China is suggesting that bankers may be faced with the alternative of liquidation' (*FT*, 10 July 1999). Liu Jinbo, Chairman of the Hong Kong Association of Banks, said that he believed the chances of liquidation were not high: 'I am confident that if both sides sit down and talk again, there is still a chance to reach a consensus' (*FT*, 10 July 1999).

In early July rumours circulated that the Chinese government had decided to let GDE be liquidated (*SCMP*, 13 July 1999). This was followed by rumours that Guangnan was to be liquidated (*SCMP*, 14 July 1999). However, many analysts believed these rumours were initiated by the Chinese side simply to put pressure on the creditors. This was followed by rumours that an agreement had been reached between GDE and the creditors (*AFX*, 15 July 1999). The 'game' was being played at many different levels.

On 15 July 1999, Wang Qishan came to Hong Kong to continue the negotiations with the creditors' steering committee. At the meeting, Wu Jiesi, assistant to the Governor of Guangdong province, announced six proposals. First, GPG would make no asset injections into GDE other than the Dongshen Water Company. Second, the losses arising from the failure of GDE should be shared between GDE and the creditors. Third, the restructuring must be negotiated in private, not in front of the mass media. Fourth, the creditors should not make public complaints against the restructuring proposals. Fifth, the restructuring of GDE, GDI and Guangnan should be undertaken as a package. Sixth, the Guangdong government agreed to prevent GDE going bankrupt only if the creditors also agreed. The creditor banks were reported to be 'disappointed' that there had been 'no concessions made by the Guangdong government.'

On 23 July it was reported that the creditors had softened their approach. They were now said to be ready to have fresh talks based on the Goldman Sachs proposals made to the third creditors' meeting (reported in *AFX*, 23 July 1999).

However, the atmosphere was still so bad that on 27 July David Li called on the Hong Kong government to 'get involved in resolving the dispute between the creditors and the Guangdong authorities' (*AFX*, 28 July 1999). David Li said:

> I think the Hong Kong government has to start a dialogue with the provincial government to tell them how serious this thing can be and the effect on Hong Kong and the effect on themselves too. I consider this extremely urgent. I have talked to the Chief Executive [of Hong Kong] to urge him to convince the monetary authority to start a dialogue with the provincial government.
>
> (reported in *AFX*, 28 July 1999)

He said that the Hong Kong government should 'warn the Guangdong provincial authorities of the consequences of not honouring what "most people consider" to be the sovereign debt of Guangdong Enterprises Ltd.' David Li warned that 'Guangdong province will find banks unwilling to lend if it fails to repay loans made to GDE, which creditors assumed had implicit government guarantees' (quoted in *AFX*, 27 July 1999). He noted China-related loans were down almost 12 per cent compared with the same period in 1998.

On 28 July the breakthrough finally arrived. The Guangdong government sent a letter to the creditors asking them to sign an agreement accepting in principle that they would make an economic loss on their investments in GDE. The Guangdong government added that they would be willing, in their turn, to make concessions on the proposals for repayment that would reduce the size of the planned preference share issue from the current 46 per cent of debts owed, to closer to the 25 per cent demanded by the creditors. Under the revised scheme, cash repayment would remain the same, but the authorities would seek to generate higher cash flow levels for creditors from the Dongshen water project that was to be injected into GDI. Additionally, the arrangements on tenure and the interest rate paid on the shares 'might be improved.'

At the ensuing press conference, the creditors acknowledged that they must give up their position of refusing to accept any haircut. Both sides were reported to now be prepared to enter a long negotiation phase. Almost at once, the restructuring entered a new phase. One international banker commented, 'There is give and take on both sides now. Before we just hated each other.'

In early September it was reported that the negotiations between the Guangdong government and the creditors' steering committee were 'progressing well' (*Oriental Daily*, 2 September 1999). However, a final agreement still appeared some way off.

Meanwhile, the extent of the corporate governance difficulties at Guangnan deepened. In December 1998 Guangnan's Assistant General Manager, Li Ruihua, had been arrested in Hong Kong (he subsequently jumped bail) and in June 1999, Hong Kong's ICAC had arrested eight people from Guangnan for their part in an alleged 'enormous' embezzlement. On 23 August 1999 Sun Guan, the former Chairman of Guangnan Holdings, resigned as a Director of GDI. It was reported that he had been detained by Chinese authorities, who were said to be investigating him 'in relation to stock trading' (*Reuters*, 22 August 1999). On 9 September 1999 James (Xiaojiang) Huang, former General Manager of Guangnan, was arrested in Hong Kong and charged by the ICAC with embezzlement.

The difficulties at Guangnan appeared to be part of a wider problem of corporate governance in Hong Kong's red chip companies. Zhu Xiaohua, Chairman of China Everbright, resigned in July 1999 and was rumoured to be under investigation in the mainland. Also in 1999, Jin Jianpei, former General Manager of Hubei province's bankrupt 'window' company, Yi-F Trading, was prosecuted in the mainland for embezzlement. In 1998, Jin Deqin, former Honorary Chairman of Kah Wah bank, was arrested for alleged commercial crimes, and Fang Dacheng, former Senior Executive of Onfem Holdings, was arrested for embezzlement. The *SCMP* commented:

> The pervasive nature of the difficulties [in Hong Kong's mainland corporates] which have affected both listed and unlisted firms backed by the central government and provinces, long-established mainland businesses and recent arrivals, indicates governance problems may be widespread and rooted in culture and management structure.
>
> (*SCMP*, 9 September 1999)

On 14 December 1999 there was a report in the *Hong Kong Economic Times* that the Chinese central government would lend RMB 45.8 billion (US$ 5.5 billion) to the Guangdong government 'to pay the debts of Guangdong

Enterprises Holdings Ltd, Guangdong International Trust and Investment Corporation and other associated companies' (*AFX*, 14 December 1999). The news was interpreted to be 'aimed at boosting the confidence of foreign banks and foreign investors.'

Fourth creditors' meeting

The fourth creditors' meeting was held on 16 December 1999. It was presented with a framework agreement, consisting of a complex restructuring package. The framework agreement was formally signed at the meeting. It followed the main principles of the package presented to the third creditors' meeting but with some significant modifications. In exchange for their existing debt, the banks were to be offered a package of instruments including notes from Dongjiang Water Supply Company (Dongshen), which was to be injected into GDI, various debt instruments of GDE, real estate and equity participation in certain related companies. The debt restructuring would share the losses between the Guangdong provincial government and the creditor banks.

The Chairman of the creditors' steering committee, E. M. Williams said: 'This is another step in the long road to solving this complex issue. The working group of banks believes that this proposal is an appropriate one under the circumstances' (quoted in *AFX*, 12 January 2000). He said that he considered the terms of the proposal to constitute an improvement for the creditors compared with that presented to the third creditors' meeting. In fact, obtaining final approval from over 120 creditors proved more complex than anticipated. There was prolonged argument about minute details of the final restructuring proposal, and the final agreement was not signed until one year later.

Simultaneously with presenting the restructuring proposal, Wang Qishan confirmed that the Guangdong provincial government had borrowed RMB 38 billion from the central government to help solve the financial crisis in Guangdong. He said that the funds were to 'help boost confidence in the province while stopping further corporate bankruptcies.' Guangdong would repay the funds over an eight- to nine-year period (*AFX*, 16 December 1999).

On 2 September, it was reported that there were clashes between two of the 'big five' accountants, Ernst and Young and Deloitte, and the Hong Kong Society of Accountants (HKSA). The HKSA responded to 'immense pressure from the stock exchange and the media' to instigate an investigation into Ernst and Young and Deloitte's audits of accounts of two red chip companies, Cosco and GDE respectively (*SCMP*, 2 September 2000). Each of the accountancy firms fiercely resisted such an investigation. However, the investigation was deemed necessary by the HKSA. It was acknowledged in the Hong Kong press that Hong Kong was 'a veritable pariah in terms of reining in directors,' and that there was serious concern about the 'too cosy relationship between auditors and their clients' (*SCMP*, 2 September 2000).

The final restructuring deal was agreed on 22 December 2000. The total amount of GDE and Nam Yue's debt was confirmed by both sides to be US$ 4.9 billion. Of this total, bank creditors amounted to US$ 2.87 billion, note holders to US$ 1.11 billion, other creditors to US$ 576 million and the Guangdong provincial government to US$ 385 million.

The final package was immensely complex in its details (Wu, 2002). However, the essence of it was relatively simple. Both bond holders and bank creditors were to receive a package for every US$ 100 owed them by the GDE Group. The package consisted of a bond certificate in Dongshen with a face value of US$ 45, a GDE security with a face value of US$ 10–12, and US$ 10 in cash (*SCMP*, 7 December 2000). The final 'haircut' for the creditors as a whole was estimated by the Guangdong provincial government to be 43 per cent, with a recovery rate of 57 per cent. For bank creditors and note holders alone, the haircut was estimated to be 38 per cent, corresponding with a recovery rate of 62 per cent. The slightly higher recovery rate for bank creditors and note holders was mainly due to the fact that they received interest payments in cash, whereas the Guangdong provincial government, in its capacity as a creditor participating in the restructuring and other non-financial creditors, did not receive such interest payments in cash.

The total contribution of the Guangdong provincial government (GPG) to the debt restructuring amounted to a gross figure of over US$ 3.02 billion, including over US$ 2.2 billion for the injection of the Dongshen water project, US$ 479 million in interest payments, US$ 109 million in advisory fees and US$ 232 million in other advances. During the reconstruction process, the GPG was able to recover US$ 1.01 billion, making a net contribution of over US$ 2.01 billion to the restructuring. The GPG estimated that the haircut of the whole class of creditors was US$ 2.12 billion: 'Generally speaking the results were in line with the overall restructuring objective that the Guangdong provincial government and the creditors would both share the economic loss' (Wu, 2001: 129).

Postscript

On 23 February 2000, the Executive Vice-Governor of Guangdong province, Wang Qishan, listened to Wu Jiesi's work report on restructuring GDE. Wang Qishan commented:

> GDE after restructuring has three challenges. The first challenge is how to manage the current businesses well. Within five years, GDE must professionally deal with the Trust and Investment Companies, some of the assets of the new company and the none-core businesses of Guangdong Investment. This will decide whether the old debts can be repaid on schedule; therefore, it is closely related to the success or failure of GDE's debt restructuring. In addition, the assets that are currently in

nearly 500 enterprises should be merged into tens of enterprises according to different business categories. These assets should be managed professionally and have added value.

The second challenge is to establish a modern enterprise management system that is compatible with the market mechanism in Hong Kong. This is the key issue that will determine whether GDE is able to hold its position in the intense market competition, seek development and avoid slipping back to the old way.

The third challenge is to set the direction for future development, seize the opportunity, and look for new areas for profit growth. In the aspect of developing new businesses, GDE must centre itself on the economic development plan for the whole province, seize the opportunity for foreign businesses provided by our country's entry to WTO, clarify the core businesses, and strengthen itself while promoting the economic development in Guangdong province.

Among the three challenges, the most difficult one is to establish a modern enterprise system. Without an internal management system of business vitality and strict discipline, even the current businesses cannot be managed well; let alone the development. Some people say that after GDE's debt restructuring, the key is business development. I don't agree with this view. I think the key lies in internal management. I hope from now on, you begin to research various regulations and rules of the new GDE with regard to human resource management, income distribution, capital management and investment management, and set up an inter-related management system. If the management is good, there is no worry for development. Therefore, the most important content of GDE restructuring is to establish an internal management system that is compatible with the environment of an economic and commodity market.

(Wu, 2002: 233–4)

In March 2001, the *International Financial Law Review* and *Asia Law and Practice* journals selected the GDE debt restructuring as the winner of, respectively, the 'Restructuring Deal of the Year' and the 'Best Restructuring Deal in Asia in 2000.' The reasons cited were that, first, the GDE debt restructuring was the largest ever undertaken by a Chinese state-owned entity. Second, restructuring had taken two years to complete and was 'widely touted as a landmark case for reviving confidence in the investment arms of Chinese provincial and municipal governments.' Third, a large number of people in numerous intermediaries were at different times engaged in working on the debt restructuring. Finally, it involved complicated cross-border issues. A detailed account of this immensely complicated process concluded: 'In fact, not only was the GDE debt restructuring the winner among Asian restructuring deals, it was also a landmark deal in the history of world corporate restructuring' (Wu, 2001: 1).

In early 2002 it was announced that in the first eleven months of 2001, 'New GDE' had made a pre-tax profit of HK$ 520 million, excluding the revenue from the Dongshen water project. This compared with a loss of HK$ 202 million in the same period of 2000. Wu Jiesi estimated that 59 per cent of the improvement was due to the successful debt restructuring. In addition, he considered that the improvement was assisted by the implementation of the 'Seventeen Prohibitions.' He also noted that in the year 2001, New GDE had dealt with and closed a total of eighty loss-making enterprises, which had drained around HK$ 600–800 million in ready cash out of GDE. It had reduced employment in New GDE from around 3,000 to around one-half that number. It had fired senior managers who were not able to do their job properly, and had substantially increased the remuneration for the remaining senior managers.

On 31 October 2000, Kang Dian, Chairman of Guangnan and Deputy Chairman of GDI, announced his resignation from both positions. He told reporters that he was submitting his resignation to GDE, the parent of GDI and Guangnan, 'because the GDE restructuring is close to completion' and he would 'like to spend more time with his wife, who has been ill since 1997' (*Reuters*, 31 October 2000). On 1 November, Wu Jiesi announced Kang Dian's resignation and stated:

> The Directors of the Company [GDI] would like to express their gratitude to Mr Kang Dian for his devotion and dedication to the Company and its subsidiaries (the 'Group') over the years. Mr Kang Dian's significant contribution towards the business management of the Group during the time when he acted as Executive Deputy Chairman and his positive contribution to the Group's restructuring are also greatly appreciated.

During the course of GDE's restructuring, Zhong Guanchao, Chairman and General Manager, suffered a stroke and had been reduced to the state of a human vegetable.

At that time, Sun Guan, former Deputy General Manager of GDE and Managing Director of Guangnan, was reportedly living in Guangzhou, with a warrant for his arrest issued by the Hong Kong police. There were arrest warrants outstanding in Hong Kong for fourteen other senior managers of Guangnan.

What kind of firm was GDE?[14]

The red chips grew from being 'window' companies in Hong Kong in the early stages of China's system reform into a far wider concept. As they gained autonomy in the 1990s, and were able to tap international capital markets, they developed into 'boundary-less conglomerates.' The stated ambition for a significant group of red chips was to create a group of globally competitive Chinese conglomerates to rival those in other parts of East Asia, including Hong

Kong itself. A close examination of the nature of GDE is especially useful as it provides insights into the nature of the large Chinese state-owned firm as it increases its business activities outside the regulatory constraints of the Chinese mainland, with its overseas branches operating in a quite different business culture and regulatory environment. This issue has become increasingly important in recent years as China's large state-owned firms have expanded their international operations under the 'going out' (*zou chu qu*) policy.

Business structure

The GDE Group as a whole had over 500 subsidiaries. This is a large number for any company. It is a huge number for a company of GDE's size. Why did GDE establish such a large number of subsidiaries? The subsidiaries operated in a wide range of businesses, including finance, hotels, tourism, infrastructure, manufacturing, real estate, trade and retailing, transport, beer, tanning and construction materials. The overlap of businesses within each sector was enormous, with consequent inefficiencies. In the finance sector there were fifteen companies (thirteen in GDE and two in GDI). In hotels and tourism there were eighteen companies (four in GDE and fourteen in GDI), and in beer alone, there were six companies. Each company was an independent legal person with its own interests. Each of them used the overall 'GDE' brand to do business. They typically used the name of GDE to borrow, so that the contingent liabilities of GDE greatly exceeded its direct liabilities. Moreover, the subsidiaries often acted as guarantors for each other's borrowings and for those of the other red chips.

Well before the restructuring process had been concluded, the Guangdong government introduced major reforms to GDE's management system. These were termed the 'seventeen prohibitions' announced in March 2000. They shed considerable light retrospectively on the way that GDE had been run. The 'seventeen prohibitions' required 'strict control over the establishment of subsidiaries and other organizations.' Henceforth, no individual, including even the Chairman or the General Manager of the Group, would have the authority to approve the establishment of companies or offices anywhere:

> The establishment of any company at any level, including project companies or organizations such as offices, must be first thoroughly considered and approved by the Board of the company, then further reviewed and analyzed and then approved by the Board of the holding company.
> (Wu, 2001; 157)

In other words, before the seventeen prohibitions, companies had been established on a widespread basis by GDE's subsidiaries in order to serve the personal interests of individuals and groups within GDE.

GDE had no fewer than eight tiers of companies, including the so-called 'project companies.' Even excluding the 'project companies,' the GDE group had a total of five tiers. The management at each level had the authority to establish new companies below them or to set up branches or representative offices. This resulted in a proliferation of organizations and increased duplication in management, leading to 'a complete breakdown of management control' (Wu, 2001: 157). Various companies in the GDE Group had thirty-three individual offices in Beijing, Shanghai, Guangzhou and Shenzhen, with twenty-two of them concentrated in Guangzhou alone (Wu, 2001: 157). These thirty-three offices employed 177 people and owned fifty-eight vehicles, four motorcycles, forty-seven apartments and several office buildings.

When Goldman Sachs began work at GDE they were staggered by the 'mind-boggling complexity of the company. We had never seen a company like it.' They had never encountered a company with such a vast number of subsidiaries. They found that the whole GDE Group had no fewer than 572 constituent enterprises. Goldman Sachs spent a long time placing the key facts of each of the many hundreds of subsidiaries onto filing cards and then sorting them into shoe boxes, each of which represented a different category of business: 'It was sheer hard slog, ten to twelve or even more hours each day, sifting through the company records, just trying to get a clear picture of the assets and liabilities.' By the end of this process, Goldman Sachs believed that they knew far more about the company than anyone else: 'No-one else understood what GDE really was.'

By the time Goldman Sachs had finished their investigation, they concluded that GDE itself (as opposed to the whole Group) had 207 enterprises. Of these fifty-four were incorporated in the mainland and 152 in Hong Kong and overseas. If the head office of GDE was counted as a first-tier enterprise, then there were thirty second-tier enterprises, 126 third-tier enterprises, thirty fourth-tier enterprises, ten fifth-tier enterprises, six sixth-tier enterprises and four seventh-tier enterprises.

Guangnan alone had sixty-six enterprises in operation and/or holding assets, of which nineteen were incorporated in the mainland and forty-six in Hong Kong and overseas. Counting the head office as the first tier, there were thirty-five second-tier enterprises, fourteen third-tier enterprises, ten fourth-tier enterprises, one fifth-tier enterprise and five sixth-tier enterprises.

However, even this large number was greatly exceeded by GDI (Guangdong Investment) which had no fewer than 247 enterprises in operation and/or holding assets, of which sixty-nine were incorporated in the mainland, and 177 in Hong Kong and overseas. Counting the head office as the first tier, there were forty-six second-tier enterprises, 119 third-tier enterprises, forty-four fourth-tier enterprises, twenty-seven fifth-tier enterprises, four sixth-tier enterprises and six seventh-tier enterprises.

Nam Yue, which was merged with GDE during the restructuring, and was also owned by the Guangdong government, had fifty-two enterprises in operation and/or holding assets, of which sixteen were incorporated in the mainland and thirty-five in Macao, Hong Kong and overseas. Counting the head office as the first tier, there were three second-tier enterprises, eight third-tier enterprises, twenty-four fourth-tier enterprises, eleven fifth-tier enterprises and five sixth-tier enterprises.

The international experts working on the GDE restructuring concluded that there were essentially 300 operating companies, and that the headquarters had 'no control over them at all.' They frequently borrowed with GDE as the guarantor, but without any formal process of project appraisal and approval.

Numerous subsidiaries do not necessarily mean that a company is badly run. Many Hong Kong-based companies have numerous subsidiaries. For example, in 2001 Hutchison Whampoa had a total of almost 170 'principal subsidiary and associated companies' (Hutchison Whampoa, 2001: 109–115). However, the turnover of Hutchison Whampoa was far greater than that of GDE. Moreover, the key questions are the purposes for which the subsidiaries were established, the degree of control over their establishment and the degree of monitoring of their business behaviour by the parent company. Goldman Sachs asked themselves why GDE had established such a large number of subsidiaries. They concluded that 'at least to some degree it was in order to perpetrate fraud.'

Well before the onset of the Asian Financial Crisis, GDE's management had become aware of deep internal problems due to the sprawling and uncontrolled structure of innumerable subsidiaries. Between 1995 and 1997 it had attempted on several occasions to introduce reforms. It tried to regroup the second-tier companies by core business types and establish each group as a management, financial and profit control centre for the respective companies. GDE was intended to provide centralized direction of policy and 'mediate and control the finances of the group companies.' GDE's headquarters also 'requested that the third-tier companies focus on management and withdrew their right to establish new group companies under them' (Wu, 2001: 7). It was proposed that existing companies under the third-tier subsidiaries be abolished. At the same time, it was proposed that several changes be made to GDE's salary system, financial management system and internal controls of the group. In fact, these proposed reforms mostly were not implemented:

> Some of the reform measures failed because of opposition from within all levels of the group. They were often delayed by internal resistance and eventually abandoned. Other reform measures were not implemented in time before the impact of the Asian Financial Crisis began to be felt by the group.
>
> (Wu, 2001: 8)

Business behaviour

Insider control

The seventeen prohibitions of March 2000 banned GDE's directors from holding directorships in more than one company at any given level and from holding directorships across different levels. The penalty for violation of the ban was being fired. The system prior to the restructuring of GDE had allowed the growth of a 'black box' of internal control by a powerful group of people within GDE.

The overlapping offices of the senior managers of GDE and its subsidiaries created large problems for corporate governance. The boards of directors in reality 'were really controlled by "insiders", and the executive directors-cum-managers acted as the *de facto* "owners" of the companies' (Wu, 2001: 151). In Wu Jiesi's view, insider control was exercised at the level of the main subsidiaries, namely GDI and Guangnan, rather than GDE itself: 'GDE, as the majority shareholder of Guangnan and GDI, basically had little control over the directors that it nominated to the Guangnan and GDI boards.' He considered that as a result of this, 'GDE also had little say over the appointment or removal of the management of GDI or over their business activities': 'for a long time, the companies under the GDE Group all acted independently,' and 'even appointed the auditors and accountants of their choice' (Wu, 2001: 151).

GDE made many disastrous investments. For example, from 1992 to 1998 there were numerous transactions between GDE and Nanfang International (*Nanfang Guoji*), a property development company listed in Hong Kong. These transactions totalled around HK$ 11 billion. They included GDE buying shares in Nanfang, guaranteeing borrowing by Nanfang, acting as guarantor to Nanfang's stock purchases and directly lending to Nanfang. The largest set of transactions came in 1997 when GDE and GDI together invested a total of HK$ 1.6 billion in Nanfang. GDE loaned HK$ 600 million to Nanfang and bought a 20 per cent ownership share in it. At the same time GDI also bought a 10 per cent ownership share in Nanfang. The investments were followed by a large increase in Nanfang's share price. In July 1998, there was 'wild sale' of Nanfang stock with the shares losing 90 per cent of their value almost overnight. Rumours later circulated in Hong Kong's financial circles that GDE insiders had personally benefitted from their own company's investments in classic 'insider trading' fashion. It was rumoured that insiders had taken gains personally from the stock appreciation stimulated by the investment decisions they had made on behalf of the companies that employed them. They then allowed their employer company to bear the losses for the subsequent collapse in the stock price.

It is clear, even from the publicly available documents, that certain senior managers of GDE and its main subsidiaries had strong interests in the lower-level subsidiary companies and their associated companies. The whole GDE Group had a total of 1,509 company director positions, and the number of people who occupied directorship positions totalled 548 (Wu, 2001: 160). In other words, each person held an average of 2.8 directorships. The person holding the most directorships within the GDE Group held a total of seventy-nine directorships! This structure created the possibility for a small group, perhaps just two or three senior officers within the company, to create their own power bases outside the supervisory control of the parent, GDE:

> For example, if the group chairman or the group general manager also acted as the director of a third-tier company, then by virtue of the personal power and influence of this director, this third-tier company would become outside the supervisory control of its parent, even though the parent, being a second-tier company within the group and the immediate holding company of the third-tier company in question, would need to be able to exercise control.
>
> (Wu, 2001: 160)

Numerous discussions with different people looking at the issue from different angles within GDE and its subsidiaries suggest that at least by the time of the GDE restructuring, the central leadership within GDE had lost control of Guangnan. The widespread view within the Group is that Guangnan persistently hid information from the parent company.

Off-balance-sheet accounts

The seventeen prohibitions stipulated: 'No individual, including the chairman or general manager of the group, has the authority to establish, for whatever reason, off-balance-sheet assets or special bank accounts outside of the normal formal accounts.' Anyone violating these regulations was to be fired and 'reported to the relevant judicial organs for possible corruption and embezzlement enforcements and investigation.' The use of 'off-balance-sheet accounts' (*zhang wai zhang*) was widespread, not only in GDE, but also in Chinese state-owned enterprises generally, both on the mainland and in mainland Chinese enterprises overseas. Wu Jiesi recognized that there was a widespread attitude that 'as long as I have not put money directly into my own pocket, there is no problem' (Wu, 2001: 158). The off-balance-sheet accounts allowed others outside the company to benefit through collusion with those working inside the company: 'The use of off-balance-sheet "accounts-outside-accounts" not only led to the loss of state-owned or corporate assets, it also led, more seriously, to the interests of enterprises becoming alienated from those of its management and employees' (Wu, 2001: 158).

When these problems came to light among mainland firms in Hong Kong, the typical way of dealing with them was to re-assign the offenders back to the mainland. However, it was difficult for the mainland authorities to collect evidence about their behaviour from regulatory authorities in Hong Kong or elsewhere overseas. Consequently, there was no serious deterrent to such behaviour. Moreover, they were often typically appointed to their position due to their political connections in the mainland. These same connections typically enabled them to escape police, Party or judicial action on their return to the mainland. It was possible for employees of red chip companies to be wanted for arrest in Hong Kong for alleged economic crimes but simultaneously to escape investigation or prosecution in the mainland due to their political connections. If offenders within red chip companies were, indeed, dealt with by the government on the mainland, then they were typically required to undergo 'political thought reform' and 're-education through self-criticism,' rather than investigation or dismissal from the company. In other words, there was little serious penalty for breaking the law: 'This is an important reason why the practices of special accounts or "little treasure chests", in all its different guises, was impossible to stop' (Wu, 2001: 158).

Lack of control over personal expenditure

The seventeen prohibitions outlawed the use of company credit cards other than in accordance with company regulations. Failure to comply would result in dismissal. It was difficult to control the use of company credit cards among PRC-owned enterprises in Hong Kong. The PRC companies were owned by the state. It was unusual for the chairman of a PRC company in Hong Kong to have the determination to confront the managers about credit card abuse. Moreover, the culture that had developed in the red chip companies was such that the chairman and general manager themselves often misused the company credit cards. How to deal with this issue was 'a matter that confounded the majority of management of PRC-owned enterprises in Hong Kong' and 'GDE was no exception' (Wu, 2001: 159).

A further prohibition contained in the seventeen prohibitions related to various other 'irregular expenses.' Henceforth, all reimbursements of expenses were to be submitted to, and processed in, the company where the individual drew their salary. This included the group directors and the directors at all levels. Those who violated the rule were to be fired. The rules governing expenses in Hong Kong were relatively relaxed compared to many other countries. PRC-owned companies operating in Hong Kong developed a lax approach towards the reimbursement of personal expenses. Some people claimed reimbursement for their own family expenses. Some people used photocopies of the same receipt to claim reimbursement from different companies within the GDE group. This phenomenon is called 'eat one, get two more for free' (Wu, 2001: 159). Some paid for items with a company credit card and then used the receipt to claim reimbursement from the company.

Within PRC-owned companies it was widespread for the group employees to eat free in the company's hotel and restaurant subsidiaries. Under the seventeen prohibitions this practice was banned, and those who violated the regulation were to be fired. It was illegal in both Hong Kong and the mainland to accept bribes and to steal. However, it was not illegal to eat, drink and be 'entertained' at the company's expense. While it may be hard to ruin a company's balance through lavish corporate entertainment, these practices had a corrosive effect on the corporate culture of PRC-owned firms operating in Hong Kong.

Remuneration and motivation

To what degree did the level of remuneration in PRC-owned companies operating in Hong Kong in the 1990s affect the employees' behaviour? The annual remuneration for company directors and senior managers in international financial institutions operating in Hong Kong was normally several million Hong Kong dollars. The remuneration of their counterparts in PRC-owned firms was usually a small fraction of this, less than HK$ 200,000 per year. On the mainland this was regarded as a high salary and an object of envy. However, in Hong Kong it was a relatively low salary. The senior managers of PRC-owned companies in Hong Kong had to deal every day with people who earned vastly greater salaries than themselves. This helped to undermine their moral resolve. They felt that they had responsibilities that were at least equivalent to those of their counterparts in global corporations, and this helped to justify behaviour that was contrary to the rules of the companies they worked for. Moreover, the phenomenon was a collective one. As long as others within the PRC companies in Hong Kong behaved in this way, there was little point for any individual not also to behave in this way. Much of the rule-breaking required the cooperation of others within the firm, so there was heavy pressure on all within the company to break the rules. Those who did not participate were a threat to those that did break the rules. The punishments for breaking the rules were so small, or even non-existent, that they did not constitute a credible threat to the individual's behaviour.

Failings among financial officers

One of GDE's seventeen prohibitions required that GDE companies at all levels should employ, through an 'open selection process,' accountants who were locally qualified in Hong Kong. The PRC-controlled companies in Hong Kong typically appointed a financial controller who was a government official or executive in an SOE in the mainland. They were frequently not qualified as accountants even in China, and rarely qualified in accountancy in Hong Kong: 'The degree of professionalism and the standard of professional ethics tend to be higher among Hong Kong qualified accountants generally' (Wu, 2001: 160).

Failure to have joint verification of external payments

The seventeen prohibitions forbade the making of external payments without the joint verification and approval of the general manager, the financial controller and the general manager of the finance department of each company. All cheques were to be signed jointly by them: 'Trust cannot, and should not, replace a proper system of checks and balances' (Wu, 2001: 161). Clearly, GDE had relied on 'trust' rather than 'a proper system of checks and balances' in the exercise of the key function of financial control.

Absence of controls over investment loans and guarantees

The seventeen prohibitions introduced the principle that all GDE's investments, loans and guarantees of listed companies within the GDE group should be formally considered and approved by the board of directors of those companies. Those of other companies within the group should first be considered by the board of the company concerned and then approved by the intermediate holding company and, then, ultimately, approved by the board of GDE. The penalty for failure to observe this rule was dismissal. In the past, all of the GDE companies had the authority to make these decisions independently, without formal discussion or approval procedures. This was a central issue in GDE's loss of control over its investments. Under the new regulations, companies at the third tier or below had no authority to make outside investments, borrow money or provide guarantees. Second-tier companies wishing to make outside investments, loans or guarantees needed first to undertake formal feasibility studies, which should then be presented to the board of directors before being submitted for approval to GDE's headquarters for discussion and approval.

The shift in business mentality

One view of GDE is that its business ethos altered substantially over time. For example, in the case of Guangnan, one commentator's view was that its listing in 1994 was highly successful. However, after the listing, Guangnan expanded over-aggressively. It made a succession of investments that were far beyond its management capability, independently of any other aspect of company behaviour. Most of the projects undertaken by Guangnan in the mid-1990s ended in failure. Following the listing, Guangnan found it easy to raise money on the international markets. This stimulated the development of a 'gambling mentality.' Finally, as it became apparent that the gambles were less and less successful, Guangnan moved towards criminal and fraudulent activities, which ultimately pushed it into a dead-end.

Government monitoring

In order to understand the behaviour of GDE, it is necessary to consider carefully its relationship with the Guangdong government. Were GDE's difficulties due to excessive interference by the provincial government? Were they, instead, due to lack of interference from the provincial government that allowed GDE to operate as a 'feudal' independent kingdom, or, even, to lack of oversight by GDE over its own subsidiaries, which in turn operated as independent kingdoms?

GDE's relationship with the Guangdong government was close. In the view of Wu Jiesi (2001), the relationship of the Guangdong government with GDE went through a number of different phases. In the first phase of

Guangdong's development in the early 1980s, the world knew little about China and vice versa. In this phase the concept of an 'enterprise' was only weakly developed in China. In this phase, Wu Jiesi believes GDE did serve as a true 'window' company, with great benefit to Guangdong province. However, in the mid-1980s, the concept of industrial enterprise reform emerged in China. During the second half of the 1980s, government control over GDE 'declined drastically' as it came increasingly to resemble a real enterprise. In this period GDE developed its own rights and connections with the international economy. In Wu Jiesi's view, out of GDE's total debt of around US$ 6 billion, only one-sixtieth (US$ 0.1 billion) was attributable to following government instructions for the use of funds for specific purposes. At the end of the 1980s, GDE rapidly developed its capital operations, which were the key to its rapid growth.

In the second phase, although the government was not permitted by Chinese law to provide formal guarantees of international borrowings, GDE used the name of the Guangdong government to attract capital from abroad. The enterprise pursued international capital to support its own expansion but used the reputation of the provincial government to do so. This approach of using the provincial government's reputation to borrow expanded rapidly during the 'bubble' in Guangdong in the early 1990s. At this time, it was the international lenders themselves who suggested the device of the 'comfort letter' from the provincial government. The combination of the relatively high rate of interest, and government 'support' through the comfort letter, made it attractive for international financial institutions to lend to GDE.

By 1994, GDE's degree of insolvency was already 'very serious.' An internal report within GDE said that the chosen method of growth ('high speed, high tempo, high debt') was unsustainable. In order to continue in this fashion, it was crucial to have the cooperation of the accountants who audited the books. The provincial government may have been kept ignorant of the true internal state of affairs at GDE from as early as the mid-1980s.

There were numerous issues involved in the failure of supervision of the different levels within GDE. It is indeed the case that GDE's top managers were appointed directly by the governor: 'The Guangdong government, through its beneficial ownership of all GDE's outstanding share capital, has the power to elect all of the members of the board.' Technically, GDE was required to report directly to the Guangdong Provincial Governor. However, the Governor had many other issues with which to concern himself. Moreover, GDE was registered in Hong Kong. The Governor only visited Hong Kong once or twice a year, and then had only a couple of hours each time to visit GDE. Each year, the head of GDE made a visit to Guangzhou to report. This also was only for a couple of hours each time. The Vice-Governor of Guangdong was in no better position to directly supervise the activities at GDE. Like the Governor he was not appointed for his professional training in business management or accounting. GDE was regarded as a 'bureau' (*ting* or *ju*) within the Guangdong provincial government, and other bureau at the same horizontal level in the Guangdong power structure had no right to interfere in or monitor it.

Did GDE's restructuring change it into a real firm?

GDH

The restructured GDE holding company (including Nam Yue and Dongshen Water Supply) was re-named simply 'Guangdong Holdings' (GDH). The ultimate goal of the Guangdong government in GDE's restructuring was not just to restructure the company's debt but also to restructure the whole operating mechanism of the company. Guangdong's provincial leaders made this abundantly clear to Wu Jiesi from early on in the restructuring process. In the words of Executive Vice-Governor Wang Qishan: 'In a nutshell, the most important aspect of the GDE restructuring is the building of a management structure system that is compatible with the market economy environment.' We have seen that Wang Qishan declared that the goal of the restructuring was to 'turn GDE into a real company, like Hutchison Whampoa.' Wu Jiesi outlined the changes that would be necessary to achieve this goal:

> As long as the new GDH group, as a whole, has learned from past experience and promptly comes up with a management system that is compatible with the competitive market economy environment, has in place a set of practical and effective internal incentive and supervisory systems, prepares and implements relevant company regulations, promotes a corporate culture that is based on solid business performance, steers the group towards becoming a focused specialized group, and adheres strictly to the relevant laws and regulations from top to bottom, then the new GDH is bound to rise again from the ruins of GDE.
>
> (Wu, 2001: 156)

Simply to set out these conditions for the revival of GDE was to recognize the size of the task that faced the new management of GDH. Even after the restructuring, GDH was 100 per cent owned by the Guangdong provincial government, and it retained control of the restructured subsidiaries, GDI and Guangnan. Achieving the 'separation of government and enterprise' necessary to produce a modern management system was a great challenge for the new management of GDH. The Chairman of GDH, Wu Jiesi, was the former assistant to the Governor of Guangdong province, and the General Manager of GDH was Li Wenyue, Vice-Secretary of the Guangdong provincial government. The Board of Directors 'representing the shareholders' interests' and the management remained inextricably connected. Prior to the restructuring, GDE's offices in Hong Kong also served as the offices of the provincial government in Hong Kong. Nominally, the restructuring was accompanied by a re-location of the offices of the government. In fact, they remained at GDE. In this sense, the relationship of the Guangdong government with GDE could not have been closer.

There was considerable scepticism in Hong Kong business circles that restructuring GDE was likely to produce a viable and competitive company:

> What is more important to the banks than the debate about whether there is a haircut is what kind of animal GDE will become after the restructuring. GDE's operating structure and management made it impossible to make the company commercially viable even if it had been under the control of a genius.
>
> (analyst, quoted in *AFX*, 24 May 1999)

Few people believed that the injection of a single large asset, the Dongshen Water Company, was sufficient to restructure GDE's business fundamentally, as opposed to restructuring its debts: 'Even if they get enough to pay back interest and principal, the future of the company is not so bright' (*FT*, 25 May 1999). One analyst observed: 'The key question for the GDE group of companies is that they are poorly run. If nothing is done to revamp the management, the group might end up in a similar situation again five years down the line' (quoted in *AFX*, 26 May 1999).

The preceding pages examined a number of the 'seventeen prohibitions' at length. However, after they were introduced, even some of GDE's senior staff admitted that they were 'not taken seriously by GDE's staff working in Hong Kong.' To change this culture required more than a set of regulations. How could the new regulations be taken seriously when everyone in the company knew that the key members of the 'black box' of inner control that Wu Jiesi discussed in his book (Wu, 2001) had not suffered any apparent punishment other than being required to return to live in the mainland? Some observers considered that the regulations were window-dressing put into place for the specific case of GDE, solely because it was forced through a humiliating public restructuring. The task that faced the new management at GDH was enormous. Wu Jiesi, the new Chairman, hoped that the company could 'do better than before', but had 'no idea if it [could] solve the problems.' However, the Chairman's hands were closely tied in many key respects. For example, despite the fact that everyone connected with the GDE case recognized that the low wage levels of the mainland employees in Hong Kong were a serious difficulty in trying to obtain honest behaviour, there was no sign that the basic system would be changed. Even after the restructuring, the Chairman of GDH would still earn only HK$ 20,000 per month, compared to a competitive market wage in Hong Kong of HK$ 200,000 for a senior manager in a similar position. It was impossible for the international branches of mainland companies to adopt international wage standards until the mainland parents had also adopted global standards.

Wu Jiesi was asked what fundamental institutional change could guarantee that New GDE would 'rise from the hell of restructuring' and become a 'phoenix,' a mythical animal that no -one has ever seen. He answered that the key to building a successful 'New GDE' was the 'ideological consciousness' of the new leaders. In the 1950s and 1960s, the 'ideological consciousness' might have been able to resolve many difficult problems that could not be solved through having the correct institutional arrangements, but it was questionable whether that approach could succeed in the twenty-first century.

GDI

After the restructuring, GDI was to focus on infrastructure and utilities, and Guangnan on food. Within the restructured GDI, much the largest single part of the business was the Dongshen Water Project. With projected annual revenues of around HK$ 2.1 billion, it accounted for almost one-half of GDI's total turnover. The Water Project supplied around three-quarters of the water consumed by Hong Kong and was the only external supplier of unprocessed natural water. Thus, the core business of the restructured GDI was a virtual monopoly. This near-monopoly business, together with most of its management team, was injected intact into GDI. It provided a large potential revenue stream but made no contribution to changing the management culture in GDH. Even the future revenue stream was uncertain. The price of the water supply needed to be renegotiated. Also, there were uncertainties about the costs that would be incurred in maintaining water quality to meet Hong Kong's environmental standards and to deal with the heavy pollution in the area that supplied water to the Project.

Guangnan

Prior to the restructuring, Guangnan had high ambitions to become a large, diversified Hong Kong conglomerate. It was highly rated by investment bankers as pursuing an apparently rational strategy of vertical integration within the food business, including food production, trading and sales through its supermarkets. During the restructuring, various discussions were held about trying to cooperate with other Hong Kong-based companies to develop the food trading business into a more broadly based frozen food business. However, the potential partner(s) in the end could see no commercial argument for this. Guangnan's supermarket business made a loss in 1999, and the business was mostly sold during the restructuring in order to help free Guangnan of debt. Guangnan considered seriously the possibility of developing e-business. However, despite significant investments in this area, and heated internal discussion about the feasibility of this strategy, this path was rejected.

The restructuring drastically changed the nature of the company. It substantially reduced Guangnan's total debt, from HK$ 4.2 billion to HK$

0.93 billion. As part of the restructuring it sold off a relatively large number of assets, including most of its supermarkets. Its assets shrank from HK$ 3.16 billion to HK$ 1.44 billion immediately after the restructuring. Guangnan's net assets rose by H$1.59 billion, from minus HK$ 1.08 billion to plus HK$ 0.51 billion. After the restructuring, it had no outstanding debt to the bank creditors or the note holders. However, the scope of the company had shrunk greatly and its ambitions contracted drastically. Its annual sales revenue fell from a peak of HK$ 8.16 billion in 1997, to HK$ 2.76 billion in 2000.

Fifty-seven per cent of Guangnan was now owned by GDH, which was, in turn, a state-owned enterprise. Guangnan was now a quite narrowly focused firm, running a near-monopoly business selling food from Guangdong into Hong Kong. Its ambitions to become a major force in supermarkets, food production and food processing, and even in the new economy, had disappeared.

The medium-term prospects for Guangnan's food sales to Hong Kong were uncertain. In the early phase of Guangnan's development it had a *de facto* monopoly on almost every kind of fresh food sold to Hong Kong from Guangdong province. The market for the sale of fish, fruit and vegetables was liberalized gradually in the 1990s. As the market was liberalized, Guangnan's share of the sales of each of these products to Hong Kong dropped to virtually zero. The remaining virtual monopolies were on the sale of pigs and chicken, but the profit from these was only around HK$ 10–20 million per annum. Given Guangnan's past record of competing in the sale of live food once the monopoly rights were withdrawn, this would leave Guangnan with almost no business at all.

In the mid-1990s, Guangnan had been touted by global investment banks as one of the most dynamic shares in Asia. Prior to the Asian Financial Crisis Morgan Stanley had recommended the stock as one the world's 'top fifty SMEs.' After the restructuring the company was on its last legs. Extensive criminal elements in the company had retired or been fired. In that sense it was a 'normal' company. However, beyond that, it was hard to see what function its existence served for the Guangdong government. What was the point of 'saving' Guangnan if it was to remain a *de facto* state-run trading company? What was the point of returning Guangnan to the situation it had been in at the start of its life? What was the point of 'saving' the company if its prospects were so poor?

Criminality

General

The KPMG report on GDE, undertaken for the Guangdong provincial government, revealed a shocking picture of unprofessional management practices at the company. However, the problems were more serious than simply unprofessional conduct. KPMG showed that the GDE Group internally had experienced a 'serious problem with the falsification of accounts' (Wu, 2001: 150). The leadership of 'certain enterprises' had tried to cover their losses from their mistakes by falsifying profits. The KPMG report stated that under Hong Kong law, 'such activities constituted criminal fraud.'

A total of thirty-five people from GDE were either arrested or had warrants for their arrest from ICAC, of which eighteen were from Guangnan. Much of the discussion concerning criminality and GDE revolved around the case of Guangnan. No serious public allegations of criminal misconduct were made about GDI, though few would deny that there were also serious professional shortcomings in the management of GDI. To some degree the close analysis of the Guangnan case was because it became the centre of a major court case initiated by the ICAC (see below). It is a moot point how much information about Guangnan would have emerged without the case. If there really is a sharp contrast between the degree of criminality at GDI and Guangnan, then this raises the puzzle of how the children (GDI and Guangnan) of the same parent (the Guangdong provincial government) both 'living in the same place' (Hong Kong) could be so different.

Taking action against criminal penetration of GDE was made more difficult by the fact that by the 1990s organized crime had significantly penetrated the public services. So deep had the level of corruption become in the Guangdong police and judiciary that it was hard for honest officials in the Guangdong government or within GDE to initiate actions to pursue criminals in the company. In the words of one senior GDE official: 'I called 110 [the police hotline] many times when I or my family have been threatened by the criminals, but they don't respond to my calls.' They had no way to rely on the honesty of the officials they were dealing with. The very criminals who were pressurizing company officials to cooperate in illegal investments could simultaneously be members of the public security apparatus.

The case of Guangnan

In 2000–1 ten cases were brought before the Hong Kong courts relating to the case of Guangnan, including two former directors of Guangnan, a former assistant financial controller and the manager of one of its subsidiaries. The cases involved 'conspiracy to defraud' and 'conspiracy to steal.' They involved also charges against another eighteen people employed by other companies who had been partners in the criminal activities at Guangnan being tried by the Hong Kong courts. The sums involved in the charges totalled HK$ 2.22 billion (US$ 282 million).

Warrants were issued for the arrest of another fourteen members of Guangnan and two directors of associated companies. Those being sought by Hong Kong police included Sun Guan, the former Chairman of Guangnan, and six other former directors of Guangnan, the former Financial Manageress and a former Assistant Financial Controller of Guangnan.

In December 2000, Huang Xiaojiang and Xie Ping, former Executive Director and Deputy Financial Controller at Guangnan Holdings, respectively, were found guilty of conspiracy to defraud and false accounting. They were sentenced in a Hong Kong court to six years and four years in jail, respectively. The trials of the others were to follow, as well as further charges against Huang and Xie.

As revealed in the Hong Kong High Court, many types of financial crime took place at Guangnan.

Insider investment

Insider investment is a common procedure in insider theft and it was found frequently within the GDE group, often involving large sums of money. The procedure involved a member at a high level in the group making a personal equity investment in a given company 'X' through a relative or friend. That person then persuaded the Board of the GDE group, or company within the group, such as Guangnan or GDI, to make equity investments in the original company 'X' in which he has made his personal equity investment. The investments by GDE, GDI or Guangnan provided a boost to the share price of the original invested company 'X.' The high-level member of the GDE Group was then able to sell his personal share purchase at a profit.

Insider lending

The web of subsidiaries and related companies created an environment in which 'insider lending' could thrive. Most of GDE's leaders held numerous directorships of subsidiaries and related companies. In order to perpetrate 'insider lending' fraud, it is not necessary to be directly involved. The fraud can just as easily be perpetrated via a trusted third party, especially a relative. Bringing company outsiders into the web is a standard procedure of entrapment and the creation of dependence, which can be either of the insider on the outsider, or vice versa.

In a typical case from Guangnan, one of the leaders might authorize a loan to a company that had no real business, but whose assets were fraudulently verified by an 'accountant.' On the basis of the false valuation, the Guangnan leader might authorize Guangnan to make a substantial loan to the company concerned. In one case, it was found that Guangnan had loaned RMB 68 million to a business the value of whose assets was allegedly HK$ 200 million, but which turned out to be worth less than HK$ 20 million. The company concerned might then make a loan to a third company of which one of the Guangnan leaders was the chairman or director. The money might then simply disappear into an offshore bank account. The chain of relationships and transactions was likely to be so technically complex that it was impossible, impossibly costly, or politically pointless, for the Hong Kong or the mainland police to investigate separately, and to do so effectively might anyway require close, complicated and costly cross-border cooperation across police jurisdictions. The loan to the original company then appeared as simply another 'bad debt,' and the Guangnan leader and his accomplice were personally better off in proportion to the 'contract' agreed between them in advance.

There were 'countless' such examples of fraud and theft in Guangnan.

Falsely inflated profits

Under the 'instruction' of its Chairman Sun Guan and Director Du Nanhai, Guangnan's Board of Directors conducted a 'conspiracy to falsely inflate the profits of Guangnan and its subsidiaries' (Hong Kong High Court indictment). Sun Guan and Du Nanhai, 'among others,' 'worked out the overall false targeted figures' at a series of meetings of senior officials of Guangnan:

> Du Nanhai distributed the false figures set out in all these meetings among the subsidiary companies according to the nature of their past business performance. The whole scheme was endorsed by Sun Guan and others involved. They, together with the Financial Department of Guangnan, then supervised the execution of the scheme in relation to each of the subsidiary companies involved.

Various forms of fraudulent practices were performed by the conspirators and the staff of the subsidiary companies. The size of existing business transactions was inflated in order to increase profits. Staff were 'instructed to alter various genuine commercial invoices and re-write the accounts.' The conspirators and their subordinates 'altered existing sales contracts, invoices and vouchers and made false account entries.' The staff of the subsidiary companies were instructed to 'locate and recruit accomplices for the purpose of creating bogus commercial transactions as sellers of goods.' These goods were 'purportedly purchased by the subsidiary companies by way of letters of credit, either by using Guangnan's facilities or their own facilities with the local bank.' Bogus commercial transactions were prepared by 'showing non-existent goods sold to the subsidiary companies which were then re-sold to fictitious buyers in the mainland.' Such buyers were either 'the trading partners of Guangnan and its subsidiary companies, or close associates of the conspirators or parties being made use of by the conspirators.' In this way, false profits were generated. Prior to 1998, 'almost all the subsidiary companies ... were involved in the scheme of false letters of credit.' As well as creating false documents to support the fictitious purchase of goods in order to obtain letters of credit, Guangnan's senior managers created documents of sale of the same goods.

Due to these fraudulent schemes, the subsidiary companies were left with substantial sums of 'payment receivable.' In order to cover up in the face of possible auditors' queries, senior managers of Guangnan arranged for the remittance of funds from Guangnan or various other sources to the subsidiary companies, purportedly as payments received from various buyers. Eventually, such sums were reverted to Guangnan for further disbursements. This would enable the subsidiary companies to balance their accounts when the moneys were injected. However, another set of bogus accounts was created when such sums were disbursed back to Guangnan.

Embezzlement

The judge at the trial of Huang Xiaojiang and Xie Ping in December 2000 said that they had embezzled funds from Chaozhou Industries, one of Guangnan's subsidiaries, in order to 'gamble them on the stock market,' 'ignoring the company law as if it was a children's game' (quoted in *SCMP*, 7 December 2000). Huang and Xie, together with a director of Chaozhou, Chen Libun, admitted embezzling more than HK$ 46 million from Chaozhou for share speculation: 'There is no doubt whatever that the funds were used for personal gain.'

Huang and Xie were Directors of both Guangnan and its subsidiary, Chaozhou Industries Holdings (Ltd). Through a series of complicated manoeuvres, Huang transferred HK$ 26.78 million from Chaozhou into a company privately owned by him (50 per cent) and three other associates, in order to speculate in shares through another company, C.A. Pacific Securities (CAP) (Hong Kong High Court Indictment). The illegal transfer was covered up through the issuance of a false account from a subsidiary of Chaozhou, called Mexxwin, to another firm, Win Master, for the purchase of 4,251 tons of 'white fish meal' for HK$ 26.78 million. The transaction was entirely false, and required substantial matching documentation in the form of various vouchers evidencing the alleged payment and matching account book entries in the two firms. Between October 1997 and February 1998 Huang made 115 purchases of shares to a total value of HK$ 63.39 million and eighty-one total sales, to the value of HK$ 51.52 million. Chaozhou 'had not received payment or restitution in any manner of the sum of HK$ 26,780,652.90.'

Huang and Xie were found guilty of a parallel crime of fraud and embezzlement. On 4 December 1997, a sum of HK$ 10 million was instructed by Sun Guan and Chen Libun, to be transferred from Chaozhou to World River Trading, 'which was at all times a company acting on the instructions of Xie Ping.' On 5 December a sum of HK$ 9.6 million was instructed by Xie Ping and Chen Libun to be transferred from Chaozhou to Well Truth, 'which was at all times a company acting on the instructions of Xie Ping.' The two companies were then instructed by Xie Ping to transfer a total of HK$ 19.6 million to Chartwise, a company incorporated in the British Virgin Islands and owned by Xie Ping, via a member of his staff, acting on his instructions. The sum transferred 'was used continuously by Huang Xiaojiang and Xie Ping for share speculation until March 1999.' Xie Ping 'took his instructions from Huang Xiaojiang.' In order to cover up the illegal transfer, a false invoice was issued purporting to show that Mexxwin was indebted to Well Truth of the sum of HK$ 19.6 million for the purchase of 2,800 tons of 'white fish meal.'

In order to complete the accounts records, Xie Ping, as Financial Controller of Chaozhou, 'arranged to fabricate a resale of all the purported purchases of the 4,251 tons and 2,800 tons of 'white fish meal.' False documents were prepared to purportedly show that 7,051 tons of 'white fish meal' were sold to Zhongshan Aquatic Import and Export Company of Zhongshan city in Guangdong province for a price of HK$ 51.02 million.

Responsibility for regulatory failings in regard to Guangnan

A major issue arising from the Guangnan case is the degree of culpability and responsibility of auditors and non-executive directors. In 1997, Guangnan had three 'independent non-executive directors.' These were Carson Wen, a Hong Kong solicitor; Nam Keung Tsang, a Hong Kong banker; and David (Kwok Po) Li, the Chief Executive of the Bank of East Asia, based in Hong Kong. There is not a great deal that an independent non-executive director can do in the absence of accurate accounts. The non-executive directors do not have the time, or often possess the requisite technical experience, to investigate the veracity of accounts certified by reputable, qualified accountants. Nor is there any reason for them to doubt the veracity of the audited accounts. A major issue in the Guangnan case was the apparent failure of the company's auditors over many years, namely Deloitte Touche Tohmatsu, to provide an accurate set of audited accounts. Deloitte withdrew their accounts for Guangnan for the year 1997. Wu Jiesi's account of the GDE restructuring asks the question:

> If the Guangnan management was able to 'fool' its external auditors over a period of years, by providing large quantities of false information, how could KPMG have found so many problems in the accounts within a little over a month through a special audit?
>
> (Wu, 2001: 151)

Distribution of responsibility within GDE

Wu Jiesi argues that GDE was unable to exercise control over Guangnan, with Guangnan acting as an uncontrolled independent kingdom:

> GDE as the majority shareholder of Guangnan and GDI, basically had little control over the directors that it nominated to the Guangnan and GDI boards. As a result, GDE had little say over the appointment or removal of the management of Guangnan or GDI or over their business activities.
>
> (Wu, 2001: 151)

However, the Chairman and Executive Director of Guangnan, Sun Guan, was also, simultaneously, a Director and Deputy General Manager of

GDE. Chen Maoqi was also, simultaneously, an Executive Director of both Guangnan and GDE (Merrill Lynch, 1997). Numerous people connected with GDE and Guangnan, who have a variety of different perspectives, believe that GDE's headquarters did, indeed, lose control of Guangnan. The judge presiding over the case heard in Hong Kong in December 2000 accepted that none of the three accused was the ring-leader, and was not personally enriched by the 'rotten, corrupted and dishonest scam.' The court was told that 'they committed the offences on instructions from top management.' Hong Kong's *South China Morning Post* commented, 'Former Chairman of Guangnan, Sun Guan, believed to be the mastermind of the fraud, remains at large' (*SCMP*, 7 December 2000). He was widely thought to have returned to Guangzhou.

Character of criminal activity at Guangnan

One international expert who worked on the GDE restructuring commented, 'Guangnan can best be understood as a large-scale collectively-organized fraud company.' Another described it as 'a criminal enterprise to generate private wealth for those who ran it.' However, in the view of one expert, it is important to distinguish the kinds of crime at Guangnan from 'mafia' or 'triad' activity. The key to the kinds of fraud perpetrated at Guangnan is to be able to work with other professional people, such as accountants and clerks. The crimes do not involve vice, drugs, 'protection,' night clubs and other such 'fixed assets.' This expert considers such crime to be 'opportunistic,' undertaken when 'no-one is watching them' and the economy is booming. The ultimate objective of the perpetrators of letters of credit–type frauds in the red chip companies in Hong Kong was to return to China to a safe position within the government.

Responsibility for regulating Guangnan

The perpetration of letters of credit fraud raises issues of the breadth of responsibility for this criminal activity. There were a large number of falsified letters of credit used by Guangnan, with many banks involved and illegal activities spanning many years: 'During all this time, none of the banks ever raised any query whatsoever regarding these transactions' (Wu, 2001: 151). The normal practice in issuing a letter of credit is to scrutinize and verify the authenticity of the relevant documents, such as sale and purchase contracts and bills of lading:

> Such verification should not be too difficult. For example, a telephone call or a letter by the bank to the shipping agency will quickly verify if the shipment is in fact being made as it should be. Regrettably, no-one at any of the banks did any such thing.
>
> (Wu, 2001: 151–2)

Although there was no legal responsibility for the banks to do this, the failure to undertake such checks at all suggests a 'serious defect in the internal management control systems of these banks' (Wu, 2001: 152).

China's Phoenix

On 15 February 2000, in his capacity as newly appointed Chairman, Wu Jiesi made a report on GDE's debt restructuring to Li Changchun, member of the Chinese Central Committee's Politburo and Party Secretary of the Guangdong Communist Party of China. Party Secretary Li gave Wu Jiesi guidance about reforming the management system of the restructured GDE (GDH).

> Not only Guangdong province, but also China as a whole and the international financial markets would be watching closely to find out whether the restructured GDE (as GDH) will become merely a debt-repayment machine, or whether it will instead continue to grow and expand to become a vital, modern corporation operated and managed according to international practice.
>
> (Wu, 2001: 153)

Secretary Li 'urged the new GDH management to learn from the past experience and lessons of GDE' and to 'follow international practices to build a genuine modern enterprise.' He emphasized this as 'the crux of the GDE restructuring' (Wu, 2001: 153).

The main function of the 'window' companies was to collect funds from international markets for their mainland parents, either governments or government-owned institutions. Their original purpose was not to establish real firms. It was an immense challenge to try to transform the ashes of GDE into a real, globally competitive firm like Hutchison Whampoa. Wu Jiesi's account of GDE's restructuring was optimistically entitled 'China's Phoenix' (Wu, 2001). The phoenix is a mythical animal. To change GDH into a real, living animal was a huge challenge. It was an open question whether the company had established a management system and a business structure that would enable it to become a successful globally competitive corporation, rather than a 'debt-repayment machine.'[15]

4 The third step

Cleaning up the local financial institutions

Introduction

The cases of GITIC and GDE mainly involved international creditors. During the AFC and Hong Kong's financial crisis, the most urgent matter was to deal with the international debts that had fallen due. At the end of 1999, as soon as the bankruptcy of GITIC and the restructuring of GDE were in motion, the Guangdong provincial government's working team immediately began the 'third step' to resolve the financial crisis, namely, dealing with the payments crisis in the local ITICs, TICs, UCCs, RFAs and the local branches of the state-owned banks. This was a non-stop battle without pause for breath or rest. Apart from the international trust and investment companies, the debts of local NBFIs were mainly from within China. Speculative funds from enterprises and institutions all over the country were mixed with the deposits from local residents. Legal depositors receiving the official interest rate were mixed with the massive deposits promising a higher interest rate. Normal deposit and loan business was mixed with illegally raised funds. Legal businesses were mixed with businesses outside the scope officially approved in the business licences. The profit and loss inside the accounts was mixed with financial relationships outside the accounts. Mismanagement in businesses was mixed with corruption, embezzlement and criminal activities. All these intertwined and became 'like a hemp rope.' Although the 'third step' was hardly noticed in the outside world, its level of complexity and its impact upon Guangdong's economic development and the daily life of ordinary people were much greater than that of the 'first step' and the 'second step.' The constant runs on financial institutions and mass protests caused a 'serious and terrifying impact upon social order.' This required the government to provide a clear and specific plan to resolve the problems at once.

The spreading fire

The Asian Financial Crisis revealed that the problems in Guangdong's local financial sector were far deeper than anyone had imagined. On the eve of the Asian Financial Crisis, Guangdong alone had twenty-five TICs, including seventeen ITICs, with forty-eight securities business branches. It had an estimated 886 rural financial associations (RFAs) (*nongcun jinrong jijinhui*), and 147 urban credit cooperatives (UCCs) (*chengshi xinyongshe*) with 1,063 branches. It also had a large network of rural credit cooperatives (RCCs) (*nongcun xinyongshe*), a separate institutional category from the RFAs. These formed a complex network of debt and credit relationships with enterprises and networks not only within the province but also across the whole country. The main SOE banks all had large-scale operations in Guangdong through their numerous subsidiaries. These were enmeshed in complicated relationships with the local NBFIs.

As we have seen, in the course of China's high-speed development in the 1990s, serious problems developed in the local financial sector across China, and, especially, in China's fastest-growing province, Guangdong. Due to the fact that it is adjacent to Hong Kong, Guangdong was the lightning conductor through which the AFC penetrated mainland China. The problems arose especially because of the unsustainable 'Ponzi-type' characteristics of the process through which funds were attracted. The insolvency of Enping's local financial institutions was a leading example of a widespread phenomenon, even before the AFC. However, the AFC greatly exacerbated an already difficult situation. As we saw in Part 1, throughout Guangdong province, as the Asian crisis hit the region in 1997, growth rates faltered and property prices crashed. The AFC revealed Guangdong's local NBFIs, including TICs, UCCs, RFAs and even the RCCs, to be insolvent on a widespread scale: 'The total level of insolvency was incredible.' Guangdong was at the centre of the emerging national problem with the NBFIs. It accounted for around one-sixth of the total national deposits with the officially approved RCCs, which nationally totalled around RMB 200 billion at the time of the crisis, growing to around RMB 230 billion in early 2001.

The ability of local governments to intervene to support their local NBFIs was limited. Not only did the respective local governments have normal constraints upon their budgets, in addition, the typical local government in Guangdong, especially in richer areas, also had its own 'window' companies in Hong Kong. There were almost 2,000 such 'window companies.' Although they came from across the whole of China, a disproportionately large share was from Guangdong. They had large debts and had engaged heavily in speculation, especially in property and the stock market, based largely on borrowing from Hong Kong financial institutions. A large number of the small local government 'window' companies were rendered insolvent by the collapse of Hong Kong's stock market and property market. Therefore, the local governments had to deal with two sets of insolvent financial institutions, for both of which it was directly responsible. Solving the problems of insolvent local NBFIs was made even more complex because of the criminal nature of many of their activities and the close involvement of local officials in these activities.

In the late 1990s, there was a series of runs on local financial institutions. In Guangdong province alone, there were over sixty such local 'bank' runs. These were associated with widespread social disorder. Every day there were serious demonstrations from angry depositors, including big demonstrations outside the government offices in Guangzhou, the provincial capital. The initial response of the NBFIs was often to set limits on withdrawals, such as 'no more than 50 *renminbi* per day.' In a pattern common throughout history in such circumstances, these actions inflamed the situation and 'destroyed people's confidence in the financial institutions.' It intensified the panic, prompting still further 'bank runs' on the local financial institutions and stimulated further social disorder across the province. The intensity of depositors' feelings was illustrated vividly by the situation in early 1999 at the Liwan District branch, in Guangzhou, of the Guangdong Securities Company:

> Confidence has already crumbled. The brokerage firm's walls are covered with slogans scrawled in red paint. 'They stole our blood and sweat', says one. An angry crowd outside the brokerage firm distributes copies of a much-photographed petition to the government signed by more than 100 investors holding defaulted bonds. 'You cannot imagine the misery we've felt in our hearts', it reads. 'When ordinary people's peace of mind is ruined, how can you expect stability in society?' A young woman in a red quilt jacket says she comes every day in hopes of recouping her father's life savings. 'The only thing my father ever believed in was the government, but he doesn't even believe in that anymore', she says.
>
> (*Wall Street Journal*, 23 February 1999)

Simply following the dictates of the market, and allowing them to go bankrupt, would have caused great social instability, as many people would have lost their savings. The *Wall Street Journal* graphically indicated the nature of the crisis that was emerging among China's numerous small banks and NBFIs. They contrasted the consequences for the big international banks stemming from the ITIC and red chip problems, with the consequences for ordinary Chinese of the failure of the local financial institutions:

> Beijing has seen enough to calculate that many foreigners want to be in the China game so badly that they'll take any amount of pain and still come back. The tens of millions of ordinary Chinese who have put their money into banks and related enterprises is a different story. Scorch them and you have a revolution on your hands.
>
> (*Wall Street Journal*, 9 February 1999)

The parallel with the US Savings and Loans scandal was widely referred to by Chinese government officials especially in terms of the scale of government intervention necessary to solve the problem. Moreover, it was feared that the contagion would spread to the main state-owned commercial banks. The central government agreed to the Guangdong government's proposal to borrow from the central government in order to try to solve the urgent problem. Those responsible for this decision were acutely aware of the 'moral hazard' problem, that using state funds to save the local financial institutions would simply encourage wasteful lending practices in other parts of the financial system and by local governments in the future. Instead, the central government and the Guangdong government wished to try as far as possible to ensure repayment of loans, which had been used to clear bad debts to the NBFIs and pay back the depositors.

Establishing the battle plan

The battle plan of the Guangdong provincial government with the support of the central government was drawn up in the face of the perilous situation in the local financial institutions. The Guangdong government's resolute response to the crisis 'made history.' There is a Chinese saying, 'using the sharp knife to cut the tangled rope,' analogous to 'cutting the Gordian knot.' This is a good way to describe the 'third step.' On 23 November 1999, Guangdong established the 'Working and coordinating team to deal with financial risks in local small and medium financial institutions and rural financial associations in Guangdong,' headed by Wang Qishan.[16] By October 2000, less than a year later, Guangdong had borrowed a package of RMB 45 billion from the central government and ordered the cessation of business to allow rectification of the innumerable local financial institutions. This was a resolute decision and the best approach to resolve the crisis – boldly and resolutely 'using the sharp knife to cut the tangled rope.' Following the eruption of the crisis in Guangdong, the provincial government led a movement to achieve an emergency 'clean-up' of the local financial institutions across the whole province. Wang Qishan emphasized repeatedly that the funds made available to 'put out the fire' should be used to 'buy coffins,' not as a 'means to help the patient get better' (*Caijing*, 5 May 2001). He said that the available funds should not be provided as 'blood transfusions to keep the terminally sick local financial institutions alive.' He argued that the province should learn from the case of Hainan Development Bank. The PBOC had spent hundreds of millions of *renminbi* to try to keep it alive, but in the end had failed, and it had to be closed down anyway.

The provincial government set up an emergency team to lead a massive effort to deal with the crisis in the province's NBFIs. This 'battle' took place under tight, unified leadership from the provincial government. The members of the coordinating team included leaders from the general office of the provincial government, from the provincial court, the provincial procuracy, the Department of Propaganda of the provincial CPC committee, the provincial Department of Agriculture, the provincial Department of Finance, the provincial Department of Auditing, the provincial Department of Public Security, the provincial Department of Supervision, the provincial Department of Labour, the provincial State Assets Administration Bureau and the provincial Development Research Centre, as well as from Guangfa Securities, the provincial ICBC, Guangzhou Foreign Exchange Administration Bureau, the provincial PBOC and the provincial branch of the Agricultural Bank of China. This was a battle under unified leadership covering the whole province. Closing down up to a thousand enterprises and institutions at one time required the mobilization of an elite force of cadres from every government department to form a working team at each level. For example, Huizhou mobilized 400 cadres, Jiangmen mobilized 200 cadres and Jieyang mobilized 138 cadres. It was estimated that more than 2,000 cadres participated in the battle. Before deciding on the correct policy to adopt, the coordinating team launched a massive province-wide investigation of all the RFAs and UCCs in the province, in order to provide the necessary technical information on which to base its strategy. Only then did it decide that massive closure was the only way forward, the 'choice of no choice.'

The provincial government allocated specific tasks to different state-owned financial institutions in cleaning up the different sectors affected by the crisis. BOC was given responsibility for the TICs, the Industrial and Commercial Bank of China (ICBC) for the UCCs, the Agricultural Bank of China (ABC) for the RFAs and Guangdong Guangfa Development Bank (*Guangdong Fazhan Yinhang* – Guangfa) was given responsibility for Enping.

Support from the central government was vital to resolving the crisis. In order to prevent the spread of the payment crisis, after intense debate the central government decided to loan RMB 38 billion to Guangdong province (through the PBOC in Beijing) specifically to help it to solve the problem of the local NBFIs. Borrowing *renminbi* from the central government would not affect the country's foreign exchange reserves and the central government would not need to revise the financial budget, as the assistance was in the form of loans rather than budgetary transfers. The loans were used to pay out the obligations of the local NBFIs, in order to quell the social upheaval. The beneficiaries were supposed to be limited to 'individual and legal deposits' (Zhang, 2001). Of the total amount made available to resolve the crisis in Guangdong's local financial institutions, by May 2001, RMB 19.4 billion had been used to pay out the depositors in the UCCs; RMB 7.1 billion for the RFAs; another RMB 4.8 billion for seventeen TICs and fourteen branch offices; and RMB 0.54 billion for the relatively small category of local securities firms (*Caijing*, 5 May 2001). The central government provided a further RMB 7 billion through the local branch of the PBOC for dealing with the payment crisis in the local branches of state-owned banks (for example, the Enping Branch of the China Construction Bank). This brought the total amount of loans from the central government and the

PBOC to around RMB 45 billion (the equivalent of around US$ 5.4 billion). The loans were guaranteed by financial support from governments at each level in Guangdong. The annual interest rate for the loan was 2.25 per cent with no compound interest. The loans were supposed to be repaid within nine years beginning from 2001. The annual repayment was RMB 4.7 billion. This was feasible for Guangdong with an annual tax revenue of over RMB 110 billion.

The central government lent to almost all provinces and directly administered cities to help solve the problem of the local NBFIs. However, none received nearly as large an amount as Guangdong. The central government provided loans to solve the problems of the local financial institutions in proportion to the severity of the problem they faced, not with regard to their capability to repay the funds. The extent of the problem was far deeper in Guangdong, but also the province had a much greater capability to repay the central government. There was great jealousy of the fact that Guangdong had received such large assistance from the central government. Moreover, there was anger that China's richest and most autonomous province should have allowed the growth of such poorly monitored institutions, necessitating such large-scale intervention from the central government. One can say that 'other people's money,' in this case, the money of the rest of China, was used to try to solve the problems of the richest and most free-wheeling part of China.

Even worse, there was accumulating evidence that a significant fraction of the funds attracted by Guangdong's local financial institutions had been appropriated by local officials, their friends and relatives, and would be almost impossible to recover. In other words, it was increasingly obvious that the NBFIs had at their core a large-scale 'Ponzi-type' scheme based around the myth of super-high returns in the super-fast growth region of Guangdong province. This myth was nurtured by the apparent benefits of the free market and proximity to the global bastion of the free market, Hong Kong. However, the central government had to decide which was the lesser of the two evils. It decided that preserving the country's financial system and social order intact had priority over other considerations. It did so fully aware that the Guangdong government and the local governments under its supervision didn't 'deserve' to be supported, due to the failure by the Guangdong government and Guangdong's local governments to monitor their own financial institutions. It did so fully aware of the dangers this path posed in terms of 'moral hazard.' The central government refused to write a blank cheque in order to repay the depositors and creditors of Guangdong's local financial institutions, and the Guangdong provincial government refused to write a blank cheque to repay the depositors and creditors of financial institutions under local governments within the provinces. The different levels worked together to produce a solution that forced each level to play a full part in solving the crisis, including the relentless pursuit of debtors, within the financial institutions that were within its jurisdiction.

The 'lightning attack'

A great amount of work was required to deal with Guangdong's twenty-five trust and investment companies, 147 urban credit cooperatives and 886 rural financial associations, as well as the network of rural credit cooperatives. There were millions of ordinary households which formed extremely complex debt and credit relationships with enterprises and institutions all over the country. In order to maintain social stability, before undertaking the closure of a local financial institution, the working team, under conditions of top secrecy, carried out a general investigation of the financial institutions that needed rectification. Based on the result of the investigation, the coordinating team was to give first priority to residents' deposits and to international debts, and then proceed to deal with other depositors' interests. The residents' deposits were subdivided into several categories depending on the size of their deposits. The majority of the depositors had small deposits and were to be paid out first. By doing so, social disturbances were lessened as far as possible. In addition, the employees who became unemployed due to the closure of their companies were to receive proper arrangements. In practice the implementation of these principles became more complex and colourful. They had eight distinctive characteristics.

First, there was the question of finding the correct way in which to deal with the different categories of depositor in order to minimize social disorder and 'calm the tumult.' A major part of the clean-up operation involved each work team building up a meticulous classification of depositors (and borrowers), and then making differentiated payments to depositors. For example, the thirteen UCCs in Shaoguan alone had 200,000 depositors. In order to maintain social stability, before the massive closure under conditions of extreme secrecy, the working team carried out a searching investigation of the financial institutions that needed rectification. For this purpose, they compiled data showing details of individual loans by category and data showing details of depositors by category. These were then handed over to the ICBC. Based on the result of the investigation, the residents' deposits were further divided into several categories: above RMB 100,000, RMB 5,000–100,000, RMB 2,000–5,000, RMB 1,000–2,000 and below RMB 1,000. The majority of the depositors had small amounts of deposits and these were paid first.

The typical practice was to pay back the smallest depositors in full immediately while other legal individual depositors were paid in instalments. For example, in resolving the crisis in the case of the RCCs at Enping, there was total reimbursement in the first year for depositors with less than RMB 10,000 in the RCC. This was the majority of the depositors. Those with larger legal deposits were to be reimbursed RMB 10,000 in the first year, and thereafter, 20 per cent of the total deposit each year until the total deposit was repaid after five years. Such evidence as exists suggests that within only a few months, a large fraction of the small depositors had their deposits repaid by the local NBFIs (Table 2.4).

Table 2.4 Average payment scale for selected small and medium financial institutions that were closed down in several cities of Guangdong

	Category	*Up to date (dd/mm/yy)*	*RMB (million)*	*No. of households*	*Average size of payment per household (RMB)*	*% of payment*	*% of households*
Zhongshan RFAs	Individual equity	24/01/00	183	9,430	19,406	43	52
Meizhou RFAs	Individual equity	25/01/00	16	750	21,333		
Chaozhou RFAs	Individual equity	06/00	125.43	9,325	13,450	62.4	86.5
Chaozhou ITIC	Individual debts	06/00	332.62	10,183	32,665	99.49	99.48
Zhongshan ITIC	Individual deposits	30/05/00	198.85	2,330	85,343		

Second, the measures adopted ensured that the extent of payments and the loss of state assets were tightly controlled. The government at each level was required to provide a guarantee for the timely repayment of the loans that the central government had provided in order to solve the crisis in the NBFIs. This reduced the incentive for the local governments to expand the size of payments made at the grass-root level. The investigation of up to a thousand RFAs and UCCs before the closure provided the data needed for the forthcoming tasks. The fact that this massive campaign was conducted so effectively and professionally meant that the possible loss of assets during the take-over and payout process was minimized. It also helped to contain the extent of the total level of payouts, reinforcing the effect of placing clear responsibility for timely repayment upon each successive lower level of government.

The Guangdong provincial government learned from the working style of the Hong Kong liquidators during the GITIC bankruptcy: impartial and incorruptible, acting 'as swift and powerful as thunder and lightning.' The whole closure process needed to be conducted at high speed in order to prevent widespread loss of state assets. Across the length and breadth of the province the work teams carried out simultaneous lightning attacks: 'The thunder was so swift that people had no time to cover their ears.' All of a sudden, they launched into the enterprises and institutions. They took them over without warning and sealed off the accounts, forms, seals, certificates, licences, guns and bullets, computers and data archives.

The provincial-level working team was set up on 23 November 1999. The following day, the Guangdong government convened the 'working meeting to resolve the risks in Guangdong's local small and medium financial institutions and RFAs.' By 5 December, only ten days later, more than thirty securities businesses' branches owned by ten TICs in Zhuhai, Shantou, Nanhai, Zhanjiang, Foshan, Zhaoqing, Zhongshan and Jiangmen had been transferred to Guangfa Securities as going concerns. By 24 December, in only eighteen days, the working team took over and sealed off 147 UCCs (with 1,063 branches) across the whole province.[17] By 31 January 2000, in only two months, including the Chinese New Year holiday, the UCCs across the province had paid out RMB 16 billion (US$ 1.9 billion), accounting for 83.3 per cent of the total task. This ability to conduct a 'lightning battle' showed that in the course of many years of gradual reform in moving towards a market economy, the capability of the Chinese bureaucracy had in certain respects improved greatly. The Chinese bureaucracy was continuing to follow its long tradition of dealing with economic crises and natural disasters in a sophisticated, subtle and comprehensive fashion.[18]

Third, the Guangdong government undertook a clear, in-depth and large-scale propaganda campaign to explain its policies on closing the local NBFIs. This helped to reassure the mass of the population and reduce the public's nervousness resulting from such a huge shock to the local financial system. During the payments crisis precipitated by the AFC there were frequent runs on local NBFIs. The sweeping closure of the RFAs and restructuring of the UCCs was a shocking bolt from the blue for the ordinary people, who were already extremely anxious. As a result of this nervousness, there was large-scale transfer of deposits from those RCCs and the city commercial banks that were not scheduled for closure. The participation of some government departments in this process aggravated the tense social atmosphere. For example, Shaoguan found that fourteen institutions, including the State Tax Bureau, railway and road authorities, Lechang Prison, Lechang State Tax Bureau, Finance Bureau, Life Insurance Company and the Telecommunication Bureau, informed their subordinate institutions to transfer RMB 11.41 million out of the RCCs. In some places, there were panic runs on the local RCCs and city commercial banks. The government at each level fully mobilized the propaganda machines, including announcing detailed news in the newspapers, answering telephone enquiries and publishing interviews to explain what was happening. Local broadcasting stations and television stations as well as Cable TV stations broadcast information on the relevant policies and regulations non-stop day and night.[19] Leaders at each level made speeches, wrote memorials and wrote articles. Provincial Governor Lu Ruihua and Executive Vice-Governor Wang Qishan gave strong, favourable opinions about the RCCs in the *Nanfang Daily*, which is the main daily newspaper in the province. Detailed accounts of the closure policies and regulations, and detailed accounts of the nature and rationale for the closures, were made known to every household so that the population's fears were calmed and possible disastrous social disturbances were avoided.

Fourth, the provincial work teams guided the public understanding of the subtle distinction between illegal speculation and legal deposits.

The numerous small depositors' legal deposits were given the first priority in paying out the funds owed by the local NBFIs. They formed the largest social group that could affect social stability. This group contained a vast number of people. Their deposits were normally their lifetime savings. They would have been infuriated if they had lost their lifetime savings. Most of these ordinary people with a relatively limited size of individual deposits were judged to have legal deposits. The deposits were paid out, but did not include the illegal element of high interest due to *gaoxi lanchu*. Ordinary depositors were reassured by this, feeling that the provincial government had carefully and fairly considered their interests. They were also relieved that they had not forfeited their savings in bankrupt institutions. Although the pay-outs did not include the high return in excess of the official interest rate, people were sincerely convinced by this action. Once this part of the payment was completed smoothly, the victory of the third step in dealing with the financial crisis was in prospect.

The most difficult problem to deal with was the identification and treatment of the individual big depositors. Guangdong's growth had been based heavily on private enterprise in small, individual businesses. There was a huge number of deposits under individual names. It was almost impossible to differentiate between 'normal deposits' and funds deposited for speculation by an individual enterprise. In the course of this process, the treatment of the so-called *da hu shi* was comic. The term da hu shi ('office for big account holders') originated from the special preferential treatment that securities trading branches had given to their big speculative clients, including individual offices, use of computers and free drinks. In a parallel fashion, in the process of liquidation and repayment, the preferential treatment given to the big depositors assumed the same form, and with a similar logic, but with a different nature and purpose. A great deal of the speculative funds seeking high returns was considered to be 'immoral wealth' arising from illegal sources and avoiding official taxes. If the parties concerned did not have the courage to walk into the *da hu shi* within the officially specified dates, to register with, and to be approved by, the departments of industry and commerce, taxes and legislation, the debts were automatically written off. In the early 1990s, when Wang Qishan had served as Governor of the China Construction Bank (CCB), he had received orders to take charge of and close down the China Agricultural Trust and Investment Corporation, which he had earlier established. This was the approach he had adopted at that time. Some large deposits were never claimed by anyone and were written off. This was practised widely in Guangdong during the closure campaign. The payment plans submitted by each level of governments were, by and large, consistent with the principle that they should not exceed the total of the deposits identified during the work team investigations prior to the closures. This saved the expenditure required by the Guangdong provincial government to resolve the financial crisis.

Fifth, having fought to ensure that urgent payments were dealt with in a timely and flexible fashion the next step for the provincial team was deciding how to deal with the illegally raised funds from enterprises and institutions. It was decided that these should be frozen. The policy that individual deposits were paid in categories depending on their size, and in instalments, and that the deposits of enterprises and institutions were temporarily frozen, caused inconvenience for some individuals, enterprises and institutions. For example, the naval station at Xuwen Xilian Dajin could not draw the living expenses for officers and soldiers due to the closure of the local UCC. After the Zhanjiang government asked for instructions from the coordinating team, the matter was resolved by borrowing from the local banks. Some of the teachers and students from Shaoguan University had deposits in a local UCC which were frozen. Thanks to careful ideological work among them, they were persuaded not to take to the street in protest. The UCCs in Xingning had a large number of deposits from enterprises and institutions. Due to their closure, a lot of offices and departments could not pay salaries to their employees. To deal with the problem, the city work team, led by the court, organized the recovery of debts. The Shaoguan government required public services such as the electricity supply, water supply, telecommunications, property administration and the road authority to allow institutions that had no other source of income than the funds frozen in the UCCs to postpone paying fees for three months and waive the fines for late fee payment so that the affected institutions could continue to operate normally.

Sixth, during the closure there emerged complex issues concerning the creditors' rights involving litigation with entities outside the province. Up to a thousand small and medium financial institutions not only raised funds, invested, deposited and loaned in Guangdong, but also had massive credit and debt relationships with financial institutions all over the country. This caused numerous cases of litigation during the process of closure and restructuring. For example, Shantou ITIC defaulted on the payment of US$ 400,000 to Zhongyuan ITIC in Henan Province. The intermediate court of Zhenzhou city was forced to transfer RMB 400,000 from Shantou ITIC's guaranteed funds account and RMB 3.52 million from the liquidation account of Shantou ITIC's Haibin Securities Branch. A complex adjudication took place between Zhuhai ITIC and Shaanxi ITIC over an investment fund. The *xian* (county) intermediate court sealed off 20,000 square metres of land owned by a subordinate company under Zhuhai ITIC and authorized the piece of land to be auctioned on the spot. The intermediate court of Wuhan City transferred RMB 890,000 of deposits from the Shenzhen Branch of Huaqiao ITIC, seized the accounts and books and sealed off the offices. Many of the litigation cases had been ongoing from before the closure. For example, Zhuhai ITIC alone had forty ongoing cases of litigation. The litigation cases across different regions caused huge problems for the Guangdong government in the process of clarifying assets and debts.

Seventh, following a common practice in Chinese administrative traditions, the overall policy guidelines set by the provincial work team were adjusted according to local conditions (*yin di zhi yi*). For example, in the case of Shantou, when the local UCCs were closed down the Shantou government injected assets of RMB 2 billion including local infrastructure projects, as well as mobilizing the financial capabilities of local large SOEs and government departments. Its decision to merge twenty-one local UCCs into a single commercial bank as a going concern also reflected this approach. When closing down the RFAs, Shantou paid back the small and medium depositors immediately but paid back the large depositors in instalments. In Maoming, the RFAs simply paid out the 'equity shares' (i.e. *de facto* deposits) with no interest payment, while in Foshan the RFAs paid both the 'equity shares' and the legal interest but not the high, illegal, interest. When paying out the individual equity depositors in the Huangqi RFA in Nanhai, the work team deducted the 'high interest' of RMB 45.64 million that had been paid over several years. A crucial condition for such a decision was that the accounts were clear and reliable.

The advantages of adjusting measures to local conditions were obvious. The development of UCCs and RFAs was uneven between different areas. Also, the extent and degree of their impact upon social stability was different. Since the local governments at each level guaranteed and paid back the debts, it was not necessary for the provincial government to formulate a detailed, unified plan. With the same basic principles and actions of unified leadership, space was left to adjust the specific measures to local conditions. This also meant that the government at each level shared responsibility for the outcome. Even if some parts of the masses were dissatisfied with the specific solutions, they would be less likely to take their grievances to the provincial government.

Eighth, as far as possible a balance was struck between resolving the crisis and avoiding moral hazard. The fact that the central government lent a massive amount of money to resolve the crisis presented a severe challenge in terms of moral hazard. The central government could not afford the payment crisis to remain unresolved. The non-stop runs on local NBFIs and large-scale protests had a frightening impact on social stability. Both the Guangdong government and local governments at sub-provincial level had to accept responsibility for their failure to monitor adequately the institutions under their control. Many hundreds of NBFIs were under the control of local city or township governments. Local cadres typically occupied the leading positions in the local NBFIs. Chaotic management often became the cover for criminal behaviour, for which there could be no amnesty. Moreover, the legal debts of the local small and medium financial institutions had to be honoured. If the debtors were able to evade responsibility for repaying their debts, moral hazard would be worsened.

The Guangdong provincial government itself was required to pay back its loans to the central government over an eight-year period. The rate of interest was 2.25 per cent per annum (simple, not compound, interest), making an annual repayment of RMB 4.7 billion. The repayment principle was 'first repay the principal and then repay the interest' (*Caijing*, 5 May 2001). The Guangdong provincial government in its turn required the governments at each level to guarantee to repay the borrowings that had come from the central government within eight years through local financial revenues. This increased the enthusiasm of governments at each level to sell the assets of the small- and medium-sized financial institutions that had been closed, and to recover debts owed to the institutions. To some degree, this formed a 'compensation for moral hazard.' Local governments at each level were required to provide detailed debt recovery plans. Although it was impossible to avoid moral hazard entirely, such measures were better than doing nothing.

Wang Qishan repeatedly emphasized the critical importance of moral hazard in dealing with the financial crisis in Guangdong province: 'In terms of the significance of different levels of financial risk, moral hazard is the most fundamental' (quoted in *Caijing*, 5 May 2001). He emphasized that the example of Guangdong demonstrated that each level of government must find a way to solve the problem through its own budgetary means. During the process of lending to the local governments to solve the payments crisis, each city was required to pledge formally to repay its borrowings as a condition of receiving the loans from the provincial government. If they failed to repay to the provincial government at the agreed dates, then the province had the right to deduct the amount from the amount of tax income that would normally be returned to them through the provincial budget. If they really did have demonstrable budgetary difficulties as a consequence, then the province could advance them a further repayable loan. This essentially was a method of prolonging the period of repayment, thereby preventing ambiguity and sophistry designed to avoid payment obligations. In Wang Qishan's words: 'This "debt cap" (*zhe ding zhai mao zi*) must be worn at all times' (quoted in *Caijing*, 5 May 2001).

This procedure provided a powerful incentive for the local government to take responsibility for its previous monitoring failures and tolerance of criminal behaviour. It provided a strong incentive for the local government to pursue the debtors to the local financial institutions. Every *renminbi* that was returned to the local financial institutions was equivalent to a one *renminbi* addition to the local budget. It gave them an added incentive to realize the maximum amount possible through the sale of any assets left within the local NBFIs. Each city within Guangdong province established an assets management office, or a special small team. They set up asset auction departments and special courts (*Caijing*, 5 May 2001). After these procedures were put into practice it was found that administrative measures tended to work better than law-based measures, 'because the debtors frequently were themselves government officials and Party cadres' (*Caijing*, 5 May 2001). Some areas adopted the practice of 'three stops and one limit' (*san ting yi xian*) with respect to cadres and public employees who had not paid back their debts. These were 'stopping employment position,' 'stopping salary payments' and 'stopping work,' and 'limiting the period of repayment.' Under this type of pressure, the contradictions in relationships between the local financial institutions and the debtors came to the surface. These measures reduced the possibility that under the cover of the massive closure programme, local governments might allow a *de facto* amnesty for criminals associated with the local NBFIs. This pressure pushed local governments at each level to devise specific approaches to recover debts appropriate to local conditions. Although it was impossible to avoid moral hazard, the steps taken helped to reduce this aspect of the campaign: to do something in this regard was better than to do nothing.[20]

There was also the danger that the clean-up might encourage 'morally hazardous' behaviour by depositors. These had been attracted by unrealistically high rates of interest earned through breaking the law. The fact that the local NBFIs were controlled by the local governments appeared to provide some form of insurance against loss of the deposits should the NBFI fail. We have seen that a large fraction of the deposits from outside the region was from large institutions, especially SOEs. Within the region, a large fraction was from local individuals or small businesses. The government needed to deal with the extensive illegal activity associated with the operation of the NBFIs, including the illegal methods used to attract deposits. The way in which the crisis was dealt with had large implications for future patterns of behaviour by depositors in non-bank institutions, and, hence, for the possibility that such types of behaviours might re-surface in the future. We have seen that the Guangdong government tried to differentiate carefully between different types of depositors. We shall see also that it attempted to deal with illegal behaviour in the NBFIs.

All these grave decisions and complex policies were made public one after another. Under immense pressure at the moment of greatest severity in the crisis, the Guangdong provincial government's work team to deal with the financial crisis made great efforts to achieve a balance between these complicated and often conflicting objectives.

By the spring of 2000, the tide had turned and systemic risk had ebbed (*Caijing*, 5 May 2001). The focus of the work to reduce risk in Guangdong's financial system had shifted to seeking the return of assets owed to the local financial institutions. This was to be a long-drawn-out process. By March 2000, deposits in Guangdong's RCCs had risen by RMB 6.9 billion compared with March 1999 (*Caijing*, 5 May 2001). Deposits in RCCs rose in direct proportion to the degree of severity of the problems in the RFAs. Around 30 per cent of the returned 'equity deposits' from the RFAs were transferred to relatively trusted banks. The recovery of the RCCs and urban commercial banks was a manifestation of the ebbing of the tide of large-scale systemic risk. As the domestic risk ebbed, so the provincial government felt itself in a stronger position to deal with the international financial crisis.

Trust and investment companies

Guangdong was in the vanguard of a sweeping nationwide clean-up of the entire trust and investment sector in the wake of the AFC. Cleaning up Guangdong's TIC sector in its turn formed part of the massive integrated programme to clean up the whole of the province's local financial institutions. GITIC's bankruptcy and GDE's restructuring provided the models for 'stopping businesses and rectifying' (*ting ye zheng dun*) (actually, administrative closure) at the other TICs and for debt restructuring. By 11 March 2000, Guangdong's seventeen city-level TICs had stopped business and begun rectification, including four TICs in Guangzhou and one TIC in each of the following cities: Shanwei, Shaoguan, Meizhou, Chaozhou, Zhanjiang, Zhongshan, Zhaoqing, Shantou, Foshan, Zhuhai, Jiangmen, Maoming and Huizhou.

The restructuring process was easier for those TICs which had mainly domestic debts. This was the case for the TICs in Chaozhou, Leizhou, Shanwei and Shaoguan. By early 2000 they had basically completed the process of 'ceasing business and rectification,' with individual debts registered and the process of asset recovery under way. For the ITICS and TICs with extensive foreign debts things were more complicated. The rectification revealed that there had been widespread use of 'borrowing new funds to repay old debts' leading to an accumulation of debts. GITIC's bankruptcy had changed the position of all the TICs in negotiation with international creditors and GDE's restructuring provided a model of how to implement a 'haircut' through negotiation. The approach typically followed was to 'cancel interest payments and repay a reduced amount of the principal.' Against the background of GITIC's bankruptcy and GDE's restructuring, the foreign creditors 'evidently did not wish to again become entangled in a legal battle over which debts were legal and which were illegal' (*Caijing*, 5 May 2001). They basically agreed to a rational commercial negotiation outside the law courts.

Zhuhai, Jiangmen, Zhongshan, Foshan and Shantou ITICs were revealed as having international debts of US$ 254.45 million. In each case the outcome was broadly the same. After difficult and extensive negotiation, the foreign creditors agreed to the cancellation of interest payments and a 30 per cent reduction in repayment of the principal. The provincial-level Huaqiao ITIC had an excess of debts over assets totalling RMB 3 billion. After the provincial government injected RMB 2 billion and the international creditors accepted a 'haircut' of 30 per cent, Huaqiao ITIC paid back all the domestic Chinese residents' deposits. Its business licence was taken away and the company was restructured into an industrial company. Guangzhou's flagship ITIC, Guangzhou International Trust and Investment Corporation (GZITIC), offered its creditors the alternative of accepting either a full repayment of the principal over a period of not more than ten years, or to be repaid only one-half their money in about six months

(*SCMP*, 26 August 2000). Creditors choosing the full repayment would be repaid their outstanding principal over no more than ten years. Of this amount, 70 per cent would be in cash in equal payments funded from a combination of the sale of 'certain GZITIC assets' as well as 'financial support' from the Guangzhou municipal government. The balance would be repaid after ten years through instruments in a joint venture bank set up by GZITIC and its owner, Guangzhou municipality.

The forty-eight securities businesses' branches owned by TICs in various locations in Guangdong transferred their securities business to Guangfa Securities Company as a going concern, following the GITIC example. The misused shareholders' guarantee funds were recovered and transferred with the support from the central government's loans.

Prior to the restructuring, Guangdong province had twenty-five trust and investment companies, of which sixteen were ITICs, including the massive GITIC. After the restructuring process was completed in Guangdong it was found that just four TICs ran their business well and were re-registered to continue operation (*gui fan bao liu*). Two were in Shenzhen, one in Guangzhou municipality and one in Dongguan county. The Guangdong provincial government was confident that the remaining TICs would be 'strictly controlled' within the guidelines of the new regulations from the central government.

Although Guangdong was in the forefront of the difficulties in the trust and investment sector, there were severe problems in the sector across the entire country. In the late 1980s the number of TICs nationwide had reached over 1,000 and following successive rounds of rectification, on the eve of the Asian Financial Crisis there were still more than 200 TICs (including ITICs). The drive to undertake root and branch reform of the TICs and other NBFIs was spearheaded by Premier Zhu Rongji. In early 1999 he declared that the government should 'inspect and rectify non-bank and local financial institutions and reduce the risks of financial institutions': '[China should] separate the operation and administration of the banking, securities, insurance and trust sectors, and implement the responsibility system for financial supervision and control.'

In early 1999, the PBOC issued *Guidelines for Restructuring Trust and Investment Companies*. The key elements in the guidelines were the following. First, the TICs' owners, mainly local governments, were to be held responsible for restructuring the companies with the supervision and approval of the central bank. Second, the number of TICs was to be reduced from around 240 at the peak to around 70–80, through merger, closure and some conversion to other lines of business. Third, every TIC was required to go through a re-licensing process in accordance with new tightened requirements. These requirements included a minimum amount of RMB 300 million in capital after writing off bad loans and investments; qualified shareholders and senior managers approved by the PBOC; an 'appropriate organizational structure and management system'; and a 'sound internal risk control mechanism.' Fourth, the business scope of the re-licensed TICs was to be limited to 'trust' business only, defined as 'managing entrusted money and assets for others.' TICs were no longer allowed to engage in commercial banking and securities activity, and were to be barred from taking deposits, making commercial loans, underwriting and trading securities and engaging in property development. Finally, TICs that failed to meet re-licensing requirements as trust companies could be converted into securities firms, finance companies, property developers, or even commercial banks, if they satisfied regulatory requirements of the respective industries. For those that were considered beyond any restructuring attempts, closure and bankruptcy remained an option.

The overall objective was to 'retain a few TICs with bigger scale, better returns on assets, strict corporate governance and running genuine trust businesses' (*Editorial Board*, 2000: 150). To support the process of cleaning up the TICs, the PBOC instigated a nation-wide process of verification of assets and assessment of capital for the whole TIC sector. The PBOC endeavoured to establish unified national accounting standards for this work. Xia Bin, the Head of the PBOC's NBFI sector, declared that the bank was planning to 'put everything right once and for all' (quoted in *SCMP*, 20 October 2000).

Although the original plan was to complete the reduction in the numbers of trust and investment companies across the country to just 70–80 within one year of the closure of GITIC, the pace of restructuring was much slower than had been hoped. By the end of 1999 only forty-eight TICs had completed restructuring and were approved by the regulatory authorities. It became obvious that the TICs' problems involved not only debt negotiation and debt restructuring, but also large-scale business restructuring. The TICs' accounts were often in a chaotic state. Moreover, in the course of debt and business restructuring, it became obvious also that there was widespread criminal activity and corruption among Party and government officials. One 'step' in solving the impact of the AFC led to another. In this sense the path of reform in the TICs was similar to that in the other NBFIs. A further reason for slow progress in restructuring the trust and investment companies was the sheer complexity of negotiating with international creditors. The local government refused to pay the TICs' debts in full. However, they did not wish to see their local trust and investment company bankrupted. Although the international creditors were reluctant to accept large 'haircuts,' they were unwilling to go through a bankruptcy proceeding in Chinese courts.

GITIC was a powerful object lesson for the international creditors to consider. At a widely reported press conference immediately after the Second Session of the Ninth National Party Congress in 1999, Premier Zhu Rongji bluntly linked the GITIC case with the need for international banks to negotiate with the TICs in order to avoid even greater losses through bankruptcy. Zhu said that he 'didn't expect to see too many bankruptcies of financial firms in the future and maybe there will be none.' But he warned, 'the precondition is that the creditor banks should not press too hard for the debt repayment beforehand or in advance. If you press too hard, they will have no choice but to apply for bankruptcy.' Zhu said:

> [that if] everybody can just sit down and have a talk according to international practice, for instance to recapitalize the firm or to inject fresh capital into it or to swap the debt for equity, then the problem can be settled and there is no need to apply for bankruptcy.

The decision to place GITIC in bankruptcy and the restructuring of GDE together had a profound effect on the way in which the international debts of the trust and investment company sector were dealt with. It forced the international creditors onto the back foot, greatly weakening their bargaining position with every local government TIC owner in China. It enabled the TICs to enter prolonged bargaining in order to postpone and restructure their international debts. In this sense the GITIC bankruptcy acted as an 'umbrella' over the whole TIC debt restructuring process. It allowed the central government time also to attempt to undertake deep structural reform of the whole sector, proceeding at its own pace to deal with the immensely complex issues of regulatory failure, mismanagement, corruption and criminality.

In December 2000, Xiao Gang, Deputy Governor of the PBOC, was optimistic that the main problems of the ITICs had been solved (interview).[21] He pointed out that several factors were likely to prevent serious difficulties emerging again in the sector. First, the capital market was now far more developed, so it was not necessary for localities and enterprises to raise capital through the intermediary of the TICs. Second, the regulatory framework had substantially improved. Third, the different levels of government now had a much deeper understanding of the potential problems of the sector. Finally, the creditors were now much more cautious about lending to the TICs. He pointed out that the Chinese government had worked 'tirelessly' to rectify and clean up this sector.

Further regulations were put into place in early 2001 to govern the operation of the trust and investment sector. These included the 'Trust Law,' the directive on 'Management methods for the trust and investment companies,' and the directive on 'Temporary management methods for the trust and investment companies' fund investment business.' This flurry of legislation 'basically concluded three years of sector rectification' (Xing, 2002) and 'substantially limited the scope of [the TICs'] business' (World Bank, 2001). The TICs were now barred from accepting deposits, issuing bonds or borrowing from abroad: 'The new regulations will tightly narrow the scope of business of the TICs. The minimum capital was confirmed at RMB 300 million. Fixed assets were not allowed to exceed 80 per cent of capital.' In the view of the World Bank, the new regulations were 'consistent with the strategy to reduce the number of TICs from 240 to about forty' (World Bank, 2001).

The international financial community followed closely the way in which the smaller TICs across the country dealt with their international debts. In a succession of cases, the central government indicated that it was not willing to pay the international creditors the full amount they were owed and that the local government 'parent' of the respective TIC should take responsibility for its own 'child.'

In September 2000, it was announced that the Dalian International Trust and Investment Company (DITIC) was to be declared bankrupt after paying 60 per cent of its US$ 150 million in debt arrears. Six Japanese banks had agreed in June 2000 to forgive US$ 36 million of their combined US$ 90 million in loans to DITIC that were in arrears (BBC, 17 September 2000). A similar arrangement had been reached with sixteen Hong Kong, European and US banks for the remaining US$ 60 million in debt arrears. This was interpreted by international analysts as a compromise solution, indicating a softening of approach towards international creditors compared with that adopted with GITIC, in which there was no settlement prior to bankruptcy:

> By bankrupting DITIC only after honouring its agreement to pay the trust's sovereign creditors 60 per cent of what they are owed, the government is saving them the considerable effort and expense of having to slug it out with DITIC's domestic creditors in a bankruptcy court for a much smaller share of the company liquidated.
>
> (*SCMP*, 18 September 2000)

The relatively high level of repayment, 50 cents in the dollar if accrued interest payments were subtracted, was thought to 'show a willingness on the part of Chinese government entities to make a deal' (*FT*, 9 August 2000). One foreign analyst commented: 'The Dalian government were very keen to resolve this. They didn't want the reputation of the city damaged' (quoted in *FT*, 9 August 2000). The deal was reported to have the approval of the central government, 'which is eager to see a speedy resolution' (*FT*, 9 August 2000). However, even this 'haircut' caused great indignation among Japanese banks: 'DITIC has become an emotional as well as a financial issue for the Japanese. Many Japanese bankers say Dalian's government could have easily helped its cash-strapped offspring' (*Asian Wall Street Journal*, 31 August 2000).

In October 2000, Hainan ITIC (HITIC) defaulted on a coupon payment on a Japanese bond (*SCMP*, 20 October 2000). The central government apparently refused to step in to support the repayment of HITIC's foreign debts. HITIC's creditors were forced to declare the company in default. Shortly afterwards, HITIC attempted to get the creditors to accept a 'haircut' of 40–50 per cent on the face value of the bonds.

During his visit to Japan in October 2000, that coincided with the HITIC default, Premier Zhu Rongji said that on his return he would 'urge the Hainan provincial government to deal with the HITIC problem' (quoted in *SCMP*, 16 October 2000). If the creditors pursued the debts through the courts, the case of GITIC showed that it would take a long time, with the risk of an even bigger haircut. The Hainan provincial government had tried for more than a year to restructure eight local trust and investment companies: 'That campaign is now in tatters' (*SCMP*, 20 October 2000). Japanese bankers and officials responded angrily to the failure of the Chinese central government to step in to support HITIC. One Japanese official said: 'Because the amount is small, we don't understand why China's central government can't help solve the problem. It would be much wiser for China to solve the problem, rather than lose credibility in the long run' (*Reuters*, 12 October 2000). Another analyst commented bluntly:

> It is doubtful that China will show any change of stance over international trust and investment corporations. China acknowledges that its credibility may be hurt, but the central government wants to demonstrate its commitment to minimal government interference in local affairs.
>
> (quoted in *Reuters*, 12 October 2000)

The refusal of the Chinese government to 'play an active role in resolving the long-standing credibility problems irked both Japanese financial institutions and the Japanese government' (*Reuters*, 12 October 2000). The objective of the Hainan government with HITIC appeared to be the negotiation of a debt repayment 'haircut' rather than outright closure, with the threat of liquidation, bankruptcy and prolonged court battles as the credible threat hanging over the creditors, inducing them to accept the 'haircut.' The example of GITIC was in everyone's mind.

The issue of repayment by the ITICs was particularly important for Japan. The total registered external debts of the ITICs stood at around US$ 6.5 billion at the end of 1999 (*Reuters*, 12 October 2000). The unrecoverable loans of Japan's top banks were estimated to stand at around US$ 1.5–2 billion (*Reuters*, 5 October 2000). In the view of one Japanese analyst, 'the issue appears to undermine the fundamental principle of a market economy, such as making payments on time' (quoted in *Reuters*, 5 October 2000). This raises the question about what, indeed, are the 'fundamental principles of a capitalist economy'? Is the fundamental principle to ensure that all debts are repaid, even if this means the central government stepping in to ensure repayment of international debts contracted by autonomous, albeit state-owned, firms? This would enshrine 'moral hazard' as the fundamental principle of capitalism.

The way in which the central government dealt with the problems of China's trust and investment companies was in many ways highly successful.

It represented an important example of the use of administrative measures to solve unanticipated problems in the course of Chinese economic reform and opening up. The PBOC commented: 'If the economy is still in transition and the market remains imperfect, certain administrative measures may be necessary to contain the contagion of financial risks and minimize their impact' (PBOC, 2000: 20). The crisis in the sector made clear the crucial nature of state intervention to maintain system stability. It demonstrated that the spontaneous play of the invisible hand of market forces was likely to produce undesirable results from many points of view. Most Chinese officials were well aware that the US government had not so long previously intervened on a massive scale to solve the problems of the 'Savings and Loans' affair. Hundreds of billions of dollars of US government funds were used to solve the crisis. Clearly, the problems of unregulated financial markets were not simply those of a 'transition' economy. However, the central government was acutely aware of the dangers of moral hazard. It was adamant throughout the crisis in the trust and investment sector that it would not solve the problems of financial institutions under the control of local governments by simply repaying international creditors with funds from the central government's budget.

By 2001 the 'trust and investment company problem' appeared to have been fundamentally solved. The World Bank (2001) believed that, 'with the exception of a handful of institutions (e.g. CITIC), TICs will be marginalized in China's financial sector.' By 2002 the total number of TICs had been reduced to sixty, with one or two for each province, directly administered city and autonomous region (Xing, 2002). This was far behind the original schedule, but the complex restructuring task was near 'completion.'

Urban credit cooperatives (UCCs)

The large state-owned commercial banks paid relatively little attention to the borrowing needs of innumerable small businesses that boomed in the 1990s. The failure of modern banking to provide adequately for the needs of small-scale businesses in a developing economy is a well-known problem. Modern sector banks in developing countries typically are uninterested in taking deposits from, or lending to, large numbers of relatively poor people or small businesses. Such businesses or individuals often have little collateral and rarely have professional audits of their accounts. Evaluating the status of a large number of small 'informal sector' borrowers causes high transaction costs per unit of loans made. These widespread difficulties were exacerbated in the 1990s in China by the fact that government policy dictated that a large proportion of the loans from state-owned banks were directed to large state-owned enterprises. In theory, in the countryside the RCCs were supposed to meet the rural credit needs, but they encountered many difficulties. In the urban areas, the booming small businesses and the growing affluence of a segment of the city population left a large gap in the financial system during the 1990s. The 1990s spawned a new form of local financial institution, the UCC, which developed in response to these needs. By the time the AFC struck, Guangdong province alone had around 150 such institutions and across the whole country there were around 5,000 UCCs.

The total debts of the UCCs in Guangdong were substantially greater even than those of the rural NBFIs. Also, protests by urban residents are more politically dangerous than those in scattered rural locations. Consequently, as we have seen, out of the total of RMB 38 billion in loans from the central government to the Guangdong government to help them through the crisis of restructuring the NBFIs, the majority, around RMB 24 billion, was allocated to help settle the problems of the UCCs' insolvency. The central government used the experience of Guangdong province to develop measures to try to reduce risk in the management of the UCCs in other parts of the country. It organized a nationwide verification and classification of assets in the sector, in order to deal with those UCCs considered to have high risks. It suspended or consolidated 'those UCCs whose behaviour resulted in a sustained regional payments crisis' (*Editorial Board*, 2000: 141). After receiving the report from the respective provincial government, the PBOC would allocate, through the commercial banks, central bank loans to settle the outstanding payments and market exit problems of the high-risk UCCs. Each provincial government was charged with the duty of drawing up plans to 'dispose of the UCCs in the province' (*Editorial Board*, 2000: 141). A number of measures were enacted to increase the level of monitoring by the PBOC of the UCCs, including early warning systems to identify risk, regular on-site inspections and closer monitoring of the background and performance record of UCCs' senior management personnel (*Editorial Board*, 2000: 142–3).

During the clean-up, 'those UCCs whose behaviour resulted in a sustained regional payments crisis' and were considered to have high risks, had their licences suspended or were consolidated with other entities. Twenty-one of Guangdong's 147 UCCs were liquidated. Thirty-six were judged to be 'good,' and were restructured, but were merged with local RCCs. Another group was restructured, but was allowed to continue to operate independently. These were often combined to form a new 'city bank.'

'Restructuring' the UCCs often involved amalgamating the pre-existing UCCs into a single much larger entity and re-classifying it as a 'city bank,' as in the case of Shantou (see below). This practice was widespread across the country. For example, in Wenzhou after 1998, forty-seven of the fifty-one UCCs were merged to form a single new entity, the Wenzhou Commercial Bank (*SCMP*, 2 December 2002). Moreover, many of the small urban financial institutions took over responsibility for the 'restructured' rural NBFIs. The precondition for remaining in business independently was that the respective UCC had a 'healthy' balance sheet and a capital of more than RMB 100 million. This was a critically important condition for allowing the UCCs to continue as an institutional form. 'Several' of the UCCs in Guangdong were merged with the local city commercial banks.[22] Each of the UCCs typically had many branches. During the clean-up a total of 1,063 branches of UCCs in Guangdong province were withdrawn from operating in the financial market (Zhang, 2001).

Despite the major reforms in the late 1990s, with extensive closure and merger of insolvent UCCs, China still had a huge number of small- and medium-sized local urban financial institutions. At the end of 1999 it was reported that the country had not only ten joint-stock commercial banks but also ninety city commercial banks, each based in a particular city, and 836 'prefecture-level urban credit cooperatives' (PBOC, 2000: 24). In 1999, the city commercial banks had assets officially totalling RMB 555 billion (US$ 67 billion), with liabilities of RMB 523 billion (US$ 63 billion). The officially reported assets of the prefecture-level UCCs totalled RMB 120 billion (US$ 14 billion) and liabilities of RMB 121 billion (US$ 15 billion) (PBOC, 2000: 25). The incentives for local urban NBFIs to raise funds illegally were no less than those affecting the local rural NBFIs. Similarly, they were deeply enmeshed in the local power structure, which had a strong impact on the lending policy of the UCCs. They also were heavily involved in lending to fund the speculative bubble in real estate in the early 1990s. Estimating the true extent of risk would involve deep investigation into the dimensions of non-performing loans.

UCCs: the case of Shantou

When we conducted our research in Guangdong in 2000/1 the issue of local financial institutions was extremely sensitive. During our fieldwork in Shantou we stayed in a hotel overlooking the South China Sea. We were the only occupants of our block in the hotel. Numerous armed soldiers surrounded the adjacent block with guns at the ready. Inside the building was an investigation team from Beijing conducting their own enquiry into the local financial institutions. A short time before their arrival, two officials from Beijing had burnt to death in a fire in a local hotel, which had been where we had originally been booked to stay.

The UCCs in Shantou city in eastern Guangdong were particularly highly developed. In Shantou, as elsewhere in the province, the UCC developed fast in order to meet the needs of small-scale, often private, businesses. Such businesses boomed in Shantou under the policies of 'reform and opening-up,' especially following Deng Xiaoping's 'Southern Journey' in 1992. The UCCs in Shantou were created to 'meet the needs of the collective and individual economy in the city,' which were not being adequately met by the main state-owned banks. A special element in the rapid development of the UCCs in Shantou may have been the powerful role played by overseas Chinese in the political economy of this important region within Guangdong province. Over hundreds of years, there had been large-scale migration overseas from the Shantou-Chaozhou district. Deng Xiaoping approved the opening up of Shantou through the establishment of a Special Economic Zone. Although the zone was only around one square kilometre in total area, its establishment was highly symbolic. A major reason that Deng supported the opening up of Shantou was to take advantage of the strong links between the local and the overseas Chaoshan people. Overseas Chaoshan people provided a major source of capital for the region's high-speed growth in the 1990s. They felt comfortable investing in businesses within their own culture. It is likely that one of the factors stimulating the growth of local financial institutions was to escape the constraints and inadequacies of the formal, state-controlled commercial banking system. An additional factor in the growth of the network of the UCCs was the greater potential for escaping surveillance than was possible within the formal banking sector. It can be imagined that this sector provided a greater opportunity for local individuals and business people to hide transactions from the authorities in Guangzhou or Beijing, enabling evasion of taxation, foreign exchange controls and other unwelcome intrusions into the financial affairs of the local business people.

Numerous UCCs sprang up in Shantou during the 1990s, totalling more than a dozen by 1996, with a network of over seventy branches across Shantou district. Shantou had a total population of 1.1 million. Each of the UCCs was established as an independent 'first grade legal person.' Their development was given the green light by the central government. When the AFC hit Guangdong, the Guangdong government and the PBOC in the province initiated a comprehensive reform and restructuring of the Shantou UCCs. In 1996 and 1997 it organized a merger of thirteen UCCs in the city. They formed a new entity, the Shantou City Enterprise Bank (*Shantou chenghsi shiye yinhang*) (SCSY). At the time of its establishment in 1997, the SCSY had total deposits of RMB 6 billion, double the size of the largest local branch of a national commercial bank, namely the BOC. This amounted to an average of RMB 5,500 (US$ 660) per person in Shantou, but of course, the amount per depositor was far greater than this. In 1997, the newly established SCSY reportedly made a profit of RMB 135 million, while most of the other financial institutions in Guangdong made losses. The SCSY ranked in the top ten among the national UCCs in 1997, and had the largest market share of any financial institution in Shantou.

In 1999, as the restructuring of local financial institutions across the province gathered momentum, depositors became nervous about the prospects for any financial institution other than the main commercial banks. They withdrew deposits on a large scale in order to switch them to the main banks, causing severe difficulties for the SCSY. A payments crisis erupted in July 1999 and the bank basically became insolvent. The SCSY authorities set a limit of RMB 3,000 in withdrawals per month, which could only be withdrawn in specified small amounts per day. This provoked great anger among the depositors, threatening the city's social stability. In July 1999, the PBOC gave instructions that an accelerated programme of restructuring should get under way. The restructuring involved close cooperation between the city government and the PBOC.

Leading businesses and institutions in Shantou were persuaded to become major shareholders, or to increase their shareholdings. These included the local branch of the China Huaneng Group (*Zhongguo Huaneng Jituan*), which generates and distributes electricity across the country, Shantou City Financial Bureau, CITIC Guoan Company and 'some other well-established enterprises in Shantou.' Between them they contributed an extra RMB 400 million in capital to the SCSY. This was designed to raise the level of 'trust' (*xinyi*) in the bank. The Shantou City government injected RMB 2 billion (US$ 240 million) in high-quality assets into the company, including bridges, highways and other reliable infrastructure projects, that could easily be converted to cash and could produce a reliable income for the SCSY. This further strengthened the close relationship between the bank and the local government. The restructuring involved also an attempt to strengthen the collection of receivables from borrowers. The number of branches was pruned from seventy-three to fifty-nine, and the number of employees reduced from 2,058 to 1,180, which produced a substantial reduction in costs.

A central part of the restructuring involved gradually reimbursing depositors who wished to withdraw their savings from the bank. During the course of the restructuring after July 1999, around RMB 1 billion was paid out to individual depositors. It appears that little assistance was provided from the provincial capital. Instead, the SCSY had to rely on the Shantou government 'mobilizing' local SOEs and government departments to make deposits in the bank. The fact that the provincial government forced Shantou to resolve its problems in the UCCs out of its own resources was strongly resented: 'If the central government had not encouraged the growth of these institutions, then the problems would not have arisen. It is not fair to shift the burden for resolving this problem entirely onto our shoulders locally.' However, this approach was consistent with the overall philosophy of the 'three steps' (*san bu zou*) to solve the financial crisis in Guangdong.

Rural financial institutions

Alongside the sweeping reform of the rural financial associations, it was recognized that the countryside had special needs for credit provision. Farming communities have special financial needs stemming from the pronounced seasonal characteristic of agriculture as well as the diverse needs of rural SMEs. The main commercial banks were unable and unwilling to meet fully the needs of millions of small rural businesses and hundreds of millions of farmers. Since the 1950s, the main institution in which farmers could make deposits, and from which they and small rural businesses could borrow, were the rural credit cooperatives (RCCs). Originally, the RCCs were genuinely 'collective' institutions. Increasingly, they lost their collective character, as their function merged with that of the peoples' communes and the supply and marketing cooperatives, to form a single system. From 1980 to 1996, authority to manage the RCCs (*dai guan*) was handed to the ABC. The RCCs effectively became base level branches of the ABC (*Caijing*, 5 June 2002).

Even before the onset of the AFC, it was widely recognized that there were fundamental problems with the RCCs. Well before the crisis the central government began a programme to reform them. The key document for the reform was published by the State Council in August 1996, entitled 'Resolution (*jueding*) on the reform of the rural credit cooperatives.' The objective of the reform was to establish cooperation as the foundation of rural finance, in order to achieve a mutually beneficial division of labour between commercial finance and policy finance. The relationship between the RCCs and the ABC was to be ended. Instead, supervision of the RCCs was to pass jointly to the PBOC and the *xian*-level (county) network of RCCs. In advanced areas, in which the RCCs were already relatively commercialized, following rectification (*zhengdun*), the RCCs were to become 'rural cooperative banks' (*Caijing*, 5 June 2002).

At the end of 1999 there were around 42,000 RCCs with 642,000 employees across the country. Their total assets were RMB 1.430 trillion (US$ 173 billion), total deposits were RMB 1.34 trillion (US$ 161 billion) and outstanding loans were RMB 923 billion (US$ 112 billion) (PBOC, 2000: 25).

In 1998 and 1999, the PBOC undertook a comprehensive national survey of the assets and capital of the RCCs. Each RCC, including those in Guangdong, was then classified into one of five categories with appropriate treatment. Those placed in the first two categories were 'urged to expand their business and improve financial services' (PBOC, 2000: 22). Those placed in the third and fourth categories were required to 'improve internal controls and work out mechanisms to regain profitability.' Those in the fifth category were 'disposed of through acquisition by the first two categories' and their independent legal person status was annulled. In those areas with a high concentration of RCCs in the fifth category, the grass roots cooperatives were 'consolidated into a single legal person within the whole county.' In the course of this complicated process of consolidation, the PBOC provided some RCCs with 'timely assistance' in the face of 'temporary liquidity crises in the process of consolidation' (PBOC, 2000: 22). In the course of 1999, over 2,200 RCCs across the whole country had their legal person status cancelled and were merged with other RCCs (*Editorial Board*, 2000: 148). The government paid close attention to the implications for the RCCs of the dissolution of large numbers of RFAs, and their being placed under the supervision of the RCCs.

The cooperative principles of the RCCs were emphasized during the clean-up process, including improvement in their share-holding structure. The PBOC attempted to establish or improve the management system, recruiting people with higher educational qualifications to raise their management quality. The RCCs were encouraged to develop a comprehensive range of financial services for the rural community. The main focus of the RCCs' lending was intended to be towards the needs of rural production. At the end of 1999, loans from the RCCs for agriculture totalled RMB 304 billion (US$ 37 billion) and loans for the township and village enterprises totalled RMB 419 billion (US$ 50 billion) (*Editorial Board*, 2000: 145). In addition, the RCCs were encouraged to 'extend their service scope from production to consumption,' making loans to farmers to build or buy houses, purchase consumer durables, meet educational fees and other consumption needs (*Editorial Board,* 2000: 146). Further, an advanced group of six well-run and wealthy RCCs was authorized to conduct foreign exchange business, including those in Shenzhen, Shunde and Dongguan in Guangdong province. A group of eight associations of RCCs, including those in Guangzhou, Shenzhen and Dongguan in Guangdong province, were authorized to become members of the nation-wide interbank bond market and underwrite and sell treasury bonds (*Editorial Board*, 2000: 146).

The problems of rural credit were exacerbated by the reforms in the four big commercial banks. In the wake of the AFC, with a massive problem of non-performing loans, and facing the prospect of increased competition from the global giant banks within China in a short period of time, the big four undertook a comprehensive restructuring of their rural operations. From 1998 onwards, they closed or merged over 30,000 branches at the level of *xian* (county) or lower. In order to lower their costs, they basically stopped making loans at the level of the *xian* or below (*Caijing*, 26 March 2003). Following the AFC, it was reported that there was a large net flow of funds out of the villages to the urban economy. The main burden of financing agriculture was now firmly in the hands of the RCCs. In 2002, out of total agricultural loans of RMB 771 billion (US$ 93 billion), 81.3 per cent came from the RCCs (*Caijing*, 26 March 2003).

The rural financial associations (*nongcun jinrong jijinhui*) (RFAs) mushroomed in the 1990s in part due to the failure of the RCCs to perform their intended function. The largest single concentration of RFAs was in Guangdong province, with a total of 886 RFAs prior to the crisis, and deposits considerably greater than those in other provinces. Guangdong formed the focal point of the central government's efforts to resolve the crisis in the RFA sector. In 1999, across the whole country, the central government introduced emergency measures to shut down 'most' of the RFAs, a massive administrative undertaking, reflecting the gravity of the situation that the government faced. The general principle was contained in the State Council's document (*wenjian*) of March 1999. This specified that where RFAs had capital that exceeded their debts, they should be merged with the local RCCs or urban commercial banks. For those RFAs in which debts exceeded capital, after clearing the accounts, they should be closed down (*Caijing*, 5 May 2001). Across the whole country the PBOC closed a total of 6,700 RFAs and merged a further 4,400 into rural credit cooperatives

(PBOC, 2000: 23). As we have seen, around 800 of Guangdong's RFAs were closed down during the 'lightning attacks' of 1999–2000. The PBOC played a central role in resolving the crisis in the country's RFAs, not only in Guangdong province, but across the whole country. The practice adopted was for the PBOC to provide loans to the local commercial banks for the specific purpose of resolving the RFA crisis. The banks then took over responsibility for the RFAs' assets, including farmers' deposits, in the case of those that were performing adequately. Others were closed or merged with the local RCCs.

Although huge numbers of RFAs were closed in the late 1990s, it was possible for 'well-run' RFAs to remain in operation or be re-opened. The government allowed the possibility that 'some RFAs, that operate in line with the law, can return to the status of mutual-aided financial organizations that serve the community after a period of time' (Mei, 2000: 6). After the massive closure of the RFAs in Guangdong, there was a significant transfer of business to the RCCs. The main banks were not keen to develop their business in the rural areas, especially places like Enping in the Pearl River Delta which had gained a bad reputation for absence of a modern credit culture and extensive local government intervention in the operation of the NBFIs. For example, in Enping in the wake of the clean-up, in early 2001, out of a total of eighteen townships (*zhen*), only eight had branches of the ICBC and BOC. Another five had only postal savings services and five had no official banking service at all. This was a big handicap for rural development. The local governments were still desperate to develop their own financial institutions, in the absence of adequate provision from the main commercial banks. Still, in early 2001, officials from the PBOC in Guangdong acknowledged the heavy local pressure to develop new forms of local financial institutions that circumvented the official regulations. In order to avoid being classified as a 'financial institution,' depositors in a local 'joint-stock company' routinely became 'shareholders,' who were given 'dividends.' In fact, the 'shares' were simply deposits and the 'dividends' were the interest on deposits. The Guangdong PBOC officials commented: 'New forms of illegal, disguised forms of fund-raising (*feifa bianxing jizi*) are constantly appearing. Our policy is to constantly be on the lookout for such forms, and when we find them, kill them.'

In the wake of the clean-up, the PBOC in Guangdong and the Guangdong provincial government worked hard to prevent the re-emergence of large-scale systemic risk in the RCC sector. However, the level of risk was still acknowledged by provincial officials to be 'high.' The corporate borrowers, mainly the township and village enterprises (TVEs), were acknowledged still to have poor management and to retain a non-repayment culture from before the crisis. It is significant that the frenzy of *gaoxi lanchu* in Enping began with the RCCs, which were supposedly under the direct supervision of the ABC. This did not provide grounds for optimism about the conduct of the RCCs, compared with the RFAs, after the closure of most of the RFAs.

A report on the RCCs published in *Caijing* in early 2003 concluded that 'resolving the problems of property rights, internal governance, management systems, and handling the bad loan problem, will need a lot of patience and time' (*Caijing*, 26 March 2003).

The balance sheets of the RCCs cannot have been helped by having to absorb responsibility for a huge number of RFAs, many of which were insolvent. Guangdong was at the centre of the continuing national problem with the NBFIs. It accounted for around one-sixth of the total national deposits with the RCCs. The total of deposits in Guangdong's RCCs at the end of the year 2000 totalled around RMB 230 billion (around US$ 28 billion), compared with around RMB 200 billion at the time of the AFC. The *Financial Times* commented that the RCCs' problems were likely to intensify after China joined the WTO, as the local governments 'scramble to shore up the enterprises that they own.' In the end 'it may be the farmers who end up footing some of the bill, that is, until they can take no more, then they will protest.'

Still in 2001, it was recognized that there were significant risks present in the rural NBFIs, particularly in the RCCs. A national report in early 2001 outlined the seriousness of the problem facing the local financial institutions (cited in *FT*, 18 July 2001). It reported that the average debt of township governments was around RMB 4 million, totalling around RMB 220 billion (US$ 27 billion) for the whole country's township governments. An official report at the end of 2000 acknowledged that the total debts of rural authorities stood at RMB 600 billion (US$ 72 billion) (*FT*, 3 January 2002). This was roughly equivalent to one-half of the annual revenues of the central government. The main creditors of the local governments were the local NBFIs, principally the local branches of the RCCs. The report said that the bad debts of the RCCs amounted to 'well over 50 per cent of assets.' The 40,000 RCCs accounted for 12 per cent of all deposits nation-wide. They were reported to have a total of RMB 1,050 billion (US$ 126 billion) in outstanding loans at year-end 2000 (*FT*, 18 July 2001).

The high degree of insolvency of the RCCs was especially significant in view of the huge number of individual households that had their deposits in these institutions. Their insolvency was also deeply meaningful in terms of the attitude of the mass of the population to the Party and government. The RCCs were established in order to provide a genuinely local form of cooperative financial institution, to pull farmers out of poverty. They were closely associated with the traditions of the Communist Party in serving the rural masses. The change in their character in the era of reform and opening up, and the wide revelations of speculative behaviour to the benefit of a small group of local leading Party and government officials, were damaging to the moral standing of the Party in the rural areas. The fact that an important part of this process involved participation in the plunder of the rents from the process of *de facto* land privatization for property development was even more damaging to the Party's standing in the countryside. Collective ownership of farmland was a pillar of the Chinese path of development from the early 1950s through to the 1990s.

In early 2003, the central government announced important new measures for local financial institutions. It decided to allow the development of a new category of financial institutions, called the 'rural commercial banks' (RCBs) (*FT*, 10 January 2003). Three of these institutions were allowed to begin operations experimentally in 2002, in Jiangsu. That experiment was judged a success, according to Zhang Gongping, Director of the Department of Cooperative Finance at the PBOC: 'We want to expand the trial [of creating Rural Commercial Banks] to other provinces such as Zhejiang, Fujian and Guangdong and to some other areas along the east coast of China such as Qingdao in Shandong province' (quoted in *FT*, 10 January 2003). Local governments were to be prohibited from taking an ownership stake in the RCBs, 'the stakeholders of which should be local bank employees and farmers.' It was hoped that this structure would free local financial institutions from interference in loan practice exercised by the local government, so that 'all lending will be made on purely commercial criteria.' No single shareholder was supposed to hold more than 5 per cent of the total share capital. The new banks were to 'lend mainly to rural enterprises and other private businesses springing up in the suburbs of China's towns and cities.'

The RCBs constituted an important potential model of reform of local financial institutions. Their introduction constituted a significant effort to shift control out of the hands of local governments in credit allocation. However, there were still many hurdles to cross before this form of financial institution could be declared a success. The degree to which they were autonomous in practice remained to be seen. There were innumerable ways in which the official regulations might be circumvented. Also, if credit allocation were to be entirely according to market principles, then this would still leave open the question of how to provide credit for the mass of China's poor farmers, who had minimal amounts of collateral. Insofar as the RCBs did operate according to commercial principles, there was a strong incentive for them to allocate loans to non-farm businesses and large commercial firms.

Despite massive reform and cleaning-up of this sector after the AFC, many of the fundamental drivers of the difficulties in the local NBFI system remained. The localities still had a strong incentive to establish their own local financial institutions that were not controlled from Beijing or Guangzhou. China was a poor country, in the early stages of developing its financial institutions, and there was a powerful drive to establish local NBFIs such as the TICs, UCCs, RCCs and the RFAs. Even though hundreds of RFAs and UCCs had been technically killed in Guangdong, 'other forms will rise up: finance is the easiest way to make money.' Much of the process of closure and restructuring of NBFIs involved merging rather than true closure, because the interests of the local government were so strongly linked to having local financial institutions under their own control.

The vacuum in rural credit markets was filled rapidly by *minjian* ('inter-personal') and *qian zhuang* ('small, traditional private banks'). They charged high interest rates, as much as 5 per cent per month, which 'greatly harmed the peasants' interests.' Inter-personal loans have 'existed since the earliest times,' but underground *qian zhuang* were outlawed and had for many years been the object of attack by regulatory authorities. The central government attempted to resolve the crisis in rural credit by allowing a series of local experiments in which interest rates paid by the RCCs for deposits were allowed to float upward to the extent of 30 per cent of the official rate, and up to 100 per cent on deposits (*Caijing*, 26 March 2003). Resolving the problems of providing finance for China's huge rural population was still a work-in-progress.[23]

National state-owned banks, local financial institutions and Hong Kong

The crisis in Guangdong's local financial institutions took place in the context of a crisis in the country's national state-owned banks. Moreover, resolution of the financial crisis in Guangdong was made even more difficult due to the complicated and tangled relationship between the local branches of national banks and local financial institutions in Guangdong, as well as the complicated relationship between financial institutions in mainland China and financial institutions outside China's borders, especially in Hong Kong.

Shortly after the announcement of the US-China WTO Agreement in November 1999, the Governor of the PBOC, Dai Xianglong, promised to 'accelerate financial and banking reform to prepare for a surge of competition after China joins the WTO' (*FT*, 21 January 2000). Dai Xianglong set out a road map for reform of the 'big four' state banks. He said that the state banks had to 'slash their payrolls, clear out bad loans, and exercise strict credit discipline' before they could be transformed into 'shareholding companies.' The transition to shareholding companies was seen as a preparation for the listing of the big banks. In November 2001, Dai Xianglong issued a stark warning of the severity of the challenge that would face Chinese financial institutions inside the WTO:

> The financial industry faces good opportunity and severe challenges after China joins WTO … However, with the accession to WTO, more foreign financial institutions will enter the Chinese market. They will compete intensely with the Chinese financial institutions in the aspect of high-quality clients, talent, new businesses and new technologies, etc. This will pose new challenges for the management of the Chinese financial institutions, for the monetary policy of the central bank and for the regulations of the regulators … The next few years will be a critical period for the reform and development of the financial industry of our country. The financial industry faces an arduous task in promoting the

> strategic adjustment of the national economic structure, in abating the financial risks accumulated over many years, as well as in dealing with the challenges with the entry to WTO.
>
> (quoted in *People's Daily*, 12 November 2001)

China's giant banks still faced immense internal difficulties, with the reform process hardly begun, and its prospects highly uncertain. One Chinese government advisor noted that China had 'significantly more serious problems in its banking, financial services and industrial sectors than those which had led to the crisis in South Korea.' He noted that 'until it reformed those institutions, China would have to weigh up carefully the risks of opening up its economy' (Fan Gang, Director, National Economic Research Institute, quoted in *FT*, 23 November 1998).

Non-performing loans

Non-performing loans were the most visible manifestation of the weak state of China's banks. In 1999–2000 around US$ 170 billion in NPLs were removed from the balance sheets of China's main commercial banks. However, this had not resolved the problem.

After the removal of the first large tranche of NPLs there remained strong political pressure upon the state-owned banks at all levels to lend to loss-making SOEs. It was feared that China's entry into the WTO would worsen the competitive situation and increase the losses of China's large state-owned industrial enterprises, which accounted for most of the loans from the main banks. If the SOE banks continued to support loss-making industrial SOEs, which themselves faced severe competition within the WTO from giant international firms, then the consequences for the balance sheets of the main banks would be serious. This would further reduce the main banks' attempts to become competitive with the global giant banks, by deepening their difficulties with NPLs. In the view of Crédit Lyonnais Securities Asia (CLSA), China's big four banks were 'still adding to the NPL stock at a significant rate' (quoted in *FT*, 30 October 2002).

The main body of the loans from state-owned banks were made to SOE industrial enterprises. In 1999, it was estimated in Chinese official circles that the country's state banks had non-performing loans (NPLs) totalling the equivalent of around US$ 250 billion, approximately 25 per cent of bank assets (*FT*, 25 February 2000). However, most commentators believed that the true level of NPLs was much above this figure. Indeed, Moody's believed that the true levels of NPLs at the 'big four' banks were 'much worse than the most pessimistic of the official indications' (*FT*, 16 July 1998), probably as high as 40 per cent of bank assets (*FT*, 12 May 2001). The extent of bad loans revealed at GITIC and GDE reinforced these fears.

The problems that were exposed at the country's NBFIs shed light on those in the country's formal financial sector. In April 1999 Nicholas Lardy warned of the wider significance of the shortcomings in China's trust and investment sector: 'Although international trust and investment corporations account for a small part of China's financial sector, their problems are evidence of loose controls over lending on a larger scale' (quoted in *AFX Europe*, 29 April 1999). He pointed out that during the course of the sale of China Investment Bank to the State Development Bank in 1999, it gradually became clear that more than 70 per cent of the foreign currency lending by the China Investment Bank was in default:

> The China Investment Bank was created in the 1980s to carry out the re-lending of World Bank loans. So the projects funded by the China Investment Bank were very carefully vetted. They were subject to international feasibility studies and approval by the Chinese government.

In Lardy's view, 'this suggests that some of the problems are not only found at GITIC but also in other institutions, even those that appear to be very carefully supervised and have a high degree of international participation.' Lardy noted the fact that GITIC operated in China's most economically successful province, but still managed to invest large amounts of money in projects that proved non-viable, which 'bodes ill for financial institutions operating in other parts of the country.' He concluded: 'I don't think you will find, at the end of the day, that GITIC was an isolated occurrence, but, rather, symptomatic of some of the things that have been going on.'

In 1999–2000 four specially established asset management companies (AMCs) took around RMB 1,400 billion (US$ 170 billion) in bad loans off the balance sheets of the big four banks. The companies whose bad loans were taken over by the AMCs comprised more than 600 of the state's worst enterprises, in areas ranging from heavy engineering to glass-making to retail stores (*FT*, 10 May 2001). It was intended initially to sell a 'significant part' of the bad debts to foreigners, recovering as much of the value of the loans as possible: 'Investors have the opportunity to get into a treasure chest,' said one foreign commentator (quoted in *FT*, 10 May 2001). Foreign investors were to have the opportunity to convert debt into equity and take controlling stakes in enterprises. However, selling the assets through the AMCs proved to be 'an uphill struggle' (*FT*, 14 May 2001). One foreign expert commented that it was not easy to see how foreign investors could make money out of buying bad loans: 'A corporate turnaround is difficult to achieve in the US. A turnaround in China, where ownership of the equity is often unclear and the ability to lay off workers is circumscribed, can be very tough indeed' (Tim Clissold, partner in Asset Management and Recovery, quoted in *FT*, 10 May 2001).

The initial roadshow to sell the AMCs' debt was planned to involve only US$ 2 billion-worth of debt, a tiny fraction of the total. The first two packages of NPLs were sold during the second half of 2001. MSDW bought US$ 1.3 billion-worth of NPLs and Goldman Sachs bought US$ 250 million-worth.

It was reported that they paid around 9–10 per cent of the face value, so the total purchase price paid was only around US$ 150 million (*FT*, 21 December 2001). There remained around US$ 170 billion-worth of NPLs on the books of the asset management companies, so these initial sales did nothing substantial to resolve the issue.

The main interest among foreigners in buying the bad debt lay among 'strategic' investors who planned to convert their debt into equity and 'then try to break up the company and sell off its best assets' (*FT*, 24 May 2001). In the United States in the 1980s, forced liquidation lay behind the success of the Resolution Trust Corporation that dealt with the fallout from the collapse of the savings and loans companies. However, in China it was much more difficult to win court orders to liquidate bankrupt businesses, and enforcing them against entrenched local interests could be impossible: 'You are not going to get a business in which a foreigner sells off the assets and walks away with the profit while thousands of workers are left without severance payments' (Tim Clissold, quoted in *FT*, 24 May 2001). There were 'formidable' bureaucratic barriers to the sale of assets. For example, permission to sell land could not be obtained without payment of a transfer fee to the local authorities that could amount to 40 per cent of its estimated value. Moreover, the degree to which debt could be transferred into equity was still highly uncertain: 'Deciding how many shares a foreigner should get, and whether they should be sold at a discount, will prove tricky' (*FT*, 24 May 2001). A further complication arose from the fact that foreign acquisition of the NPLs was still treated as foreign debt, which involved complicated and time-consuming procedures to gain approval especially those involving SAFE.

In 2001 the Bank of China confirmed the worst fears about the extent of NPLs in the four big banks. BOC was thought to have one of the lowest levels of NPLs, reported to stand at only 11–15 per cent. However, in preparation for the BOC's listing of its Hong Kong assets in 2001, it was revealed that the non-performing loans of the mainland parent accounted for 28 per cent of bank assets (*FT*, 12 May 2001). The BOC's head, Liu Mingkang, was 'adamant that 28 per cent was an accurate figure calculated according to international standards and arrived at after a thorough internal review' (*FT*, 14 May 2001). The revelation from the BOC could be interpreted in a positive light, as giving evidence that the Chinese government was 'preparing a new programme to clean up its state banking system' (*FT*, 12 May 2001). The first step in this process was to acknowledge frankly the full extent of the problem with the banking system. The Bank of China was to be the vanguard of improvements in the performance of the four big banks. It was widely regarded as 'by far the strongest and best run among the top four banks' (*FT*, 12 May 2001). The revelation of the full extent of the BOC's non-performing loans caused international analysts to express renewed concern at the ability of China's banks to withstand competition within the WTO (*FT*, 14 July 2001).

The announcement that the BOC had NPLs of 28 per cent of assets lent support to the likelihood that the level of NPLs at the other three 'big four' banks was much higher than had previously been acknowledged. CLSA concluded that the total NPLs in China's banking system were the equivalent of around US$ 450 billion, or 37 per cent of GNP (CLSA, 2002). The fact that the level of NPLs for the big four banks appeared now to be confirmed as above 30 per cent, was interpreted by some analysts as necessitating China's integration into the global financial system proceeding at a much slower pace than many had formerly thought desirable. The exposure of the full extent of the NPL problems at BOC meant that 'the ability of the state banking sector to withstand the competition from China's entry to the WTO is set to come under greater scrutiny' (*FT*, 14 May 2001).

In 2004 and 2005 a second round of NPLs totalling RMB 1.3 trillion (US$ 160 billion) were acquired by the asset management companies (Walter and Howie, 2010: 58), and in 2007 the ABC spun off another US$ 112 billion preparatory to its listing (Walter and Howie, 2010: 41). It is estimated that between 2000 and 2007 a total of around US$ 480 billion in bad loans was removed from the balance sheet of the four main commercial banks (Walter and Howie, 2010: 41). By the end of 2006 the recovery rate on these loans was reported to be around 20 per cent (Walter and Howie, 2010: 65).

It was thought that the asset management companies would have to provide a discount of up to 90 per cent in order to have a chance of selling the bad debts that they had taken off the books of the state banks. In the end the asset management companies were themselves owned by the state. This meant that the Ministry of Finance would need ultimately to foot the main part of the bill for removal of the bad loans. The head of Huarong Asset Management Company commented: 'If we can't sell the bad loans, we will take some losses, but it will actually be the state that pays for them' (Yang Kaisheng, quoted in *FT*, 24 May 2001). The bill for cleaning up the bank's NPLs needed to be paid from China's 'strained fiscal revenues,' which raised the spectre of 'domestic debt levels that approach those of Japan today' (*FT*, 24 April 2001). Government revenues as a proportion of GNP rose significantly from 10.7 per cent in 1995, a low point during the reform years, to 17 per cent in 2001. However, Nicholas Lardy warned that China was in danger of suffering a fiscal crisis sometime around 2006–8 unless the state banks developed a credit culture and the government was able to raise its tax take as a share of GNP still further: 'If new bad loans continue to emerge at the rate of the past few years it would still appear that the fiscal deficit is unsustainable' (quoted in *FT*, 30 October 2002).

The problems of non-performing loans in the formal banking sector were not confined to the major banks. In the 1990s, local city banks proliferated. In the year 2000 it was reported that China had a total of eighty-eight city commercial banks (*chengshi shangye yinhang*). As we have seen, one of these, Shantou City Commercial Bank, was insolvent in the late 1990s, and had experienced a serious run on deposits, necessitating large-scale intervention by the provincial authorities. By international standards, at the end of the 1990s, the whole city commercial bank sector was insolvent. At the end of 1998, the sector had total assets of RMB 494 billion but bad debts officially totalled RMB 471 billion, a staggeringly high ratio of bad debts to assets (*FT*, 6 June 2000). It was announced that some banks would be closed, while others would be merged. The PBOC took the decision to reinvigorate the city commercial banks due to their acknowledged importance in stimulating the supply of capital to the non-state sector firms that formed an important part of their client base. The State Development Planning Commission called for greater credit support for private enterprises. Dai Xianglong, Governor of the PBOC, declared that the central bank would 'ensure that the city commercial banks could honour their payment obligations' and then would extend them credit 'when they were short of funds to lend to quality borrowers.' International analysts expressed concern that the PBOC's planned support for the city commercial banks 'could end up becoming a significant drain on central bank and municipal funds' (*FT*, 6 June 2000).

Corruption and criminality

The urgent need for financial sector reform was reinforced by a series of reports by the Chinese National Audit Office. In 1999, the Audit Office revealed accounting abuses involving a 'staggering RMB 400 billion' (US$ 48 billion) at two of China's 'big four' state banks, in an unprecedented report 'illustrating the extent to which corruption has eroded Beijing's executive power' (*FT*, 17 December 1999). Investigations at 4,600 branches of ICBC and 1,700 branches of CCB found that the two banks had overstated their assets by RMB 200 billion and run off-book accounts (*zhang wai zhang*) comprising another RMB 200 billion: 'The implications of the huge amount of off-book loans uncovered were that many of them were running a parallel banking business by lending people's deposits and pocketing interest payments for themselves' (*FT*, 17 December 1999).

The central government was concerned about the case of GITIC long before the crisis finally erupted in 1998. Numerous investigation teams were sent to explore the problems of internal management, but achieved little progress. During the 'clean-up' of the local NBFIs and GDE in Guangdong, it became obvious that there were problems of criminality and corruption in this sector. However, it gradually became clear that there were fundamental failures in corporate governance not just at the local level as revealed in Guangdong, but at the very highest levels in the country's banking sector. In the course of the clean-up of the country's financial institutions, three high-profile senior banking officials encountered serious difficulties, namely those of Zhu Xiaohua, Li Fuxiang and Wang Xuebing: 'All three were close associates. All spoke excellent English and had cultivated relationships with many of the world's top bankers to whom they seemed to embody the market-savvy face of a new China. The illusion is now shattered' (*FT*, 16 January 2002).

The problems facing the three bankers had a big impact on the way in which China's banking system was viewed outside the country. The *Financial Times* commented:

> China must rapidly overhaul its financial system if it is to prevent corruption, inefficiency and gross misallocation of capital from wrecking the creation of a modern economy...The combination of policy lending and corrupt practices has eaten away the banks' balance sheets and their hopes of squaring up to foreign competitors which gain access to the Chinese market under the WTO rules within five years.
>
> (*FT*, 18 January 2002)

Zhu Xiaohua, Li Fuxiang and Wang Xuebing were part of Premier Zhu Rongji's team of four 'can-do-commanders' (*gan jiang*) who were used by Zhu to attack issues of critical importance in China's financial reforms.[24]

From 1993 to 1996, Zhu Xiaohua held the positions of Deputy Governor of the PBOC and head of the management of China's foreign exchange reserves. In 1996 he was appointed Chairman of China Everbright Bank (CEB). CEB was founded in 1992. It was one of the group of innovative state-owned banks that was allowed to operate 'free from the mountains of non-performing loans that characterize the traditional big four state banks.' In 1999, Zhu Xiaohua vanished from public view. It was reported in the international press that an investigation into his 'alleged misdeeds,' was apparently hampered by his 'fragile mental state' (*FT*, 16 January 2002). For three years there was no news about him in the official Chinese media. Then, in August 2002, several key aspects of his story emerged in the mainland press. It was revealed that in July 1999 he had been placed under house arrest and required to confess to his mistakes. In December 2000 Zhu Xiaohua's wife, Ren Peizhen, committed suicide by jumping from a building in Chicago. Zhu's daughter, Zhu Yun, suffered a mental collapse. In May 2001 Zhu Xiaohua was arrested and placed in Qincheng prison near Beijing.

China Everbright Bank had planned to launch an IPO in 2003, but in early 2002 it was announced that the IPO had been 'postponed indefinitely' (*FT*, 13 August 2002). It was reported that the bank had been subjected to a sweeping government investigation, involving a team of up to 500 officials, who had uncovered 'many improprieties' (*FT*, 13 August 2002). In August 2002 it was announced that Zhu Xiaohua had been expelled from the Communist Party and would stand trial for 'absolutely vile' crimes. It was reported officially that Zhu 'took huge kickbacks worth several million Hong Kong dollars and violated credit rules to approve loans worth hundreds of millions of Hong Kong dollars' (*FT*, 13 August 2002). On at least four occasions after his disappearance from public view, it was rumoured that Zhu was about to be brought to trial, but each time the trial was not brought to fruition for 'mysterious reasons.' Finally, on 20 August 2002, at 8.30 am, Zhu's trial began at the Beijing Middle Level People's Court.

On 10 October 2002, the official Chinese news media broadcast that Zhu had been sentenced to fifteen years imprisonment for crimes committed while Chairman of China Everbright Bank, including taking a bribe of RMB 4 million (*FT*, 11 October 2002).

Li Fuxiang was formerly the head of the Bank of China's foreign exchange dealings in New York, and subsequently became the official in charge of the State Administration of Foreign Exchange, following Zhu Xiaohua. In May 2000 he committed suicide by jumping out of the seventh-floor window of a hospital in Beijing as investigators moved in. The official reason given for Li's death was depression. At the time of his death he was being questioned about his conduct at both the Bank of China and at SAFE: 'Questions over what happened to the billions of "missing" reserves remain unanswered to this day' (*FT*, 16 January 2002). In 1998, it was estimated that over the course of the whole year, the combined total of foreign investment and the trade surplus was US$ 89 billion. However, the foreign exchange reserves grew by only US$ 5.1 billion. In 1999, the foreign exchange reserves grew by US$ 9.72 billion, compared with a trade and investment surplus of US$ 76 billion (*FT*, 16 January 2002). Most observers believed that a substantial part of the discrepancy could be attributed to capital flight, propelled by concern over the possibility that China might devalue the *renminbi*. However, estimates of capital flight account for only around US$ 35–40 billion a year, according to some analysts, leaving unexplained the remainder of the discrepancy (*FT*, 16 January 2002).

The case of the Bank of China

The case of Wang Xuebing was closely bound up with the complex story of BOC. In the struggle to reform China's four big banks in time to face the expected onslaught of competition by global giant financial institutions within the WTO, it was widely believed that BOC was the best-run, with the best chance of becoming an internationally competitive financial firm.

In early 2002 it was revealed that Wang Xuebing, who was then President of China Construction Bank, was being investigated for 'credit problems' at the Bank of China branches which had occurred during the period from 1993 to February 2000 when he had been President of the Bank of China. It was later revealed that Wang Xuebing had been detained in 2001 on corruption charges, and was 'assisting investigators from within Qincheng prison,' a high-security prison on the outskirts of Beijing (*FT*, 9 June 2003). In July 2002 it was reported Wang and other senior managers had been arrested for their role in alleged fraudulent transactions involving BOC's New York branch. In 2002 Wang was expelled from the Communist Party for 'taking bribes, leading a decadent life style and breaking financial rules.' On 10 December 2003 Wang Xuebing was sentenced to twelve years in jail for 'taking bribes.'

However, shortly after China joined the WTO it emerged that BOC had further serious corruption problems. In 2002, the National Audit Office

(NAO) completed an audit of BOC from the period 1992 through to the year 2000. It covered the head office and seven provincial branches of BOC. The NAO identified twenty-two possible incidents of fraud or misconduct with respect to transactions totalling RMB 2.7 billion. Many officials at different levels in the company faced prosecution.

At the end of December 2002 it was announced that the former chief of BOC's Zhanjiang (Guangdong) branch had been given a life sentence in a Guangdong court for corruption and malpractice: 'The court found the defendant Fan Shourun guilty of embezzlement and misallocation of bank funds, breaching loan extension rules, issuing illegal financial bills and in possession of huge amounts of assets whose sources could not be ascertained' (Xinhua reported in *SCMP*, 30 December 2002). Fan was head of the Zhanjiang branch of BOC between August 1993 and June 1996. He was found guilty of embezzling HK$ 650,000 during his tenure.

Following the Zhou Zhengyi scandal (see below) it was revealed that other questionable loans had been made by the Shanghai branch of BOC. In early July it was announced that the general manager of the Shanghai branch, Zhou Lu, had been sacked (*SCMP*, 15 July 2003). The reason given was that he had made 'irregular credit extensions' to a Shanghai company, the Wan Tai group.[25] BOC had already made nearly RMB 800 million-worth of loans to Wan Tai when Zhou Lu took over. Under Zhou Lu's leadership, a further RMB 600 million-worth of loans were made. In total the BOC Shanghai branch had loaned Wan Tai the equivalent of around US$ 170 million. The ostensible purpose of the loans made by Zhou Lu was for property projects. In fact, they had been used to finance stock market trading, and the acquisition of three listed companies, two in Hong Kong and one in Shanghai (*SCMP*, 15 July 2003).

BOC's Kaiping branch

The deficiencies in corporate governance within the local branches of the main state-owned banks were exposed vividly by the case of the Kaiping branch of BOC. In early 2002, it was revealed that five bank officials at the BOC branch in Guangdong's Kaiping city had stolen the equivalent of 'nearly US$ 500 million.'[26] This was the biggest embezzlement case since the founding of the PRC. Kaiping is the neighbouring city to Enping, en route to Enping from Guangzhou, about two hours' bus ride southwest of the provincial capital. They are both in the Jiangmen City administrative district.

Xu Chaofan was the Branch Manager at Kaiping in the early 1990s, until he was promoted to BOC's offices in Guangzhou. His successors were Yu Zhendong and then Xu Guojun. According to Hong Kong government officials the three were 'already well-prepared' as their families had already been sent abroad using false passports (*FEER*, 30 May 2002). It is alleged that on 25 October 2001, the three fled to Hong Kong, also using fake documents. From there, they were reported to have fled to the United States and

Canada. Some of the money was laundered through Macao as well as in Las Vegas (*FT*, 16 March 2002). Hong Kong police said that they had arrested two solicitors and a barrister in connection with the laundering of money from the Kaiping branch. The three former managers and their two accomplices were said to have been 'doing this for nine or ten years': 'These guys were massive high rollers. They were gambling and travelling overseas with their families' (investigator, quoted in *FEER*, 30 May 2002).

Relative to the size of Kaiping city, this was a huge theft. Kaiping had a population of only around 680,000 people. The theft was the equivalent of around US$ 740 for every citizen of Kaiping. In 2000, Kaiping's GDP totalled US$ 1,080 million, and its total residents' savings totalled (the equivalent of) US$ 1,130 million (SSBG, GTN, 2001: 631 and 655). The theft was the equivalent of around one-half of Kaiping's GDP and one half of its total savings. Immediately after the managers fled, rumours began to circulate about the alleged theft. On 17 October depositors started to queue at the branch, and the authorities were forced to send in truckloads of cash to meet demands for withdrawals. The *Far Eastern Economic Review* commented: 'Calm was restored within days, but the incident shows how wary the government is of any loss of public confidence in the banks. Some analysts warn that a run on China's debt-laden banks might spark a nationwide financial crisis' (*FEER*, 30 May 2002).

The publicly available information made it impossible to identify exactly how the three managers had exploited loopholes in BOC's internal accounting systems and escaped detection for so long. BOC(HK)'s listing prospectus in 2002 simply said that the theft had taken various forms, including 'foreign exchange trading activity in violation of regulations, off-balance sheet loans, and the diversion of bank funds to third parties.' Chinese and Hong Kong investigators said that the three men had 'established a pipeline into the Bank of China's foreign currency reserves in Beijing' (*FEER*, 30 May 2002). One method that investigators said was used by Xu Chaofan to shift money offshore was through issuing bogus loans to local township and village enterprises, which then transferred the funds as payment for orders of raw materials to companies controlled by Xu in Hong Kong (*FEER*, 30 May 2002). Veteran police investigators in Hong Kong said that it was 'highly unlikely that the three managers had acted alone.' Other managers were replaced in a 'sweeping clear-out of local [BOC] branches' (*FEER*, 30 May 2002). By May 2002, the Hong Kong police had arrested four people in connection with money laundering associated with the case, and further arrests were expected. The Royal Canadian mounted police were reported to be investigating a number of people in Canada in connection with the case (*FEER*, 30 May 2002). Part of the embezzled funds was used to build a luxury hotel in Kaiping and a 22-storey office block that housed the BOC office. The hotel manager was a former BOC employee. After the scandal erupted, he committed suicide by jumping from one of the hotel windows (*FEER*, 30 May 2002).

In 2002, as the revelations about failings of corporate governance at BOC emerged, BOC's Governor, Liu Mingkang, emphasized that the bank was determined to stamp out graft and improve management: 'The Kaiping affair shows that [BOC] has a long way to go' (*FEER*, 30 May 2002). In its report on the Kaiping scandal, *Caijing* (5 May 2002) concluded that the Kaiping scandal illuminated the 'terrifying complexity and scale of the challenge facing China': 'Only by drawing a lesson from this bitter experience and facing reality bravely will the Chinese banking industry be able to make up for lost time' (quoted in *FEER*, 30 May 2002).

In 2004 Xu Chaofan, Xu Guojun and Yu Zhendong, along with the wives of Xu Chaofan and Xu Guojun, were arrested in Nevada. They appeared in court in Las Vegas and were charged with engaging in a RICO (Racketeer Influenced and Corrupt Organizations Act) conspiracy that began in 1991 and continued until their arrest in October 2004. Yu Zhendong pleaded guilty to a racketeering charge and returned to China voluntarily where he was convicted for his role in the Kaiping BOC theft. Xu Chaofan and Xu Guojun were convicted of charges of 'racketeering, money laundering, international transportation of stolen property as well as passport and visa fraud' (Department of Justice, 2009). Evidence presented at the trial established the 'elaborate scheme to defraud the Bank of China of at least US$ 485 million,' orchestrated by Xu Chaofan, Xu Guojun and Yu Zhendong. The evidence demonstrated how the former BOC Kaiping bank managers 'created a number of shell corporations in Hong Kong and with assistance from others funneled the bank's money into these companies as well as numerous personal bank and investment accounts.' Assisted by their wives, relatives and others, the former bank managers then laundered the stolen proceeds through Canada and the United States. The government of the People's Republic of China, in particular the Ministries of Justice and Public Security, along with the Hong Kong Department of Justice and the Hong Kong police force, provided 'substantial assistance in producing evidence and making witnesses available.' US District Judge Philip M. Pro sentenced Xu Chaofan to twenty-five years in prison and Xu Guojun to twenty-two years in prison. Their wives were each sentenced to eight years in prison. In 2018 Xu Chaofan was returned to China to face charges of embezzlement and corruption. The CPC's Central Committee for Disciplinary Inspection said, 'The successful repatriation [of Xu Chaofan] is considered an important achievement in Sino-US anti-corruption law enforcement cooperation.'

Flotation of BOC(HK)

The operational risks for China's banks as they began to expand their international operations were exposed vividly by the case of Bank of China (Hong Kong). A key part of the Chinese government's strategy to improve the operational mechanism of China's main commercial banks was to allow them to float part of their share capital on international markets. The flotation of BOC(HK) in mid-2002 was intended to be a milestone in this process. It was thought that BOC(HK) would benefit from shareholder scrutiny, from the publicity and regulation consequent upon operating in Hong Kong. It was hoped that this would facilitate progress in the parent company, BOC, assisting it to become a modern, professional, globally competitive financial firm, which would pave the way for an eventual international listing of part of the equity of BOC's mainland operations. BOC(HK) was formed from the merger of eleven different local banks formerly under BOC(HK), making it Hong Kong's second largest banking group. BOC(HK) was the 'cream of the BOC group,' accounting for almost 80 per cent of the profits of the whole group in 2001 (*SCMP*, 26 June 2002). BOC(HK) was subject to supervision by the Hong Kong Monetary Authority rather than the mainland regulators. Many commentators expressed the belief that this would have a strong positive effect on the operational mechanism of BOC(HK).

BOC's flotation was strongly supported by leading Hong Kong businesses. Li Ka Shing's companies, Hutchison and Cheung Kong, were reportedly ready to invest US$ 200 million in the issue, and a further seven companies, 'mostly Hong Kong property groups,' offered a total of around US$ 550 million (*FT*, 27 July 2002). This followed the same pattern as other large-scale Hong Kong listings by mainland companies. This practice was criticized by some commentators: 'This is precisely the antithesis of how the free market is designed to operate … It's *guanxi* basically. Curry favour with the right people in China and basically business will be easier for them' (quoted in *FT*, 26 July 2002). It is paradoxical that a process that was supposed to signal major progress in BOC's corporate governance should have been so dependent on 'connections' with Hong Kong business leaders. The BOC flotation in July 2002 was greatly oversubscribed.

Public investors were reassured to learn that BOC(HK) would have as independent non-executive directors, prominent Hong Kong business people. These were: Chia Pei-yuan, former Vice-Chairman and a Director of Citigroup; Victor Fung, Chairman of Li and Fung; Shan Weijian, Managing Director of Newbridge Capital; and Tung Chee Chen, Chairman of Orient Overseas, and former Chairman of the Hong Kong Shipowners' Association. Anthony Neoh, former Chairman of the Hong Kong Securities Regulatory Commission, was senior advisor to the board.

The flotation of BOC(HK) raised US$ 2.8 billion through the sale of 30 per cent of the firm's equity (*FT*, 26 July 2002). The mainland parent company, BOC, retained ownership of 70 per cent of BOC(HK)'s equity. It appeared that BOC had put behind it some serious problems, and was now able to devote itself to proving itself as a model of Chinese enterprise reform in the financial sector. BOC was widely regarded as the best of the big four Chinese banks and BOC(HK) was by far the 'best' operating unit within BOC. Having successfully completed its flotation, and operating in the transparent business environment of Hong Kong, subject to full scrutiny by Hong Kong regulatory authorities, with a high-quality team of local independent directors, and subject to scrutiny from its public shareholders, BOC(HK) was to be the flagship of China's banking reform, the key litmus test of the ability of large Chinese financial institutions to reform through privatization and achieve the ability to compete with the global giant financial institutions.

However, numerous issues concerning failures of corporate governance in BOC were brought into the public domain in connection with the listing. BOC(HK)'s listing prospectus in 2002 admitted the serious problems that had been experienced at its Kaiping branch, as well as recognizing that 'incidents involving embezzlement, misappropriation and bribery by BOC officers and employees, as well as parties outside BOC' had also 'occurred at other BOC branches' (BOCI, 2002: 169).

The revelations about BOC's operations within China were accompanied by other serious allegations relating to BOC's international operations. In January 2002, BOC's New York branch agreed to pay a record US$ 20 million in fines to the US Office of the Comptroller of Currency (OCC) for 'alleged misconduct throughout the 1990s' (*FEER*, 28 February 2002). The OCC and the PBOC announced that an investigation had found BOC's New York branch management guilty of misconduct between 1991 and 1999 (*SCMP*, 26 June 2002). In response to OCC's investigations, in early 2001 BOC launched legal actions against two of its clients, alleging it had been the victim of fraud. In January 2002, they in turn filed a complaint with the Manhattan district court that named BOC(HK) as defendant (*FEER*, 28 February 2002). The litigation was in relation to 'seventeen complex currency and interest rate [arbitrage] transactions in 1999.' As a result of these court actions, 'hundreds of pages of court documents' came into the public domain, 'opening a rare window on corporate culture in the branch [BOC(HK)] and possibly across the Bank of China' (*FEER*, 28 February 2002).[27]

BOC and the Zhou Zhengyi scandal

The tangled and messy relationship between the international operations of China's main SOE banks and their domestic operations was exposed vividly by the Zhou Zhengyi scandal. Only a year after its flotation, another huge scandal rocked BOC(HK). The scandal revealed the close relationship between China's banks and property development, and shed light on the complicated web of financial relationships between Hong Kong and the mainland. The Chief Executive of BOC(HK), Liu Jinbao, was at the centre of the scandal.

Liu Jinbao had been the Chief Executive of BOC's Hong Kong branch since August 1997 and was also Vice-Chairman of BOC, BOC(HK)'s parent company. During that time he had also been head of the Bankers' Association of Shanghai. He was personally responsible for the comprehensive restructuring of BOC's Hong Kong operations, which paved the way for the formation and subsequent flotation of BOC(HK). He was the Chief Executive of BOC(HK) at its flotation. Liu Jinbao's CV reads like a model of a modernizing CEO of an international financial services company. He was forty-nine years old at the time of BOC(HK)'s flotation, with a PhD from the Shanghai Academy of Social Sciences. He was the Chairman of the Hong Kong Enterprises Association, a non-executive director of several leading Hong Kong financial firms and a member of the Hong Kong government's Exchange Fund Advisory Committee, Land Fund Advisory Committee and Commission on Strategic Development. His positive public image was an important part of the successful flotation of BOC(HK).

In May 2003 Liu Jinbao was recalled to Beijing from his post as Chief Executive of BOC(HK), just one day before BOC(HK)'s annual general meeting. It was reported that he was under investigation by the Party's Central Discipline Commission for allegations concerning questionable loans made by BOC in Shanghai between 1994 and 1997, when Liu had been head of BOC's Shanghai branch (*FT*, 9 and 10 June 2003). Audit officials said that a total of US$ 59 million had gone missing, that RMB 200 million-worth of loans had been made illegally and 'some RMB 200 million was still unaccounted for' (*FT*, 9 June 2003). At the same time it was reported that mainland investigators were 'tracing RMB 200 million (US$ 24 million) and US$ 59 million that went missing from BOC's Shanghai branch' (*FT*, 10 June 2003). In August 2005 in a mainland Chinese court Liu Jinbao was convicted of embezzlement and given a two-year suspended death sentence. Liu was convicted of receiving US$ 173,000 in bribes and embezzling US$ 2.7 million on his own and with others.

A key part of the mainland investigation into Liu Jinbao concerned his links with Zhou Zhengyi, a Shanghai property developer. In early June 2003 it was reported the Zhou Zhengyi had been arrested in mainland China (*FT*, 11 June 2003). In 2004 he was sentenced to three years in jail on a charge of stock market fraud and released in May 2006. In early 2007 Zhou was re-arrested and in January 2008 was sentenced in a Shanghai court to sixteen years in jail. He was found guilty of five charges including misappropriating funds and forging VAT receipts.

When Liu Jinbao had been head of the BOC's Shanghai branch, he had 'provided massive loan guarantees' to Zhou Zhengyi to 'play the Hong Kong stock market' (*SCMP*, 16 June 2003). In 2002 *Forbes* named Zhou as the 'eleventh richest man in China.' Zhou was an 'uneducated dumpling shop operator,' who had 'worked his way up in various businesses from karaoke to saunas and stock trading' (*SCMP*, 16 June 2003). Eventually he was able to finance property purchases, which he, in turn, mortgaged to BOC Shanghai. These mortgages were 'exchanged for counter guarantees to the BOC Hong Kong branch, which agreed to loan [Zhou] HK$ 1.7 billion for hi-tec company speculation' (*SCMP*, 16 June 2003). This piece of mortgaged property 'was his downfall.'

In 2002, Zhou Zhengyi had won the right to consolidate eight pieces of prime real estate in Shanghai's central Jingan District into a single 63,000 square metre development. On 1 May, hundreds of angry demonstrators massed near the residential compound of Shanghai's top leaders to protest against being evicted from their homes. The Shanghai City Government was reported to have arrested more than one hundred of the protestors. The protestors claimed that they had been moved under false pretences, with officials claiming that the land was to be used for public parks or new roads, but, instead, private apartments were built on the land. The protestors claimed they were only paid RMB 2–3,000 per square metre, only around one-half of the market price: 'Many of the developers that swindled us were state-owned, but even the ones that were not state-owned had very close ties with the government,' said one protestor. The protestors said that they tried to pursue their claims through the local courts, but 'they always ruled in favour of the developers.' Eventually, a group of residents went to Beijing to protest about their alleged mistreatment at the Ministry of Construction (*SCMP*, 26 June 2003).

The city government subsequently announced that they were investigating Zhou Zhengyi's flagship enterprise, the Shanghai-based Nongkai Development Group. Zhou was 'one of a number of multi-millionaires who built their fortunes in Shanghai by getting an inside track on the city's rapidly developing private property market' (*FT*, 4 June 2003). Shanghai developers, including Zhou, filled many of the top positions in the *Forbes* annual list of the richest people in China: 'Although they are private businessmen, the key to the success of entrepreneurs such as Mr Zhou is their relationship with the government officials who control the sale of land' (*FT*, 4 June 2003). Shanghai's land market was 'dominated by insiders' (*SCMP*, 11 July 2003). Officials and industry executives said that 'backroom property deals' like that involving Zhou Zhengyi were 'endemic in the city and much of the country' (*SCMP*, 13 June 2003): 'Everyone involved gets kickbacks. Judges and other high officials are given free units in new apartment blocks' (*SCMP*, 11 July 2003).

In the wake of the revelations about BOC's lending to Zhou Zhengyi, it was revealed that other Shanghai banks had also made large loans to Zhou Zhengyi. The CCB alone was reported to have made loans totalling RMB 3 billion, and the total amount for banks in Shanghai was estimated as RMB 10 billion (around US$ 1.2 billion) (*SCMP*, 21 June 2003). A senior banker said: 'Every bank used to scramble to do business with tycoons like Zhou [Zhengyi]' (*FT*, 13 June 2003). Between 1998 and 2003 prices in the Shanghai land market rose by over 60 per cent. Even after the Zhou Zhengyi scandal erupted, local banks, with few profitable alternatives for lending, were still 'competing aggressively for mortgage lending': 'The hottest game in town remains unchecked by a scandal that seems likely to register barely as a blip on the screen of massive building and capital accumulation' (*SCMP*, 11 July 2003).

Following the 'deepening corruption scandal' the Shanghai government announced that it was 'reviewing all large commercial transactions involving local property developers, banks and municipal officials' (*FT*, 13 June 2003). The government pledged to review all major land transactions signed since May 2001. Under Article 30 of the Ministry of Land and Resources, which came into force in July 2002, all land suitable for development was supposed to be either auctioned or sold through a transparent bidding process. However, despite an 'open bidding system,' the city government could ignore the highest bidder without giving reasons: 'Some land is always given away at low prices to some developers who make huge profits afterwards' (Cai Yutian, head of the Shanghai Housing and Land Administrative Bureau, quoted in *FT*, 13 June 2003). The PBOC issued 'Document 121' which demanded tighter controls on lending to 'prestige projects,' and those which 'aim to glorify particular officials, projects that pose as parks and campuses, but are in fact ordinary real estate, those on collective land, those outside official plans and those that are illegal and improper' (*SCMP*, 12 July 2003).

Initially, the enquiry into the Shanghai land scandal was based on the activities of BOC's mainland office in Shanghai under Liu Jinbao's stewardship, but it quickly broadened out to include the activities of BOC(HK) while Liu Jinbao had been Chief Executive.

The tangled web of relationships between Zhou Zhengyi's operations in Shanghai and those in Hong Kong was shown to be even more complicated when the Hong Kong authorities arrested Zhou's wife, Mo Yuk-ping, on 2 June 2003. Mo was the Chairwoman of Hong Kong listed Shanghai Merchants Holdings (*FT*, 3 June 2003). Hong Kong's anti-corruption body, ICAC, had launched an investigation of an alleged loan fraud involving Mo Yuk-ping. Mo and eighteen others were arrested for suspected 'granting of banking facilities and conspiracy to defraud' (*FT*, 3 June 2003). Eventually, a total of twenty-seven people were arrested by the ICAC in connection with the case (*SCMP*, 18 June 2003). On 2 June shares in Shanghai Merchants Holdings were suspended after it was discovered that two of its subsidiaries had made 'unorthodox' loans totalling RMB 650 million (US$ 79 million) to two mainland entities in Shanghai (*FT*, 11 June 2003). It was reported that they had borrowed the money from 'Shanghai financial institutions' and on-lent it to two unidentified 'mainland entities' (*SCMP*, 14 June 2003). Shortly afterwards the shares in Shanghai Land Holdings, Shanghai Merchants' sister company in Hong Kong, were suspended and they were both placed in receivership (*SCMP*, 18 June 2003). During the ensuing case in the Hong Kong High Court, it was revealed that a number of the accused, including Mo Yuk-ping, Chairwoman of Shanghai Merchants, Managing Director Yang Rui, Financial Controller Carrie Ng Wai-ling and Assistant Financial Supervisor Anna Yu, had conspired to siphon several million (US) dollars-worth of funds out of the company (*SCMP*, 17 July 2003). Mo Yuk-ping was sentenced to three years in jail.

In June 2002, just one month before it was listed, BOC(HK) loaned HK$ 1.77 billion (US$ 25 million) to New Nongkai Global Investment, a Hong Kong company then controlled by Zhou Zhengyi. The money, which was used by Zhou to buy a 75 per cent share of Shanghai Land (see previous paragraph), was secured against Zhou's shares in New Nongkai, and against New Nongkai's 75 per cent ownership share in Shanghai Land, valued at HK$ 789 million (*FT*, 10 June 2003). In other words, the security was provided substantially by the assets that had been purchased with the loan. BOC(HK) accepted risky shares as collateral for its loan, and 'appeared to turn a blind eye to [Zhou's] investment strategy, which was essentially to liquidate profitable Hong Kong property assets and invest the proceeds in speculative Shanghai real estate projects.' New Nongkai Global Investment was placed in receivership at the request of BOC(HK) (*SCMP*, 18 June 2003). Goldman Sachs' analyst, Roy Ramos, observed that BOC(HK)'s loan went 'against the grain of sensible and prudent lending practices':

> Given the questionable nature of the underlying purpose and collateral of the loan, we question why this loan request was not rejected or more vigorously resisted by the BOC(HK)'s independent risk management department, which in turn is chaired by the Chairman of BOC(HK).
>
> (quoted in *SCMP*, 12 June 2003)

Accepting shares as collateral for a loan is generally undesirable, since shares fluctuate in value, 'particularly shares in companies involved in speculative property deals' (*SCMP*, 18 June 2003). In addition, the shares were not in a company unrelated to the borrower, but were in the borrower itself: 'If anything goes wrong, both the loans and the shares were likely to go south' (*SCMP*, 18 June 2003). Even worse, as an equity holder, the bank would be last in line for any assets if the borrower went bankrupt: 'Banks in the West don't make too many loans secured on shares' (*SCMP*, 18 June 2003). It was not clear whether BOC(HK) took a close look at the property deals that Shanghai Land became involved in: 'A loan of this size backed by shares in a company that transformed from a Hong Kong asset-holder into a speculative property investor in Shanghai certainly would have drawn the attention of Western auditors' (*SCMP*, 18 June 2003). The Zhou Zhengyi case drew closer attention to the nature of BOC(HK)'s loan portfolio. Even more than is normal in Hong Kong, BOC(HK)'s loans were heavily concentrated in the property sector. Seven of the bank's top outstanding loans were granted to property companies, 'raising red flags about over-concentration in one industry' (*SCMP*, 18 June 2003). At the end of 2001, BOC(HK)'s non-performing loan ratio stood at 11 per cent. Even after the sale of HK$ 7.4 billion in NPLs to the Cayman Islands branch of its parent, the NPL ratio still stood at 8.5 per cent, far above the Hong Kong average of 4.5 per cent (*SCMP*, 26 June 2002). Goldman Sachs estimated that at the end of 2001, 33 per cent of BOC(HK)'s NPLs were to mainland borrowers, including 'Hong Kong flagships of mainland localities, red chip, H-shares and ITICs' (*SCMP*, 26 June 2002). Around 32 per cent of BOC(HK)'s loans were in property development.

Standard & Poor revised its outlook on BOC(HK)'s 'BBB+' long-term counter-party rating from stable to negative amid concerns about the effectiveness of BOC(HK)'s credit approval controls (*SCMP*, 12 June 2003). Standard & Poor observed that the fact that the loan to New Nongkai became problematic in less than a year raised questions about the adequacy of BOC(HK)'s loan-approval controls, which were thought to be of a higher standard than those of the twelve commercial banking operations of the former Bank of China in Hong Kong that were merged to form BOC(HK): 'Whether certain loan problems are isolated incidents or reflect a bigger issue of execution problems by bank officials is of bigger concern' (quoted in *SCMP*, 12 June 2003).

Implications of the case of BOC(HK)

The scandal over BOC(HK) sparked widespread concern about corporate governance standards in China's commercial banks, since BOC(HK) was supposedly 'the best part of China's best bank.' The initial investigations suggested 'a troublesome lack of attention to the important details of how to run a bank' and did 'not bode well for China's bid to reform the banking sector' (*SCMP*, 18 June 2003). In 2002–3, several high-profile cases of corruption within BOC exploded into public view, including, the investigation of the BOC's New York City branch for fraud; the massive theft from the BOC's Kaiping branch; as well as the complex dealings between BOC and Zhou Zhengyi, both in Shanghai, with the BOC's local branch, and in Hong Kong with BOC(HK). One international commentator observed that there was 'no reason to assume that China's banking system will not follow the downward spiral of Japanese banks,' in fact, 'their mistakes may be on an even grander scale': '[C]leaning up China's banking system is not just a question of competition, but survival' (Laurence Brahm, in *SCMP*, 16 June 2003). The scandal at BOC(HK) placed a question mark over the Chinese government's strategy to accelerate reform of the four big banks through listing on international stock markets: 'A scandal at the first key bank listing overseas calls these goals into question' (*SCMP*, 18 June 2003).

The scandal brought into the open the problematic aspects of the relationship between mainland and 'overseas' Chinese entities. The main body of this study examined the complex financial web that binds together the financial institutions in Guangdong province and Hong Kong. The scandal surrounding BOC(HK) revealed that this complex web extended deeply into the mainland, indeed, into the very heart of the Chinese commercial and financial system in Shanghai. One observer described this 'fascinating and inscrutable mess' as follows:

> 'One country two systems' has never been so complicated: a prominent Hong Kong-based Beijing banker and a Shanghai businessman are detained on the mainland to facilitate investigations there; the

> businessman's wife is arrested in Hong Kong; and receivers of the businessman's Hong Kong firm are chasing its Shanghai subsidiaries for millions of *yuan* in missing loan proceeds.
>
> (Tom Mitchell in *SCMP*, 14 June 2003)

The case of Zhou Zhengyi exposed a core part of the process of 'primitive capital accumulation' in the Chinese 'transition' process, namely the appropriation of the rents from the privatization of urban land: 'Across China, in every city, there is the same network of local state officials, banks and criminals, working together to profit from the privatization of publicly owned land.' We could see this process at work at the local level in the Pearl River Delta, but the case of Zhou Zhengyi demonstrated that this same network was present even in China's most commercially developed and 'well-run' city.

The main body of this study included an examination of corruption in Guangdong province. A widely held perception was that the Shanghai business environment was markedly less corrupt than that in Guangdong. However, the Zhou Zhengyi case, and the other cases which came to light as a result of it, demonstrated that Shanghai also was deeply mired in corruption. A local state newspaper expressed alarm that the explosion of financial crime that had been revealed in the city was 'threatening the city's rise as a financial centre' (quoted in *SCMP*, 16 July 2003). It was reported that the city's courts had handled 35,669 cases of financial crime in the years 1997–2002, an increase of 93 per cent on the previous five-year period. The city's authorities were reported to be 'overwhelmed by the sheer volume of cases,' and 'could not anticipate being able to investigate them all' (*SCMP*, 16 July 2003).

The case of Enping: unravelling the Gordian knot[28]

The messy and complicated relationships between rural financial institutions and the local branches of the main SOE banks were exposed vividly by the case of Enping. When Dr Wang Xiaoqiang and I got off the bus in Enping, we expected to be conducting research into the notorious rural financial associations in Enping. Instead, we found that the rural financial associations were embedded in a tangled and nearly impenetrable relationship with the local branches of SOE banks and the rural credit cooperatives.

Enping is a county in the southwest corner of Guangdong's Pearl River Delta, the fastest-growing area in the whole country in the 1990s. It has an area of 1,698 square kilometres, eighteen small towns (*zhen*) and a population of 470,000 resident in the county. There are estimated to be 300,000 overseas Chinese from Enping. Up until the mid-1980s it was mainly an agricultural county. From 1984 onwards, the speed of development picked up, with bank loans playing a key role in the county's growth. In the early 1990s, financial institutions in Enping began secretly to offer illegal high rates of interest to attract depositors (*gaoxi lanchu*). The Enping case figured prominently in the national level discussion of problems of rural finance exposed during the AFC. The real situation turned out to be even more complicated than it appeared from accounts in the national press.

China Construction Bank

The Enping branch of the CCB was extremely active in soliciting deposits. Enping may have been unusual in that the local branch of one of the big four commercial banks seems to have been the initiator of the local competition for deposits. The practice of attracting funds using interest rates far above the official, legally stipulated interest rate began during the period in which Zheng Rongfang was head of the Enping CCB. Originally, he had been secretary of the Communist youth league in Enping. Then he had worked as a hired labourer, and after that entered the Enping CCB as a driver, gradually working his way up through a succession of positions, until eventually becoming head of the local branch of the Communist Party of China.

From 1988 to 1993, the Enping branch of the CCB offered interest rates of over 30 per cent to attract billions of *renminbi* of deposits. During this period, not only did Enping RCC solicit huge deposits illegally, in addition, the head of the CCB in Enping, Zheng Rongfang, was 'not only fishing for profits through the RCC,' but simultaneously was supposed to be the regulator of the CCB through his position as the deputy head of Enping city government. The CCB's head office and the Guangdong Party committee sent several reports on the problems in Enping to the Party's central disciplinary commission, including even to Premier Zhu Rongji. However, nothing was done until it was too late, and a crisis had erupted.

Under Zheng Rongfang in the late 1980s and early 1990s the annual interest rate on deposits reached as high as 36 per cent, and Enping's CCB attracted around RMB 1.6 billion in deposits. By the mid-1990s, only 20 per cent of the deposits in the Enping CCB were from within Enping, and the rest were from outside. Enping's branch of the CCB collected funds 'from every part of China except for Tibet.' Increasingly, the offer of rates of interest far above the official rate became more open. In the avid pursuit of deposits, a new class of financial dealer (*jinrong fanzi*) emerged, who specialized in attracting funds from across the country. They brought deposits not only from individuals but also from large institutions in North China, including many SOEs, who believed they could get a far better return by investing in the booming Guangdong economy via the CCB branch of Enping than by investing in their own businesses. A considerable part of the funds deposited in Enping must have had its origin in loans from state banks to SOEs in other parts of China. The brokers were routinely rewarded with bonuses proportional to their success in attracting funds to the Enping CCB.

The illegal high rates of interest offered by Enping CCB were paid on separate deposits from the regular legal deposits. These 'off-balance-sheet deposits' (*zhang wai zhang*) were widely used across China. Zheng Rongfang is credited with 'inventing' them in Enping. In 1994, the head of Enping CCB changed to Hou Chunxin. He followed the same path as Zheng Rongfang but in an even more extreme way. Under his leadership, in 1994, Enping CCB collected around RMB 3.5 billion in 'off-balance-sheet accounts.' Following the lead of the CCB, Enping's branch of the ABC and the rural credit cooperatives (RCCs) followed suit, and through *gaoxi lanchu* raised around RMB 6–7 billion in deposits. A complete system of 'off-balance-sheet' accounts made it hard for superior levels to check up on the practices of subordinate entities for which they were responsible.

By 1995, the official deposits in the Enping CCB branch stood at RMB 150 million, compared with no less than RMB 3.5 billion (over US$ 400 million) in 'off-balance-sheet-accounts' or around US$ 850 per resident of Enping. In the midst of the booming national economy of the 1990s, it was easy to attract money to Enping. Across China, it was well known that the economy of the Pearl River Delta was the fastest-growing in China. It seemed rational to depositors that such a fast-growing region would be able to pay much higher rates of interest than the regular, official rate. It seemed logical that the local financial institutions would be able to obtain high returns from their loans enabling them to justify paying such high rates of interest.

The official deposit rate in 1993 was around 10–11 per cent, but the Enping CCB was offering a rate of 16–17 per cent above the official rate. This was enticing for the depositors. They hoped to take advantage of the explosive growth in Southern China to earn easy money for themselves. Not only was the local CCB involved in *gaoxi lanchu* but so also was the local branch of the ABC, in order to be able to compete with the CCB. An interest rate of 30 per cent seems to have been normal in order to attract depositors in the mid-1990s, with payment of interest on deposit, so that instantly, the sum deposited would have 30 per cent added to it.

A crisis finally erupted in May 1995, when the CCB was unable to meet the demands of depositors who wished to withdraw their money. At that point the total loans of the CCB in Enping were around RMB 5.5 billion (US$ 660 million). The immediate cause of the crisis was the tightening of overall control of the money supply in China. A large gap began to appear between the deposits and the repayment commitments of the Enping branch of the CCB. The social crisis was 'very severe,' with people violently protesting outside the office of the CCB, throwing stones at the building. The CCB's response was to send funds to the Enping branch to alleviate the immediate local crisis. The CCB's head office in Beijing sent RMB 2.2 billion to defuse the crisis. It was technically a loan from Beijing to the Guangdong branch of the CCB, which in turn made a loan to the Enping branch of the CCB. In addition, Guangdong province and Jiangmen city (under whose jurisdiction Enping falls) together provided RMB 0.7 billion, and Enping city itself provided RMB 0.3 billion. At first, the CCB tried to distinguish between true individual depositors and institutional depositors, by only repaying those with deposits of less than RMB 1 million. However, this met with an outcry. The social crisis was so severe that they decided to repay all the depositors, regardless of the size of the deposit. 'Calming the tumult' took precedence over the niceties of moral hazard.

Immediately afterwards, the CCB withdrew the branch status of the CCB in Enping and declared it to be an 'office' (*banshichu*) without autonomy or independent legal standing. However, the fact that the CCB superior office had stepped in to solve the problems of the insolvency of the Enping branch of the CCB had a perverse 'moral hazard' effect. It made the depositors even more willing to deposit their funds in the local branch of the ABC, which also used *gaoxi lanchu* to attract funds through *zhang wai zhang*. The depositors benefitted from the high interest rates offered by both the ABC and the CCB. They interpreted the actions of the higher levels of the CCB as indicating that the state banks would always step in to guarantee repayment in order to avoid 'social instability.' Indeed, it may have created the perverse incentive of actually encouraging social disorder in order to frighten the authorities so that they would step in to ensure that the state bank's debts to depositors were always repaid, even if they were illegal.

The fact that the depositors were repaid did not solve the problem of the bad loans. At the end of 1996 it was estimated that the Enping office of the CCB alone had a total of RMB 3.3 billion in non-performing loans, in other words, around 60 per cent or more of outstanding loans. In 1998, Xinda Asset Management Company took over RMB 2.6 billion in bad loans from the Enping office of the CCB. Across the whole of China in 1998, Xinda took over around RMB 250 billion in bad debts from the CCB, of which around RMB 46 billion were for Guangdong province alone.

In the 1990s, Guangdong was China's fastest-growing province, given special privileges by the central government in terms of autonomy in economic policy. It had achieved the highest level of income of any province in China by a considerable margin, around 60 per cent higher than the national average, and more than double that in the poorest provinces. It had only around 5.7 per cent of China's total population. However, it was responsible for 18.4 per cent of the bad debts due to the CCB that were taken over by Xinda. In the 1990s, Enping was one of the fastest-growing counties in Guangdong province, along with several others in the Pearl River Delta. It had only 0.64 per cent of the total population of Guangdong province, but it accounted for 5.7 per cent of the total bad debts of the CCB absorbed by Xinda in Guangdong. It is striking that some of the fastest-growing and highest-income parts of China should have been least able to ensure that debts to state banks were repaid. Local institutions and individuals in fast-growing, high-income regions had borrowed relatively large amounts from the state which they had not repaid and for which there seemed little likelihood of repayment occurring. For the Enping branch of the CCB to have accumulated such a huge proportion of NPLs in the midst of the fastest-growing region of the whole world, suggests that there were deep problems with the nature of the process of credit provision and loan monitoring. It suggests strongly that there were 'Ponzi'-type criminal processes at work, with funds being lent to insiders who had no intention of repaying. The concept that these unpaid debts could be considered as 'theft' is strengthened by the few details that were available concerning the amount and use to which the loans were put.

A central problem in the Enping case was the lack of a credit repayment culture with its matching legal system and incentives to use the system to ensure repayment. Enping's entrepreneurs 'don't care about loan repayments,' even if they were making profits. They 'don't repay their loans on time, and typically refuse even to pay their electricity bills.' It was difficult to use the legal system to obtain repayment, even if the local branch of the banking system had wished to do so. Numerous popular sayings in Guangdong during this period reflected the *de facto* legal theft from the local financial system, with huge amounts of borrowing with no intention of repaying. The local people spoke of loans from the bank as *aye de qian*, or 'father's money,' which does not therefore need to be repaid. They spoke also of *chi tangsheng rou*, or 'eating *tangsheng* meat,' after the monk in 'Journey to the West.' Those who ate his 'meat' would live forever. Those who ate the bank's 'meat' also could live forever, because the loans would just be endlessly rolled over with no intention of repaying or incentive to do so.

The process through which these 'non-repayable, interest-free grants' were allocated was strongly influenced by local networks of relationships, especially by family ties. A large proportion of the CCB's loans went to building cement factories (see below). Alongside the growth of the cement factories went a substantial change in their property rights regime. During the 1990s, most of the cement factories ceased to be collectively owned and run. Instead, they were predominantly leased to individuals, often to the township head or Party secretary. The terms under which the factories were leased were typically highly advantageous to those who took over the leases: 'You can easily imagine the processes through which the leases were determined.' Over much of the Pearl River Delta during this period, after Deng Xiaoping's 'Southern Journey,' almost all the true SOEs were sold. There was said to be 'zero public bidding involved.' The process was heavily criticized as 'open, large-scale, public robbery.' Leading Chinese economists defended the process arguing that if some mistakes were made during this process it was a price worth paying for establishing a market system based on private property.

Much of this loan activity was funded through *gaoxi lanchu* operations across the length and breadth of China. The probability of the benefits being distributed equally among the local inhabitants was small. Of the total of RMB 5.5 billion in loans outstanding to the Enping branch of the CCB in 1998, at least two-fifths were 'bad loans.' It was estimated by an insider from the financial system that only around one-third of the Enping CCB's loans were put to 'productive' use. The remaining two-thirds 'just disappeared,' 'taken by the brokers' (*jinrong fanzi*), lost in 'corruption,' or 'used to set up networks.' Following the crisis, many of the *jinrong fanzi* fled to foreign countries, including even Latin America, often using their connections with overseas Chinese.

One can say that there were two financial 'games' being played by the CCB in Enping. One was the 'deposit' game. The local branch of the CCB felt confident in paying high rates of interest to attract deposits from across China, because in the end they had no intention of paying back the depositors. They knew that in the end the higher levels of the CCB would step in to settle the debt. The other side of the 'game' was the lending game. The borrowers didn't care if they were charged a high rate of interest, because they had no intention of paying back the bank. They didn't mind if the loans were rolled over and the total debt kept escalating. At the height of the crisis, the total interest payments owed by local borrowers were as large as the original debt.

Agricultural Bank of China and the Rural Credit Cooperatives

Up until 1996, the ABC and the RCCs essentially constituted a single entity across the whole country. The latter were formally under the control of the ABC and were required to hand over their surplus each year to the ABC. All their business was supposed to be overseen by the ABC. In Enping the two bodies had 'a single door, but two signs over the door.' The staff each had two 'hats,' one for either body. Basically, each township in Enping had a single RCC branch, with a total of over 1,000 staff, and 141 sub-branches across the county. It seems that the local branches of the RCC were the prime movers among the local financial institutions in the struggle to attract funds to Enping. During the 1990s, the struggle to attract deposits became increasingly severe, with growing competition between the different financial institutions for local depositors.

By late 1996, as the financial crisis intensified, the RCCs in Enping had a total of RMB 6.69 billion in loans (over US$ 800 million), and RMB 6.7 billion in deposits. Of the deposits, RMB 5.5 billion were 'personal,' within which RMB 5.3 billion were in 'discount' deposits which offered a *de facto* premium above the legal state-fixed rate of interest (*tieshui cunkuan*). This practice was reported to have begun in Enping's RCCs in October 1994. Competition for local funds was intensifying, with other local financial institutions beginning to offer a premium on the state-fixed interest rate as financial controls relaxed in the interests of 'promoting development' across the Pearl River Delta. At first the premium was relatively small, around 3–4 per cent above the state-fixed deposit rate which was then around 10 per cent. Before this, the most that any bank or quasi-bank had dared to offer was a 'small gift' to depositors. The RCCs quickly raised the premium to 7 per cent above the state-fixed legal rate, rising to 8 per cent in early 1995, and by the end of the year they were offering a *de facto* premium of 10 per cent above the state-fixed rate, in other words, around 20 per cent.

At this point, a crisis loomed. Early in 1996 Enping's RCCs found that they were unable to obtain an adequate repayment from borrowers, and faced the prospect of not being able to meet the demands of their depositors for withdrawal of funds. They responded by raising the premium they paid over the state-fixed deposit rate to 12–13 per cent (i.e. an effective interest rate of 22–23 per cent). Moreover, by this point the rate of price inflation had sharply fallen from the peak in 1993–5. The Guangdong provincial retail price index surged to an annual increase of over 18 per cent in both 1993 and 1994, falling to 11.6 per cent in 1995, but by 1996 it had fallen to just 4.4 per cent, and in 1997 was just 0.1 per cent. Consequently, the effective real interest rate being offered by the RCCs in 1996 surged to around 20 per cent. However, this still failed to attract sufficient deposits to enable Enping's RCCs to meet their payments requirements from depositors wishing to withdraw funds. The ability of Enping's RCCs to attract deposits was, naturally, hard hit by the crisis in the local branch of the CCB. The local RCCs raised the rate offered to depositors even further, first to 18 per cent, and then, finally, hit a peak at the end of 1996, of a premium of 22–23 per cent above the official interest rate, which stood at 10.98 per cent for depositors at that time. In other words, the nominal interest rate surged to around 33–34 per cent, or a real interest rate of around 30 per cent. This was unsustainable. The RCCs had become enmeshed in a form of 'Ponzi' scheme using new deposits to pay off old depositors who wanted to withdraw funds.

Quite rapidly, the Enping RCCs were unable to meet their withdrawal demands. The depositors reacted with massive displays of anger. The Guangdong government was forced to act. Enping became a model of how to gradually clean up the immensely complicated problems of the local NBFIs. Enping was an extreme example of a widespread problem within Guangdong province. The long and complicated clean-up in Enping prefigured the massive operation to clean up the entire local NBFI sector in the province and, eventually, across the whole country.

The licence of the Enping RCC was withdrawn by the PBOC. The responsibility for the disorder at Enping's RCC was firmly in the hands of its supervisory body, namely the local branch of the ABC. We have seen that at the time of the crisis in 1996, the RCC in Enping had outstanding loans of RMB 6.7 billion, compared with total outstanding loans of all financial institutions in Enping of around RMB 11 billion, or around three-fifths of the total. Following the crisis, the Guangdong provincial government appointed the Guangdong Guangfa Development Bank as trustee of the RCC in Enping.

As of August 1996, there were deposits in Enping's RCCs totalling RMB 2.53 billion that were officially stamped with the seal of the ABC. The ABC had clear responsibility for these. Accordingly, when disorder broke out in late 1996, the ABC intervened and sent a work team to try to deal with the crisis. This was termed a 'liquidation' group (*qingsuan zu*), in the sense of 'clarifying the accounts,' not implementing legal bankruptcy. This included the head of the Guangdong provincial ABC, which is a measure of the seriousness with which the situation in Enping was regarded. Between October 1996 and 28 April 1997 the liquidation group reimbursed depositors to the extent of RMB 2 billion. This dampened the worst of the immediate anger of depositors. The funds were provided by the Guangdong branch of the ABC. The liquidation group declared that the interest offered above the official rate was illegal. This group of depositors were repaid both their principal and 'normal' interest. After 28 April 1997, subsequent repayments did not include interest due. In December 1997, in response to the public announcement of a repayment, depositors queued from midnight until ten in the morning. After they had been paid, a riot erupted, with the masses of depositors screaming that the deposits were their money and they wanted not only their deposits back but also the interest they felt they were owed (*Caijing*, 5 May 2001).

As of 8 December 1998, there still was RMB 3.2 billion in RCC deposits in Enping unpaid. Presumably, the bulk of these were illegal deposits without a certificate from the ABC, in other words, *zhang wai zhang*. Responsibility for these deposits was ambiguous. Although they were not officially stamped by the ABC, the ABC and the RCC were intimately inter-twined, with the same personnel in key positions in both institutions. The burden for the repayment of these outstanding amounts was divided between three different entities. First, the Guangdong Guangfa Development Bank took over the trusteeship of the Enping RCC, and assumed responsibility for RMB 1 billion of the debts. In return for this, the Guangdong provincial government provided the Development Bank with an exemption from the industrial and commercial tax, and the turnover tax for a period of five years. Second, the Enping and Jiangmen city governments together decided to establish a new commercial bank which would take responsibility for RMB 1 billion of the deposits of Enping's RCC. Third, the PBOC agreed to transfer RMB 1.2 billion in loans to the Guangdong Guangfa Development Bank, in order to deal with this part of the deposits problem. It was estimated that it would take a total of around five years to complete the process of paying back the depositors for their funds in the RCC. As of January 2001, only around RMB 100 million in past debts had been paid back to the RCC by borrowers, less than 2 per cent of the total. In other words, if this situation were allowed to persist, the equivalent of around US$ 800 million would have been provided in *de facto* 'interest-free grants' to those segments of the Enping population that were in a position to obtain loans from the RCC. Up until early 2001, not a single debtor enterprise had been taken to court for non-payment of debts to the RCC in Enping. The debts were simply rolled over.

Cement factories

Enping is rich in limestone, and the deposits are close to the surface, so extraction costs are low. The cement industry was an important one around which to base the county's advance. From the mid-1980s right up to the eruption of the Asian Financial Crisis, Enping's cement factories kept expanding. Eventually, the county had twenty-five factories, with a total of thirty-seven production lines, and a capacity of five million tons.

During the economic boom in the 1990s in the Pearl River Delta in Guangdong province, demand for cement surged. There was a frenzy of road and bridge building. However, the most powerful driver of demand was the property boom with a surging demand for cement to construct buildings of all sorts. This was the 'main pulling force' for the explosion in the number of cement factories in the Pearl River Delta. The cement plants in Enping ought to have made substantial profits, due to their advantageous local raw material conditions and consequent low costs, alongside booming demand. In the mid-1990s, at the height of the boom, the average cost per ton of cement in Enping's cement plants was reported to be around RMB 200 per ton, but the selling price was around RMB 500 per ton.

Each of the three main financial institutions in Enping collected funds to invest in the cement factories. The Enping branch of the ABC reportedly loaned around RMB 4.5 billion (over US$ 500 million) for their establishment. This accounted for around 70 per cent of the total amount of loans made by the Enping branch of the ABC. The Enping RCCs were reported to have loaned around RMB 5.5 billion to the cement factories, amounting to around 80 per cent of its total loans. As well as the loans from the ABC and the RCCs, the CCB also loaned around RMB 1 billion to the cement plants. It is possible that as much as RMB 11 billion may have been lent to the Enping cement plants during the mid-1990s, though the actual amount may be somewhat less than this, due to a certain amount of double-counting in relation to the reporting of loans from the ABC and the RCCs.

In other words, by August 1996, somewhere between US$ 800 million and US$ 1.3 billion was loaned by local financial institutions to establish Enping's cement factories. Even though there were thirty-seven production lines, this is still an amazingly large sum to develop the cement industry in a single county, amounting to between US$ 1,700 and US$ 2,800 for each of the county's residents. The gross value of industrial output in Enping in 1999 was reported to be only the equivalent of US$ 600 million, and the total combined value of industrial and agricultural output was only the equivalent of US$ 750 million. In fact, it is clear that only a proportion of the loans to establish cement factories were used for the ostensible purpose for which the loans were provided. Rough estimates suggest that the cost of establishing the entire system of thirty-seven cement production lines in Enping would have been around RMB 1–1.5 billion (US$ 160–180 million), far below the amount that was loaned to build the cement factories. A substantial fraction of the loans to 'establish cement factories' was in fact used for other purposes. The ostensible loan purpose was a method of satisfying the formalities that the local financial institutions were required to fulfil in order to satisfy their superiors. This required suitable paperwork to specify the purpose of the loan. In Enping, the standard purpose for most large loans was simply 'establishing a cement factory.' In other words, the 'cement factories' were the vehicle through which the loans were channelled. Given the hugely inflated size of the loans in relation to the ostensible purpose for which the loans were made, it suggests a complete absence of normal loan procedures. Instead, it suggests that both the financial institutions and the borrowers were wholly aware of the 'game' that was being played. A 'game' on such a magnitude had to involve the main members of the local political establishment.

The AFC and the collapse of the property bubble had a huge impact on Enping's cement factories. By 1999, only a few of them were operational, and this was still the case during our fieldwork in Enping in January 2001. The huge loans made to the cement factories were largely not repaid: 'The depositors couldn't get back their deposits and the banks couldn't get back their loans.'

Dealing with corruption in Enping

From 1996 up until the end of 2001, thirteen separate work groups had been sent to try to deal with the problem of the local financial institutions in Enping. These included representatives from the PBOC in Beijing, which at that time was the ultimate regulator of China's financial services industry; the People's Procuracy in Jiangmen City (the capital of the district in which Enping is located); the Central Government's Inspection Committee (*jiancha bu*) from Beijing; the Public Security Bureau from Jiangmen; a special workgroup from the Guangzhou provincial government, including senior officials; and a team from the Guangdong Communist Party Disciplinary Commission. In other words, this was treated not only as a serious issue for the province, but also of considerable significance for the whole country's financial system reform and development.

As a result of the investigations into the activities of the different financial institutions in Enping, a large group of people was arrested. The head of the RCC for Enping 'fled.' Two deputy heads of the RCC were arrested. Others removed from their posts included the General Managers of both the ABC and the BOC in Enping. The head of the Enping branch of the CCB was arrested.

Numerous officials in the CCB branch of Enping and in Enping local government were arrested as a result of the investigation that followed the crisis. The best-known was Zheng Rongfang, head of the branch before the crisis. He was a former driver for the CCB in Enping, who rose to become Director of the local branch. Zheng was so 'successful' at bringing capital into Enping that he was appointed Deputy Mayor of Enping county. During the crisis, Zheng Rongfang was forced to resign as Deputy Mayor of Enping. It was decided that he should be brought to trial. He learned that he was going to be arrested and escaped to Guangzhou. He tried to leave China by sea and was arrested at the port together with his wife and mistress, carrying an alleged amount of HK$ 700,000. In 1998 he was sentenced to twenty years in jail. In October 1999, he was tried on a further set of charges, and he received a death sentence, suspended for two years. Other local officials arrested for their roles in the Enping case included Li Guanghua, former Mayor of Enping, and Kuang Ren, the former Deputy Party Secretary of Enping. Kuang Ren had been promoted to be Deputy Mayor of Jiangmen City (which included Enping).

The affair raised fundamental questions about the nature of local politics. The Enping case demonstrated how close was the relationship between local financial institutions, including branches of the state banks as well as the 'cooperative' institutions, and the local government and the Communist Party. Other senior local political figures caught up in the case included Kuang Ren, the former Deputy Party Secretary of Enping, who was promoted to be Deputy Mayor of Jiangmen City. He was arrested for his role in the Enping scandal and sentenced to four years in prison for 'serious misconduct.' The former Mayor of Enping, Li Guanghu, was arrested for his role in the affair, and also sentenced to four years imprisonment.

Over the years, through *gaoxi lanchu*, Enping's financial institutions (CCB, RCCs and ABC) attracted a total of around RMB 11 billion in deposits. This compares with Enping's annual GDP of around RMB 4 billion in the mid-1990s. However, if unpaid interest is included the total climbs to an astonishing figure of around RMB 20 billion (US$ 2.4 billion), an incredible sum for a small county in a developing country, with a population of fewer than half a million people. A significant part of this represented the 'theft' of savings lured from across China by the greed of depositors who hoped to make easy money by lending at such high rates of interest. Essentially, a large fraction of the borrowers was able to use these relatively large amounts as interest-free grants. We have seen that it is almost certain that a large fraction of the loans was allocated to a tiny fraction of the local residents, which included significant numbers of overseas Chinese business people. The large inequality in the benefits from *gaoxi lanchu* helped to make local popular anger even stronger in the face of the local NBFIs inability to repay depositors.

The financial crisis in Enping was of great significance for the local economy. It caused such a severe contraction of credit that it 'set the economic development of the city back by a decade.' A major part of the government 'clean-up' of the problems in Enping involved investigations into corruption and criminal behaviour. In other words, the 'clean-up' in Enping involved a sequence of steps: 'fire brigade' work to quell social disorder, next the restructuring of the debts, and then the restructuring of the local financial firms' business structure, and, last, trying to solve the problem of criminality and corruption. This was a long, complex process.

5 Conclusion

The achievement of 'cutting the trees to save the forest' (*kan shu jiu lin*)

Fighting fires

The axe is the forester's most symbolic professional possession. It is the key to protecting the forest, used to cut down trees in order to preserve the forest's valuable resources. The trees constitute both a rich resource and the instrument through which the fire spreads to destroy that resource. In countries at all levels of development, the most important method to prevent the spread of forest fire is to construct fire-breaks, destroying large quantities of valuable forest resources in order to protect the main part of the forest. Mostly, this laborious process is carried out in advance of a fire by cutting fire-breaks. In high-income countries, it is common to deliver water from planes and helicopters to try to extinguish the flames. In severe fires that rage for a long period in developing countries, it is impossible to move large quantities of water deep into huge forests to drench the fire. The only way to stop the spread of large fires is to destroy trees to save the forest. A common method used in crisis situations is 'back-burning,' employing controlled burning to deliberately lay waste to an area of trees in advance of the main fire, so that there is nothing left to burn when the main fire arrives. Controlling forest fires is dangerous. Fires do not rest at night, and neither do firefighters. Many forest firefighters have lost their lives. A sudden shift of wind is especially dangerous.

In early modern cities, fires were a great hazard. A common strategy for firefighters was to pull down buildings to stop the fire spreading. This meant destroying valuable property, which had taken many years to construct, in order to try to save the rest of the city. In September 1666 the Great Fire of London raged for four days. It destroyed a large part of the City of London, then Europe's leading commercial and financial centre. During the night of 2 September, the Lord Mayor of London, Sir Thomas Bludworth, was called to the scene of the initial fire in a small group of houses. He was advised to pull down the group of houses surrounding the fire. However, firefighters who pulled down buildings to create a firebreak were liable to find themselves taken to court by the owners of the property and compelled to pay the cost of the rebuilding. The Lord Mayor rejected the advice to pull down the buildings, asking: 'When the houses have been brought down, who shall pay the charge of rebuilding them?' (quoted in Porter, 2001: 27). Bludworth is reported to have said on his arrival at the scene of the fire that 'a woman might piss it out' (Porter, 2001: 2).[29] In the aftermath of the Great Fire, Bludworth was 'much blamed' for 'not pulling houses downe time enough' (quoted in Porter, 2001: 45). Samuel Pepys condemned the Lord Mayor as 'a mean man of understanding and despatch of any public business' (Pepys, 1995: 190).

Extinguishing the fire of the AFC in Guangdong involved cutting down the province's 'tall trees,' GITIC and GDE, as well as 'cutting down' hundreds of smaller local 'trees' in the shape of the financial institutions that were the proud possession of local governments. Through timely and decisive action to 'cut the trees to save the forest,' the threat of financial crisis was averted in Guangdong. The dangers of contagion across the country's financial system was stopped in its tracks and a considerable contribution was made to calming the financial turbulence in Hong Kong.

Suiting measures to local conditions

'Suiting measures to local conditions' (*yin di zhi yi*) is one of the most important precepts of China's political tradition. For 2000 years the central government has enunciated the principles and promulgated the regulations for the whole political-economic system. However, from the top to the bottom of the bureaucracy, government officials have had individual responsibility for putting these principles and regulations into practice in the light of concrete local conditions and problems. Government officials at different levels are evaluated in relation to their success or failure in meeting the specific challenges in the locality to which they are sent. They must work within, and continuously interact with, a local bureaucratic structure with its own history and traditions. The way in which the impact of the Asian Financial Crisis upon Guangdong province was resolved provides an example in a modern context of the operational practice of the Chinese bureaucracy over the course of 2000 years.

In December 1997 Wang Qishan was sent by the central government to become a member of the Guangdong provincial Party committee. One month later he was appointed Executive Vice-Governor of the province. The main task was to deal with Guangdong's fragile financial institutions, and to prevent the province experiencing a financial collapse such as was taking place in the countries surrounding China. Dealing with the impact of the Asian Financial Crisis upon Guangdong was the core task of the provincial government over the next two years. Throughout the crisis Wang Qishan appeared frequently before the public and the mass media in Guangdong and Hong Kong. Standing behind him was the 'five-member leading team of the provincial CPC committee.' It consisted of team-leader Lu Ruihua, Governor and Vice-Secretary of the provincial CPC committee; Chen Shaoji, Vice-Secretary of the provincial CPC committee and Secretary of the political and legislative committee; Liu Fengyi, Vice-Secretary of the provincial CPC committee and Director of the CPC's provincial organization department; Wang Qishan himself, member of the standing committee of the provincial CPC committee and Executive Vice-Governor; and Wang Huayuan, member of the standing committee of the provincial CPC committee and Secretary of the provincial disciplinary and supervisory committee. Implementation of the 'three steps' to solve the crisis was under the direct leadership of the political and legislative committee, the organization department of the CPC and the disciplinary and supervisory committee. The 'three steps' involved decisive measures in the face of the raging fire of the Asian Financial Crisis. The decision to 'cut down the tall trees' of GITIC and GDE was humiliating for Guangdong province. The bankruptcy of GITIC and restructuring of GDE took place in the full glare of the global media. At least as important was the 'third step,' namely restructuring over 800 local rural financial institutions. The three steps included a massive clean-up of corruption and criminality. Implementation of the 'three steps' was only possible thanks to leadership by such a politically powerful team.

One country, two systems

The Hong Kong Basic Law, agreed between China and the UK, states: 'The socialist system and policies shall not be practised in the Hong Kong Special Administrative Region, and the previous capitalistic system and way of life shall remain unchanged for fifty years.' The Handover of Hong Kong to Chinese rule took place on 1 July 1997 and within hours the Asian Financial Crisis had begun to unfold with the currency crisis in Thailand. Within a few weeks the AFC had erupted in Hong Kong itself. Under 'one country, two systems' the Chinese government now had formal responsibility for Hong Kong as well as the mainland. During the 1990s the economic, financial and human links between Hong Kong and the mainland had become steadily deeper. By the end of the decade a wide array of Chinese business activities took place in Hong Kong. Chinese firms were an important part of the Hong Kong stock market. Global firms, including financial institutions, had greatly increased their presence in Hong Kong. Investment from Hong Kong in the mainland had grown enormously, notably in the Pearl River Delta. Millions of mainland workers were employed in enterprises owned by Hong Kong business people. The workers had been educated in Chinese institutions. The water, electricity and transport systems for the factories were provided by the mainland. The Chinese police force ensured that the factories and surrounding areas were safe. GITIC and GDE had deep tentacles in both Hong Kong and the mainland. The bankruptcy of GITIC and restructuring of GDE involved Hong Kong creditors, audit firms, lawyers and investment banks. The 800 local financial institutions in Guangdong, especially those in the Pearl River Delta, were connected with Hong Kong through financial, trade and personal relations. The eruption of the AFC in Hong Kong made it dramatically clear that 'capitalist' Hong Kong and 'socialist' China had become inextricably intertwined. Through the ever-advancing mechanism of trade, finance and movement of people, the 'two systems' of Hong Kong and the Pearl River Delta were ever more closely interwoven. This presented great opportunities for the development of the 'Greater Bay Area.'[30] It also presented great governance challenges for both Hong Kong and Guangdong. Effective implementation of the 'three steps' contributed to the stable economic development of the whole Greater Bay Area.[31]

Moral hazard

By the late 1990s there was an extensive group of 'red chip' companies and 'international trust and investment companies' (ITICs) operating in Hong Kong, with a large quantity of offshore borrowings in foreign currency. If the central and local governments had stepped in to support repayment of the international debts contracted by Chinese firms in Hong Kong, it would have had serious consequences for government budgets. The total foreign currency debts of red chips and ITICs in Hong Kong were equivalent to around one-half of China's total foreign exchange reserves. In other words, treating the foreign currency debts as China's sovereign debt would have reduced the government's ability to defend the value of the *renminbi* during the AFC. It would have had even more serious long-term implications in relation to 'moral hazard,' encouraging reckless borrowing by government-backed entities in the mainland and reckless lending by international financial institutions in Hong Kong, confident that the Chinese government would ensure repayment of their loans. In other words, commercial lending with commercial interest rates would have been treated as *de facto* sovereign debt. The decision for GITIC to declare itself bankrupt caused an immediate, decisive change in the outlook of both lenders and borrowers. The decision by the Guangdong government not to acknowledge the debts of GDE as sovereign debt, but instead to go through a prolonged restructuring with the creditors, further reinforced the principle that both lenders and borrowers should base their decisions on the business case for the financial transaction, rather than relying on the government to guarantee debt repayment. These decisions radically transformed the landscape in relation to moral hazard. They not only changed the landscape in the attitude of international financial markets towards lending to Chinese firms. They also served as a powerful example for domestic banks and state-owned non-financial firms of the government's determination to drive moral hazard out of the economic system. Even 'tall trees' owned by the government would need to avoid 'moral hazard' in their borrowing and lending practices. If they failed to do so, they risked being cut down.

Corporate governance

The bankruptcy of GITIC and restructuring of GDE involved deep investigation into the internal workings of major state-owned enterprises, far beyond that involved in listing selected parts of large SOEs on international stock markets. The investigation involved international auditors, law firms, investment banks and law courts. They revealed in both companies tremendously complex business structures with hundreds of subsidiaries operating in a wide range of businesses, without coherent central leadership or clear business objectives. The complex structures facilitated a high degree of waste; uncontrolled borrowing by subsidiaries using the parent company's 'name' and reputation; uncontrolled lending, frequently based on relationships rather than a robust business case; and, not least, extensive fraud and criminal behaviour. GITIC's bankruptcy and GDE's restructuring remain the only examples of deep exposure of Chinese SOEs to international scrutiny. The shocking revelations about the two flagship companies in China's most commercially sophisticated province demonstrated the urgent need for corporate governance reform at China's SOEs, especially those in the financial sector.

'Going out'

The process of 'going out' by Chinese firms gained momentum in Hong Kong in the 1990s. It included the flotation of 'H-share' companies, the growth of 'red chip' companies and ITICs in Hong Kong, alongside the development of a wide variety of other business activities by mainland firms in the territory. Under British rule Hong Kong was widely regarded as a model of the 'rule of law' and best international practice for regulation of financial markets. Under this secure legal and regulatory structure, the 1990s witnessed the rapid expansion in Hong Kong of the activities of Western financial firms, dominated by those from the United States. Under the 1984 Handover Agreement between China and the UK, global financial firms were confident that these structures would remain in place for fifty years after 1997. This structure seemed also to provide a safe legal and regulatory environment within which mainland Chinese firms could begin their long journey of expansion in international markets. Instead, the Asian Financial Crisis exposed huge shortcomings in the corporate governance of Chinese firms operating in Hong Kong and deeply problematic interactions between them and the international financial firms operating in the territory. The shocking revelations produced during GITIC's bankruptcy and GDE's restructuring demonstrated to China's policy-makers the grave dangers involved in large-scale 'going-out' by Chinese firms in the absence of comprehensive reform of their corporate governance. They also raised uncomfortable questions about the real nature of Hong Kong's political economy under British rule.

Hard budget constraint

In the 'transition' process in the former Soviet Union and Eastern Europe the main body of international advisors argued that a 'hard budget constraint' was an essential part of the capitalist system. Across the high-income countries small- and medium-sized enterprises frequently go bankrupt and cease operation. However, bankruptcy and liquidation is infrequent among large firms with an important position in the economy. In the United States insolvent firms typically enter the Chapter 11 process, which provides protection from creditors. Eighty to ninety per cent of large US firms emerge safely from Chapter 11. Indeed, some firms have entered Chapter 11 on multiple occasions. In Europe bankruptcy and liquidation among large firms is also rare. In Europe the solution to insolvency in large, systemically important companies is typically some form of government-orchestrated rescue, through state investment, sale at a 'firesale' price to a competitor, or, increasingly, to a private equity firm. The most extreme recent example of state intervention to resolve the problems of large, systemically important insolvent firms was the large-scale state-orchestrated rescue of insolvent financial institutions in the United States and Europe during the Global Financial Crisis.

In the 1990s China was groping its way towards suitable procedures for insolvent firms and modification of its bankruptcy law. The GITIC bankruptcy was the first occasion on which the Chinese government had refused to bail out a major SOE. Indeed, it was the first major bankruptcy in the history of the PRC. It was essentially carried on according to the 1986 Bankruptcy Law. The law was widely recognized to have many shortcomings, but this was the law that had to be applied. The Chinese government wished the bankruptcy process to be conducted in a manner that international creditors would perceive to be reasonable. This was a major reason for the close involvement of international auditors, lawyers and investment banks. Since the case of GITIC there have been innumerable bankruptcies of small- and medium-sized Chinese firms. However, GITIC remains a rare example of bankruptcy and closure of a major state-owned Chinese enterprise. In China, as in the West, insolvency of large, systemically important firms is typically resolved through rescue of the firm through state-orchestrated solutions. In most countries, insolvency of a major company with deep roots in the surrounding economy involves complicated political decisions and is rarely a simple matter of applying the bankruptcy law.

Financial crisis and social stability

During the Asian Financial Crisis, the Guangdong government confronted an immensely complicated situation in relation to the interests of the mass of the population, not only in their own province, but also in relation to Hong Kong. Throughout the whole process of the 'three steps' tremendous care was taken to deal with their implications for different segments of the population. These had widely disparate interests, ranging from the leaders of giant financial firms in Hong Kong to local, law-abiding depositors in Guangdong's rural financial institutions, who faced the prospect of losing their family's savings. In between these two extremes there was a complex tapestry of financial interests, both domestic and international, with a great variety of legal and ethical relationships with the insolvent institutions. At every stage, great care was taken to investigate the reasonableness of creditors' claims, whether a global bank or an individual household. Whether in the case of the GITIC bankruptcy, GDE re-structuring, or the re-structuring of 800 local financial institutions, the Guangdong government's objective was to reach a just solution to financial claims that would make sense both legally and ethically to all creditors, whatever their size or nationality. This approach was essential to maintaining social stability not only in Guangdong but also in Hong Kong. In the wake of the 1997 Handover it was essential that international financial firms felt that they were being treated fairly, even if this meant sharing with the Guangdong government the pain of a debt 'haircut.' Within the province avoidance of socio-economic instability required all interested parties to understand the logic and justice of the solution adopted for each situation in relation to their particular interests, even if the solution involved financial loss for them.

Global financial risk

The impact of the Asian Financial Crisis served as a vivid reminder for the whole of Asia of the dangers of close integration with poorly regulated international financial markets. By the late 1990s global financial markets had been transformed compared to the 1970s. Liberalization of financial markets across the high-income countries had resulted in a large increase in the level of debt, credit and asset prices, and in the corresponding role of capital markets. Liberalization was to a considerable degree a result of 'regulatory capture' by giant financial firms, with Wall Street firms and their offshoots in London and Hong Kong at their core. In the 1990s high-level Chinese policy-makers had warned of the dangers of instability inherent in de-regulation of the global financial system. The explosion of the Asian Financial Crisis and its powerful impact on Guangdong province through the medium of Hong Kong reinforced their apprehensions about the dangers of close integration with global financial markets in the absence of an effective global regulatory structure. It greatly reinforced the argument that close integration with the global financial system would only be safe if there was significantly improved international regulation.

Breathing-space for financial reform

By early 2001, the fire of the Asian Financial Crisis had been extinguished. The storm had passed over Guangdong. The bankruptcy of GITIC had been concluded. The long-drawn-out process of negotiating with the creditors of GDE had been completed, and its debts restructured. Many hundreds of local financial institutions across the province had been closed down or restructured. Most of the province's ITICs had been shut or merged with other ITICs. The serious threat to the province's social stability had been quelled. The Chinese government had helped to limit the damage the AFC had wrought on Hong Kong. The promised threat of a drastic decline in international capital flows to China had failed to materialize. Executive Vice-Governor Wang Qishan had returned to Beijing to take up the position of Minister in charge of the System Reform Commission under the State Council. The task of steering Guangdong through the Asian Financial Crisis had been accomplished.

In the late 1990s China's state-owned banks had high levels of non-performing loans and were not yet in a condition to compete directly with leading international financial firms from high-income countries. The Asian Financial Crisis revealed deep-seated problems in the local branches of the big commercial banks, in local financial institutions, and NBFIs, including trust companies and rural financial associations. These problems were compounded by the large foreign currency debts contracted with foreign banks in Hong Kong. There was a danger that the impact of the crisis mediated through Hong Kong would de-stabilize the whole Chinese financial system. The 'three steps' eliminated this possibility and enabled not only Guangdong province, but also the whole country, to come safely through the 'fire' of the Asian Financial Crisis. Not least, it set the pattern for large-scale debt restructuring of the international debts of large numbers of ITICs and red chip companies. Most importantly, the huge bureaucratic effort and bold decisions undertaken in the 'three steps' provided a breathing space for China to enter a period of comprehensive reform from top to bottom of the country's financial institutions

Notes

1 He held this post until November 2002.
2 The name list was ranked according to the member's position within the Party instead of their administrative position.
3 Under the system of government structure led by the CPC, the CPC political and legislative committee is responsible for guiding all the government departments, including public security, prosecution and court. The organization department is in charge of the appointment of cadres for all the government departments and CPC. The discipline and supervision committee is responsible for supervising and disciplining leaders and cadres at each level within the CPC.
4 In fact, as was pointed out in Part 1, I cannot think of any example of a European SOE that has been declared bankrupt. The normal practice was, indeed, for the respective national government to take responsibility for the SOE's losses without letting the enterprise go bankrupt. Repeatedly, the taxpayer picked up the bill. This was a major argument about moral hazard in SOEs.
5 In fact, in the case of GITIC, it was the government, not the enterprise, that determined that it should declare itself bankrupt.

6 The bankruptcy of GITIC's Hong Kong red chip subsidiaries was carried out according to Hong Kong law.
7 Other significant loans included US$ 32.6 million to the San Mao Railway Company for the construction and operation of the Sanshui-Maoming Railway; US$ 35 million to the Maoming Chemical Fibre Factory for the purchase of an acrylic fibre production line; US$ 30 million to China United International Leasing Company as working capital; US$ 20 million to the GITIC Shantou Real Estate Development Corporation as working capital; US$ 26.6 million to the Pearl River Tunnel Company for the construction of the Pearl River Tunnel; and US$ 20 million to the Guangdong Highway Corporation for the construction of the 286-kilometre Shenzhen-Shantou highway.
8 Other significant guarantees included US$ 90 million to the Nanhai Power Plant Company for the purchase of power generation equipment; US$ 60 million to the Zhongshan Ja Fa Electric Power Company for the purchase of power generation equipment; US$ 59 million to the Jingguang Development Company Limited for the construction of the Beijing Jingguang Centre; US$ 45 million to Beijing Hua Qiao Mansion Company Limited for the construction of Beijing Hua Qiao Mansion; US$ 38 million to Dalian Furama Hotel Company for the construction of Dalian Furama Hotel; US$ 35 million to Nanhai Dali Power Company for the acquisition of power generation equipment; US$ 35 million to Dongguan Donghua Electricity Company for the purchase of power generation equipment and US$ 34 million to the Guangdong Floating Glass Company for the acquisition of a glass production line.
9 These included minority equity shares in Ping'an Insurance Company (6.8 per cent), China Southern Glass Holding Company (12 per cent), Guangdong Southern Soda Ash Company (20 per cent), Shenzhen Sungang Leasing (19 per cent), Guangdong Teem Group Department Store (11 per cent), Huitong Dyeing and Finishing Company (20 per cent), Shenzhen Yifeng Department Store (22 per cent), Guangdong Overseas Chinese Investment Company (8 per cent), Foshan Fost Motorcycle Company (40 per cent) and Guangdong Jianlibao Beverage Company (15 per cent).
10 These included representatives from the Provincial Judicial Affairs Bureau, the Party's Disciplinary and Inspection Committee, and from the Guangdong Provincial Planning Commission and Audit Bureau.
11 These included one representative from the City Planning Commission and one from the Audit Bureau.
12 It was in fact registered before its parent, GITIC.
13 Unless specifically indicated, 'GDE' is taken to mean GDEHL throughout this Part. GDE is the name by which most analysts refer to GDEHL
14 Wu Jiesi's study (2001) provides a detailed insight into the nature of GDE. Wu Jiesi was former Assistant Governor of Guangdong. He was head of the government group to deal with the GDE and GITIC issues, and Chairman of GDE's Liquidation Committee. He became the Chairman of the 'New GDE.'
15 Almost a decade after the restructuring, GDH remained far removed from its intended benchmark, Hutchison Whampoa. Hutchison Whampoa is the main part of the Cheung Kong Group, which is run by Li Ka Shing and his family. It is one of the world's most powerful conglomerates. It has its headquarters in Hong Kong and has a portfolio of businesses in each of which it is a world leader. These include energy, infrastructure, ports, property, hotels, telecommunications, soft drinks manufacture, life sciences and retail. In 2008 Hutchison Whampoa had a turnover of US$ 30.4 billion and a market capitalization of US$ 20.9 billion. Moreover, Hutchison Whampoa owns 84.6 per cent of Cheung Kong Infrastructure and 39 per cent of Hong Kong Electric. In 2009 they

had market capitalizations of US$ 19.9 billion and US$ 13 billion respectively. The Cheung Kong Group as a whole employs around 24,000 people worldwide, and has a total market capitalization of around US$ 100 billion. In 2009 GDH had a total turnover of US$ 2 billion, of which GDI amounted to US$ 750 million, Guangnan to US$ 300 million and Kingway Breweries to US$ 197 million. The combined market capitalization of the three companies totalled US$ 3.7 billion. In 2015, it was still the case that 64 per cent of GDI's turnover was derived from the Dongshen Water Project. In 2004, Heineken had acquired 21 per cent of Kingway's equity. Thereafter, Kingway's revenue had grown quite rapidly, though it was still a small company in global terms. In 2018, 89 per cent of Guangnan's turnover came from its recently established tinplate company. Its flagship was the Qinghuangdao Tinplate Company, in which South Korea's Posco owned 34 per cent of the equity. Over three-quarters of the turnover of the whole GDH group was in the mainland, with negligible international competitive capability. In sum, the 'phoenix' was very far from the globally competitive East Asian conglomerate that had been the declared goal at the time of restructuring.

16 The Vice Heads were Wu Jiesi, assistant to the Governor; Jiang Chaoliang, Director of PBOC Guangzhou Branch (assistant to the Director of PBOC); and Liu Xingqiang, Director of Guangzhou Securities Administration Office.

17 Including the three UCCs in Heyuan City that had been closed for rectification.

18 See, for example, Will's account of the way in which the traditional Chinese bureaucracy resolved the threat of famine in the eighteenth century (Will, 1990).

19 For example, by 16 January 2000, within a little more than one month, news units in Chaozhou had broadcast and published ninety-three announcements and notices, and the local UCCs had 'distributed 29,202 pieces of propaganda material and received 29,420 people for consultation'.

20 For example, Pingyuan county used a variety of methods depending on the type of debt. For government units, cadres and employees, the Pingyuan county CPC committee and the county government each sought relevant responsible personnel in charge of the units to urge debt repayment. The UCCs were made responsible for recovery of debts from its own employees. The PBOC was responsible for the recovery of debts from its employees and departments. For small debts, the approach was to pursue repayment through personal visits. Many larger debts that could not be recovered by other means were pursued through the courts.

21 Xiao Gang, President of the Bank of China between 2004 and 2013. Between 2013 and 2016 he was Chairman and Party Secretary of the Chinese Securities Regulation Commission.

22 These also were required to have a 'healthy balance sheet' in order to continue in operation.

23 Zhao (2011) provides a vivid account of the continuing struggle to ensure safe and reliable finance for China's rural population.

24 The fourth member of this group was Wang Qishan, who led the clean-up and financial restructuring in Guangdong, the analysis of which forms the core of this book.

25 The Wan Tai Group was headed by Qian Yongwei, who came from a poor peasant family in the Shanghai suburbs. He had made his initial fortune speculating on raw materials trading during the period of the 'dual track' price system. He also speculated in futures and stocks. In July 1998 Qian acquired 56 per cent of a Hong Kong listed company, Sui Chong Holdings (re-named Sun Man Holdings), and in January 2002, he acquired a 28 per cent share of another Hong Kong-listed company, Pearl Oriental (re-named Sun Group).

26 Initial reports suggested that as much as US$ 725 million had gone missing (*FT*, 16 March 2002, and *FEER*, 30 May 2002). In its listing prospectus in July 2002, BOC(HK) referred to the 'Kaiping incident', acknowledging that there had been 'embezzlement or misappropriation of funds from the BOC's Kaiping branch amounting to approximately US$ 500 million, from 1993 to 2001' (BOCI, 2002: 168).

27 The case was complicated. It centred around currency and interest rate arbitrage, intended to benefit from the low Japanese interest rate, and a possible weakening of the *yen* against both the US and Hong Kong dollar. In fact, the scheme failed due to unanticipated currency movements. It involved a subsidiary of BOC in Hong Kong, namely the Kwangtung (Guangdong) Provincial Bank, which was later merged into BOC(HK), as well as BOC's New York branch. BOC alleged that it was the victim of a fraud perpetrated by businessman John Chou and his wife, Sherry Liu, through a 'metal trading' firm, NBM, and their Cayman Island–registered firm, confusingly named 'BOC Co.' Chou and Liu alleged that the scheme originated from the top of the New York branch of Bank of China itself, which 'lined up support for the deals from Bank of China branches in Tokyo, the Cayman Islands and Hong Kong' (*FEER*, 28 February 2002). They allege that 'BOC Co' in the Cayman Islands was set up with the active involvement of Bank of China's Cayman Islands branch. Both sides agreed that some US$ 50 million in Japanese *yen* was borrowed by Chou and Liu's firm, NBM, from the Bank of China's New York branch to pay for Certificates of Deposit (CDs) that BOC Co (Cayman Islands) bought in Hong Kong. Bank of China (New York) claims that it was led to understand that the loans were to be used for import and export of metals. Chou and Liu claim that Bank of China (New York) was fully aware that the loans to NBM were low interest rate loans (benefitting from low Japanese interest rates) to be used to fund speculative arbitrage deals (*FEER*, 28 February 2002). Whatever the real background, the US Office of Currency Control criticized the loans as 'unsafe and unsound banking practices' (quoted in *FEER*, 28 February 2002). One of Moody's analysts commented that BOC had 'done a lot towards becoming a commercial-oriented entity.' However, he questioned whether 'the operating culture has changed sufficiently' (quoted in *FEER*, 28 February 2002). Some analysts expressed concern at the 'lack of outside hiring at the upper management level' (quoted in *SCMP*, 26 June 2002).

28 Phrygia was the dominant kingdom in Western Anatolia between 1200 and 700 BC. At one point the Phrygians were without a king, but an oracle decreed that the next man to enter the capital city driving an ox-cart should become their king. A peasant farmer named Gordias drove into town on an ox-cart and was immediately declared king. Out of gratitude, his son Midas dedicated the ox-cart to the Phrygian god Sabazios (whom the Greeks identified with Zeus) and tied it to a post with an intricate knot of cornel bark (*Cornus mas*). The knot was described as comprising 'several knots all so tightly entangled that it was impossible to see how they were fastened.'

29 This incident is thought to have lain behind the famous scene in Jonathan Swift's satire *Gulliver's Travels*, published in 1726, in which the giant Gulliver puts out a fire in the queen's palace by urinating on it. It was effective in putting out the fire. However, it so angered the queen due to its 'rudeness' in polluting the palace, which had 'cost so many ages in erecting,' that the event became the basis for Gulliver's impeachment (Swift, 1967: 104–5).

30 The concept of the 'Greater Bay Area' was not formally announced until December 2016. However, the concept of integrated, mutually beneficial development of the whole Pearl River Delta Area had been part of Chinese government thinking from the late 1970s onwards. The city of Shenzhen was established in 1979 in the county of Bao'an, which is adjacent to Hong Kong. The development

of Shenzhen was a key part of the overall strategy of 'Reform and Opening-up' promulgated in 1978. The Pearl River Delta area has historically been one of China most commercially advanced regions, with deep connections with international trade across the South China Sea.

31 The relationship between 'socialist' China and 'capitalist' Hong Kong became even more complicated after 1997. It reached a new stage in 2019 with the eruption of the protest movement in Hong Kong. For many supporters of the protest movement, the objective was to use 'capitalist' Hong Kong as a lever to de-stabilize 'socialist' China. Kevin McCarthy, Republican leader of the US House of Representatives, believed that the US Congress' Hong Kong Human Rights and Democracy Act would perform the same function as the Reagan administration's support for the Solidarity movement in Poland in the 1980s (McCarthy, 2019). In McCarthy's view, Solidarity 'played a decisive role in the downfall of communism' in Eastern Europe and the USSR: 'Its defence of the ideal of self-determination made it a powerful symbol of resistance to Soviet domination.' He considered that the 'standard of freedom is being unfurled in Hong Kong' and the US government should 'stand with the people there' in the same fashion that President Reagan had supported the Solidarity movement in Poland

Postscript

Finance and the real economy

China and the West since the Asian Financial Crisis

Introduction

In the depths of the Asian Financial Crisis few people could have imagined the tremendous transformation that would take place in the financial systems in China and the West in the following two decades. In the late 1990s China was preparing to join the WTO. It seemed that under the WTO agreement China's financial firms would soon be competing directly with their global counterparts. The AFC starkly revealed the weakness of China's financial institutions, including giant state-owned banks, local financial firms and non-bank financial institutions operating outside China. Through the medium of Hong Kong the Asian Financial Crisis threatened to destabilize the financial system in the neighbouring Guangdong province, and even damage the financial system across the whole of China. The 'three steps' (*san bu zou*) to solve the financial crisis in Guangdong – bankruptcy of GITIC, restructuring GDE and restructuring hundreds of local financial institutions – stemmed the crisis not only for Guangdong, but for the whole country. The crisis provided a vivid demonstration of the potentially unstable nature of the international financial system and the damage that instability could cause to China. The impact of the crisis upon the Chinese financial system convinced China's policy-makers of the need to keep a barrier between the main body of China's financial system and the global financial system until such time as the reform of the country's domestic financial institutions had been completed. The crisis in Guangdong made it clear that this would be a long process. 'Cutting the trees to save the forest' provided a breathing space for the whole Chinese financial system to undertake comprehensive reform. The Global Financial Crisis provided an even greater shock to China's policy-makers. After the GFC China persisted with deepening reform of the country's financial system. The country's financial system has benefited greatly from global information technologies, flotation on international stock markets, close study of international financial firms and application of the Basel Accords. However, the fundamental features of financial system regulation, operational mechanisms and corporate governance are different from those in high-income countries. Ten years after the GFC the West's financial system stands on a knife-edge. The way in which the Chinese and the West's financial system interact with each other constitutes a central issue in global political economy in the years ahead.

The West

The real economy

The transformation of global finance since the 1970s is closely linked to the parallel transformation of the real (non-financial) economy. Two competing frameworks have influenced academic analysis of the real economy in the era of globalization. Variants of the dominant, mainstream approach view market structure through the lens of Alfred Marshall's famous analogy of the 'trees in the forest,' in which diseconomies of scale limit the growth of firms beyond a certain height. Variants of the non-mainstream approach view market structures through the lens of Karl Marx's 'law of concentration of capital.' Economies of scale and scope, especially in relation to innovation and technical progress, result in there being no limit to the growth of the firm.

Evidence from the current era of globalization supports both perspectives. After forty years of globalization it remains the case that the vast majority of firms and employment are in the SME sector. For the most part, the sector is characterized by low technology and absence of brands, alongside low-paid, insecure and often dangerous conditions of work. 'Small' is rarely 'beautiful.' This is, indeed, the world of Marshall's 'trees in the forest.' However, in the high-technology and branded products sector, which produces goods and services for other global firms and for the global middle-class, Karl Marx's 'law of concentration of capital' operates. As global markets for goods and capital liberalized, industrial concentration advanced across almost every sector, from aerospace and autos, to pharmaceuticals and beverages. In each sector a small group of firms, with focus on clearly identified 'core business,' dominate the 'commanding heights' of the sector. Through the weight of centrally coordinated procurement budgets, the 'system integrator' firms have exerted tremendous pressure, which 'cascades' downwards through their suppliers, nurturing and stimulating industrial concentration deep in the value chain. Fierce oligopolistic competition characterizes business relations at each level of the business system within each sector. There is a high degree of industrial concentration in research and development spending, including the IT sector, which is at the heart of competition in the global business system: the top 500 firms, mostly from the high-income economies, account for 82 per cent of global corporate R&D spending (EU, 2017).

Financial sector

Transformation of the real economy has gone hand-in-hand with transformation of the financial sector. A powerful stimulus to financial sector concentration arose from the wide array of services that the financial sector performs for global firms in the real economy. These include trade finance; hedging risk in foreign exchange, commodity and bond markets; payrolls and cash management; tax payments; project finance; restructuring through mergers and acquisitions, IPOs and divestitures; corporate bonds; and syndicated loans. Performance of these functions is the 'glue' that helps to bind together the global business system in the real economy. An increasingly important function is wealth management for the global elite, who work in the upper reaches of global firms. There are strong economies of scale and scope in global financial services, including spending on IT hardware and software, as well as the ability to attract the best talent from across the world.

There are a huge number of SME financial firms occupying geographical and sectoral niches. However, after the 1970s there took place a relentless consolidation at the core of the global financial system. By 2018 the top twenty-five global banks accounted for over 40 per cent of the total assets of the 'Global 1000' banks; the top fifty asset managers, all from the high-income countries, accounted for 65 per cent of the total assets of the top 500 asset managers; the top fifteen firms, all from the high-income countries, accounted for 53 per cent of global bond markets; the top ten firms, all from the high-income countries, accounted for 59 per cent of global equity markets; the top twenty firms, all from the high-income countries, accounted for 66 per cent of total global investment banking revenues; the top ten firms, all from the high-income countries, accounted for 67 per cent of the total foreign exchange market; and the top four asset custodians, all from the high-income countries, accounted for 66 per cent of the global assets under custody. In wealth management the top ten firms are all from the high-income countries. In other words, the core of global 'capital markets' is highly concentrated and dominated by a small group of firms, mainly American, from the high-income countries. It is self-evident that in the world's capital markets in the era of globalization, the 'law of concentration of capital' applies as much as it does in the real economy.

Liberalization of financial markets

The 'Washington Consensus' institutions, notably the IMF and the World Bank, have been dominated by the developed countries since their inception right through to the present day. A key policy advanced by these institutions, strongly supported by the leading global financial firms, was the proposition that developing countries which privatized their financial firms and allowed free access to global financial firms would out-perform economies that kept their financial firms under state ownership and isolated from the 'global level playing field' of competition in financial services. It was argued that global financial firms from the high-income countries were subject to close and careful regulation in their home markets and more immune to pressure for imprudent lending and less liable to suffer from 'moral hazard' than financial firms in developing countries.

During the era of globalization there developed a growing influence among academics and policy-makers of the view that financial markets are inherently efficient and self-regulating, requiring only 'light' government regulation. Increasingly powerful global financial firms, with those from Wall Street at the epicentre, played a key role in nurturing this view through the process of 'regulatory capture.' The alternative view, that financial markets are inherently unstable, prone to vicious circles of asset price inflation and debt increase, was marginalized and regarded as out-of-date for the analysis and regulation of modern, technologically driven financial markets. Government controls over financial markets were removed progressively. So-called 'independent' central banks were established, instructed by governments to set interest rates in order to control consumer price inflation, but excluded from considering asset price inflation as part of their responsibility.

The era of globalization witnessed unprecedented expansion of asset prices and debt across the high-income countries. Between 1980 and 2003 the total global financial stock increased from 109 per cent of global GDP to 326 per cent (Table P.1). The vastly increased role for 'capital markets' was welcomed enthusiastically by global financial firms. The main body of citizens welcomed the 'wealth illusion' arising from inflation in the price of their financial assets, which they either held directly or increasingly through intermediary institutions such as pension funds and investment funds. It

Table P.1 Growth of global financial stock relative to GDP, 1980–2003

	1980		*2003*	
	$ trillion	*% Global GDP*	*$ trillion*	*% Global GDP*
Total financial stock	12	109	118	326
Bank deposits	5.4	53	35	97
Government debt securities	2.2	22	20	55
Private debt securities	1.7	17	31	85
Equity securities	2.8	28	32	89
World GDP (nominal)	10.1	–	36.1	

Source: McKinsey, 2003, *$118 Trillion and Counting: Taking Stock of the World's Capital Markets*, London: McKinsey Global Institute.

seemed as though the 'Great Moderation' had banished financial crises in the West and made everyone better off through increased wealth.

Policy response to the GFC

In the autumn of 2008 asset prices collapsed across the high-income countries. After years of lecturing developing countries about state intervention in the financial sector and the dangers of moral hazard, large parts of the West's financial system only survived the crisis thanks to massive government support and extensive state ownership. In response to the crisis the Bank for International Settlements (BIS) produced a revised set of Basel Accords which introduced more stringent bank capital requirements, and more stringent minimum leverage and liquidity coverage ratios. It placed severe restrictions on the use of complex mathematical models to evaluate banks' capital requirements. It introduced additional measures to reduce risk at a group of 'systemically important financial institutions,' which included the leading global financial firms. However, the new rules gave favourable treatment to sovereign debt in relation to bank capital, which created an 'adverse feedback loop.' 'Sovereign debt' is never risk-free. There are numerous examples of governments defaulting on 'sovereign debt,' including domestic debt. The increased role of 'sovereign debt' in bank capital tied the fortunes of national governments and large banks closely together. The risk of a 'doom loop' between sovereign debt and the financial system is higher in those countries that have a larger financial sector.

The policy response of governments to the GFC across the high-income countries followed a common path. They chose not to use fiscal policy in order to redistribute income and wealth, strengthen social welfare systems and expand infrastructure. Instead, they focused on policies which had the objective of 're-igniting asset prices' and thereby stimulating economic growth through the effect on wealth and consumer spending. The core policy was for central banks to lower the policy rate of interest to close to zero and add further downward pressure on interest rates through central bank purchase of government debt. Under the 'quantitative easing' (QE) programmes central banks across the high-income countries greatly increased their holdings of bonds issued by the national treasuries.

Debt

In the decade following the GFC (2008–18) in relation to global GDP financial sector debt declined significantly, falling from 91 per cent to 81 per cent, mainly due to more stringent Basel regulations; household debt increased slightly, rising from 58 per cent to 60 per cent; while corporate sector debt, fuelled by near-zero interest rates, rose rapidly, increasing from 72 per cent to 90 per cent. In the face of heavy pressure to maintain social stability Western governments maintained relatively high levels of social welfare

Table P.2 Global debt, 1997–2018

	1997		*2008*		*2018*	
	$ trillion	*% Global GDP*	*$ trillion*	*% Global GDP*	*$ trillion*	*% Global GDP*
Total	74	235	178	280	247	318
Non-financial corporates	21	66	46	72	74	90
Government	19	61	37	58	67	87
Financial corporates	19	61	58	91	61	81
Households	15	48	37	58	47	60

Source: Institute of International Finance (IIF), *Global Debt Monitor*, July 2017 and July 2018, Washington DC: Institute of International Finance.

spending, government debt ballooned from 58 per cent to 87 per cent of global GDP (Table P.2). In the 1970s global debt stood at around 130 per cent of GDP. By 1997 it had risen to 235 per cent and by 2008 it reached 280 per cent, a level unprecedented in peacetime. In 2018 it stood at 318 per cent, significantly above even the level on the eve of the GFC. In 2018 the vast bulk of global debt (72 per cent) was still in the high-income countries.

Asset prices

Asset prices recovered in line with the policy-makers' hopes. In high-income countries stock market capitalization had risen from 52 per cent of GDP in 1990 to 126 per cent in 2007, before plunging to 63 per cent in 2008. By 2017 it had rebounded to 138 per cent of GDP, far above the level before the GFC (Table P.3). Property prices in global cities plunged during the GFC. By 2017 real house prices in most 'global cities' had surpassed their pre-GFC peak and stood at two to three times their level in 2000 (Table P.4). Between 1980 and 2003 the total value of debt securities (government plus private) rose from 39 per cent to 140 per cent of GDP. By 2018 the total global bond market stood at 215 per cent of global GDP, with high-income countries accounting for 88 per cent of the total global bond market. In 2018 in the United States, the world's largest bond market, total debt securities stood at 208 per cent of GDP (Table P.5). The so-called QE programme helped to stimulate a frenzy of bond purchase, driving bond prices ever higher and pushing yields downwards. By 2016 around 30 per cent of total bonds were 'negative-yielding' and by 2019 the total of negative-yielding bonds surpassed the previous peak in 2016. In the era of financial globalization, instead of financial assets such as equities and bonds being acquired for their dividend and interest return, assets have been acquired increasingly for speculation on asset price increase and 'total returns.' The possibility of 'snap-back' and a 'great rotation' in bond prices and interest rates was widely discussed among fixed income analysts and regulators.

Table P.3 Stock market capitalization (% GDP in each area/country)

	1990	*2000*	*2006*	*2008*	*2017*
United States	53.2	154.7	147.6	80.4	165.7
UK	85.8	178.7	159.6	69.3	n.a.
Germany	21.2	66.8	56.5	30.4	61.5
Euro Area	21.7	87	81.2	37.9	n.a.
High-income economies	51.6	117.8	126.1	62.9	138.4

Source: World Bank, *World Development Indicators*, various years.

Table P.4 Real house price index, Q4 2017 (2000 = 100) [a]

New York	138	London	251
Los Angeles	158	Amsterdam	158
Toronto	236	Geneva	216
Vancouver	303	Copenhagen	229
Auckland	253	Stockholm	266
Hong Kong	270	Paris	257
Shanghai	135	Brussels	220

Source: *Economist*, Real House Price Index, 2018.

a Nominal house prices deflated by the retail price index.

Table P.5 Bond market in selected high-income economies[a]: outstanding debt securities (2018, Q2)

	$ billion	*Of which: general government (% total)*	*Total debt securities/ GDP (%)*		*$ billion*	*Of which: general government (% total)*	*Total debt securities/ GDP (%)*
France	4,606	49	178	UK	5,917	46	226
Germany	3,615	51	98	Australia	1,945	33	147
Italy	3,225	71	167	Canada	2,361	52	127
Netherlands	2,171	18	263	Japan	12,978	75	266
Spain	1,970	60	150	United States	40,330	45	208

Source: BIS, Debt securities database.

a High-income countries with over US$ 1 trillion in outstanding debt securities.

Wealth

The vast increase in the extent of global capital markets relative to the real economy provided rich opportunities to 'earn money from money.' By 2000 global wealth already stood at 348 per cent of global GDP. This increased to 394 per cent by 2007 and by 2018 global wealth had risen to 419 per cent of global GDP. The global Gini coefficient of wealth distribution stands at the astonishing level of 92.7 per cent: the top one per cent own 47 per cent of total wealth, the top 10 per cent own 85 per cent and the bottom 50 per cent own one per cent.

Economic stagnation

The stated economic logic behind the Western governments' drive to push down interest rates was to stimulate economic growth through the impact on wealth and consumer demand. In fact, the rate of growth of GDP in the high-income economies failed to return to the trend before the GFC. In the G7 countries the average annual growth rate of GDP declined to 0.7 per cent in 2007–18. In 1980 the G7 group of countries accounted for 51 per cent of global GDP (in PPP dollars). By 2007 their share had fallen to 38 per cent. By 2018 it stood at just 30 per cent. The West's financial system stands on a knife-edge. If confidence in asset prices were to be shaken, and real interest rates were to return to their long-run normal level, the resulting financial crisis would shake the entire financial, economic, social and political systems of the high-income countries.

China

Financial system fragility

Ever since China began its long-term policy of 'Reform and Opening-up' international experts have warned that the political and economic system faced imminent collapse. For many years there has been a wide agreement among international commentators that the economic collapse would stem from the financial sector. The impact of the AFC upon China was little recognized in the West. However, the deep impact of the GFC and China's response to it was visible to the world. In response to the crisis, China implemented a huge rescue package, with infrastructure construction at the core. China's investment rate soared to levels rarely seen anywhere in the world, and the incremental capital-output ratio increased significantly. It is widely thought that the rescue package facilitated 'wasteful, debt-fuelled investment' on a massive scale, facilitated by the close relationship of the state-owned banks to state-owned non-financial firms, which starved the non-state sector of financial resources. It is argued that this led to the 'advance of the state [sector] and retreat of the private [sector]' (*guo jin, min tui*). The accumulation of local government debt was considered to be a danger to the financial system. Local government financing platforms are widely thought to be prone to corruption and weak performance monitoring by lenders.

The role of 'shadow banking' increased rapidly after the GFC. Wealth management products offered interest rates far above official deposit rates in banks. They were issued by a wide array of financial institutions, including banks, trust companies, asset management companies and insurance companies. In addition, informal P2P lending expanded rapidly making use of the explosive advances in internet-based technologies. China's banking system remains dominated by state ownership, not only in the giant 'Big Four' banks, but also in the joint-stock banks and the wide network of city commercial banks. China's banking sector is substantially isolated from international competition. The CPC controls appointments to leading positions in the major state-owned banks, which means that political considerations, rather than technical competence, play a role in senior bank appointments. The CPC occupies a dominant position within the banks, formalized in the recent change in the articles of association. The main customers of the state-owned banks are SOEs in the non-financial sector. These features of the Chinese banking system are widely thought to inhibit competition and 'distort the process of loan allocation.' China's debt-to-GDP ratio climbed steadily in the early 2000s, before accelerating from 160 per cent in 2008 to 298 per cent in 2018. A chorus of international commentators warns that China faces the prospect of a major financial crisis.

Financial system strength

In fact, unlike the West and numerous developing countries, China has not experienced a financial crisis throughout the past forty years. The systems strengths are rarely appreciated outside China. Moreover, the huge rescue package put into place during the GFC played a key role in stabilizing the global economy at its most dangerous point. During the whole period 2008–18, China has accounted for 30 per cent of global GDP growth compared with 20 per cent for the G7 countries. China's state-owned banks played a central role in financing the tremendous investment in Chinese infrastructure since the GFC. This has been widely criticized as wasteful and inefficient, preventing the economy re-balancing away from investment towards consumption. Since the GFC China's electricity, transport, housing, sewage system, water supply and information technology infrastructure, as well as the education and health infrastructure, have expanded at a tremendous speed. This expansion has provided wide-ranging welfare improvement for the mass of the population. China is far ahead of India in its provision of the infrastructure necessary to meet the welfare needs of the mass of the population (Table P.6). Moreover, the huge progress in infrastructure provides extensive support for the non-state sector, which produces the major part of national output and employs the great majority of the workforce. China's SMEs and large non-state sector firms have access to state-of-the-art infrastructure, far ahead of most developing countries. Indeed, in many respects, such as telecoms, internet and high-speed rail, China is ahead of the 'developed' countries in terms of infrastructure. China has firmly grasped the 'advantage of the latecomer,' employing the most advanced global technologies throughout its infrastructure. Its high rate of investment means that a large fraction of its infrastructure employs cutting-edge technologies.

In the late 1990s the prospects for China's financial system looked bleak. After China joined the WTO in 2001 fierce pressure was exerted on the Chinese government to privatize and break up the country's main banks, and open the financial sector to international competition on the 'global level playing field' in financial markets. In fact, China's leaders decided to follow an independent path of gradual reform, modernization and restructuring of the financial sector, substantially shielded from direct competition with global financial firms. China's leaders decided that the Big Four banks would

Table P.6 Economic development and social welfare in China and India, 2017

	China	*India*
Population (millions)	1,386	1,339
Gross National Income, pc. (PPP dollars)	16,750	7,060
Manufacturing value-added (US$ billion, 2015)	3,250	323
Merchandise Exports (US$ b.)	2,263	299
High-tech exports (US$ b.)	504	14
High-tech exports (% manufacturing exports)	24	7
Energy use p.c. (kgs oil equivalent)	2,237	637
Electricity consumption p.c. (kwh, 2014)	3,927	806
Electricity transmission and distribution losses (%)	5.5	19.4
Port container traffic (m.TEU)	214	13
Air passengers carried (m.)	551	140
Mobile cellular subscription (no/100 people)	105	87
Internet use (% population)	54	30
Gross enrolment in tertiary education (% relevant age group)	51	27
Health expenditure p.c. (US$ PPP, 2015)	762	238
Health expenditure (% out-of-pocket, 2015)	32	65
Infant mortality (no/1,000 live births)	8	32
Life expectancy at birth (years)	76	69
Poverty (% population)		
<US$ 1.90 p.d.	0.5	21.2
<US$ 3.20 p.d.	7	60.4
<US$ 5.50 p.d.	27.2	86.8

Source: World Bank, *World Development Indicators*, 2018.

be 'reformed as single entities' (*zhengti gaige*). In 2003 China established the China Banking Regulatory Commission (CBRC), which has exerted close control over the country's banks.[1] It decided to limit the ownership share of foreign banks in individual Chinese banks to 20 per cent for a single foreign bank and 25 per cent for a group of foreign banks combined. China's main banks have made huge investments in IT systems, which have mainly been purchased from US companies, and have arguably overtaken their global peers in terms of the technical level. A succession of Chinese banks has restructured and floated minority shares on international stock markets. This has not only raised capital but also subjected the banks to close scrutiny from international investors and the international financial media. CBRC has encouraged competition between the different segments of the financial industry, facilitating a steady diminution of the share of total assets held by the Big Four state-owned banks and a corresponding increase in the share held by the joint stock banks and city commercial banks. China's main banks have made great strides in transforming corporate governance, including the way in which board meetings, subsidiary committee meetings (especially audit and risk) and annual general meetings are conducted. The level of professional competence in the upper reaches of Chinese banks has progressed steadily, with great emphasis on training courses both within China and in leading international universities. The central role of the CPC within China's banks has imparted a powerful sense of common purpose among the staff. China's bank employees are aware that China's financial institutions have a moral purpose to serve the interests of the real economy and improve the welfare of the whole society. China's banks have played a vital role not only in funding welfare-enhancing infrastructure, but also in supporting the modernization of a group of state-owned enterprises, with the objective of competing directly with leading global companies on domestic and international markets.

International critics who express fears about the shadow banking sector rarely appreciate the positive role that the sector can play through lending to millions of small and micro businesses. Firms in this vast sector find access to credit from the formal banking system difficult in all economies, whatever their level of development. The Chinese government has acted effectively to modernize the regulatory structures in order to meet the rapidly changing demands from P2P finance, facilitated by explosive changes in internet communication technologies. In addition, China's bank regulators have put into effect policies to bring off-balance-sheet shadow banking products onto bank balance sheets. Despite the large increase in bank credit, the level of bank sector NPLs remains relatively low and stable. The performance of China's leading banks has been completely transformed since the late 1990s and early 2000s. China possesses five of the world's top ten banks in terms of market capitalization. Their performance in terms of standard indicators of efficiency (capital-assets ratio, profits on capital, return on assets and NPL ratio) bears comparison with their leading international peers (Table P.7).

Table P.7 Performance of largest Chinese and US banks, 2017

	Assets ($ billion)	*Soundness: capital-assets ratio (%)*	*Pre-tax profits ($ billion)*	*Profits on capital (%)*	*Performance: return on assets (%)*	*NPL to total loans (%)*
ICBC	4,007	8.09	56	17.28	1.4	1.56
CCB	3,398	8.01	46.1	16.92	1.36	1.49
BOC	2,990	7.51	34.2	15.26	1.15	1.45
ABC	3,234	6.74	36.8	16.87	1.14	1.81
JPMorgan Chase	2,534	8.24	35.9	17.21	1.42	1.44
Bank of America	2,251	8.39	29.2	15.26	1.28	1.23
Wells Fargo	1,952	9.13	27.4	15.36	1.4	2.22
Citigroup	1,842	8.95	22.7	17.43	1.23	1.12

Source: *The Banker*, July 2018.

Interaction between China and the West

Counter factual

Despite fierce pressure from both outside and inside the country, China's leaders decided not to open up the country's financial sector in the same fashion as Latin America and Eastern Europe. The decision to reform the Big Four banks as single entities and maintain majority state ownership across the financial system was of great significance, not only for China but also for the whole global financial system. It meant that China was able to withstand the tremendous pressure exerted upon the country by the GFC and initiate a massive rescue package. The package formed the foundation of China's development in the decade after the GFC. It made a major contribution to the stability of the whole structure of China's political economy. An important question to consider is: what would have happened to China and the global financial system if China had followed the path that was urged upon it by the international community in the years leading up to the GFC?

Two different systems

In 2018 China announced a wide array of measures that promised to open up the country's capital markets to international firms. Chinese officials are confident that the country's financial firms have radically improved their performance compared to ten to fifteen years ago and will be able to compete effectively with their global peers, both within China as well as in international markets. However, despite the GFC, global financial firms, especially those from the United States, dominate the commanding heights of global capital markets, including investment banking, asset management, foreign exchange, and commodities trading, wealth management and custody, as well as corporate banking in areas such as trade finance, project finance and cash management. Global firms also dominate the activities that are ancillary but essential to capital markets, such as legal services, audit, consultancy, data provision and ratings agencies. The core information technologies that have contributed to the rapid modernization of China's financial sector are mainly purchased from leading Western suppliers. In many respects the operational mechanism of China's financial firms is different from that of the leading global firms. SOEs are still the principal customers for the five big banks. Non-interest income is still a relatively small share of their revenues. Their international operations are proportionately much smaller than for their global peers. The proportion of non-Chinese employees is very small. Their senior executives are paid tiny salaries compared to the leaders of global financial firms. The central role of the CPC means that the corporate governance is fundamentally different from that of their global peers. These differences and the fact that China's financial firms operate in an environment that has been largely protected from international competition, mean that the struggle between Chinese and foreign firms on the 'level playing field' of global capital markets will be long and complex.

Fragile international financial system

China's commitment to open its capital markets to international firms takes place at a point of great fragility in the international financial system. In the late 1990s China was preparing to open up its financial markets to global competition. The explosion of the AFC provided a vivid illustration of the dangers of close integration with a poorly regulated international financial system and the alarming speed with which a financial 'fire' could spread and leap across national boundaries. At the same time, the competitive weakness of China's domestic financial firms was sharply exposed. In the following decade China conducted extensive restructuring and international flotation of the leading banks, and established an effective system of financial sector regulation under the CBRC. China once again considered the possibility of opening the financial sector to international competition.

In 2007, a few months after he had been appointed US Treasury Secretary, Hank Paulson, who had been CEO of Goldman Sachs (1999–2006), 'decided to try to influence the [Chinese] leadership by launching a campaign on capital markets reform.' In a speech at the Shanghai Futures Exchange on 8 March 2007, he told the audience:

> If China wants to live up to its promise, it should quicken the pace of financial services reform. Efficient capital markets, based on transparency, clear property rights, strong institutions, and robust supervision, drive economic growth. They funnel money to the best ideas and allow people to invest in their country's future.
>
> (Paulson, 2015: 206)

One year later, the GFC began to unfold with the collapse of Bear Stearns in March 2008. The explosion of the GFC shocked China's leaders and deeply affected the Chinese economy. During the Strategic and Economic Dialogue in June 2008 Vice-Premier Wang Qishan told Hank Paulson: 'You were my teacher, but now I am in my teacher's domain, and look at your system Hank. We aren't sure we should be learning from you any more.' Paulson notes: 'The crisis was a humbling experience, and this was one of the most humbling moments' (Paulson, 2015: 240). Opening up the country's capital markets to international competition was once again postponed and reform of domestic financial firms made steady progress in a heavily protected home market.

In 2019 China once again stands on the threshold of opening up the country's capital markets. The policies adopted in the West in response to the GFC have re-ignited asset prices, but the unprecedentedly low rates of interest have stimulated an even deeper extent of debt in relation to the real economy than before the GFC. The West's financial system stands on the edge of a precipice. At the same time the stability of the West's social structure is being undermined by the forces of globalization and the political systems of the West are being swept by the tide of populism. The relative decline of the West has accelerated since the GFC, leading to a widespread psycho-social crisis.

Awareness is gaining ground in the West that after 200 years of comprehensive Western dominance of the global economy, business system, innovation, military and culture, the world stands at a crossroads of civilization. There is a growing realization that for 2,000 years before the British Industrial Revolution China was at the centre of the world economy, innovation and culture, and that it is steadily returning to this role. The West's democratic system is of recent origin, coming into existence only at the end of the nineteenth century. The system worked well for the West as long as it dominated the world through economic, cultural and military power, mediated through colonial and post-colonial structures of global governance. It is questionable whether the system is equipped to deal peacefully with the relative decline of the West. Hostility to China has gained force across the West, with widespread discussion of the possibility of a new 'Peloponnesian War.' If another financial crisis were to erupt in the West, the consequences for economic, social and political stability would be enormous. Serious financial turbulence in the West would place its political-economic system under severe strain, with unpredictable and potentially dangerous results. The 'rising tide' of asset price inflation conceals deep socio-economic fissures hidden beneath the calm surface of the water. If the tide of asset price were to reverse direction it is likely that the 'rocks' would appear (*shui luo shi chu*). This has the potential to flow into international relations in a dangerous fashion, most obviously in relation to China.

Regulating money: different philosophical foundations

The West

Since the Ancient world of Classical Greece and the Zhou Dynasty, attitudes towards 'money to make money' have diverged fundamentally in the West and China. In the West there has been a deep-rooted Manichean conflict between those who regard the pursuit of 'money to make money' as immoral and sinful, deserving a place in hell, and those who regard the individual's unfettered pursuit of money as the foundation of a successful economy and a free society. In the West, right through to the present day, these two perspectives have been fundamentally opposed to one another. The Book of Revelation provides a terrifying, apocalyptic vision of the destruction that will be wrought upon a society dominated by money-making. It still inspires those who wish to 'de-throne mammon.' The only substantial era in which 'mammon' was 'de-throned' in the West was in the Soviet Union and Eastern Europe. The Leninist-Stalinist interpretation of Karl Marx viewed money-making and the pursuit of profit as wholly incompatible with a 'good society' that served the interest of the mass of the population.

In fact, for most of the history of the West there has been minimal restraint on the financial sector's activities. In Ancient Greece and Rome, the land- and slave-owning ruling class was deeply involved in financial activities without significant restraint. In the late Middle Ages and early modern period, merchants and financiers held the fate of cities and nations in their hands through the loans they provided to warring entities - 'money is the sinews of war.' During the modern era of democracy the financial sector has continuously exercised powerful influence upon the decisions taken by legislators and regulators. This was somewhat moderated in the wake of the Wall Street Crash and the Great Depression. However, that influence became even greater in the recent era of globalization.

De-regulation of the financial sector in the era of globalization has been driven by regulatory capture exercised by the emergence of global financial institutions with their headquarters in the high-income economies. Capital markets have been the central force driving the ever-increasing role of finance relative to the real economy during the recent era.

As financial firms increased in size, especially through mergers and acquisitions, they were able to exercise even greater pressure on governments to liberalize the financial sector and give support to capital markets. A significant part of the population was a willing accomplice, happy in the 'wealth illusion' and the increased borrowing capacity that it produced. Nominally 'independent' central banks regularly made small adjustments to the policy rate of interest in response to changes in consumer prices while the 'fire' of asset price inflation raged around them in de-regulated financial markets. Credit and debt expanded in proportion and the era witnessed a cultural revolution in the high-income countries, intimately linked to the revolution in asset prices, debt and credit.

Financial commentators routinely refer to 'markets' and 'investors' as if they were abstract, neutral entities. In fact, they are concrete institutions. The real-life firms that are the core of capital markets have acted as the 'bullies' of democratic governments and central banks.

A vast terrain of capital markets business has grown into being in the world's financial centres in the high-income economies, with New York and London at the centre, closely bound together by global financial firms. The firms that inhabit different overlapping segments of capital markets include not only retail banks and investment banks, but also a panoply of interconnected nonbank financial institutions, including asset managers, mutual funds, money market funds, pensions funds, insurance companies, asset custodians, hedge funds, private equity and sovereign wealth funds. Surrounding these firms is a thick layer of firms that work with capital markets, including financial hardware and software providers, law firms, audit firms, trading platforms, analysts, data providers, consultants and head-hunters. The share of these institutions in terms of employment and income within the high-income economies has marched forward in lock-step with the increase in the relative importance of capital markets.

The financial system in the West has demonstrated its capacity to cause immense harm to the 'real' economy and there is a high chance that it will do so again. Instead of the human species controlling its own destiny through intelligent regulation of the financial system in the common interest, the financial system in the West has become a 'Frankenstein' monster, created by our collective endeavour, but out of our collective control, setting the direction of travel for the whole structure of political economy: 'Modern bourgeois society with its relations of production and of exchange, is like the sorcerer, who is no longer able to control the powers of the nether world whom he has called up by his spells' (Marx and Engels, 1848: 49).

China

China's approach to 'making money from money' has almost always been pragmatic rather than ideological. 'Making money from money' has not been regarded as sinful and those who do so have never been threatened with a place in hell. The bureaucracy has consistently viewed the pursuit of profit and money-making as a powerful positive force that should be nurtured and respected. Apart from the Maoist era between 1956 and 1976 there have never been direct attacks on commercial activities and money-making. However, ever since the Zhou Dynasty, the bureaucracy has viewed commerce and finance as requiring regulation in the common interest. The idea that commerce and finance should control government policy and practice is anathema in the Chinese political tradition. The only point at which this was the case was during the short-lived Republican Era of KMT rule (1927–36), when finance and government were deeply intertwined and served the interests of a small group of powerful families (Song-Kong-Chen). Since the Ancient world, Chinese political theory and practice has consistently held that the meritocratic bureaucracy should be independent of control by commerce and finance. The bureaucracy has always controlled the country's ideological foundation and value system. The most highly respected social position is that of the educated scholar official, the 'Gentleman' (*junzi*), who earns his place in the ruling bureaucracy on merit. The highest moral duty of the Gentleman is to serve the interests of the mass of the population, not to make pursuit of money the goal of life.

During forty years of Reform and Opening-up China has sought to find a Middle Way in reforming the financial system. It has followed the bureaucracy's long tradition of encouraging commerce and money-making while simultaneously experimenting with methods of regulating the financial sector to serve the welfare of the whole society. The CPC has been at the core of the long, experimental reform process, including regulation of the financial sector to serve the common interest. Restructuring, modernization and flotation of the country's main financial firms has been pursued alongside a continued role for state ownership and control over the financial system through the CPC. Regulation includes the role of the CPC's Central Organization Department in selecting and evaluating the performance of senior executives and the role of the Party committee formalized in the articles of association of financial firms. The main regulatory body, the CBIRC, is under the control of the CPC, as is the PBOC, which oversees the whole financial system. Under Reform and Opening-up the space to 'make money from money' has greatly increased. Many of the richest people in the world are Chinese who have profited from this process. However, the ideology and regulatory structure is under the firm control of the bureaucracy, which has become steadily more professionally capable and able to manage the financial system effectively.

Management of the ideology and the practical realm of money-making in China is based on a fundamentally different philosophical foundation from that in the West. The management and regulation of the financial system and the financial firms is not driven by 'regulatory capture.' As China's capital markets open up further, the giant global firms that dominate global capital markets outside China can make a valuable contribution to modernizing the country's financial system. However, they will operate in a different environment from that in the West. As they expand in China, they have no choice but to accept that regulation of the country's financial system is under the leadership of the CPC in order to serve the interests of the welfare of the mass of the Chinese population. Neither 'Wall Street,' the 'City of London' nor the 'Hong Kong Financial District' can expect to exert 'regulatory capture' over the Chinese financial system. China already has a 'voice' in the international institutions that influence the way in which money is governed across the world, including the IMF, World Bank and the Basel Committee. However, these institutions are still firmly controlled by a small group of high-income countries: the head of the IMF is still a European; the heads of the World Bank and the Financial Stability Board are both American. The voice of China and other developing countries in the institutions of global financial governance is almost certain to increase. However, the eventual shape of global governance of 'money' is unclear, but is likely to look very different from that of today

Note

1 In 2018 CBRC was merged with the insurance regulator to form CBIRC.

Bibliography

Bergère, M.-C. (1986) *The Golden Age of the Chinese Bourgeoisie, 1911–1937*, Cambridge: Cambridge University Press.

Berthier, S. (2002) 'Hong Kong's difficult transition', Hong Kong, *Asian Affairs*, No. 19, 2002/3.

BNP Peregrine Research (1999).

BOCI (2002) *BOCI Report*, Bank of China International.

Brahm, L.J. (ed.) (2001) *China's Century*, New York: Wiley.

Calavita, K., Pontell, H.N. and Tillman, R.H. (1997) *Big Money Crime*, London: University of California Press.

Capital Markets (1996) *China: 1996, the Year of Infrastructure Development.*

Chan. T., Tracey, N. and Zhu, Wenhui (1999) *China's Export Miracle*, Basingstoke: Macmillan.

Chang, G.C. (1998) 'GITIC lenders learn the value of compliance with foreign exchange rules', *China Law and Practice*, December 1998–January 1999.

Chang, G.C. (2001) *The Coming Collapse of China*, New York: Random House.

Che, Waikin (2000) 'The crime scene in Guangdong province', in Cheng, J. (ed.), *Guangdong in the Twenty-First Century: stagnation or take-off?* Hong Kong: City University of Hong Kong Press.

Chen, E. and Ng, R.C.W. (1999) 'The financial sector and economic development in Hong Kong: implications for developing countries', in Masayuma *et al.* (eds), *East Asia's Financial Systems*, Singapore: Institute of Southeast Asian Studies.

Cheng, J. (ed.) (2000) *Guangdong in the Twenty-First Century: stagnation or take-off?* Hong Kong: City University of Hong Kong Press.

Cheng, J. (2000) 'Guangdong's challenges: organisational streamlining, economic restructuring and anti-corruption', in Cheng, J. (ed.), *Guangdong in the Twenty-First Century: stagnation or take-off?* Hong Kong: City University of Hong Kong Press.

Claessens, S., Djankov, S. and Lang, L. (2000) World Bank Discussion Paper No. 409, Washington, DC: World Bank.

Crédit Lyonnais Securities Asia (CLSA). (2002) *Banking in China*, Hong Kong: CLSA.

Crédit Suisse First Boston and Bear Stearns & Co. (1993) *Guangdong International Trust and Investment Corporation*, Bond Offering.

Delhaise, P. (1998) *Asia in Crisis: The Implosion of the Banking and Finance System*, Singapore: Wiley.

De Trenck, C. *et al.* (2000) *Red Chips, and the Globalisation of China's Enterprises*, Hong Kong: Asia 2000 Ltd.

Department of Justice. (2009) 'Former Bank of China Managers and their wives sentenced for stealing more than US$ 485 million, laundering money through Las Vegas casinos', Office of Public Affairs, 6 May.
Editorial Board. (2000) *Almanac of China's Finance and Banking*, Beijing: Editorial Board.
European Commission (EU). (2017) *EU R&D Scoreboard*, Luxembourg: EU Publications.
Fairbank, J.K. (2002) *Guan Cha Zhong Guo* (Observing China), Beijing: World Knowledge Press.
Faure, D. (1996) 'History and culture', in Hook, B. (ed.). *Guangdong: China's promised land*, Hong Kong: Oxford University Press.
Gu, Minkang (2000) 'Legal developments and new challenges in Guangdong Province', in Cheng, J. (ed.), *Guangdong in the Twenty-First Century: stagnation or take-off?* Hong Kong: City University of Hong Kong Press.
Guangdong Enterprises (GDE) Research Department. (1997) 'A brief introduction to the Guangdong's economic development, to the GDE Group, GDE Investment and the Guangnan Group', 27 June.
Guangdong Enterprises (Holdings) Ltd. (GDEHL). (1998) *Annual Report, 1997*, Hong Kong: Guangnan (Holdings) Ltd.
Guangnan (Holdings) Ltd. (1998) *Annual Report for 1997*, Hong Kong: Guangnan (Holdings) Ltd.
Holz, C. (2001) 'China's monetary reform: the counter-revolution from the countryside', *Journal of Contemporary China*, No. 10, pp.189–217.
Hook, B., ed. (1996) *Guangdong: China's Promised Land*, Hong Kong: Oxford University Press.
Hu, Shuli (1999) *The Explosion Beginning in 1998* (in Chinese), Beijing: World Knowledge Press.
Huang, Weiding (2001) 'Fighting corruption amidst economic reform', in Brahm, L.J. (ed.), *China's Century*, New York: Wiley.
HutchisonWhampoa Limited. (2001) *Annual Report, 2000,* Hong Kong.
Institute of International Finance (IIF), *Global Debt Monitor,* July 2017, and July 2018, Washington DC: Institute of International Finance.
Kang, Dian (2000) 'A study of red chip companies in Hong Kong', mimeo, Cambridge: Judge Business School.
Krugman, P. (2000) *The Return of Depression Economics*, Harmondsworth: Penguin Books.
Lardy, N. (1998) *China's Unfinished Revolution*, Washington, DC: Brookings Institution.
Lewis, A. (1954) 'Economic development with unlimited supplies of labour', *Manchester School*, May.
Liu, Zhifeng (ed.). (1998) *Towards Judicial Justice* (*Zouxiang cifa gongzheng*), Beijing: Materials Publishing House.
Marx, K., and F. Engels (1968) *The Communist Manifesto*, in Marx and Engels, 1968, Selected Works, London: Lawrence and Wishart (originally published 1848).
Masayuma, S., Vandenbrink, D. and Yue, C.S. (eds). (1999) *East Asia's Financial Systems*, Singapore: Institute of Southeast Asian Studies.
McCarthy, K. (2019) 'America must respond to the pleas of Hong Kong People', *Financial Times*, 10 September.
McKinsey (2003) *$118 Trillion and Counting: Taking Stock of the World's Capital Markets*, London: McKinsey Global Institute

Mei, Xingbao (2000) *Measures to Avert the Dangers Threatening China's Rural Financial Institutions* (*Wo guo nongcun jinrong fengxian de fangfan yu huajie*), Beijing: Zhongguo Jinrong Chubanshe.
Merrill Lynch, Lehman Brothers, Morgan Stanley & Co. (1996) *Guangdong International Trust and Investment Corporation*, Offering Circular.
Merrill Lynch (1997) *Guangdong Enterprises (Holdings) Ltd.*, Hong Kong.
Mitchell, T. (1998a) 'Tick, tick, tick…', *Economist Intelligence Unit: Business China*, 12 August.
Mitchell, T. (1998b) 'Riddle, mystery, enigma', *Economist Intelligence Unit: Business China*, 17 August.
Mitchell, T. (1998c) 'Goodbye GITIC', *Economist Intelligence Unit: Business China*, 26 October.
Moody's Investors Service (1998a) 'Banking system outlook: International Trust and Investment Corporations (ITICs)', April.
Moody's Investors Service (1998b) 'Fall from grace: Moody's comments on the closure of Guangdong International Trust and Investment Corporation', October 23.
Moody's Investors Service (1999) 'In the twilight zone: International Trust and Investment Corporations', June.
Moody's Investors Service (2000) 'International Trust and Investment Corporations (ITICs) in China: banking system outlook', July.
Morgan Stanley Dean Witter (MSDW) (1998) *Asia Pacific Investment Research*, 8 June.
Ng, E. and Chen, R.C.W. (1998) 'The role of monetary policy under a linked exchange rate regime: the case of Hong Kong', in Kwan, *et al.* (eds), *Coping with Capital Flows in East Asia*, Singapore: Institute of Southeast Asian Studies.
Nolan, P. (1983) *Growth Processes and Distributional Change in a South Chinese Province*, London: Contemporary China Institute.
Nolan, P. (2008) *Integrating China: towards the Coordinated Market Economy*, London: Anthem Press.
Paulson, H.M. (2015) *Dealing with China: An Insider Unmasks the New Economic Superpower*, London: Headline Publishing.
People's Bank of China (PBOC). (2000) *China Financial Outlook, 2000,* Beijing: PBOC.
Pepys, S. (1995) *The Diary of Samuel Pepys, 1666*, Berkeley, California: University of California Press.
Porter, S. (2001) *The Great Fire of London*, Stroud, Gloucestershire: Sutton Publishing.
Qin, Xiao (2004) *The Theory of the Firm and Chinese Enterprise Reform*, Abingdon: Routledge.
Research Department of GDE Financial Holdings. (1999) *The Battle to Defend Hong Kong's Exchange Rate.*
Soros, G. (2000) *Open Society*, London: Little Brown.
Standing Committee, China National People's Congress. (1986) *Bankruptcy Law of the People's Republic of China (trial implementation).* Beijing: China National People's Congress,
State Statistical Bureau (SSB). (2000) *Chinese Statistical Yearbook* (*Zhongguo Tongji Nianjian*) (ZTN), Beijing: Zhongguo Tongji Chubanshe.
State Statistical Bureau of Guangdong (SSBG). (2000) *Guangdong Statistical Yearbook* (*Guangdong Tongji Nianjian*) (GTN), Guangdong: Zhongguo Tongji Chubanshe.

State Statistical Bureau of Guangdong (SSBG). (2001) *Guangdong Statistical Yearbook* (*Guangdong Tongji Nianjian*) (GTN), Guangdong: Zhongguo Tongji Chubanshe
Stiglitz, J. (2002) *Globalisation and its Discontents*, London: Penguin Press.
Strange, S. (1997) *Casino Capitalism*, Manchester: Manchester University Press.
Swift, J. (1967) *Gulliver's Travels*, London: Penguin Books (originally published 1726).
Wade, R. (1998) 'From "miracle" to "cronyism": explaining the Great Asian Slump' *Cambridge Journal of Economics*, Vol. 22, No. 6, pp. 693–706.
Walter, C. and F. Howie (2010) *Red Capitalism: the Fragile Financial Foundations of China's Extraordinary Rise*, Singapore: Wiley.
Wang, Gungwu (1998) *The Nanhai Trade: the early history of Chinese trade in the South China Sea*, Singapore: Times Academic Press.
Will, P-Et. (1990) *Bureaucracy and Famine in Eighteenth Century China*, Stanford: Stanford University Press.
World Bank (1997) *China's Non-bank Financial Institutions,* Washington DC.
World Bank (2000) *World Development Report*, Washington DC.
World Bank (2001) *Quarterly Report: China*, March.
World Bank (2018) *World Development Indicators*, Washington DC: World Bank.
Wu, Jiesi (2001) *Chinese Phoenix: the debt restructuring of the Guangdong Enterprises Group*, Hong Kong: ISI Publications.
Wu, Jiesi (2002) *The Debt Restructuring of the Guangdong Enterprises Group* (*Yuehai Chongzu Shilu*), Hong Kong: Commercial Press.
Wulan, Mulun (1997) *Hong Kong Economy Facing the Twenty-First Century*, Beijing: Chinese Finance and Economic Press.
Xing, Cheng (2002) 'The present situation of China's trust industry and the development strategies of China's trust and investment companies', *Tianjin Trust Development Report*, September.
Yeung, G. (2001) *Foreign Investment and Socio-Economic Development in China: The Case of Dongguan*, Basingstoke: Palgrave.
Yeung, G. (2004) 'Inequality in Hong Kong', *mimeo*, Cambridge: Judge Business School.
Zhang, Jiwei (2001) '"Mine clearance" in Guangdong's financial industry', *Caijing*, No. 5, pp. 72–73.
Zhang, Xianchu (2000) 'Guangdong and the challenges of the twenty-first century: the legal perspective', in Cheng, 2000.
Zhao, Yuepeng (2011) *China's Rural Financial System*, Abingdon: Routledge.

Index

Note: **Bold** page numbers refer to tables and page numbers followed by 'n' denote endnotes.

For Product Safety Concerns and Information please contact our EU
representative GPSR@taylorandfrancis.com
Taylor & Francis Verlag GmbH, Kaufingerstraße 24, 80331 München, Germany

www.ingramcontent.com/pod-product-compliance
Ingram Content Group UK Ltd.
Pitfield, Milton Keynes, MK11 3LW, UK
UKHW020154200926
475702UK00016B/2705

9780367523398